Theory and Research in Mass Communication

Contexts and Consequences

Second Edition

30130503969929

oR 2/03

302.2301
PER   HE
        SHL

LEA's COMMUNICATION SERIES
Jennings Bryant/Dolf Zillmann, General Editors

Selected titles in the Communication Theory and Methodology subseries (Jennings Bryant, series advisor) include:

Berger • *Planning Strategic Interaction: Attaining Goals Through Communicative Action*

Dennis/Wartella • *American Communication Research: The Remembered History*

Ellis • *Crafting Society: Ethnicity, Class, and Communication Theory*

Greene • *Message Production: Advances in Communication Theory*

Heath/Bryant • *Human Communication Theory and Research: Concepts, Contexts, and Challenges, Second Edition*

Olson • *Hollywood Planet: Global Media and the Competitive Advantage of Narrative Transparency*

Riffe/Lacy/Fico • *Analyzing Media Messages: Using Quantitative Content Analysis in Research*

Salwen/Stacks • *An Integrated Approach to Communication Theory and Research*

For a complete list of titles in LEA's Communication Series, please contact Lawrence Erlbaum Associates, Publishers.

Theory and Research in Mass Communication

Contexts and Consequences

Second Edition

David K. Perry
University of Alabama

LEA LAWRENCE ERLBAUM ASSOCIATES, PUBLISHERS
2002   Mahwah, New Jersey   London

Lawrence Erlbaum Associates, Inc., Publishers
10 Industrial Avenue
Mahwah, New Jersey 07430

Cover design by Kathryn Houghtaling-Lacey

Library of Congress Cataloging-in-Publication Data

Perry, David K.
   Theory and research in mass communication : contexts and consequences /
David K. Perry.—2nd ed.
      p.   cm. — (LEA's communication series)
   Includes bibliographical references and index.
   ISBN 0-8058-3937-2 (cloth) — ISBN 0-8058-3938-0 (pbk.)
   1. Mass media—Philosophy.   2. Mass media—Research.   I. Title.   II. Series
P90.P378   2001
302.23′01—dc21   01-033193
                                                                         CIP

Books published by Lawrence Erlbaum Associates are printed on acid-free paper,
and their bindings are chosen for strength and durability.

Printed in the United States of America
10   9   8   7   6   5   4   3   2   1

Contents

00069787790010

Preface

This book constitutes an attempt to promote "socialized intelligence," to borrow a phrase from Robert Westbrook (1991, p. 436). Traditionally, books dealing with mass communication theory and research have been largely designed for students who intend to take jobs with the media industries. My aim is wider: I want to help make this body of knowledge accessible to much larger groups of people, beginning with college students in general. Our research often has implications for the lives of everyone.

In attempting to reach a wider audience, I have continued in the second edition to rely on ideas from the philosophical tradition known as American pragmatism. Pragmatism "may best be characterized as the attempt to assess the significance for human values of technology in the broadest sense" (Kaplan, 1961, p. 14). In this sense, technology includes not only the mass media, but scientific research. In comparison to the first edition, however, I have placed more emphasis on ideas from the *Social Pragmatists* (see Campbell, 1995). For example, readers can find a discussion of the social, symbolic nature of mind in chapter 1. I used this to help set the tone for the entire book. I also review the implications of the nominalism and realism debate in philosophy, an ancient issue interwoven with ideas about individuality and community. The idea comes up repeatedly in the text, in areas where it helps shed light on existing literature. I have not tried to include it at every conceivable opportunity, however. This issue also ties in with the pragmatist-inspired civic journalism movement (e.g., Merritt, 1998). As I argue in chapter 1, this book is designed as a civic journalism presentation of research in our field.

My argument is that researchers, like journalists, need to connect with the broader communities in which they live. However, this should not be taken as advocacy of abandonment of what Kaplan (1964) called the *autonomy of inquiry*. Of course, the various sciences, taken together, must work independently of external controls. In fact, history shows that scientific progress depends on a lack of subservience to ideological, philosophical, political, and religious ends. Rather, the argument is that scientists should not avoid a concern with the potential real-world implications of their work that people in the broader community may value. Researchers need to connect in part as a means of increasing public support for their work, perhaps avoiding a future financial depression similar to what the universities experienced during the early 1990s.

A number of other changes from the first edition appear. Chapter 1 includes an expanded discussion of the history of the field. I have placed an increased emphasis on the details of theory construction in chapter 2. Chapter 5 includes a discussion about patterns of media ownership. Chapter 9 has been expanded to include discussion of Putnam's (e.g., 2000) controversial work about TV and social capital as well as the possible implications of the Internet for human communities. Chapter 10 includes a rather extensive update of the TV violence controversy. Readers may also find additions of recent research throughout the volume.

As with the first edition, a guiding principle of the book is that the broader society in which we live conditions and (at least potentially) is conditioned by research. In other words, the social and historical contexts of our lives contribute to (without necessarily determining) social science theory and research, which in turn can have important consequences for society. Hence the title phrase, contexts and consequences. In discussing the possible consequences of research, I assume the Deweyan argument "that whenever technological institutions fail to enhance desirable human goals there needs to be more, not less, technology" (Hickman, 1995, p. 86). In short, assessing the impact of research on society potentially can help prevent undesirable consequences.

A number of the chapters follow the logic of the pragmatist maxim, which Charles Peirce first formulated in 1878 and on which many others have elaborated. According to one version, the meaning of an idea comes from the difference it would make for us if it were true. For example, what are the empirical consequences of the idea that TV contributes to crime? How might this help us in future research or in understanding the world in which we live? At least as important, how might we use such knowledge to improve our lives?

In this light, theory and research are not seen as a means by which the human mind mirrors an external world. Rather, in Rorty's (1982) words, they can be seen as "vocabularies as instruments for coping with things"

(p. 198). Like all human products, they are fallible. An acquaintance with the work of philosophers in the pragmatist tradition makes it seem very unlikely, and probably impossible, that science could provide certain, infallible conclusions about media issues, such as the impact of televised violence. This applies, as well, with arguably more settled issues such as those concerning the impact of smoking on cancer rates or sexual behavior on AIDS transmission. A possible doubt always is possible. We have to ask ourselves instead if such doubts are reasonable. Then we have to do the best we can with what we know.

Acknowledgments

Although only one person is listed as the author of this book, many others contributed to its existence. Among those who provided useful comments regarding drafts of chapters in the first edition were several of my colleagues in the College of Communication (now the College of Communication and Information Sciences) at the University of Alabama: Jennings Bryant, William Melson, Yorgo Pasadeos, Joe Phelps, and David Roskos-Ewoldsen. John McNelly, professor emeritus at the University of Wisconsin–Madison, commented on a number of chapters. Various graduate research assistants at Alabama also helped out. These included Clay Rossi, William Self, and Shyam Sundar Sethuraman. In completing the second edition, my research assistants John Carmichael and Peiqin Zhou helped me locate pertinent literature. Finally, the author wishes to thank the Erlbaum staff and three Erlbaum reviewers for their many helpful comments concerning the first and second editions. Of course, these people bear no responsibility for whatever mistakes remain.

1

Introduction and the Historical Contexts of Media Theory and Research

Citizens, policymakers, and communication practitioners who are concerned about mass communication issues often turn to the academic community for answers. Their questions often involve such things as whether, to what extent, or why media violence or sex contributes to antisocial or criminal behavior among audiences. The answers often are not as simple or consistent as they might like. As one scholar put it:

> only after much research has been completed does a statement come to be viewed in the scholarly community as true—a status very few communication theories are ever likely to reach. Even then, the truth value is to be found more in the degree of agreement among scholars, an intersubjective criterion, than in any ultimate reality. (Chaffee, 1991, p. 11)

Definitions of *truth* as scholarly consensus are often found in modern literatures of the history (e.g., Kuhn, 1970) and philosophy of science (e.g., H.I. Brown, 1977). They are not a product of the present century. During the 19th century, pragmatist philosopher Charles Peirce (1878/1957) defined *truth* as that "opinion which is fated to be ultimately agreed to by all who investigate" (pp. 53–54). Peirce believed that proper inquiry (at least if carried on to infinity) could lead members of a scientific community, who initially might disagree, to reach inevitable conclusions. His stress on consensus simply assumed that many heads are better than one and that truth is a product of many minds.

Of course, as Peirce recognized, it is perhaps best not to define truth solely in terms of whatever a community of inquirers accepts. For example, one must exclude the possibility that scientists will accept fraudulent research. Similarly, political or religious dogma sometimes may determine the conclusions of scholars, most obviously in totalitarian societies. Hence, notions of usefulness and/or some sort of correspondence may remain necessary (see the appendix). In fact, scientists often consider a scientific idea valid or true because they find it useful and/or believe that it corresponds to the external world (Kaplan, 1964).

Today, Peirce's consensus criterion may seem too optimistic. Serious doubts persist that science progresses by attaining ever closer approximations of any ultimate reality (Hesse, 1980; Kuhn, 1970). Rather, different ideas about phenomena may gain currency at different time periods before sometimes falling out of favor and perhaps reappearing later in a modified form. In short, research frequently shows no signs of satisfying what Dewey (1929) called the *quest for certainty*. Because of this, scholarly disagreement perhaps may always exist about the degree of truth in almost any social scientific idea. Faced with this, how might those who would like to use research react to the available, but less than certain, conclusions of scholars? Perhaps another pragmatist, William James, provided an answer. Until and unless inquiry attains Peirce's ideals, "we have to live to-day by what truth we can get to-day, and be ready to-morrow to call it falsehood" (James, 1907/1975, p. 107).

Here, as elsewhere in their work, Peirce had his eye on truth as generality, and James focused on what works in particular situations. Their positions display two different philosophical viewpoints — realism and nominalism — found within both pragmatism and philosophy more generally (Lewis & R.L. Smith, 1980). Realists such as Peirce argue that universals (e.g., scientific laws or essences of objects such as blue jays) exist separately from the human mind. In contrast, nominalists like James deny their existence or see them (but often not the physical world) as mind-imposed. The phrase *"only particulars exist"* (Pepper, 1942; p. 214; italics original) effectively captures the nominalist view.

This issue (see also the appendix) has many implications for both communication research and life more generally. References to it arise at various places in this book. For example, the United States is a quite socially nominalistic society (see Lewis & R.L. Smith, 1980). Its culture emphasizes individuality more than commonality or community. Taken in moderation, nominalism probably has positive consequences, encouraging individual initiatives that benefit all. However, certain forms of community ties, which some forms of mass media may disrupt (see chap. 9), appear to promote economic prosperity, human health, and public safety (Putnam, 2000).

In his most famous essay, "The Will to Believe," James (1898/1960) addressed the problems people face when they must respond to uncertain situations, such as whether to believe in God. Written in the late 19th century, the essay primarily referred to moral and religious questions, rather than to scientific ones. His essay explicitly rejected scientism, the "pernicious exaggeration of both the status and function of science in relation to our values" (Kaplan, 1964, p. 405).

James began by defining a *live* hypothesis as a proposal that seems possibly true, and hence a potential guide to action, to a person considering it. For example, a researcher, policymaker, or consumer who reviews evidence concerning the long-term behavioral impact of exposure to television and televised violence on the young (see chap. 10) might find two live hypotheses. Perhaps exposure early in life increases the total amount of violent, criminal behavior that young people engage in when they reach the crime-prone ages of late adolescence and early adulthood (Centerwall, 1989). Yet it may have no long-term effect on aggressiveness (Milavsky, Kessler, Stipp, & Rubens, 1982). In contrast, any idea that such exposure reduces overall behavioral violence now seems quite implausible. In James' terms, it seems a *dead* hypothesis.

Two competing live hypotheses do not necessarily present a genuine option, according to James. To do so, the choice must involve two additional conditions. It must have momentous (or perhaps at least nontrivial) consequences, and some decision between the hypotheses must be inescapable. Obviously, in a purely intellectual sense, one can easily suspend one's judgment.

However, someone who does so may face a "real-world" decision. A parent may wonder whether to limit a child's exposure. A network executive or government policymaker may consider a plan to restrict the amount of violence during prime-time hours. In James' terms, these choices certainly are more genuine than was the intellectual one. They may or may not be momentous depending on the actual consequences of both mediated violence and the contemplated action. Nonetheless, the person must either act or fail to act. Hence, James' (1898/1960) central thesis:

> Our passional nature not only lawfully may, but must, decide an option between propositions, whenever it is a genuine option that cannot by its nature be decided on intellectual grounds; for to say, under such circumstances, "Do not decide, but leave the question open," is itself a passional decision,—just like deciding yes or no,—and is attended with the same risk of losing the truth. (p. 11)

In emphasizing the function of values in everyday life, James was responding to scientistic thinkers of his day who argued that it is always wrong to believe anything, such as the existence of God, without conclusive evidence. Such thinking reflects a value that a person is better off to risk failing to detect truth than to risk making an error about it. By its nature, science usually proceeds cautiously. According to its dominant values, the judgment of the scientific community in some ways should resemble that of a jury, which must acquit a criminal as long as any reasonable doubt exists of the person's guilt. Those responsible for public policy sometimes proceed in a similar fashion. According to Rowland (1983), the less-than-conclusive results of past media violence research sometimes have allowed policymakers to appear concerned and avoid taking regulatory action. Nor is this necessarily inappropriate. Restricting media violence by law or public policy could have dangerous consequences for other civil liberties, for instance. Perhaps because of this, and the influence of powerful commercial television industries, possibly "the level of 'proof' demanded goes well beyond what is usually accepted in less controversial social science research" (Huston, 1987, p. 942).

Audiences are not bound to the same standards, however. After weighing both the evidence and potential consequences of allowing a child to view violence without restriction, the parent might or might not decide to limit exposure. For example, he or she might restrict viewing based on research after recognizing that children do not have the same legal rights to view media contents as do adults. Nevertheless, the parent might find the evidence less than convincing or decide that only a slight chance exists that television will affect the child negatively. Thus, he or she might conclude that no restriction is needed. In any case, the parent's concern is with a specific situation.

James came to regret the title of his essay. It left him open to charges of encouraging wanton or wishful thinking. He believed that the phrase "Right to Believe," instead of "Will to Believe," better summarized its theme (Murphy, 1990). In short, people can base their actions on whatever evidence is available, as well as their values. Thus, mass communication consumers today have a right to believe or not, and to act or not, after taking evidence into account. In such a light, this book is intended for a very broad audience, including scientists, teachers, students, and anyone else concerned with mass communication issues.

THE FIELD OF MASS COMMUNICATION RESEARCH

The term *communication* has two different meanings, historically. It is rooted in the Latin word *communis*, which refers to "communion or the idea of a shared understanding of, or participation in, an idea or event" (Office of Technology Assessment, 1990, p. 31). By the late 17th century, "the notion of imparting, conveying, or exchanging information and materials was incorporated into the concept" (Office of Technology Assessment, 1990, p. 31). The two meanings do not exclude one another. Hence, Dewey's (1916) comments about the social import of communication:

Society not only continues to exist *by* transmission, *by* communication, but it may fairly be said to exist *in* transmission, *in* communication. There is more than a verbal tie between the words common, community, and communication. Men live in a community in virtue of the things they have in common; and communication is the way in which they come to possess things in common. (p. 5)

Communication depends on people's ability to use widely understood symbols. To many pragmatists, the concept of mind refers to this capability. Here, not entirely unlike pragmatist philosopher John Dewey (Lewis & R.L. Smith, 1980), I combine influences from nominalism and realism (for a justification, see the appendix). Contrary to ideas from ancient philosophy, I do not treat the mind as a substance that can exist independently of the body. Instead, it is a functional entity in two senses of the word (Morris, 1932).

In the first sense, mentality has the purpose of helping humans adjust to their environment by solving problems in specific contexts. This is an instrumentalist view of mind, shared by many pragmatists and philosophers such as Friedrich Nietzsche. Given its focus on individual problems and adaptation, it has rather obvious links to nominalism and Darwinian theory. In the second sense, the mind performs a role, such as a stone that a person uses as a paper weight (Morris, 1932). As Peirce said, all thinking involves signs—symbols that stand for something else. In this regard, mind refers to the human capacity for symbolic communicative behavior, including language use, which is seen as social (i.e., realist) in origin. According to Lewis and R.L. Smith (1980), "the efficacy and utility of symbols requires the reality of what we have called 'limited generals' " (p. 131). Such universals need not have unlimited scope; they may apply within only specific temporal boundaries. For example, blue jays may evolve into another species in a few hundred thousand years, but for the time being they remain blue jays. This idea allows realism to remain plausible in the face of experience that contradicts notions of "an immutable universe controlled by eternal laws of limitless scope" (p. 21).

Explaining this concept of mind, according to its elaboration by pragmatist philosopher George H. Mead (1934) and his student, Charles Morris (1934), involves a number of concepts such as the gesture, the significant symbol, self, and society. The types of gestures employed represent a key difference between animals and humans and hold the key to the evolutionary emergence of mind. A cat, for example, may curl its back when it becomes frightened. As best we know, however, the cat does not comprehend the meaning of the gesture, although another cat might respond to it. Humans routinely use widely and reciprocally understood gestures, however. If a bicyclist extends his or her left arm, few (and least of all the bicyclist) will fail to understand the bicyclist's intention to turn left. Such gestures contain a significant symbol. "The individual must know what he is about; he himself, and not merely those who respond to him, must be able to interpret the meaning of his own gesture" (Morris, 1934, p. xxi).

The use of socially understood symbols indicates the emergence of mind, which therefore becomes inherently a social entity. "Mind is the presence in behavior of significant symbols" (Morris, 1934, p. xxii). In Mead's work, vocal gestures are especially significant. "No other gesture affects the individual himself so similarly as it affects others. We hear ourselves talk as others do, but we do not see our facial expressions, nor normally watch our own actions" (p. xxii). Thus, "the vocal gesture is the actual fountainhead of language proper and all derivative forms of symbolism; and so of mind" (p. xxii). As Mead (1934) put it:

> Only in terms of gestures as significant symbols is the existence of mind or intelligence possible; for only in terms of gestures which are significant symbols can thinking — which is simply an internalized or implicit conversation of the individual with himself by means of such gestures — take place. (p. 47)

Similarly, language makes possible the emergence of the self and consciousness via the role taking involved in the significant symbol. "In so far as one can take the role of the other, he can, as it were, look back at himself from (respond to himself from) that perspective, and so become an object to himself" (Morris, 1934, p. xxiv). The self consists of two components: the subject "I" and the object "me." The nominalist "I" is the individualistic, creative, and impulsive component, whereas the more realist "me" represents the influence of society and its norms. In this way, society does not merely reproduce itself in its members, but also guarantees itself a means of evolution and change. It

> can rationally wish to do no more than present to each of its members, through the "me," the social setting within which conduct is to take place, and to make each responsible for the social values affected through this action. Under the penalty of stagnation, society cannot but be grateful for the changes which the moral act of the creative "I" introduces upon the social stage. (p. xxvi)

In short, biological evolution has given humanity the ability to use significant symbols, but culture provides the symbols often in the form of language. A boy raised by wolves, for instance, presumably would not possess a mind.

In the broadest sense, *mass communication* refers to communication activities that involve large numbers of people. Traditionally, mass communication has been conceptualized as a process involving messages that are sent to fairly general groups of people. For example, Blumer (1946) identified a mass as consisting of a very loosely organized group of people who come from all walks of life, who remain anonymous with each other, and who interact very little among themselves. Research concerning mass communication often has focused on the scientific and humanistic study of the communication media and their audiences. These media include magazines, motion pictures, newspapers, radio, television, and a variety of new communication technologies. Nonetheless, some have sharply criticized the equation of mass communication with existing mass media. According to Carter (1990), mass media represent only one potential solution to the need for mass communication. "Other solutions are potentially possible if we understand the problem well enough to invent something else" (p. 282). In short, the field has tended to focus on what is sometimes at the expense of what might be (see Carter, Stamm, & Heintz-Knowles, 1992).

Mass communication is commonly contrasted with interpersonal communication, which typically involves face-to-face interactions and much smaller audiences. In reality, the distinction involves a continuum. Hence, this book is only relatively about massified forms of communication. By necessity, it discusses work from other areas of the field as well. For instance, mass communication may influence some people directly, as when a person first learns of a news event from a story in a magazine. At other times, interpersonal communication may expand its effects. For example, a person may pass the details of what he or she reads onto others. Beyond this, today society continues to witness a demassificiation of forms of communication as cable systems permit explosive growth in the numbers of television channels and the Internet supplements existing media and threatens someday to eliminate distinctions between existing forms such as print and broadcasting. "By the year 2020, more than 90% of the words, images, sounds, videos, and three-dimensional (3D) worlds produced will be located somewhere on the Internet" (Biocca, 2000, p. 23). Most will be free or available at little cost, according to Biocca. Presumably these wide choices will diminish the extent to which people have common communication environments. Doubtlessly, these developments will continue to contribute to new forms of theory. However, futuristic predictions about communication revolutions often overstate things. Forms of mass communication will remain for a long time. What is sometimes overlooked is the increased massification of certain media today, as illustrated by the growth of nationally distributed newspapers, for example.

In large part, the field has addressed the questions posed in Lasswell's (1948) simplified, and perhaps excessively used, model:

Who
Says What
In Which Channel
To Whom
With What Effect? (p. 37)

In doing research and constructing theoretical explanations of phenomena, scholars sometimes examine the "who" — the communicator. This may involve, for example, describing the people who actually make decisions about what appears in the mass media. Scholars may look at the "says what" — the content of communication. For instance, a researcher may describe the demographic characteristics of characters appearing in prime-time television drama and compare these with the general population. They may study the "channels" — the actual technologies that deliver the message. In this regard, they may describe innovations in delivery systems. Researchers may focus on "to whom" — the characteristics of audiences and their motivations for attending to media. For instance, they may try to assess what audiences want from the media. Finally, they commonly look at "with what effect" — how audiences react to, or change as a result of, the message. For example, scholars may focus on the effectiveness of an advertising campaign or the impact that watching television violence has on the young. In fact, one could argue that, unless effects occur, the other questions contain little importance. Of course, Lasswell's model ignores certain aspects of the mass communication situation, such as the growing abilities of audiences to respond to communicators. It also ignores the "why" — "that is, Why do those in control of communication choose to use it for the functions that they do?" (E.M. Rogers, 1994, p. 221). Nonetheless, it can serve as a useful first approximation of the traditional scope of the field.

This book introduces and reviews research in most of these different areas. In particular, it tends to ignore the "who" while focusing a great deal of attention on the "with what effect?" Before discussing the products of theory and research, however, this book focuses on the contexts within which scholarly activity takes place. Later, when discussing the substance of the field, whenever possible it emphasizes the actual and potential consequences, especially for media consumers, of research. Both emphases reflect forms of philosophical pragmatism. Scholars (e.g., Carter, 1989; Delia, 1987) have acknowledged the rather profound influence of pragmatism on the field of communication studies, but seldom have they discussed the specifics of its impact (Jacobson, 1993). Instead, contemporary thinking "that tends to see social problems as being problems of communication (thus warranting the usefulness of communication studies)" (Craig, 1989, p. 102) has implied such as influence.

In particular, the emphasis on media effects, the consequences of existing forms of mass communication, fits rather congenially within certain aspects of the pragmatist tradition. Yet the lack of previous scholarly attention to the potential consequences of research seems to reflect an oddly truncated version of that tradition. Pragmatist thinkers often emphasized the harmful effects of isolating scientific means from the ends for which they were used. Therefore, the book also attempts to deal with the perennial issue of the actual and potential consequences of research, admittedly sometimes a bit speculatively, to the extent possible in light of existing knowledge.

A DYNAMIC MODEL

The history of any research field is never so simple or ordered as it might appear to an uninitiated outsider. People commonly assume that science progresses as new knowledge simply adds to or builds on previous work. In fact, historical studies of science really do not support this view. Instead, the very essence of a mature field, including its conceptions of its subject matter and how a researcher should work, often changes during different historical periods. Such changes may be fully apparent only to those working within a field.

Kuhn (1970) has rather forcefully and controversially (see the criticisms in Hunt, 1991) described this process. Kuhn argued that two types of periods, normal science and revolutionary science, characterize the history of a mature field. During times of normal science, a field relies on past achievements that its researchers see as providing the basis for further study. In short, one salient approach, or paradigm, is dominant. A paradigm consists of the definition of the subject matter of the field, its important problems, and what methods address these appropriately. Instead of continuing for all time, as commonly held views suggest, normal science periodically gives way to a scientific revolution. Anomalies, such as research findings that existing theoretical approaches cannot account for, inevitably arise from within an existing paradigm. For a time, researchers may have to live with the anomalies. When these become numerous or severe enough, alternative conceptions of the field may offer the promise of dealing with them. Then revolutionary science often occurs. Researchers change paradigms, adopting drastically revised conceptions of a field. In short, scientific order often leads to scientific chaos, which may lead back to a different sort of order, as with the movement from the Newtonian to the Einsteinian paradigm in physics. In this sense, a field revolves with time.

Kuhn's work dealt largely with the history of the natural sciences, leaving social scientists to argue about the applicability of his ideas to their work. Perhaps mass communication research has never really had a dominant paradigm (see the various discussions in Dervin, Grossberg, O'Keefe, & Wartella, 1989). Rather, a variety of preparadigms possibly have marked the history of the field. According to Kuhn, an immature field is one that has yet to develop a dominant paradigm. A variety of almost random approaches—preparadigms—characterize such a field.

This book adopts a paradigmatic view of research largely rooted in American pragmatism, sometimes also known as *contextualism* (Pepper,

1942). For the benefit of advanced students, the appendix contains a more detailed description of contextualism and other worldviews, such as mechanism. Pragmatists judge ideas, including scientific ones, largely by their consequences and practical (e.g., observational) results. Beyond this, all classical pragmatists (Dewey, James, and Peirce) expressed a number of common ideas. The following list comes largely from Almeder's (1986) summary.

1. The world contains physical objects, with knowable properties, that are not dependent on their perception by the human mind.
2. Human cognition consists of an attempt by the species to adjust to its environment.
3. Beliefs become acceptable if, when acted on, they help people deal with sensory experience.
4. Future evidence can lead to the revision of the truth value in any idea. That is to say, all beliefs are potentially fallible and subject to later revision. There are no eternal truths.
5. Only the scientific method, broadly defined, can determine the acceptability of ideas about the physical world. Experience has validated the scientific method.
6. As James put it, truth (or Dewey's fallibilist notion of warranted assertion) arises from the fruits, not the roots, of ideas. That is to say, whether a belief helps humans attain a purpose, rather than how they acquire it from sensory experience, determines its value.

One powerful implication of pragmatism concerns the common distinction between *basic* and *applied* scientific research. The term *basic research*, also known as pure or theoretical research, refers to studies that seek to understand the world without regard to practical value. *Applied studies* attempt to solve practical problems. Many pragmatists see the human mind as a participant in nature, not as something separate from it. Thus, they view science as a means of coping with the environment and tend to challenge any sharp separation of basic and applied research. In fact, much theory has developed from research designed to solve practical problems (Kaplan, 1964).

Pragmatism accordingly describes humanity as actively engaged in and with the world. It not infrequently stresses the consequences of applications of research, but it also emphasizes that scholars introduce changes into nature as they acquire knowledge. They cut things up, bounce x-rays off of objects, and so on (Kaplan, 1961). In the words of one of Dewey's closest students:

What excited me more than anything else was Dewey's revolutionary approach to philosophy that undercut all the assumptions of the classical tradition in philosophy. This view had held that man was primarily a knower and that knowledge reflected the antecedent structure and truths of the world. The mind was a spectator of what was given and discovered the truth when its ideas corresponded with the facts. The great difficulty in this approach was to account for the warranted everyday belief that thinking makes a difference to the outcomes of experience, that thought could be practical, that ideas count for something, and that ignorance and error have a price. If ideas were images, impressions, or mere effects of an external world on an organism, how could they ever change the world or modify the conditions into which we are born? The whole of education and other aspects of human experience presuppose that human reflection plays an active role in redetermining within limits not only ourselves but our society and to some extent even our natural environment. Yet the traditional conceptions of mind from Plato to Descartes make a mystery of it.

For Dewey, man is an integral part of nature, whose thinking is a form of behavior, of doing guided by words and symbols that direct and redirect differential responses. Thought is an outgrowth of the world, not a mirror image of it, as most previous empiricists believed. (Hook, 1987, pp. 88–89)

Consistent with these ideas, this book is rooted in naturalism — the idea that everything that exists belongs to the natural world. Scientific theory and research, for example, occur within nature just as much as do the wind and trees. This idea also encourages an examination of the effects of research activity on the everyday lives of human beings. In turn, such work someday may help control such consequences. Traditional thought-as-mirror metaphors could discourage such work. These are associated with Plato and Descartes and tend, at least implicitly, to separate the human mind and nature.

In some ways, such ideas are congenial with the history of media studies. For example, investigators often have not seen themselves as detached observers seeking to uncover knowledge and truth without considering its practical implications. As a result, they often have participated in policy debates by writing articles for popular magazines and testifying before legislative bodies. In addition, funding for much mass communication research has tended to arise from public concerns about the power of the media, rather than from purely theoretical considerations (J.M. McLeod & Reeves, 1980). Of course, commercial interests that wish to sell products or manipulate mass opinion also sometimes provide research funding. At bottom, the purpose behind much of what this book covers has been not only to understand the world, but to change and even at times improve it as well. The presumed mechanisms of improvement often involve public education. For better or worse, research also may change the world by increasing the impact of propagandists.

Perhaps the work of psychologist Kurt Lewin best exemplifies the use of social science to improve the world. He is remembered for his statement that nothing is so practical as a good theory. Lewin (1948) advocated treating research, practical application, and training (i.e., education) "as a triangle that should be kept together for the sake of any of its corners" (p. 211).

Figure 1.1 depicts a model for socially engaged research in the traditions of Lewin. Although scholars could assess it empirically, it is also a normative model. That is to say, portions of it may describe what might be as much as what is. Its four components represent public concerns about mass communication, research, education, and audience behavior. The history of the field and the ideas of Dewey, discussed subsequently, suggested inclusion of public concerns. The next two are elements in Lewin's triangle. Research includes studies of mass communication and its impact, as well as those that examine the impact of educating the public about such research. In Fig. 1.1, education refers broadly to any means by which people learn about such research. This includes school-related activities and others, such as reading news reports dealing with research or even talking informally with researchers. In this model, it represents a possible means of applying research. Audience behavior appears in the fourth corner. It represents all activities of audiences except those covered by other elements, such as education. For example, it includes television viewing and its possible consequences, such as behavioral aggression.

These elements form a system—an interdependent group of objects or phenomena. As an open system, outside factors can affect it. For the sake of simplicity, the model excludes other influences on the system, such as the mass media industries. There is no end to the processes represented. Instead, changes in any element may affect all others.

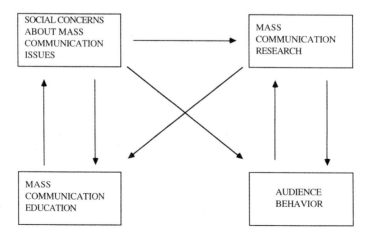

FIG. 1.1.   A model for socially engaged research in mass communication.

Sometimes one element may affect another directly. A direct effect simply involves intervening processes left out of the model. To suggest such instances, arrows link one corner with another. One arrow runs from public concerns to research. Thus, scholars may choose to study issues of widespread social concern. They may rely on polling data, or even the availability of government grants, as indications of such concerns. Another arrow links research to education. Obviously, research findings can and should influence the contents of education. One other arrow runs from public concerns to audience behavior. This assumes that persons concerned about mass communication issues may behave differently as a result.

Reciprocal arrows join public concerns and education. Widespread social concerns presumably can influence the presence of such topics in school curricula, for example. In turn, education may influence the concerns of those who are exposed to it. Similarly, research and audience behavior can affect one another directly. For instance, research might convince broadcasters to reduce the amounts of televised violence available, causing audiences to view less of it. Finally, audience behavior might affect research, as when scholars observe such behavior in natural settings.

A lack of an arrow pointing from one corner to another indicates that one might affect the other, at least primarily, by first influencing other elements in the model. Thus, research and education concerning the consequences of televised violence might influence audience behavior because they first affect public concerns. For example, persons concerned about televised violence might shun it or limit what their children see. In turn, audience behaviors such as avoiding televised violence might affect the contents of education and social concerns if research documents their "real-world" consequences, such as lower crime rates.

The model is a dynamic one. Each element may change constantly, as modifications occur in other components and as outside developments occur, such as with the forms or contents of mass communication. For example, education about the effects of exposure to televised violence (see chap. 10) may help limit these effects. Only additional research can assess the impact of education. "In an apt metaphor this ongoing change has been called the 'mountain-range effect': we climb a peak only to find other peaks beyond us; no matter when we leave off climbing, other peaks remain beyond" (Kaplan, 1964, p. 395). At bottom, as the world changes, the need for social inquiry will continue indefinitely.

CIVIC JOURNALISM AND MEDIA RESEARCH

In the field of communication, pragmatism has influenced more than formal research activity. During the past decade or so, a movement known as public or civic journalism (D. Merritt, 1998) has challenged traditional journalistic practices. Although precisely defining *civic journalism* has proved a bit elusive, its roots lie in the Deweyan idea that the human mind is an active participant in nature, not a detached spectator. More specifically, as journalists at mainstream newspapers face increased competition from online services and other technological innovations, they may have to do more than observe and transmit information about news events. Instead, they can participate in their communities by helping to solve, or at least providing a forum to address, problems. Civic journalists also tend to see their audiences as participants in public affairs, rather than as spectators (see the discussion of the Dewey–Lippmann debate in chap. 9). They also tend to promote political forms of civic engagement among citizens that some research (see chap. 9) indicates has fallen. In short, they try to build connections with the communities they cover.

Dewey's (e.g., 1927/1946) ideas about the role of journalism encompassed more than just politics, narrowly conceived. His work suggests that journalism amounts to a form of continuing education. He and his followers often pointed out that a "community was not fully democratic until it had 'socialized intelligence' " (Westbrook, 1991, p. 436). The concept of *intelligence* is central to his work. Instead of merely copying objects, it takes account "of the ways in which more effective and more profitable relations with these objects may be established in the future" (Dewey, 1925/1973, p. 54). He (1930/1981) foresaw "a time when all individuals may share in the discoveries and thoughts of others, to the liberation and enrichment of their own experience" (p. 115).

In this light, this book is intended as a civic journalism treatment of mass communication research. Its aim is to promote social intelligence based on the idea that democracy rests "as much if not more on the egalitarian distribution of knowledge" as "on the egalitarian distribution of wealth" (Westbrook, 1991, p. 53). Defining the mind in symbolic terms emphasizes that one's intellectual achievements depend on a heritage from others, magnifying the duty to share. Civic journalism has both nominalist and realistic components (Perry, 1998). It commonly, but implicitly, assumes a nominalistic Darwinian, functional theory of mind, although its frequent emphases on community and, by implication, the social nature of the mind can be seen as realistic.

THE HISTORY OF MASS COMMUNICATION RESEARCH

The Birth of a Field

An early and middle 20th-century matrix in the United States largely gave birth to mass communication theory and research. Not entirely unlike today, often contradictory forces influenced the field. These included public concerns about media effects and propaganda, desires of commercial and political interests to influence audiences, and the need of the U.S. government to mobilize wartime mass opinion. Of course, all involve actual or potential practical application.

Despite its U.S. origins, earlier work by a number of European intellectuals conditioned the field profoundly but often indirectly. These include Charles Darwin, Sigmund Freud, and Karl Marx (E.M. Rogers, 1994). Darwin and, to a lesser extent, Freud influenced researchers who use traditional scientific methods to study communication phenomena such as media effects. In addition, generally humanistic scholars attempting to use research to promote social change have relied heavily on ideas from both Freud and Marx.

At the start of the 20th century, the Industrial Revolution had turned an agrarian U.S. society into a modern, industrialized one. For the first time in history, the vast majority of the population was literate, allowing the print media to reach mass as well as elite audiences. Motion pictures had become popular, and radio soon would become a mass medium. At this time, many scholars saw the new media as vehicles for either good or antisocial manipulation, to varying extents as potential social Messiahs or Satans (or both; J.D. Peters, 1989b). Today, such blanket hopes and fears seem a bit naive because much more is known about the influence of media. Nonetheless, similar ideas continue to appear in modern research, although usually in somewhat muted and qualified forms.

In the wake of industrialization, many saw a loss of community and democracy. Private citizens no longer banded together for mutual benefit into small and self-governing units that physical distance protected from outside control. Instead, industrial progress had created problems beyond the competence of ordinary citizens to deal with, and scientists and other expert elites ran the world. Scholars debated the desirability or inevitability of this. Journalist Walter Lippmann, a student of and contributor to pragmatism (Simonson, 2001), saw the masses as chronically unable to govern themselves. He (1922, 1925) supported limited democracy and a government run by experts (see chap. 9). As an advocate of participatory democracy, Dewey (e.g., 1927/1946) disagreed.

To simplify things a bit, Dewey and Lippmann left a somewhat forked trail for the field of communication studies. Clearly, its scholars often followed Lippmann or tried to combine ideas from the two. For instance, Carey (1989) called Lippmann's 1922 *Public Opinion* the founding book of the field. J.D. Peters (1989a) described Dewey as "the path not taken by American mass communication research" (p. 201). According to E.M. Rogers (1994), Dewey's ideas exist "too far over the horizon" (p. 159) for communication scholars to recognize his sometimes indirect influence. In its civic journalism orientation, this book nonetheless attempts to chart a kind of neo-Deweyan path through the research literature.

Perceptions that industrialism and urbanism had destroyed traditional ways of life contributed to the birth and growth of the Progressive movement, which paradoxically wanted to use the tools of science and technology to help recapture the old notion of community (Delia, 1987). Some theorists believed that a kind of mass society, in which individual people are detached from their traditional social contexts, had taken hold. Thinkers such as Dewey (1927/1946) hoped that a reformed mass media could be enlisted in the cause of creating new forms of fellowship. As a young man, Dewey even helped plan a still-born newspaper designed to diffuse social scientific knowledge to the general public.

Today, scholars identify Dewey as one of the earliest U.S. communication theorists. In some ways, he exemplifies the early 20th-century Progressive intellectual. He was a native of New England, with its traditions of close-knit villages and participatory town meetings. A Darwinian who rejected the survival-of-the-fittest ethics of certain other evolutionists, Dewey supplemented Darwin's nominalism with a philosophically more realist focus on community. He (1927/1946) felt that many of the problems of his day — including World War I, political alienation and apathy, and substance abuse — resulted from the lack of new, interacting (or transacting) local, intranational, and international community structures to replace the traditional local ones that industrialism had destroyed. To Dewey, communication provided a fundamental remedy by making possible a common symbolic environment needed for a functional democracy in which the masses kept the elites — political and scientific — in touch with their problems. It alone could provide the public, disenfranchised from controlling its existence despite democratic forms such as the secret ballot, with "full publicity in respect to all consequences which concern it" (Dewey, 1927/1946, p. 127).

In short, to Dewey, modern democracy required an unshackled mass media able to disseminate the results of scientific and social experimentation to ordinary people, who then could keep the experts in touch with the salient issues in their lives, with the "real" world. This transactional dialogue between citizens and technicians would maximize the practical application of the results of science and help make democracy meaningful. Without this, Dewey believed, intellectuals might only serve as the tools of large economic interests. Dewey felt that the world progressed through *experimentation* — a term he used to refer both to scientific (see chap. 2) and less formal forms. For instance, to Dewey, only the consequences of different types of government, and not logical appeals to assumptions about human nature, could determine the most appropriate state. Education, a form of communication, also figured prominently in Dewey's hopes for the future. Despite his emphasis on mass media, Dewey saw face-to-face communication as the ultimate key to restoring the local community — to him the final source of human fulfillment and happiness.

About the same time that Dewey expressed his hopes and Lippmann his skepticism, many also feared the new mass media. During World War I, the U.S. government made wide use of persuasion techniques. After the war, a number of exposes of prevarications in it heightened interest in communication and propaganda (Delia, 1987). According to one definition, *propaganda* occurs when "the action which is the goal of the persuasive effort will be advantageous to the persuader but not in the best interests of the persuadee" (R. Brown, 1958, p. 300). Broader definitions encompass any form of persuasive communication. Among those studying propaganda was political scientist Harold Lasswell, a student of pragmatism. At times, Lasswell's work used ideas from Dewey, Freud, Lippmann, and even Marx. His ideas implied to certain later scholars a simple, powerful, and direct effects conception of mass communication:

> In the Great Society it is no longer possible to fuse the waywardness of individuals in the furnace of the war dance; a newer and subtler instrument must weld thousands and even millions of human beings into one amalgamated mass of hate and will and hope. A new flame must burn out the canker of dissent and temper the steel of bellicose enthusiasm. The name of this new hammer and anvil of social solidarity is propaganda. (Lasswell, 1927, pp. 220–221)

Again communication provided the key to a restoration of community. This implicit model of communication, however, was not participatory, as Dewey hoped, but top–down and manipulative. Rather like Lippmann, Lasswell did not want to abandon democracy entirely. Instead, he favored "a 'politics of prevention' in which therapeutic social scientists would advise elites who in turn would 'reorient minds' in order to control political conflict" (Westbrook, 1991, p. 285). Although few researchers today would describe the impact of propaganda quite as dramatically as did Lasswell, the idea that media contents contribute to more uniform perceptions among the public still appears. In particular, the mainstreaming concept of the Cultural Indicators research group and the spiral-of-silence theory of German researcher Elisabeth Noelle-Neumann (see chap. 9) have received at least partial support from modern research. Both rely on ideas of media influence that are reminiscent of Lasswell's mass society musings.

Some propaganda scholars (e.g., Biddle, 1932) wanted to teach people how to resist, or at least to assess more thoughtfully, influence attempts. Thus, findings from propaganda analysis during the 1920s and 1930s often were included in school curricula. One of the best of these studies concerned the speeches of the Reverend Charles E. Coughlin, a U.S. priest who used the radio to promote profascist ideas (Lee & Lee, 1939). The study identified a number of techniques, such as *name calling* and *card stacking*. The latter occurs when someone attempts to present the best or worst possible case for an idea or product with either facts or falsehoods. Such research, however, could not indicate to what extent such techniques proved effective.

Early Empirical Research: The Limited-Effects Generalization

To a significant extent, social science came of age during the 1920s (Schramm, 1997). At perhaps no place was this more evident than at the University of Chicago. There the famed Chicago School developed in sociology and related areas. Dewey taught at Chicago for a decade beginning in the late 1890s. Many of these scholars were intellectual collaborators with or followers of Dewey and James. Darwin exerted a powerful influence on them as well. Beginning in the 1890s, the Chicago pragmatists tended to focus on social problems in their urban environment. For example, one study concerned taxi dancers, young women who for a dime would dance with men in a mildly erotic way (Cressey, 1932/1968). These scholars often saw human thought and communication as important tools of ultimate reform. Their city included large groups of recent immigrants from Europe that provided scholars with opportunity to study possible mass society phenomena. The philantrophic wealth of oil man John D. Rockefeller, who provided founding and other gifts to sustain their university more generally, fueled portions of their research.

Although they tended to employ primarily qualitative methods, they formed a mold for later media effects research (E.M. Rogers, 1994), which often concerns "the peril and possibilities of democracy" (J.D. Peters, 1989a, p. 200). Chicagoan Robert Park, a former journalist, may have been the first mass communication theorist. He theorized about the relationship of news to mass or public opinion and social control. According to Frazier and Gaziano (1979), Park anticipated many contemporary ideas in mass communication theory. These include identifying the major functions of communication (see chap. 4) and agenda setting (see chap. 9).

As quantitative techniques of the social sciences developed, researchers inevitably began applying them to study mass media use and effects directly. Such studies largely occurred in the context of other changes within U.S. social science during the 1930s. At Chicago and elsewhere, these developments modified its Deweyan, reformist character with the ideals of the hard sciences, including rigor and freedom from values. As Rorty (1982) said:

> Both social scientists and philosophers wanted to stop striking public attitudes and start showing that they could be as thoroughly and exclusively professional, and preferably as mathematical, as the natural scientists. American sociology, whose early stages had been satirized as the expendi-

ture of a five-thousand-dollar grant to discover the address of a whore-
house, came to be satirized as the expenditure of a five-million-dollar grant
to plot the addresses of a thousand whorehouses against a multidimen-
sional array of socio-economic variables. (pp. 63–64)

Some early research in fact tended to confirm the assumed power of the
media. The Payne Fund studies were one of the first formal attempts to
document media effects. Conducted during the late 1920s and 1930s, they
examined the impact of motion pictures on children—a group that
throughout history has been seen as especially susceptible to media influence. This research, along with later work concerning children and both
radio and television, was conducted primarily to address perceived public concerns (Wartella & Reeves, 1985). Among the researchers was University of Chicago sociologist Herbert Blumer, an advocate of qualitative
methods and disciple of Mead, one of the leading pragmatist philosophers
of the time. Relying on both quantitative and qualitative techniques, such
as case studies, the Payne Fund studies provided some ammunition for
those who feared the power of the media. They also evidently contributed
to the subsequent enforcement of stringent self-regulation, which lasted
until the 1960s, within the motion picture industry.

A notorious radio broadcast in 1938 also helped support popular fears
about mass communication (Lowery & DeFleur, 1988). On Halloween
night, actor Orson Welles took his place in front of a microphone at a CBS
radio studio in New York. In his hand he held a script, Howard Koch's
version of H.G. Wells' novel *War of the Worlds*. The story concerned a fictional invasion of the United States by Martians, seemingly a perfect story
for the occasion. Nonetheless, CBS expected the show to attract little attention in part because Charlie McCarthy's program, its competition that
night, was very popular with the public.

What followed produced newspaper headlines and a variety of social
scientific investigations. Perhaps 6 million people heard the broadcast and
as many as 1 million panicked, in some instances attempting to flee the *invasion* by automobile. Many of those who panicked missed the opening of
the program, which contained disclaimers pointing out its fictional nature,
because they had listened to a popular guest on McCarthy's show. On turning their dial when a less popular guest came on, they heard what seemed
to be authentic emergency radio broadcasts concerning the *invasion*.

Hadley Cantril, a public opinion and propaganda scholar, conducted
an after-the-fact study, which largely focused on variables that predicted
whether people panicked. Cantril relied on in-depth personal interviews
with 135 persons in New Jersey and survey data collected by CBS and the
American Institute of Public Opinion. One especially important factor influencing whether people panicked seemed to be critical thinking ability,

which suggested that education could reduce the likelihood of other such incidents (Cantril, 1952).

Yet these early studies often lacked rigor, by modern standards, and other research soon suggested a markedly different picture about media effects. Today, one can applaud the increased rigor of subsequent studies while recognizing the values implicit in them. These often were those of wartime propagandists or, probably at least as often, those of the developing commercial media. By the time of World War II, the field had turned away from the concerns with audiences inherent in the work of certain propaganda scholars often in favor of research that might enhance the effectiveness of persuasive communicators. In short, significant military and industrial complexes affected it during subsequent decades.

At worst, some work may have enhanced the effectiveness of advertising and thereby contributed to public health disasters such as tobacco use. For example, field forefather Paul Lazarsfeld accepted money from a tobacco company to assess reasons that people do and do not smoke (E.M. Rogers, 1994). Philosophical views that separate facts and value judgments may have discouraged scientists from examining the consequences of their work, facilitating harmful research applications (see appendix).

Work during World War II and the cold war also attempted to develop tools of psychological warfare of benefit to the U.S. side. Funding agencies often included military and intelligence entities (see Glander, 2000). For example, after the World War II, the Central Intelligence Agency (CIA) bankrolled numerous projects, including some of Cantril's international communication work (Simpson, 1994). Simpson (1994) argued that during the cold war researchers became insulated from the sometimes violent consequences of their work in areas such as Greece and Guatemala. For instance, he claimed that they rationalized their activity with the idea that their purportedly nonviolent work differed from that of, say, developing warheads.

When viewed with the detachment that numerous passed decades makes possible, some may find the military and intelligence work more valuable than were some of the commercial efforts. As Danielson (2000) put it: "Hitler was no kindly humanist. Neither was Joseph Stalin. And cooperation with governmental efforts to win wars was not at the time considered inherently evil" (p. 533). Had the U.S. not fought World War II or the cold war, one could argue that Nazism or Stalinism doubtlessly would have spread their tyrannies much farther. Even so, the legacies of wartime research today may exert nefarious influences on U.S. democracy. For example, they may reinforce existing cultural tendencies toward authoritarian communication patterns.

Scholars (e.g., Schramm, 1997) have identified four forefathers of the field of mass communication research. These include psychologist Carl

Hovland, mathematician-sociologist Lazarsfeld, Lasswell, and Lewin. A forefather typically conducts significant early research without identifying with a field (Chaffee & E.M. Rogers, 1997). Hovland is known for his experimental work into attitudes, especially during World War II; Lazarsfeld for his early panel studies of media effects; Lasswell for studies of the significant symbols in media content and other political affairs materials; and Lewin for his gatekeeper concept (see chap. 3) and emphasis on primary groups. Rockefeller Foundation money at times propelled all four. As E.M. Rogers (1994) put it, "The field is built on a foundation provided by oil" (p. 145).

Perhaps the work of Lazarsfeld best exemplifies the early field. An Austrian who came to the United States during the early 1930s, he eventually settled at Columbia University. He had earned a doctorate in mathematics and may have invented market research (Schramm, 1997). In Austria, the young Lazarsfeld had gained experience by running a commercial research institute. Oddly enough, he offered to do research on virtually any topic as a means of financing what he really was interested in — work that might advance the cause of democratic socialism. His socialist politics appeared to fade as he examined the marketability of products such as beer, milk, shoes, and wool (Glander, 2000).

Lazarsfeld "was undoubtedly the most important intellectual influence in shaping modern communication research" (E.M. Rogers, 1994, p. 246). Yet he arrived in the United States with little appreciation for the reformist, Deweyan past of its social science (J.D. Peters, 1986). Beyond this, he apparently had little interest in communication per se. Rather, it served as a convenient means of pursuing his interest in research methods. At Columbia, he headed the Office of Radio Research, which later expanded to become the Bureau of Applied Social Research. There, along with commercial studies devoted to topics such as refrigerator purchases, he helped make the Martian invasion study possible. He often developed academic research out of commercial work after selling "overpriced research projects to corporation executives" (E.M. Rogers, 1994, p. 294). In addition, Lazarsfeld conducted what is often regarded today as the most important early mass communication research.

In 1940, President Franklin Roosevelt was seeking an unprecedented third term. His Republican opponent was Wendell Wilkie, who made the idea of a third term a major campaign issue. The United States was also on the brink of World War II. Lazarsfeld and his colleagues decided to examine empirically what influenced the voting decisions people made during an electoral campaign (Lazarsfeld, Berelson, & Gaudet, 1968). The study grew out of plans to investigate the effects of U.S. Department of Agriculture radio messages. Years later, Lazarsfeld was unable to recall just how the topic changed (E.M. Rogers, 1994).

For the study, the researchers chose Erie County, Ohio, the county seat of which is Sandusky. Some 600 persons in the county were included in a panel, a group of respondents who were interviewed seven times from May to November of that year. Other respondents were interviewed only once as a check on possible sensitization created by the panel technique.

In fact, the published study reported little evidence of media effects in the sense of changes in voting intentions among the panelists. Instead, the research suggested that the major impact of political propaganda was to reinforce a person's original voting decision (Lazarsfeld et al., 1968). Another effect of the political campaign was activation of political predispositions. Because of this, undecided voters usually wound up voting for the candidate that others with the same social class, religion, and area of residence also favored (Lazarsfeld et al., 1968, p. 73). According to J.D. Peters (1989a), the book "is an extended footnote to Lippmann's demolition of faith in the rational citizen's existence. A chief finding of the study is that the reasoning, independent voter who carefully ponders all the issues and votes accordingly is a fiction" (p. 213).

A major reason that campaign propaganda had so little influence on candidate preferences evidently was that persons most frequently reached by it usually were sophisticated and already converted (Lazarsfeld et al., 1968). Thus, it appeared that the political messages bypassed the most likely potential converts.

Another important outcome of the study concerned the role of interpersonal communication. Those individuals who changed their mind during the campaign mentioned other people as being most responsible for the decision. This certainly contrasted with ideas about mass societies and isolated individuals. The researchers noticed what they called *opinion leaders* among all occupational groups. Lazarsfeld borrowed this concept from public relations founder Edward Bernays, who got the idea while reading Lippmann's *Public Opinion* (E.M. Rogers, 1994). Opinion leaders, a distinct minority, were especially interested in the campaign. They paid a lot of attention to news and propaganda concerning it and engaged in heavy amounts of political discussion. On the basis of these data, Lazarsfeld and his colleagues formulated the famous two-step flow hypothesis — the idea that the mass media often transmit ideas directly to these opinion leaders, who in turn pass them on to the less interested. This suggests that mass media effects typically are indirect.

Shortly before the outbreak of World War II, the Rockefeller Foundation called together a number of social scientists. They initially were to examine issues of mass communication research to guide future foundation funding. In written invitations to participants, John Marshall, a Rockefeller official, invented the term *mass communication* (E.M. Rogers, 1994). The term has often served as a kind of euphemism for propaganda, by then a concept of ill repute. The group quickly focused "on how communication could be utilized by the federal government to cope with the approaching war" (E.M. Rogers, 1994, p. 220). Given the legacy of public concern about World War I propaganda and existing isolationist sentiment, the Roosevelt administration could not tackle such questions (Gary, 1996).

The participants struggled with difficult issues, such as how to develop mass morale during wartime without ruining democracy. They often drew on both the Lippmann and Dewey views of democracy (Gary, 1996). For example, sociologist Robert Lynd, author of a Deweyan critique of existing social science (Lynd, 1939), nonetheless argued for a Lippmann-like realism about the incompetence of mass opinion (Gary, 1996). Ultimately, they "helped defeat the Nazis, and probably got their hands dirty along the way, while engaging in elite research in the name of the people" (Gary, 1996, p. 146).

Scientists in the group included Lasswell and Lazarsfeld. According to Glander (2000), memoranda from discussion groups make clear that the two men

> regarded the development of conformity of opinion as the main goal of their research. Likewise, it is important to note that these views, although accentuated by the war, were not confined solely to problems of the society at war, but rather were seen as directly relevant to modern society in times of relative peace as well. (p. 47)

World War II also stimulated early experimental mass communication research. A group of psychologists, including Hovland, conducted early persuasion research for the U.S. Army. The military wanted to assess the impact of films designed to improve troop morale. Freud's ideas indirectly influenced this (E.M. Rogers, 1994). To a degree, this research (Hovland, Lumsdaine, & Sheffield, 1949) demonstrated the ability of communication to change attitudes in artificial, contrived settings. Yet it provided less evidence about what happens in more normal settings, when people engage in voluntary media-related behavior. Nonetheless, it provided the groundwork for theoretically oriented work in persuasion during subsequent decades. For example, Hovland's postwar research program at Yale University involved such topics as the impact of source credibility and fear appeals in messages and the relationship of personality to persuasibility (Hovland, Janis, & Kelley, 1953). These remain central to the modern study of persuasion and hold obvious interest to advertisers and other propagandists (see chap. 7).

Other events during the war especially helped shape the field. A man with an unusually eclectic background, Wilbur Schramm, became director of the School of Journalism at the University of Iowa. Schramm held a

Ph.D in English yet had learned social science as well, partly in postdoc-
toral study with a physiological psychologist. He had published his own
fiction writing and directed the Iowa Writers' Workshop—a graduate
program of exceptional quality for creative writers. After Pearl Harbor,
Schramm worked for a time at the Office of Facts and Figures, a government propaganda agency. He helped write some of President Roosevelt's
fireside chats, which the U.S. public heard over the radio.

Schramm represented the transition of the mass communication research from a field dominated by researchers in traditional fields such as
psychology and sociology to one with its own autonomy. His research interests also were extremely eclectic. They ranged from children and television to media and development. In the words of a biographer, Schramm

> probably did more to define and establish the field of communication re-
> search and theory than any other person. He founded two institutes of com-
> munication research (and helped found a third), wrote several basic text-
> books in a field that had none before, and trained a small army of followers
> who, for the first time thought of themselves as full-time communication
> scholars. (Tankard, 1990c, p. 239)

Schramm believed that the traditionally vocational journalism school at
Iowa should also produce both research and scholars with doctorates. He
started the first mass communication doctoral program, with courses in
areas such as communication theory and research methods. He eventually
became a central figure to such programs at the University of Illinois and
Stanford University. In some ways, Schramm's ideas resembled those of
Lippmann. According to one critic (Glander, 2000), he followed the legacy
of a neohumanists, who embraced the ideal of an aristocracy. Schramm

> carried the neohumanist legacy into the germinating field of mass commu-
> nication research. The neohumanist ideal of a hierarchical, aristocratic social
> order; the conceptualization of mass communications as a process of per-
> suading people to adopt a certain mode of thinking and behaving; and the
> emphasis on an educated elite masterminding this communication process
> were central to Schramm's thinking throughout his career. (Glander, 2000,
> p. 153)

In addition, a very different strand of mass communication research
appeared during the 1930s and 1940s. A group of leftist sociologists
known as the Frankfurt School came to the West to avoid Nazi persecu-
tion in Germany. Both Freud and Marx profoundly influenced their work
(E.M. Rogers, 1994). Most significant among them for media research was
T.W. Adorno. These scholars, with a research agenda based more within
the humanities than the social sciences, began developing critical mass media research. Critical research typically (or, perhaps more accurately, ster-

eotypically) has eschewed quantitative techniques. It has as its goal human liberation. Its practitioners often have favored qualitative descriptions of the control structures of modern media systems and the latent (rather than overt) content of media messages. Often critical scholars have merely assumed that effects flow logically from these. For example, that news organizations are operated as for-profit businesses or that their product exhibits subtle probusiness bias in the coverage of a labor dispute, at least in the mind of some researcher, may be taken to mean that news coverage will swing mass opinion to the side of business in the dispute. Perhaps ironically, some of the Frankfurt scholars served in intelligence and propaganda roles in the U.S. government. For example, Herbert Marcuse, later considered a theoretician of the 1960s U.S. New Left, served with the Office of Strategic Services, the forerunner to the CIA, during World War II and in other U.S. government offices until the early 1950s.

Lazarsfeld and Adorno collaborated briefly in a research project at Columbia. The effort ended unsuccessfully, contributing to a schizophrenia in mass communication research centered around the critical–empirical separation. Various factors — personal and philosophical — contributed. Adorno could be difficult to work with, but he also expressed disgust with the links between researchers and industry. "He felt that scholarly research should be conducted to advance the frontiers of knowledge, not so that wealthy media moguls could become wealthier" (E.M. Rogers, 1994, p. 282). Historically, critical research has dominated the agenda of many European and Latin-American researchers in the field, whereas empirical research has dominated the U.S. scene.

As the postwar campaign against communism got underway, Lasswell proclaimed the policy sciences. He identified Dewey, an ardent anticommunist, as their inspiration. Policy scientists participate in, rather than merely observe, the policy process. Their work has two dimensions. One focuses on the policy process and may help make it more rational, for example. The other aims to improve "the concrete content of the information and the interpretations available to policy-makers" (Lasswell, 1951, p. 3). During the 1950s and 1960s, in the latter sense "mass communication research developed as a policy science par excellence" (J.D. Peters, 1986, p. 535) as a weapon in the cold war. With his background in intelligence and his cold war activism, Schramm had impeccable policy science credentials (J.D. Peters, 1986). For example, he wrote an early mass communication textbook based on a training manual for the U.S. Information Agency. Of course, much other mass communication research that attempts to inform policymakers, say about the effects of mediated depictions of sexuality, also qualifies as policy science.

The field also got something of a boost from information theory (Shannon & Weaver, 1949), which is a model rather than a theory (see chap. 3). It depicted communication as a one-way phenomenon in which sources sent messages to receivers via channels. Claude Shannon, a Bell Labs engineer who worked on cryptography problems during the war, largely developed it. According to E.M. Rogers (1994), it "provided the root paradigm for the field of communication study" (p. 440). As such, it encouraged the existing focus on effects. Ironically, Shannon argued that it did not apply with ordinary human communication, but only with engineering phenomena. To him, "human meanings and interpretations were a kind of soft data that could not be reduced to precise mathematical formulations" (p. 426). Nonetheless, Schramm's enthusiasm for it contributed greatly to its visibility, although he did not see it as more than one model among many for the new field (E.M. Rogers, 1994). J.D. Peters (1986) argued, however, that the field largely used information theory for legitimization. For example, it put the concept of communication at the center of scholarly endeavor in areas as diverse as analytic philosophy, psychology, and sociolinguistics.

As the war ended, Lazarsfeld continued his research. One study, set in Decatur, Illinois, examined the two-step flow hypothesis more directly. It primarily concerned the consumer behavior of women and appeared in a book entitled *Personal Influence* (E. Katz & Lazarsfeld, 1955). The study originated from a magazine publisher's desire to attract more affluent readers. It (at least debatedly) corroborated the two-step flow hypothesis. Perhaps especially noteworthy was evidence that little overlap existed among opinion leadership in different domains. That a woman was an opinion leader concerning fashion did not predict whether she would be a leader concerning marketing or public affairs, for instance. Finally, respondents perceived personal discussion as more influential than the media in almost all domains of behavior studied. Subsequent research (e.g., Troldahl, 1966–1967) has indicated that the two-step flow idea often simplifies a much more complicated process.

To some, this emphasis on interpersonal contacts may seem Deweyan. For instance, it focused on a rediscovery of the *primary group* — a termed originated by Charles H. Cooley, an early "Chicago" sociologist at the University of Michigan. Such groups (e.g., parents and peers) are "face-to-face, intimate, and important in forming a person's social nature" (E.M. Rogers, 1994, p. 153). Yet as J.D. Peters (1989a) argued, "other than as a weapon to fend off mass society theory's gloom about the future of democracy and the fate of 'mass man,' the book lacked any theory of why community talk might be important" (p. 215).

According to Glander (2000), the Decatur study relied on a narrow conceptualization of media effects — a point that many historians have ignored or overlooked. It involved only the intended influence of persuasive communicators. Not included were notions of wider social or educational impact. As Glander wrote, "The opinion leaders concept has had enormous practical utility to propagandists and advertisers, because identifying these opinion leaders and finding particular ways in which to persuade them has led to an increased capacity to persuade the larger population" (p. 108). The possibility of such applications motivated Lazarsfeld and his colleagues (Glander, 2000).

Partly due to Lazarsfeld's research, a limited-effects generalization about media effects dominated many academic discussions for decades. So well established did the generalization seem that Joseph Klapper, the head of research at CBS, devoted an influential book to it. To Klapper (1960), "mass communication *ordinarily* does not serve as a necessary and sufficient cause of audience effects, but rather functions among and through a nexus of mediating factors and influences" (p. 8). Klapper articulated a *phenomenistic* approach, defined as "a shift *away* from the tendency to regard mass communication as a necessary and sufficient cause of audience effects, toward a view of the media as influences, working amid other influences, in a total situation" (p. 5).

Thus, the extent of media influence may depend on whether a message is in accord with the norms of groups to which audiences belong, for example. Klapper identified reinforcement as a typical outcome of media use. For instance, media use may reinforce a person's existing political orientation and his or her tendencies toward or away from delinquent behavior. Minor attitude change — as when a person who wavered between support for a political party and neutrality decides to support the party — also occurs. Evidently, this happens less often than reinforcement, he reported. Finally, conversion (e.g., from support for one party to another) can take place, but perhaps happens least often. Klapper speculated that in abnormal situations, such as times of unusual social unrest, media effects might be much more important.

The limited-effects idea has extremely important implications for policymakers and the media. On the one hand, it suggests the appropriateness of a rather libertarian approach to media content. If the media seldom influence the attitudes and behavior of audiences in substantively important ways, why worry about their content? To this extent, many media practitioners understandably view the idea as consoling. On the other hand, the idea that media effects are unimportant could destroy the economic base of the U.S. mass communication industry (McGuire, 1986a). If advertisers take it seriously, the media may have to find another means of financing their operations.

Such a generalization also threatens communication researchers, whose work may appear unimportant (McGuire, 1986a). If the media have no important effects, why study them? Scientists such as Lazarsfeld from older disciplines, such as psychology and sociology, did most of the early communication research. By the late 1950s, many (including Lazarsfeld) had largely abandoned media research ostensibly in favor of potentially more fruitful endeavors. One of the founding parents of mass communication research, Berelson (1959) even talked about the field withering away.

The Rebirth of Media Research

As of 1960, it seemed to some that empirical social science had largely dealt with the influence of mass communication by showing that effects are generally limited and benign. In itself, that would have been a useful contribution because it would have answered commonly heard concerns about the media and could help focus energy on more serious problems. Conceivably, media study could have continued without a concern with effects, but its importance would be suspect.

Nonetheless, by the late 1950s, other developments were helping to revitalize and institutionalize the field. First, television had established itself as a ubiquitous phenomenon in U.S. life. Its presence created a lot of concern about its effects, especially on children. Modern researchers have often argued that television effects are much more important than were those of media available during the 1940s. Second, university programs devoted to the academic study of the media appeared in large numbers during the 1960s. Finally, older college programs designed to train young people for mass communication careers increasingly followed aspects of Schramm's vision. For example, they have demanded that their faculty possess academic, as well as professional, credentials. Undergraduate enrollments in various areas of media and communication study (e.g., advertising and journalism) exploded from 1970 to 1990, ensuring job opportunities for the growing number of persons with doctorates in the field. All this has helped guarantee that a critical mass of scholars devotes careers to media study. In the process, both traditional skills departments and research in the field were remade (Delia, 1987). Yet some of these developments did little or nothing to encourage scholars to study the real-world consequences of their research.

By the early 1980s, numerous changes were especially evident. Technological innovations such as microcomputers (and eventually the Internet) continued to appear, and scholars did not hesitate to study them. The field also moved away from an exclusive emphasis on mechanistic ideals in favor of viewing communication phenomena contextually (Georgoudi & Rosnow, 1985a). As in other social sciences, research tended to focus more on dynamic, processual, and historical phenomena. Such an emphasis was especially salient in the noteworthy *Ferment in the Field* special issue of the *Journal of Communication* (Gerbner, 1983). This issue assessed the state of the field about 25 years after Berelson's prediction. Today, the traditional effects focus remains, but other approaches have supplemented it. These include significant studies of media content, the varied meanings people attach to the same media text, and the intellectual history of the field. According to Georgoudi and Rosnow (1985a), Berelson's talk of withering away "was more prophetic of the revolutionary metamorphosis of the field than of its stagnation and death" (p. 86).

Limited Effects Reconsidered

In this light, many modern empirical scholars (e.g., J.M. McLeod & Becker, 1981) consider both powerful-effects assumptions and the limited-effects generalization as caricatures or exaggerations. The truth often seems to lie somewhere in the middle.

Why did the limited-effects idea become so widely accepted? One possibility is that a type of media effect on researchers contributed to the original limited-effects notion (Noelle-Neumann, 1983). According to Noelle-Neumann, in the late 1960s, Lazarsfeld told her that he abandoned communication research because he could not stand the media pressure that surrounded his work. In fact, Lazarsfeld, director of a budding research institute in 1940, later admitted his need to avoid losing media support. Noelle-Neumann argued that the published results of his Erie County study may have reflected a degree of scientific self-censorship. Critical scholar Todd Gitlin (1981) alleged that certain of the findings of the Decatur study of women's consumer behavior were clearly contrary to the two-step model and consistent with notions of powerful media effects. Yet Chaffee (1988) argued that Lazarsfeld's research team really was not to blame because of the inevitable problems with early research in any field. The real difficulty involved "what the Klappers did with the Lazarsfeld results. Instead of building new and better programs of research, they extrapolated from weak findings from the pre-television era to the conclusion that television too would only have limited effects" (p. 248). Perhaps journalists, who like other mass communicators have a vested interest in avoiding government regulation, also contributed to the scientific prestige accorded limited-effects research and tended to ignore or downplay other findings (Noelle-Neumann, 1983). To what extent such influences exist today among mass communication academics, who may depend on industry sources for grants and to hire their students, remains an open question.

Yet some thoughtful psychologists still express ideas reminiscent of the limited-effects notion. McGuire (1986a) reviewed evidence concerning a wide variety of hypothesized media effects and concluded that it failed to demonstrate convincingly that massive media effects occur. He did note that research has not proved a negative—that such effects do not occur. In referring to a massive media effect, he apparently meant a situation in which media-related behavior accounts for a heavy proportion of variation in outcomes such as aggressive or consumer behavior. In this sense, he is right. As assessed statistically, media-related behavior rarely accounts for more than a few percentages of the variation in any socially significant behavioral outcome.

In fact, an almost infinite number of potential factors are likely to influence the attitudes and behavior of media audiences. For example, age, gender, physical size, personality, family socioeconomic status (SES), and intelligence all might contribute—along with exposure to media violence—to a child's aggressive qualities. In addition, in U.S. society today, virtually everyone engages in media consumption, especially television viewing. This means that researchers often have to compare the attitudes and behaviors of people who already use media substantially. Because of this, research evidence may tend often to understate media effects. Finally, no assurance exists that causal agents account for all human behavior. Behavior sometimes may occur randomly and/or spontaneously perhaps because of the controversial notion that humans possess a free will. Therefore, whether a single type of causal influence (especially a mediated one) can account for most of the variability in any socially significant behavioral outcome is often highly questionable.

What then might determine the import of an effect? Its import is not found exclusively in purely mathematical indicators such as amounts of explained variation, which relate to the accuracy of using one thing to predict another (see chap. 2). For example, medical researchers link the majority of cases of lung cancer to cigarette smoking, and smokers have a risk of about 11 times greater than do nonsmokers. Nonetheless, smoking data only explain about 1% of the variation in this disease (J. Cohen & P. Cohen, 1983). The vast majority of both nonsmokers and smokers never develop evidence of the disease, and smoking data thus allow only a slight improvement beyond chance prediction. Similarly, television and television violence may only contribute to serious violence among a small number of those exposed to it, but even this could increase the rates of such crime rather markedly (Belson, 1978; Centerwall, 1989).

Rather, the extent to which analysis of media effects can potentially contribute to some socially significant outcome, such as the reduction of aggressive or antisocial behavior in young people, is of considerable importance (Perry, 1992). In this light, the evidence indicates that the mass media today are neither Satan nor the Messiah, nor are their effects wholly without import. Instead, they represent an often potentially important mechanism that individuals and society can use to adapt to their nonmedia environment and to achieve goals, as well as a part of the broader cultural environment to which human beings sometimes must accommodate themselves, at times unfortunately. The subsequent examination in this book of media effects evidence and the extent to which society has used it sometimes may raise the question of whether the limited-effects generalization describes the societal uses of research at least as much as it does media effects.

2

Processes of Theory Construction and Research

Science consists of both processes and products. In an effort to attain goals, such as predicting when something will occur, scientists employ a variety of tools, including theory and research methods. Understanding the products of research, such as its findings and warranted theoretical propositions, requires some familiarity with its processes. To many pragmatists, distinctions between means and ends are holistic and relative (see appendix). One implication of this especially applies here. According to Shusterman (1997), "True means are not simply necessary, external conditions for the end, but rather integral parts of it — as the colors and lines that are the means of a painting also form part of its end" (p. 82). Pragmatism emphasizes "process, method, correction, change, not definitive and permanent results" (Diesing, 1991, p. 75).

The chapter partly concerns methodology — the study of scientific methods. According to philosopher Abraham Kaplan (1964), *methods* are

> techniques sufficiently general to be common to all sciences, or to a signifi-
> cant part of them. Alternatively, they are logical or philosophical principles
> sufficiently specific to relate especially to science as distinguished from
> other human enterprises and interests. (p. 23)

In short, they involve such activities as forming hypotheses, building theories, and conducting experiments. The chapter also describes, in Kaplan's terms, the specific *techniques* commonly used in empirical mass communication research. For instance, it discusses the forms of theory and experimentation that such researchers often use.

The chapter sometimes focuses on what Kaplan called a *reconstructed logic*, an idealized description of procedure, often created by a philosopher. Certainly science sometimes advances through procedures, or logics-in-use, not linked to any reconstruction. To Kaplan, methodology and philosophy should seek to improve the usefulness of methods and techniques, not enforce inflexible rules. A logic's consequences, rather than its popularity, determine its value. Perhaps the various reconstructions discussed here can help readers understand theory and research in the later sections of the book.

WHAT IS RESEARCH?

Research sometimes is defined, somewhat controversially, as the systematic generation of new knowledge with replicable (i.e., repeatable) methods. To qualify, scholarly activity must be conducted so that other investigators could essentially repeat the procedures and determine whether the results hold up. The definition also requires that the work adhere to certain formal, systematic rules. An emphasis on replicability helps specify the boundaries of truth concerning scientific ideas and thus helps guard against unwarranted conclusions based on isolated research efforts (see the discussion in Miedema & Biesta, 1994). Without it, scholarly work could reveal more about the mind of the investigator than of the phenomena of interest. In this sense, the "intersubjective becomes the mark of objectivity, for it testifies that the observation is uncontaminated by any factors save those common to all observers" (Kaplan, 1964, p. 128). Science, then, is only relatively objective (Kurtz, 1992).

SCIENCE AND THEORY

Science is a form of semantic empiricism — the view that a meaningful idea must be testable with experience (Kaplan, 1964). Much of science involves a search for laws, empirical generalizations in which scientists place a great deal of confidence. Often such laws involve causal statements of this form: If X, then Y. For example, it may be a scientific law that if children are exposed to televised violence under certain conditions, they will become more aggressive in their behavior (see chap. 10). Beyond this, science seeks theories that explain why the laws occur. For instance, seeing violence on the tube may lower children's biological or socially induced restraints against behaving aggressively.

Obviously, then, both animals and humans depend on lawful empirical regularities to survive. One cannot eat breakfast, drive to work, walk across the street, or conduct an experiment without taking them into account. In turn, theories not only help scientists make sense of their empirical findings, but they also guide empirical inquiry in ways that soon will become evident. In short, a theory is a symbolic, human invention. Its existence requires significant symbols (see chap. 1), specifically those in language. According to Kaplan (1964): "To engage in theorizing means not just to learn by experience but to take thought about what is there to be learned. To speak loosely, lower animals grasp scientific laws but never rise to the level of scientific theory" (p. 295).

P.D. Reynolds (1971) discussed various forms of theory. The *set of laws* version conceives of it as statements summarizing " a set of well-supported empirical generalizations or 'laws' " (p. 10). One simple example is that pure water boils at 212 degrees Fahrenheit at sea level. Other forms see it either "as an iterrelated set of definitions, axioms, and propositions (that are derived from the axioms)" (p. 10) or "a set of descriptions of causal processes" (pp. 10–11). For example, assumptions that observing violence diminishes a person's inhibitions against aggression may serve as an axiom for a propositional hypothesis that exposure to television violence increases children's aggressiveness. Theories in this book generally take this axiomatic or causal process form sometimes a bit informally. The following paragraphs develop the simple example about television violence.

McGuire (1983, 1986b) summarized the historical evolution that established modern science as the preferred criterion for truth. This section borrows heavily from him. Early approaches centered around nonscientific forms of deduction—reasoning from general premises to specific conclusions that follow logically. Until 1,000 or so years ago, dogmatism was the preferred truth criterion. The establishment judged an idea by whether it related logically to or contradicted a supposedly infallible doctrine, such as Christian scripture. Gradually, a more sophisticated version of deductivism, rationalism, replaced dogmatism. A rationalist begins with premises that seem convincing based on logic or experience (e.g., that all life comes from other life), rather than on faith or authority alone. He or she then deduces the logical conclusions of these premises, individually and in combination. Next, the conclusions are combined, sometimes with the original premises, and yet more conclusions result. Eventually, one constructs an elaborate logical pyramid.

Dogmatism and rationalism lack an essential ingredient for science—a place for systematic observation. By the 17th century, an early scientific approach called *positivism* gained dominant influence. To a positivist, direct sensory experience provides the source of knowledge and the test of any theory. One observes nature, supposedly without preconceptions, and induces the general laws that govern the universe. *Induction* involves reasoning from specific, concrete particulars to general principles. Thus, positivism is quite compatible with the set-of-laws form of theory. Reynolds (1971) called positivism the research-then-theory approach. It "reflects the assumption that there are 'real' patterns in nature and that the task of scientists is to *discover* these patterns, the laws of nature" (p. 147).

As such, it embodies nonpragmatist philosophical assumptions that treat the human mind as a mirror of nature (Rorty, 1979). In any case, one insurmountable problem existed with early positivism. Pure observation, unguided by any implicit expectation of what one might find or without any recognition of what one is observing and why, seems impossible.

In the early 20th century, a group of philosophers known as the Vienna Circle formulated what developed into logical empiricism. By focusing on physics, the Vienna Circle tried to reconstruct a normative descriptive of all science. In large part, Kaplan's rejection of absolutist norms of procedure amounts to a criticism of any unjustified influence from their work.

In effect, the logical empiricists combined the rationalist and positivist approaches (McGuire, 1983). Figure 2.1 illustrates an influential form of their work. In it, science begins with rationalism. Commonly, one formulates or borrows a theory, consisting of a system of general principles designed to explain why things happen. One then deduces from the theory one or more hypotheses, which are concrete logical consequences of the theory that can be assessed against formal, sensory evidence. Thus, a scientist makes explicit both what he or she expects to find and why, instead of observing the world without acknowledging such expectations.

Therefore, one might assume that people who are exposed to large amounts of behavioral violence will tend to lose some of their socially induced inhibitions about it, which in turn will make them more prone to aggressive behavior. Another premise might be that children are prone to mass media influence. From these, one could deduce the hypothesis that, as a child's exposure to violent TV programming increases, he or she will tend to behave more aggressively. Those practicing theory-then-research

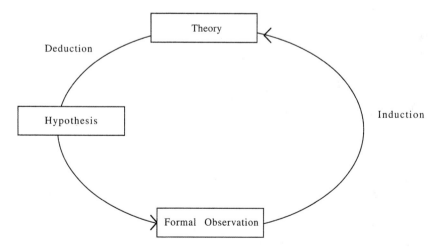

FIG. 2.1.   The circular relation of theory and research.

strategies implicitly construe science "as the process of *inventing* theories (formalizing an idea in axiomatic or causal process form) and then testing the usefulness of the invention" (Reynolds, 1971, p. 147; italics original). This reconstruction has obvious affinities with pragmatism. It generally appears more desirable than the inductivist approach, for a variety of reasons, according to Reynolds. For instance, it leads to more efficient research, it more readily permits usage of concepts (e.g., magnetism) that cannot be measured directly, and it may be especially helpful in allowing scientists to understand what they are studying.

As inquiry proceeds, scientists usually explicate the substantive concepts, such as aggression, contained within their hypotheses. Initially, one often conceptually defines the concepts using other concepts to clarify their meaning. What, for instance, is aggression? Is it limited to physical, rather than verbal, behavior? Does it require an overt attempt to harm someone else, or is the potential for harm sufficient? In one study discussed in chapter 10, Joy, Kimball, and Zabrack (1986) conceptually defined *aggression* as "physical aggression, with the potential to injure, and verbal abuse, including threats" (p. 303). Conceptual definitions allow scientists to employ a variety of different empirical indicators of a concept as long as the indicators are consistent with it. Of course, scientific progress requires a certain elasticity or tentativeness to these definitions; only research informs scientists of the usefulness of their conceptualizations. One may find, for instance, that televised violence has very different effects on levels of verbal and physical aggression in children, suggesting that research should assess the two separately. Chaffee (1991) provided a detailed discussion of concept explication in communication research.

Then formal research assesses (or, as some would say, tests) the hypotheses as directly as possible. A scientist operationally defines exposure to violent television and aggression by developing rules for observing these concepts (see the examples in Belson, 1978; Huesmann & Eron, 1986c). These rules must be consistent with the conceptual definitions, but they frequently will cover less ground. For example, one might study students at a local elementary school by sending diaries home in which their parents record details of the children's television-related behavior. These would not describe such behavior outside the home, however. From these, one would construct a measure of exposure to televised violence for each child. Then the researcher could ask each of a child's classmates whether the child has ever been known to engage in various forms of aggressive physical and verbal behavior. Finally, a statistical analysis could indicate whether those children who are heavily exposed to televised violence, on the average, behave more aggressively than do children who are less exposed. If so, the hypothesis has been confirmed or corroborated.

The fact that data support the hypothesis also helps support the theoretical premises, but only indirectly. If one properly deduces the hypothesis from the theory, the truth of the theory guarantees the truth of the hypothesis. The truth of a hypothesis does not imply the truth of theoretical premises, however. A researcher can derive any hypothesis from a virtually unlimited number of very different theories. In this case, different theories implying a causal impact of televised violence on aggression, as well as those suggesting that aggression may affect exposure instead, are also consistent with the hypothesis. For example, exposure to violence may affect aggression not because children lose socially induced restraints, but because they tend to imitate what they see on the tube (see the numerous examples in chap. 10). Or, other children perhaps ostracize kids with especially aggressive behavioral patterns, leaving the latter with few social activities that compete with watching television. Thus, support for the hypothesis only increases the plausibility of the theoretical premises. This illustrates the idea of underdetermination of theory by evidence, which claims that the same evidence can provide the basis for competing theories.

Philosophers often debate the existence of what I term *ultimate underdetermination*. This is the notion that the all conceivable observation cannot, in principle, decide the comparative acceptability of at least two logically incompatible theories (e.g., from Newtonian and Einsteinian physics). A more modest, and therefore probably less controversial, idea may apply with mass communication research. Available evidence probably always underdetermines theory and will do so at least for the foreseeable future, regardless of whether theory in principle must always remain underdetermined. Thus, one may well find a way to hold whatever position one wishes regardless of available evidence. For example, an industry executive can deny harmful effects of media violence, and a media critic can always do the opposite. Often, however, to do so may be unreasonable. To use an extreme example, one can rely on the underdetermination idea to argue that the Earth is flat. Doing so forces a person to make extremely convoluted assumptions about visual distortion in observational evidence.

As a result of difficulties with confirmationism, some philosophers (e.g., Popper, 1965) have maintained that science proceeds more by falsification of theory than by its confirmation. Science, as Popper defined it, is the practice of making bold conjectures about the world and attempting to refute them. A scientific idea must be potentially falsifiable through empirical (i.e., sensory) observation. That is to say, the idea must exclude some things from happening. Commonly mentioned examples of nonscientific ideas include forms of religious fundamentalism, Marxism-Leninism, Freudian psychology, and various debates about the existence of God. For example, one simply cannot disprove the existence of God by systematic observation of nature. Among scientific ideas, a kind of Darwinian survival of the fittest perhaps occurs. Ultimately, the falsification of any scientific idea will almost certainly occur, and something better will replace it, according to this reconstruction.

Perhaps neither confirmationism nor this form of falsificationism adequately describes scientific procedures, however. Philosopher W.V. Quine (1951/1980) suggested why. He condemned the logical empiricists' reductionism as dogmatic. In the sense applicable here, it is the notion that in science, each hypothesis, "taken in isolation from its fellows, can admit of confirmation or infirmation at all" (p. 41). Instead, Quine argued, the totality of human knowledge or belief, "from the most casual matters of geography and history to the profoundist laws of atomic physics or even of pure mathematics and logic, is a man-made fabric which impinges on experience only along the edges" (p. 42).

Conceivably, Quine's holistic notion could implicate all of science in any hypothesis test. Thus, studying the impact of media violence may also implicitly rely on assumptions and theories from diverse areas, including seemingly unrelated fields such as bacteriology, geology, physics, and so on. More modestly, when a scientist tests a theory, he or she "is actually 'testing' a host of initial conditions, measuring instruments and auxiliary hypotheses that together form the *ceteris paribus* conditions" (Hunt, 1991, p. 356). In other words, individual hypotheses and scientific statements usually become meaningful only when linked together. An exception might occur if a scientific sentence is lengthy enough to express a number of different hypotheses. In any case, if unexpected results occur, one therefore will not know why. The theory, the deductive link between it and hypothesis, the measuring instruments used, and so on could all be at fault. In short, a researcher has the ability to "adjust one strand of the fabric of science rather than another in accommodating some particular recalcitrant experience" (Quine, 1951/1980, p. 46). Thus, absolute falsification cannot occur.

In other words, evidence does not mandate one humanly invented interpretation. Instead, theories thrive or die in terms of their long-run, pragmatic consequences (Hesse, 1980; Mounce, 1997). These may include whether they prove useful in the prediction, explanation, and control of phenomena (see the subsequent section on the goals of science). Until long-run consequences become evident, how can one choose among alternatives? Following Quine (1951/1980), pragmatic values such as simplicity or maintenance of earlier belief may be influential. To reject the flat world idea allows use of much simpler observational assumptions, and it also conserves other knowledge far more readily, for example. In short, scientists have to interpret, in potentially revisable ways, Nature's responses to research questions.

Next, the researcher uses induction to reason from the results back to the more general theoretical premises, completing the circular process depicted in Fig. 2.1. Ideally, research should corroborate scientific laws and theories that apply universally across time and space. For example, the real issue concerning exposure to televised violence and aggressive behavior is not limited to a sample of children in a single elementary school. Instead, it applies to all children who will ever view the medium. Yet no logical mechanism can justify or prove such inductive conclusions. Their justification comes from evidence of pragmatic convenience (Abel, 1966–1967). In the social sciences, virtually all knowledge at most describes *quasi laws*, for which unexplained exceptions occur (Kaplan, 1964). Thus, research often helps define a limited range of situations in which theoretical ideas likely apply (McGuire, 1983). For example, aggression linked to mediated violence may occur only among children of a certain age, class, or gender.

In summary, axiomatic theory includes a number of features (see Reynolds, 1971). Among these are theoretical and operational definitions, plus a set of existence statements that describe the contexts or scope within which the theory applies. It also contains axioms, "statements from which all other statements in the theory may be derived" (p. 92). In the preceding example, these include the disinhibition idea and the notion that children are especially affected by television. Propositions, including in this case the hypothesis about television violence, should also be present. These are all "other statements in the theory, all derived from combinations of axioms, axioms and propositions, and other propositions" (p. 93). Finally, a system of logic (e.g., deduction) exists that relates concepts within various statements and allows the derivation of hypotheses.

The similar causal-process form substitutes a set of causal statements that are not separated into axioms and propositions. Each identifies the impact of one or more causal agents on one or more outcomes (see Reynolds, 1991). A simple example could consist of two statements: "If exposure to television violence, then disinhibition" and "If disinhibition, then enhanced aggressiveness." From this, one may derive the following, "If exposure to television violence, then enhanced aggressiveness." More complex examples might add processes of imitation and excitation (see chap. 10) as additional mechanisms explaining why television exposure might lead to more aggressive behavior. All together, they would yield the disinhibition-imitation-excitation theory in Fig. 2.2.

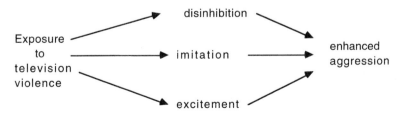

FIG. 2.2.   A causal-process presentation of theory concerning TV violence and aggression.

The work of the logical empiricists remains an important influence on much of social science, perhaps both because researchers find it useful and because of the emphasis it receives in textbooks. Yet their reconstructions have shortcomings. As McGuire (1986b) put it, often an "outcome that fails to confirm the hypothesis leads to the rejection, not of the hypothesis (as required by logical empiricism) but rather of the experiment" (p. 283). Given Quine's ideas, this is not necessarily wrong. The procedures used, including the measures, may contain flaws that prevented confirmation. Thus, however useful logical empiricism may be as an initial description of science, research does not proceed in so tight a manner as it may suggest.

McGuire (1983) advocated a contextualist revision of the logical-empiricist view of the research process. To him, all knowledge contains flaws. He argued that the seriousness of the distortion inherent in a given theory or hypothesis varies across different contexts. In fact, scientists should assume a priori that all theories and hypotheses, even contradictory ones, are both relatively true and false as situations change. In this regard, McGuire (1973b) quoted William Blake: "Everything possible to be believ'd is an image of truth" (p. 448). Instead of describing research as testing or attempting to falsify theories and hypotheses, it may be more meaningful to think of it as a process of discovery aimed at clarifying the limitations of scientific ideas, as well as helping to explicate the assumptions that one makes in asserting them. Rather than rejecting and ignoring the earlier, unsuccessful "tests," his position encourages scientists to take them as indicative of contexts in which the truth of their ideas varies. In effect, McGuire advocated replacing one reconstructed logic with another, which may be more congenial with actual scientific procedures.

By advocating what he termed *sophisticated falsificationism*, Lakatos (1970) described yet another reconstruction. According to some versions of falsificationism, "the theoretician proposes, the experimenter—in the name of Nature—disposes" (p. 95). This rests on assumptions that a natural border separates theory and fact. Instead, as Quine emphasized, scientists rely upon various theories, such as those pertaining to measurement, in determining facts. To a sophisticated falsificationist, abandoning a theory requires not just anomalies, but a superior alternative. A theory's inconsistency with pieces of evidence may not prove fatal. As it evolves, it may gain an ability to handle these. Even Einstein's work encountered numerous anomalies. A replacement not only should handle evidence supporting its competitor, but more as well. It should imply novel predictions, at least some of which are sustained.

In addition, according to Lakatos, a researcher may immunize the central core of a theory from evidence (see discussions in Diesing, 1991; Larvor, 1998). These ideas are essential to research programs, which consist of a series of historically related theories. Their abandonment would require giving up the program. Newtonian mechanics represent a good example. If heavenly bodies did not seem to move as his laws of motion and gravitation predicted, Isaac Newton could allege that "the observations must be distorted by the atmosphere or misinterpreted by poor optical theory" (Larvor, 1998, p. 52).

Programs either progress or degenerate. Progressive ones develop logically and successfully predict novel phenomena, at least sometimes. Degenerates focus rather exclusively on adjusting theories to unsupportive facts. In mass communication research, Viswanath and Finnegan (1996) described knowledge-gap research (see chap. 6) as a progressive program. Marxism and psychoanalysis fall into the latter category, according to Lakatos. Marx's predictions about revolution , as well as those of his followers, have failed repeatedly, for example. A scientist has no obligation to drop a degenerating program, which may turn progressive. Honesty about its often poor prospects is required, however.

As Lakatos (1970) put it, "The history of science has been and should be a history of competing research programmes" (p. 155). Unlike Lakatos' view of Kuhn paradigms (see chap. 1), rational procedures guide such programs. Newtonian and Einsteinian physics represent obvious examples. In addition, *the continuity in science, the tenacity of some theories, the rationality of a certain amount of dogmatism, can only be explained if we construe science as a battleground of research programmes rather than of isolated theories*" (p. 155; italics original). His ideas obviously contain a larger component of rationalism and even dogmatism than do those of many philosophers. He believed that theory could develop internally without encountering data for lengthy periods of time. Although he considered himself no pragmatist, Lakatos claimed his reconstruction combined the best elements of various orientations, including pragmatism. Those encountering controversies concerning research areas, such as media usage and social capital or cultivation effects of television (see chap. 9), may find some of his ideas useful in comprehending the evolution of these topics.

CREATING THEORY

Where does theory come from? How does one invent a scientifically promising idea? For one thing, the forms that theories take sometimes depend on the symbolic ideas that are salient in a culture at a given time. Mechanistic theories during the 19th century often resulted from the machine age. For another example, the information-processing models widely used today in cognitive psychology (see chap. 6) rather obviously did not exist prior to computers.

Traditionally, research training has tended to neglect theory creation on the assumption that creative theorists are born, not nurtured. Nonetheless, some sources (e.g., Reynolds, 1971; McGuire, 1997) have attempted to provide guidance. According to Reynolds (1971), important new ideas tend to arise from identifiable circumstances, such as from the work of a relatively solitary individual. Neither the inductivist idea of the scholar as computer who uncovers reliable empirical patterns or the theory-first notion "of an individual dreaming away in study" (p. 153) until hitting on an world-class idea quite matches available evidence.

> The overall image is that of one intelligent individual who knows what useful ideas are, who is well acquainted with the existing theories in the area he is studying, who is not committed to any of the existing theories, and who is working closely with both the theories and the phenomenon. (p. 153)

Despite the advantages of the theory-then-research approach, Reynolds (1971) endorsed a composite in which a scholar may do purely exploratory or descriptive studies to generate ideas for use in later formal hypothesis testing. Communication researchers who state research questions, rather than explicating hypotheses, may be following this strategy. An example would be: "What are the television-related motives for using the World Wide Web?" (see Ferguson & Perse, 2000, p. 158).

In this light, McGuire (1997), who for decades has argued that instruction can improve one's ability to generate hypotheses, recently listed several dozen potentially useful techniques. Some of these do not require knowledge of sophisticated research techniques. For example, one might attempt to understand why exceptions occur to general trends. Thus, a communication researcher may interview National Merit Scholars who watch unusually large amounts of television in an effort to understand contexts in which time spent with the medium may not diminish academic accomplishment. As another example, a researcher may introspectively analyze his or her own behavior in similar situations to those under study. For instance, a researcher who is interested in the contexts that enhance the impact of pressures for conformity on public expression might recall instances in which he or she has kept quiet rather than risk starting an argument. Other examples, such as mathematical modeling, require advanced research training, however.

THE GOALS OF SCIENCE

The scientific enterprise has a number of goals. One can value scientific theories and hypotheses according to their usefulness in achieving these, instead of by whether they somehow mirror reality. Reynolds (1971) listed five goals: construction of typologies, predictions of the future, explanations of the past, a sense of understanding about the causes of events, and control of phenomena studied. Of these, he identified construction of typologies, systems for classification, as the easiest to achieve. For instance, one can classify news stories by their dateline or acts of aggression according to whether they are rewarded or punished (see the examples in the *National Television Violence Study*, 1997–1998). Typologies often function to advance the other goals.

Science may also predict future events, as when meteorologists forecast tomorrow's weather. In general, the social sciences are not known for their precise predictions, although they can attain a degree of success. For example, sometimes one can predict reasonably well how aggressive a child will be (in comparison with others) later in life from his or her early behavior (see the discussion in Huesmann & Eron, 1986b). Science sometimes may explain the past, as when scholars attempt to assess why murder rates fluctuate (Centerwall, 1989) or why community ties seem to weaken (Putnam, 2000). Another goal of science—providing a sense of understanding—is the most difficult to achieve. According to Reynolds, this occurs only when one describes fully the causal mechanisms that link causes to effects. For example, describing and empirically validating the disinhibitory impact of televised violence on aggressive behavior (e.g., Belson, 1978) would provide a partial sense of understanding. It is partial because other theoretical mechanisms, such as imitative behavior, are also likely to occur. Finally, science sometimes permits some degree of control of events. In one study, intensive efforts to convince children not to imitate television violence reduced their aggression levels several months later (Huesmann, Eron, Klein, Brice, & Fischer, 1983; Rosenthal, 1986). Nonetheless, some scientific fields cannot attain this goal. Meteorological knowledge helps people prepare for bad weather, but it does not control it.

DESIRABLE CHARACTERISTICS OF THEORY

Obviously, theory becomes valuable to the extent that it helps attain these goals of science. It must be potentially refutable (at least provisionally) and help describe, predict, explain, and/or control phenomena of interest. Abstract theory, which applies broadly across time and space, is likely to be especially helpful in attaining these goals. Beyond these features, a number of other values may affect the scientific community's acceptance of a theory. These include simplicity and conservatism, which Quine emphasized. To the extent that two competing theoretical explanations of a phenomenon have the same evidentiary support, scientists sometimes favor the simpler one. Perhaps especially in the social sciences, counterintuitiveness can enhance the value of a theory. Some scholars argue that science makes its greatest contribution when it refutes commonsense beliefs, such as that the world is flat. Counterintuitive ideas that receive empirical support, such as early claims that sexually explicit materials reduce rates of sex-related crimes (see chap. 10), are likely to be both scrutinized closely and prized if they survive.

TYPES OF VARIABLES

Science is only concerned with variables—things that take different numerical values at different points in time and space. It cannot deal with constants. If one tests a causal hypothesis or theory, a presumed cause is known as an *independent variable*. The term *dependent variable* refers to the presumed effect.

Research often involves a variety of other variables. *Control variables* are those that a researcher eliminates any influence of from a study. *Intervening* or *mediator variables* come between a cause and an effect and help determine why a causal process occurs. For example, exposure to television may contribute to some health problems because it disrupts social ties (see the discussion of Putnam [2000] in chap. 9). In this case, diminished ties would be both an effect of televised and a cause of health problems. *Moderator* variables modify the extent to which a causal process occurs. For instance, exposure to televised violence might have more impact on younger children than on older ones (Paik & Comstock, 1994).

CAUSATION

To a large degree, then, science exists to explain why things happen. For example, one may be concerned about the amount of violence in society and wonder what effect the media have on this. Any discussion of media effects requires a concern with causation. Before a researcher can conclude that one concept is a cause of another, the researcher must establish three things. First, the presumed cause and effect must covary, or go together. For example, people who are heavily exposed to mediated violence should tend, on the average, to be either more or less aggressive than those who are less exposed. If aggressiveness increases along with exposure, the two variables are positively correlated or associated. If aggressiveness tends to decline as exposure increases, the two are negatively correlated. Second, the presumed cause must precede the presumed effect. Finally, a researcher must eliminate plausible rival (i.e., third variable) explanations for the observed covariation of the presumed cause and effect. This notion of causation largely originated with 19th-century utilitarian philosopher John Stuart Mill (T.D. Cook & Campbell, 1979).

For example, evidence that children who are heavily exposed to mediated violence tend also to be relatively aggressive satisfies the first condition. The two covary. Virtually all available research (see chap. 10) supports this idea. From this, one cannot determine which variable is the cause and which the effect, however. Aggression may increase exposure rather than vice versa. Both processes could even occur (see Belson, 1978; Huesmann & Eron, 1986a). Finally, something that affects both exposure and aggression may create the observed covariation. Thus, no causal relationship between the two may exist. For instance, children who live in high-crime areas may both watch a lot of TV, rather than expose themselves to danger outside, and behave aggressively as a survival skill. This may create a misleading correlation between exposure and aggression. In an absolute sense, science never proves that one thing causes another. Instead, one must look at the preponderance of evidence. This is one of the major reasons that evidence underdetermines theory, as discussed earlier.

Causal processes can take many forms, and theorists need to state precisely which of these to expect. A cause may or may not be necessary or sufficient to produce an effect. In the social sciences, almost everything has multiple causes, so scholars generally will not find individual variables that are necessary to produce an effect. A sufficient cause produces effects regardless of other factors. In addition, a cause may be deterministic or stochastic. It may always produce an effect or only increase odds of the effect occurring. For example, exposure to TV violence may slightly increase the aggressiveness of everyone, but only result in criminal violence in a much smaller number of people (see Centerwall, 1989). In addition, a cause may be reversible or not. That is to say, a theoretical orientation may predict that exposure to TV violence both increases aggression and vice versa (see Belson, 1978; Huesmann & Eron, 1986a).

Philosophers have not always accepted traditional notions of causation. Following 18th-century philosopher David Hume, hard-core empiricists have claimed that causation only involves temporal regularity, not the unseen forces implicated by common sense. Pragmatic contextualists (see appendix) may see causation as a useful imposition on data. However, they may reject mechanist ideas that cause and effect "are discrete parts that exist independently of their relations, or of the scientist's act of analyzing the whole into parts" (Hayes, Hayes, & Reese, 1988, p. 105).

RESEARCH APPROACHES

Many scholars classify empirical research techniques into three types: experimental, correlational, and descriptive. These all represent ways to bring hunches and theories about the world into confrontation with experience.

Experimental Studies

In the most general sense, experimentation involves staging one or more events and observing the consequences. Researchers conduct experiments for a variety of reasons, ranging from pretesting a research design to attempting to refine a measuring instrument (Kaplan, 1964). One common use involves testing causal hypotheses. When appropriate, a formal experiment may provide important, but not infallible, evidence of causation. To conduct one, researchers must do two things. First, they must manipulate at least one independent variable. One does not merely observe and measure an independent variable as it naturally occurs. Instead, it is controlled and varied as part of the study design. Second, chance processes must determine whether, or to what degree, an individual participant is exposed to the independent variable. This is known as *random assignment*.

For example, one could use 100 school children in a simple experiment, dividing them randomly into two groups of 50 students each. The researcher might then expose one group, known as the *treatment group*, to a predetermined amount of filmed violence. The second group, a *control group*, would not see the violence. Finally, the children could be turned loose on a playground. There, trained observers would record how frequently each child behaves aggressively. Finally, the researcher could compare the average rate among the children in each group.

Such research meets many of the criteria for causal inference. First, if more aggression occurs among children in the treatment group than in the control group, covariation is established. Second, time order is built into the design. Children are exposed to the independent variable before observation of the dependent variable. Third, by letting chance determine which of the children are in the two groups, a researcher largely controls for prior differences in aggression and for other factors that may affect it. For example, about the same average level of aggression should exist in each group prior to experimental manipulation. Also each group should have about the same number of males and females. Perfect comparability will not occur, but any preexisting differences will result from chance.

This feature allows researchers to eliminate many, but not necessarily all, plausible rival hypotheses. For example, an artifact could affect the frequency of aggression among those in the treatment group. For instance, an experimenter might accidentally cue these children that they are expected to behave aggressively. In addition, something about the experimental setting, such as different temperatures in the rooms in which the films were shown, could influence subsequent behavior. In this sense, data underdetermine any interpretation of experimental results.

This example illustrates a simple experiment. It used only one manipulated independent variable with only two levels. Normally, multiple independent variables are used in experimental research. For example, a researcher might separate the children by gender and then randomly assign within each group. Continuing the prior example, this would create four experimental groups (i.e., treatment and control groups for males and females). The resulting study would be a 2 × 2 design. Each independent variable has two levels each. Clearly, random assignment of the children to gender is impossible. Only exposure is manipulated within each gender condition. This makes any causal inference about the impact of gender on aggression problematic. Nonetheless, as long as at least some independent variables are manipulated, the design can qualify as an experiment.

The use of multiple independent variables in experimental designs is substantially beneficial. If the impact of exposure to media varies for different people, such designs allow the efficient study of these differences. For example, including both exposure to mediated violence and gender in one design permits a researcher to examine both the separate relation of each independent variable with aggression and their interaction. An interaction occurs whenever the effect of one thing on another varies according to some third variable. For instance, exposure may have more effect on males than females. Hovland and Weiss (1951–1952) conducted a famous experiment concerning the changing effect of source credibility on attitudes as time elapses (see chap. 7).

Sometimes a researcher manipulates one or more independent variables, but does not randomly assign respondents to any of the different experimental conditions. For example, a researcher may have two existing classes of elementary school students and use one as the control group and the other as the treatment group. This sort of study is known as a *quasi-experiment*. Obviously it is much weaker than a formal experiment for causal inference. There is no assurance that the groups differ only by chance at the start of the study. Joy, Kimball, and Zabrack (1986) conducted an interesting quasi-experiment in which they took advantage of a naturally occurring independent variable manipulation—the introduction of TV into a Canadian town (see chap. 10).

Because of their usefulness for causal inference, experimental studies usually are high in internal validity. Nonetheless, this strength carries a price. By definition, they involve contrived settings that may differ dramatically from the way audiences use mass communication in the "real" world. For example, exposure to TV violence normally occurs voluntarily and at home. If a researcher controls it, one has no assurance that the effects observed will apply in more typical contexts. Thus, experimental research may indicate what can happen, rather than what does happen in "realistic" settings. In this sense, it is often low in external validity, or generalizability to the "real" world. Experimental research also tends to be limited to the short-term impact of the mass media. One usually cannot manipulate and control media-related behavior for months or years.

Correlational Studies

These examine the covariation between variables, such as exposure to TV violence and aggression in children, without researcher manipulation or random assignment. Instead, a researcher usually measures the variables as they occur naturally. Such studies often fall well short of meeting the criteria for causal inference. A purely correlational study, involving measures of exposure to TV violence and aggression, was described earlier. It was a synchronic or cross-sectional study. Each variable was measured at only one time point. Putnam's (2000) study of changes in social participation in the United States used much cross-sectional data, for example (see chap. 9).

It is sometimes possible to control time order by using a diachronic study, which involves more than one time point. Measurement of theoretically important third variables, and statistical techniques, permit a researcher to control these as well. However, the number of such variables is generally so large that one cannot possibly measure all of them. Such statistical control is not likely to deal with as many third variables as does experimental random assignment.

Despite this shortcoming, correlational studies usually reflect naturally occurring processes. In this sense, they are high in external validity. In fact, many questions are examined using both experimental and correlational techniques. To the extent that each type provides similar evidence (e.g., that as a person's exposure to mediated violence increases, so does his or her aggression), the two complement each other nicely. Each is strong exactly where the other is weak.

Much work has gone into making causal inference in nonexperimental situations. Time has not been kind to certain techniques. One approach, occasionally used in media research, involves cross-lagged correlations. Here, researchers try to determine which of two correlated variables — A or B — has the strongest influence on the other. A might be exposure to TV violence and B aggression, for instance. To simplify things a little, they compare the correlation between A, as measured initially, and B, as observed later, with that between initially observed B and later measured A (T.D. Cook & Campbell, 1979). Rogosa (1980) discussed problems with this approach. Causal modeling techniques can also be problematic. They allow researchers to examine the consequences of causal assumptions. Ordinarily, these do not demonstrate which of two associated variables may be a causal agent or allow one to infer that causation exists (Asher, 1976). This is so regardless of the seductive path diagrams that often accompany such work.

Stronger techniques exist to examine causation with observational data, however. Examples often appear in panel studies, such as those concerning the effects of TV violence on the young (Huesmann & Eron, 1986c; Milavsky et al., 1982) as discussed in chapter 10. In these studies, the basic model in data analyses — to simplify things with minimal distortion — frequently involves relating initial levels of an independent variable (e.g., violence exposure) to future changes in a dependent variable (e.g., aggressiveness). This approach is a vast improvement from cross-sectional, correlational studies because it eliminates reverse causation from the design. For example, changes in a child's aggressiveness cannot affect his or her earlier exposure. In addition, third variables come into play only if they influence both initial exposure and later changes in aggressiveness. Thus, the design retains some (but not all) of the controls present in an experiment while permitting study of naturally occurring, long-term effects.

In addition, epidemiologists have developed rules for determining the presence of causality in their largely observational science. Epidemiology examines the incidence and causes of such things as death, disease, and injury. For instance, researchers may wonder whether one's gender affects susceptibility to some sort of disease. Obviously, to randomly assign people to gender is an ethical impossibility. Epidemiologists rely on a number of issues that influence the confidence with which they make causal inferences. These include how strongly variables are correlated, the consistency of their association across different contexts, the theoretical plausibility of evidence, its coherence with other knowledge, and time order of presumed cause and effect (Friis & Sellers, 1996). Such considerations have helped permit conclusions that, among humans, smoking causes lung cancer and sexual behavior spreads the HIV virus. In a controversial study, Centerwall (1989) used such criteria to conclude that the introduction of TV into the United States caused a subsequent doubling of criminal homicide rates (see the discussion in chap. 10).

Descriptive Studies

These simply describe the degree to which something is present. No attempt is made to link independent variables with dependent variables. A study concerning the amount of violence during a typical week of prime-time television (see chap. 5) would exemplify a descriptive study.

MEASUREMENT

Formally, one can define *measurement* as "the assignment of numbers to objects (or events or situations) in accord with some rule" (Kaplan, 1964, p. 177). Communication researchers use a variety of measurement techniques in their work. These range from attitudinal questionnaires to unobtrusive observation of human behavior to physiological indicators. Any research conclusion rests on an assumption that a researcher has measured variables properly. Two concerns—reliability and validity—commonly arise about the quality of measurement. Reliability exists to the extent that random measurement error is absent. Such error occurs when a measuring instrument provides data that fluctuate in no particular pattern above and below a "true" value, such as a person's weight. The best way to think of reliablity is not as something that lies outside human experience, but as the value that repeated improvements in a measure converge on (Kaplan, 1964). Reliability usually can be assessed fairly directly, as when a researcher checks to see whether an instrument provides consistent readings at different time points. For example, in his TV effects study, Centerwall (1989) used evidence that medical and police records agree about 95% of the time to establish the reliability of homicide diagnoses.

Reliability is not the key issue in measurement, however. Far more important is a measure's *validity*, commonly defined as the extent to which it actually measures what one wishes it to. Both random and systematic errors hurt validity. Systematic, or biasing, error can occur in various ways. A measure of behavioral aggression could consistently overstate people's propensities, or it could reflect something other than aggressiveness, such as nervous energy. By definition, reliability is an upper bound on validity; something can be no more valid than it is reliable. If only random error occurs, the reliability of a measure equals its validity. If systematic error exists, a measure is more reliable than it is valid.

Assessment of validity is less clear cut than that of reliability. Typically, two broad classes of measurement validity are recognized. A measure has *pragmatic validity* to the extent that it is useful in some practical sense. For example, many graduate programs use the Graduate Record Examination (GRE) to screen applicants. If the test actually predicts likelihood of success, it has pragmatic validity. In this case, one tests a hypothesis about covariation between a person's GRE score and the likelihood that he or she would complete graduate study. Ordinarily, the hypothesis would not be linked to an explicit theory. *Construct validation* is really identical to the pragmatic form, except that more explicitly theoretical research assesses it. To the extent that one's theoretically derived hypotheses receive support from research, one has evidence for the construct validity of the measures used. Evidence that exposure to TV violence and aggression in children tend to increase together as hypothesized would be evidence that the researcher used valid exposure and aggression measures.

STATISTICS

Quantitative methods, usually of statistical form, are ubiquitous in modern social-scientific research. Two types of statistics normally are used: descriptive and inferential statistics. Descriptive statistics merely reduce a body of data to manageable proportions. One of the most common of these is the arithmetic mean, or average. For example, to compare aggression among children in an experimental group with aggression among those in a control group, one almost certainly would examine their group means. The Pearson correlation coefficient is another example. It ranges from 1 to –1 and indicates the degree of covariation between two variables. A correlation of 1 (or –1) occurs only if perfect positive (or negative) covariation is present (i.e., if one can perfectly predict values of a dependent variable from knowledge of an independent variable). A correlation of 0 suggests a total absence of covariation. In mass communication research, weak to moderate correlations ranging from .2 to .4 typically occur. The relatively low correlations may occur because many factors other than media-related behavior affect commonly used dependent variables such as aggression.

By squaring the correlation, one obtains the coefficient of determination—an indicator of the extent to which knowledge of an independent variable allows a researcher to reduce error in predicting a dependent variable. This is usually stated as percentages of explained variation. For example, a correlation of .2 between exposure to TV violence and aggression would suggest that exposure explained or accounted for .04 (4%) of the variation in aggression among audience members. This does not necessarily mean that the audience would be 4% less aggressive without violence exposure. Mathematically, the measure would allow prediction accuracy to be 4% greater than otherwise. Discussion of explained variation also does not imply causation unless a study meets standard criteria for causal inference.

Inferential statistics examine the plausibility of judgments that go beyond one's data. Researchers who use random sampling often use inferential statistics. Sampling occurs when, for reasons of time or economy, a researcher examines only a subset of a concrete population. For example, a pollster might wish to describe the likely proportion of the vote that two candidates will receive in an upcoming election. He or she normally will not try to contact every potential voter—the population. Instead only a sufficient number whose responses should represent adequately those of everyone is interviewed. As long as every potential voter has an equal chance of being included in the sample, the pollster can make an educated guess about the outcome of the election. Ideally, any difference between the preferences of the sample and those of the population will occur only from chance.

Researchers often use inferential statistics without random sampling. In experimental research, this can help assess whether observed differences between or among experimental groups are likely to reflect chance variations attributable to random assignment or differences linked to the independent variables. A statistically significant difference cannot plausibly be attributed to chance. Usually such a difference is large enough that it will occur by chance fewer than 1 time in 20. For instance, assume that an experimenter compares a treatment group of children recently exposed to mediated violence with an unexposed control group. On the average, members of the first group perform two acts of physical aggression per minute of play, and those in the second engage in only one per minute. Inferential statistics indicate that chance would produce such a difference less than 1 in 20 times. Thus, the researcher can conclude that the violence manipulation likely increased physical aggression. For a similar example, see Joy et al. (1986).

META-ANALYSES

This book sometimes relies on meta-analytic results (e.g, those of Paik & Comstock, 1994) to summarize available studies concerning a research question. Meta-analysis (Hunter, Schmidt, & Jackson, 1982) is a formal research technique in which researchers analyze statistical patterns found in available research studies. It represents a formalistic, replicable version of often more impressionistic literature reviews. Researchers conducting meta-analyses nonetheless assume certain risks in common with literature reviewers. Both techniques sometimes treat all studies equally regardless of quality. Both tend to rely on the published record, which may present an unrepresentative picture because journals often refuse to publish research with nonsignificant results. Despite these shared imperfections, meta-analytic studies generally appear superior to traditional reviews as a means of summarizing the current state of knowledge (Beaman, 1991). Thus, students perhaps should regard conclusions from meta-analyses as generally less tentative than those that come from traditional reviews. Unfortunately, even a cursory comparison of *Communication Abstracts* with the *Psychological Abstracts* suggests that the field of communication lags seriously behind related disciplines in the amount of meta-analytic work available.

OTHER APPROACHES

The quantitative research techniques described in this chapter by no means exhaust those employed by modern communication scholars. Like many other social sciences, in recent years the field has gone through a period of ferment (Gerbner, 1983). Challenges sometimes reflecting both modern attacks on empiricism and ancient doubts about its usefulness in social research have appeared to traditional methods. Many researchers (e.g., Craig, 1989, 1993) have called for pluralism. For example research approaches using qualitative, interpretative approaches continue to attract a significant body of scholars (Potter, Cooper, & Dupagne, 1993). Often such studies attempt to understand human behavior from people's own frame of reference rather than to explain the laws that govern behavior.

Today scholars (e.g., Craig, 1989) often divide social inquiry into three categories. These include the empirical sciences, which seek to predict and control phenomena by the identification of general laws; the historical-hermeneutic sciences, which focus on the interpretation of texts (e.g., conversations or written documents); and critical theory, which has as its goal human emancipation. These categories are not necessarily mutually exclusive. For example, critical theorists sometimes attempt to incorporate the other two approaches into their work (see Craig, 1989). This book primarily concerns empirical research, yet one of its purposes is to encourage a critical emancipation of media consumers. Finally, writing the book required me to first interpret hundreds of texts (e.g., research articles and books), thus employing hermeneutics.

"REAL-WORLD" CONSEQUENCES OF THEORY AND RESEARCH

Social science has a potential for both use and misuse. For example, it can help solve widespread human problems or assist the powerful in taking advantage of the less fortunate. One common "real-world" function of theoretical explanation is technological, in which it may help attain ends beyond those of inquiry. Thus, scientific prediction helps people adapt to their environment (Kaplan, 1964). For example, parents may prevent their children from watching television TV because of research evidence linking it with a loss of inhibitions against behavioral aggression. If the explanation of aggression is sound, it could prevent future aggressive behavior.

Sometimes interwoven with this, a social-science explanation may have an instrumental function, in Kaplan's terms. This concerns the impact of awareness of an explanation. In the example just given, the instrumental function produced the parents' action. Beyond this, instrumental functions may even become self-fulfilling if they concern the behavior of those who learn an explanation. For instance, a journalist who studies a theory describing influences on news content (see chap. 5) may act in ways consistent with the theory.

To what extent this affects the scientific status of the theory is problematic. Obviously, this is a problem unique to the social sciences. In physical science, the objects of study cannot acquire an awareness of scientific explanations about them. In a sense, then, awareness of social science among the public could become constitutive. It potentially "influences how people in society think and talk about their own activities and thereby shapes those activities and the emergent social structures produced and reproduced in them" (Craig, 1993, p. 30).

Largely because of such considerations, Craig called for an abandonment of traditional forms of theory. As he stated,

> a theory that actively shapes the very phenomena it purportedly explains is essentially untestable and thus irreparably unscientific. Any observations that might be adduced to test predictions derived from such a theory are hopelessly contaminated, and the logic of explanation falls into a vicious circle. (p. 30)

According to Craig (1993), researchers facing this situation can do one of two things. First, they could attempt to insulate society from the influence of theory. Obviously, Craig argued, such an option is ethically ridiculous and futile, at least in an open society. Second, researchers could embrace this constitutive role of theory and take responsibility for it. Thus, he advocated social scientists to largely abandon traditional models of theory in favor of essentially normative, practical approaches (as discussed in Craig, 1989).

Yet one can dispute the merits of Craig's argument. For example, the constitutive or instrumental function of theoretical explanations may not be as important as he assumed. The only widely researched question pertinent to this involves the impact of demand characteristics, the awareness among research subjects of possible hypotheses being tested. In general, the impact of demand characteristics on human behavior often may be overstated (L. Berkowitz & Donnerstein, 1982).

A possible criticism to Craig's rejection of traditional theory on the grounds of its constitutive effects is that it fails to separate adequately the influence of theory from the impact of people's awareness of it. One could retain the scientific legitimacy of traditional approaches by simply explicating their boundary conditions—by asserting that social-scientific theory will only apply to the extent that people are unaware of it (Kurtz, 1990). As Kaplan (1964) suggested, research could then examine the impact of people's awareness of theory on the very phenomena a theory attempts to describe.

In the media-effects area, whether all this would render theory unscientific seems a bit beside the point. Perhaps social scientists would be more effective if they stopped worrying so much about being scientific (Kaplan, 1964). What really matters is whether theoretical vocabularies help solve scientific problems and improve society. Therefore, the world clearly needs more research explicitly examining the social consequences of media research. Polemical claims abound, but only a limited number of truly empirical studies exists. These range from histories of the role research has played in debates about media violence (Rowland, 1983) and children's advertising (Kunkel & Roberts, 1991) to the consequences of education about the impact of sexual media contents (Fisher & Barak, 1989).

According to Krippendorff (1989), "all scientific knowledge has social consequences. Those who generate and communicate scientific knowledge ought not to hide behind the facade of an objective reality they in effect build and then disown, but to assume responsibility for its construction" (p. 79). These responsibilities include, he argued, the kinds of technology that follow from research, such as teaching machines based on psychological models. They also include the institutions that research helps support, such as media that may benefit from learning how to control audiences more effectively, as well as the image of humans portrayed in research, he argued. "Had another theory taken hold of the conceptual vacuum that existed in Freud's times, we would presumably see ourselves differently today" (p. 79).

In discussing empirical research, critical scholars often make a potentially very important point. Media research may contribute to a manipulative technocracy—an elite that uses its knowledge of the laws of human behavior to exploit the less fortunate. This threat accounts for a good deal of the criticism of empirical research. For example, Carey (1989) suggested that the traditional, empirical social sciences are inherently antidemocratic:

> Notions of laws of behavior and functions of society pretty much obliterate the entire legacy of democracy; they substitute ideological and coercive practice for the process of consensus formation via uncoerced conversation. If behind our subjective notions of what we are up to there lie in wait our genes, our conditioning history, or the functions of society exacting their due, then our subjective life, our intentions and purposes, are just so many illusions, mere epiphenomena. The only people who grasp the distinction between reality and appearance, who grasp the laws of conduct and society, are the ruling groups and those who do their bidding: scientific, technical elites who elucidate the laws of behavior and the functions of society so that people might be more effectively, albeit unconsciously, governed. (p. 100)

In short, a successful behavioral science largely might inform the elites about how to exploit and manipulate the masses, according to Carey's arguments. Although this may happen all too often, it is by no means inevitable. In a discussion of social science and morality, Rorty (1983) described the argument between the advocates of quantitative and qualitative methods as not about methods per se, but about "the sort of terminology to be used in moral and political reflection" (p. 162). In this light, one cannot simply equate quantitative methods with domination and qualitative or psychoanalytic ones with liberation. With reference to using laws to predict human behavior, Rorty (1983) said that "it is no easier or harder to be nasty in that style than in the style of Marx or of Freud" (p. 165).

In this light, social-scientific evidence (see chap. 9) suggests that whatever issues the media emphasize during a political campaign influence what voters weigh in choosing between or among candidates. Conceivably, a political campaign director could use such research to influence press coverage to focus on trivial issues in a way that promotes a particular candidate.

Education concerning such research might help people make more sophisticated voting decisions. In this sense, by making people aware of otherwise unconscious environmental determinants to their decisions, causal analysis of human behavior could potentially enhance human freedom. Thus, research could serve an emancipatory purpose (Diesing, 1991). As Gergen (1973) surmised, "sophistication as to psychological principles liberates one from their behavioral implications" (p. 313). Empirical evidence has supported such assertions to a degree. For example, some research suggests that an awareness of research can help overcome students' psychological inhibitions against helping others (Beaman, Barnes, Klentz, & McQuirk, 1978), although perhaps not in all situations (see Katzev & Brownstein, 1989).

Thus, education may help check those who might use social research to control others. When people understand social-science theory, "they are able to join, at least in principle, the communication-community of the scientists and social engineers and thus they may emancipate themselves from the status of mere objects of science and technology" (Apel, 1977, p. 309). I hope to help readers attain such a status.

3

Mass Media Processes and Contexts

Potentially, mass communication has an important impact not only on individuals, but on social groups ranging in size from families to entire nations and cultures. Thus, unlike more traditional academic disciplines such as psychology, media research uses a broad variety of levels of analysis. In research, a *level of analysis* refers to whatever a scientist studies the characteristics of. For example, psychologists generally are concerned with the behavior of individual people, whereas sociologists typically study the characteristics of groups. A media researcher studying the impact of TV violence on the aggressiveness of individual children uses a psychological level; someone studying the impact of mass communication on the economic development of entire countries works at a sociological level.

Following French philosopher Auguste Comte, Paisley (1984) described a scientific hierarchy based on levels of analysis. Sociology rests on psychology, which rests on biology, the study of the constituents of the body. In turn, biology rests on its constituents, the subject matter of chemistry, and everything else finally rests on physics. In this light, Paisley characterized fields such as communication, political science, and economics as *variable fields*. These employ a wide variety of levels of analysis. Those that focus largely on a single level, such as psychology and sociology, are *level fields*. Generally speaking, media research involves either the psychological or sociological levels. The sociological level is extremely broad, covering groups ranging in size from dyads to entire countries. In fact, most media research is explicitly *social psychological*—a field commonly defined as the study of how individuals are influenced by other persons. Even within the field of social psychology, some researchers demonstrate a psychological bent and others a sociological one.

Someone working in a variable field must be very careful not to generalize results and theories inappropriately from one level to another. An ecological fallacy occurs when one assumes, without evidence, that a group characteristic necessarily holds true for individuals. For instance, one might find that societies that have high levels of violence in their media tend to have high rates of violent crime as well. This would not necessarily mean that violent criminals tend to see more media violence than do others. An individualistic fallacy involves the opposite (i.e., assuming that a relationship among individuals will produce an analogous pattern among groups). For instance, a political scientist may find that more affluent individuals are more likely to vote Republican than are less advantaged persons. One could not conclude that wealthier states also tend to elect more Republican candidates.

Many researchers work at only one level of analysis. Indeed, the individual is by far the most common level in communication studies. Which level one chooses depends to a degree on certain philosophical assumptions. A theorist or researcher studying groups is likely to assume that such phenomena are holistic (i.e., that a group is more than the sum of its parts). They are philosophical realists who "think of society in terms of interaction and social process" (Park & Burgess, 1921/1924, p. 36). Sometimes researchers assume the opposite — that a phenomenon at one level is reducible to another, more basic level. For example, a researcher may assume that a sociological phenomenon such as the degree of modernity in a country can be described by references to levels of achievement motivation among individuals. A psychologist may assume that one can reduce human behavior to its biological components. Reductionists tend to be mechanistic nominalists (see appendix). In sociology, for example, nominalists "think of society as a collection of actually or potentially *like-minded* persons" (Park & Burgess, 1921/1924, p. 36).

One reason to suspect that the complete reduction of social to physical science will not occur is that many forms of human preferences (e.g., clothing styles) and behavior change over time much more rapidly than does human physiology. According to Gergen (1973), physiology "can never account for the continuously shifting patterns of what is considered the good or desirable in society, and thus a range of primary motivational sources for the individual" (p. 316).

In fact, individuals and social groups exist in the context of one another. Separating the behaviors of individuals from those of groups they belong to (and vice versa) may be useful for research purposes, but treating the two as somehow dualistic (i.e., dialectically opposed to one another) risks confusing the true relationship between them. Individuals and social groups are inherently interwoven and complementary (see Dewey, 1927/1946). For example, studying the artificially separated reactions of individual people to mass media in an experimental laboratory setting may help isolate certain factors at work when people also attend to the media in real-world situations. In real life, people may attend to media along with other people or because of social motives, such as to become informed to participate as a citizen in a democracy.

By and large, the social sciences are less successful than the physical sciences, or at least many people describe them this way. Perhaps their isolation from one another contributes to this. At many universities today, one can take a course in social psychology within both a psychology and a sociology department. One may find little common material. Early in the century, Dewey (1927/1946) saw this isolation as a mark of backwardness, in contrast with the widespread intercommunication and cross-fertilization that occurs among those in the physical sciences, such as astronomy, biology, and physics.

This isolation among the social sciences, and the related separation of the social sciences from physical inquiry, has its roots in the ancient struggle between church and science, which really ended only in a highly qualified victory for science.

> In this compromise, the world, including man, even beginning with man, was cut into two separate parts. One of them was awarded to natural inquiry under the name of physical science. The other was kept in possession in fee simple by the "higher" and finally "authoritative" domain—and dominion—of the "moral" and "spiritual." In this compromise, each part was free to go its own way provided it refrained from trespassing upon and interfering with the territory made over to the opposed division. (Dewey, 1947, p. 381)

Precisely because of its status as a variable field, the study of communication today represents a potentially fertile meeting ground among social scientists. Its isolation, often reinforced by institutional structures and a culture that sometimes is as much professional as academic, perhaps has kept the field even more separated from its allied disciplines in the humanities and social sciences than the allied disciplines are from each other. Sometimes the creation of colleges containing only communication programs, from departments formerly located within liberal arts units, has removed the programs from divisions that treated them as cabooses when it came to handing out resources. Yet such separation works against cross-fertilization within the social sciences and may encourage communication scholars to follow the values and research agendas of media industries (i.e., it perpetuates an industrial complex).

MODELS OF MEDIA AND COMMUNICATION PROCESSES

Over the years, researchers have used a variety of models to study media processes and effects. Deutsch (1952) defined a *model* as "a structure of symbols and operating rules which is supposed to match a set of relevant points in an existing structure or process" (p. 357). One can view a model as a form of map, which provides a usefully simplified description of a phenomenon or phenomena. Their functions, which should become apparent in the subsequent discussion, often include helping organize empirical experience. A model also may serve as a heuristic device to help researchers discover unanticipated facts and methods (Deutsch, 1952). Whenever somebody studies communication, he or she implicitly relies on some sort of model.

> We are using models, willingly or not, whenever we are trying to think systematically about anything at all. The results of our thinking in each case will depend upon what elements we put into our model, what rules and structure we imposed on those elements, and upon what actual use we made of the ensemble of possibilities which this particular model offered. (Deutsch, 1952, pp. 356–357)

The two historical definitions of *communication* (see chap. 1) have influenced available models. Many tend to reflect a transmission view—the idea that "communication is a process whereby messages are transmitted and distributed in space for the control of distance and people" (Carey, 1989, p. 15). The information theory model (discussed later) reflects a transmission variant in which people pursue power; balance models (see the subsequent discussion) reflect a version in which they flee anxiety, according to Carey.

As an alternative to this, Carey emphasized a ritual view, which sees the highest form of communication "not in the transmission of intelligent information but in the construction and maintenance of an ordered meaningful cultural world that can serve as a control and container for human action" (pp. 18–19). Therefore, one may view a newspaper as either a vehicle for spreading news and information or a means of allowing its readers to participate in a *ceremony* that confirms a particular worldview.

Information "Theory"

Many transmission communication models traditionally have been linear ones (i.e., the models assume that mass communication is a process that unfolds over time and involves a source who does something to a receiver or an audience). An example of a linear, and obviously rather mechanistic, model is information "theory" (Shannon & Weaver, 1949). It is important to realize that the models discussed in this chapter, including the rather unfortunately named *information "theory,"* are not theories. All theories involve models, but not all models are theories (see Hunt, 1991). That is to say, models may merely suggest ways of viewing communication phenomena or suggest, without mandating, specific theoretical predictions. Additionally, many of the models are fairly general and can apply to virtually all forms of communication, interpersonal and mass. This book focuses on those models that have influenced mass communication scholars.

Anyone who has taken an introduction to mass communication class will recognize many of the concepts from the information model (see Fig. 3.1). This model exemplifies the linear, one-way characteristics that some modern scholars today tend to reject in favor of more reciprocal views.

The model begins with a source, who expresses a message chosen from among those that could have been sent. A transmitter then changes it into a signal. The signal is carried via a channel, and it may encounter noise, some form of interference. A receiver then translates the signal back into a message, carrying it to its destination, where someone interprets it. In mass communication terms, a broadcast journalist might report a news story, which gets transmitted into a TV signal. Atmospheric interference might contribute noise or distortion to the signal. Your TV set receives the signal, translating it into a visual and auditory message. You (the destination) see and hear the story, thereby interpreting it.

The substance of information theory really involves a question: What is information? The answer is reduction in uncertainty. For example, students might receive an examination that contains three types of questions: essay, multiple-choice, and true–false. In information-theoretic terms, your response to an essay item, all else remaining equal, will contain the

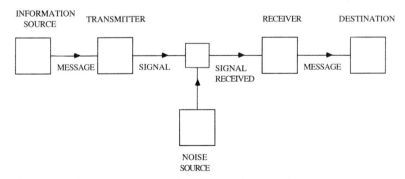

FIG. 3.1.   The information theory model (from Shannon & Weaver, 1949). Copyright 1949, 1998 by the Board of Trustees of the University of Illinois. Used with the permission of the University of Illinois Press.

most information and that to a true–false question the least. Obviously, there are only two possible responses to the latter, but an infinite variety of responses to the former can occur. This conceptualization can allow for very precise measurement of the amounts of information in a message. The technical concept of entropy, or disorder, permits such measurement.

Mass communication research has made rather limited use of information-theoretic concepts such as entropy (Finn & Roberts, 1984), although the field has employed aspects of the overall model widely to describe the communication process. Chaffee and Wilson (1977) conducted one study that used the entropy concept. They examined whether the presence of different news media in a community relates to the degree of uniformity in what issues people attached the most importance to. Consistent with assumptions of Jeffersonian democracy, persons in media-rich communities showed more entropy (i.e., diversity) in response than did those in media-poor ones.

Balance Models

Certain other models often used in media research have roots in the Gestalt tradition of psychology, which originated in Germany in the early 20th century. The Gestalt psychologists resembled pragmatists (see appendix) in that they viewed experiential events as consisting of patterned, synthesized wholes. To Gestaltists, it makes little sense to break down the event of, say, reading a newspaper into its elemental components or sensations.

Neo-Gestaltic models tend to imply that a need for order is central to human psychology—hence, they are often known as balance or consistency models. Consistency models and theories were very visible and influential within social psychology and communication during the 1960s and 1970s. Among these are the model of psychologist Fritz Heider (1946, 1958) and the A-B-X approach of social psychologist T.M. Newcomb (1953). Lewin's field theoretic orientation laid the groundwork for the balance models.

Heider's balance model focuses on the cognitive structures of individual people. It typically concerns an individual's attitudes toward another person and toward an object, as well as the individual's perception of the other person's attitude toward the object. Heider felt that it was more useful to analyze a small part of a person's cognitive system, rather than attempting, as earlier theorists such as psychoanalyst Sigmund Freud had done, to understand the entire structure. Because of the focus on perceptions within a single individual, the balance model is an intrapersonal one.

Heider felt that an individual would feel more comfortable in situations in which his or her perceptions were logically consistent or balanced. To simplify things slightly, he defined a *balanced situation* as one in which a positive product existed among the three perceptions. For instance, assume that you like your roommate, you dislike the mayor of your community, and you perceive that your roommate dislikes the mayor as well. The first perception is positive and the second two are negative. Multiplying the three signs (+ – –) yields a positive product. Hence, you should find the set of cognitions comfortable. In contrast, if you perceived that your roommate liked the mayor, a negative product would result from the three signs (+ – +). Because you like someone with whom you disagree, you presumably would experience discomfort. Implicit in the model is the idea that you would attempt to eliminate this discomfort perhaps by changing your attitude toward the mayor or toward your roommate, or by attempting to change your roommate's attitudes.

The model provides no means of predicting how you would attempt to restore balance, however. Quite likely, you might use communication, (e.g., by paying attention to the local newspaper in hopes of finding materials that would change your roommate's mind or even your own). Conceivably, if all else failed, you might even distort your perception of the roommate's opinion or even repress it. Because of the predictions about cognitive structure implied in Heider's model, it is sometimes considered a theory in its own right.

Newcomb (1953) expanded Heider's model to apply it to a dyad—a social system containing two people and their interactions. Figure 3.2 illustrates the model. It depicts two people, A and B, and their simultaneous orientation toward each other and some object, X. Unlike Heider's model, the basic Newcomb model pictures the "objective" perceptions of two people (i.e., as seen by a third observer), rather than as one of the participants might perceive them. Hence, Newcomb's model is an interpersonal one.

Newcomb used the concept of *symmetry*, rather than balance, to refer to an orderly quality within the social system. He defined symmetry as a situation in which A and B have similar orientations toward X. These orientations could include both affective and cognitive components. That is to say, they could consist of either feelings concerning the object or beliefs about its characteristics. Newcomb assumed that a change in one component is likely to change the other components. Hence, the pieces of the sys-

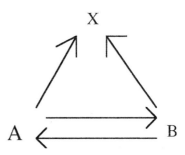

FIG 3.2.   Newcomb's (1953) model.

tem should form an interdependent whole. The term *coorientation* refers to this assumption. Presumably, then, people often feel pressure to agree with one another concerning some object, and pressures intensify to the extent that they like one another and/or value their perceptions about the object. Newcomb (1953) used the phrase "strain toward symmetry" (p. 95) to describe these situations. Under conditions of strain toward symmetry, communication may be a means of achieving agreement.

For example, assume that you and your roommate like one another but disagree concerning a candidate for student government president. The disorder in the system, a product of disagreement, may lead to communication. You might consult a mass medium (i.e., the student newspaper on your campus) in an attempt to bolster your opinion and change your roommate's. After discussing the matter with the other person, you could change your mind, change his or hers, or the two of you could alter your attitudes toward each other. If neither of you wished to find a new roommate, however, you might agree to disagree, perhaps a relatively uncomfortable semisolution, and stop discussing the matter.

The Concept of Gatekeeping
and the Westley–MacLean Model

Many models that explicitly involve mass communication make use of the *gatekeeper* concept (see Shoemaker, 1991). The concept refers to someone who makes decisions about what passes through the various gates separating potential media contents from their audiences. For example, before a story appears in a local newspaper, both a reporter and an editor have to select it from among potential alternatives. In addition, it may pass through other gates as well, such as those manned (or, in more politically correct terms, personned) by wire service personnel and editors and other newspapers who subscribe to the service. Lewin (1947) developed the gatekeeper concept, and D.M. White (1950) first used it in a research project, which concerned why an editor selected certain stories from those made available via the wire services. Among the mass communication models making use of the gatekeeper concept are those of Westley and MacLean (1957), McNelly (1959), and Bass (1969).

The Westley–MacLean (1957) model is the most influential of these. In part, it extended Newcomb's model to typical mass communication situations, which involve gatekeepers. Westley and MacLean began by recognizing two basic distinctions between interpersonal and mass communication. Usually in interpersonal communication, receivers can rely on more of their senses when evaluating a message. For example, one can only hear a message delivered via radio without seeing the communicator. In addition, less immediate forms of feedback, and typically fewer forms of it, characterize mass communication. Feedback consists of the responses of one or more receivers to a message. For instance, rather than getting immediate responses, radio and TV stations largely use ratings to gauge people's reactions to their messages.

Westley and MacLean saw communication as involving a purposive communicator (A) and a receiver (B). B may be either a person or various groups, including the entire audience for a mediated message. The model also includes various Xs, defined as "any object (or event) that has characteristics capable of being transmitted in some abstracted form" (Westley & MacLean, 1957, pp. 32–33). Sometimes, according to Westley and MacLean, the As and Xs that are important to B lie outside of B's immediate environment. As a result, they include C, the gatekeeper of Lewin and White, in their model. C is a nonpurposive communicator. To them,

C is conceived of as one who can both (a) select the abstractions of object X appropriate to B's need satisfactions or problem solutions, (b) transform them into some form of symbol containing meanings shared with B, and finally (c) transmit such symbols by means of some channel or medium to B. (p. 33)

Figure 3.3 illustrates one version of the model (for three others, see Westley & MacLean, 1957). In it, A uses a gatekeeper, such as a TV chan-

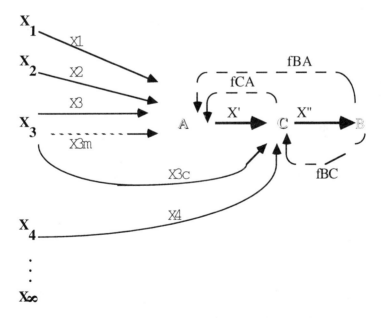

FIG 3.3.   One version of the Westley–MacLean model (from Westley & MacLean, 1957). Copyright by the Association for Education in Journalism. Used by permission.

nel, to send a message to B. For example, each January, the U.S. president delivers the State of the Union address before Congress, and the TV networks carry the speech live to the public. In the speech, the president chooses from an infinite number of Xs, such as the state of the economy, the need for health care reform, and future military appropriations. The message may be either purposive or nonpurposive. That is to say, it may attempt to change the receiver's perception of an X or it may be sent, perhaps in the form of a news story, with no such attempt. In the latter case, A disappears from the model, and the speech represents an X.

The concept of feedback is an important component of the model. Members of audiences, Bs, can respond both to the Cs, via ratings for the speech, and to the president, by writing letters concerning the speech or participating in polls concerning its topics. C also may send feedback to the communicator, for instance, by editorializing about the speech. Feedback may be either purposive, as in the letter, or nonpurposive, as when someone purchases an advertised product, and a study gauging the effectiveness of the ad detects the purchase.

Models of New Media Usage

The Westley–MacLean model appeared at a time when the massification of media was at its height. Since the 1960s, things have changed. The segments of print and electronic communication directed toward general audiences often have declined, with more material targeted at specialized groups of people. For example, because of cable, TV viewers in some areas can now choose from several hundred channels, many of which carry specialized fare ranging from music videos to religious or travel programming. Beyond this, technology has often made it easier for audiences to respond to the media. For instance, some newspapers today not only supplement their daily editions with online services, but have made it possible for audience members to communicate via computers with journalists and even with a reporter's sources. As these tendencies accelerate, new models will be necessary. For example, traditional models that draw a strict separation between source and receiver and downplay the role of audience reactions as mere feedback may no longer describe mass communication processes adequately. Media use increasingly may resemble E.M. Rogers' (1986) normative definition of *communication* as "the exchange of information among the participants in the communication process" (p. 196).

Therefore, a convergence model (Kincaid & Schramm, 1975; E.M. Rogers & Kincaid, 1981) may be increasingly appropriate. In the model, two participants, A and B, share information in an effort to reach understanding. Communication is a cyclical process, with only an arbitrary beginning, among equal partners. According to the model, Person A expresses a message, which B interprets. B then expresses a message, and A interprets it. The exchange continues indefinitely, and the participants may converge on mutual understanding. Perfect understanding cannot occur, however. The partial overlap in the circles for each party at the end of the process illustrates this. Figure 3.4 depicts the convergence model.

Given all this, new media technology likely will continue to have certain democratizing influences. For example, media audiences may increasingly make their own decisions about content, rather than relying on gatekeepers. Technology also gives them more opportunity to interact with media sources. Yet the new media may primarily benefit well-to-do people. The less affluent, who cannot afford to subscribe to online information services or sometimes even to cable TV, may remain largely left out.

Linear models have often caused researchers downplay or overlook many potentially fruitful research questions. Convergence models can help identify such questions, even in traditional mass communication contexts. According to E.M. Rogers and Kincaid (1981),

> when an automobile company aims television ads at prospective car-buyers, this situation might seem to be a source transmitting a persuasive message through a mass medium to an audience of receivers. Not necessarily. It depends on whether one defines communication as linear or convergent. Research based on a narrow, linear model of communication would ignore the effect of the advertisement on the managers of the auto company, on their competing companies, on what members of the "audience" say about the product to one another, and on the thousands of auto agency salespersons throughout the country who eventually talk with potential customers. (p. 72)

The extent that linear models have guided media research historically becomes evident from the relative lack of research concerning such questions. Inevitably, this book reflects such tendencies. On the whole, scholars have developed few general models that apply to new forms of mass communication (e.g., Office of Technology Assessment, 1990).

CONSEQUENCES OF COMMUNICATION MODELS

Obviously, communication models are important because they help determine what scholars study. For example, if one views communication in linear terms, its effects become very important topics of investigation. They often imply specific theoretical predictions. For instance, the balance models suggest the need for order in human life, as articulated in theories such as cognitive dissonance (see chap. 7).

Speculation exists about the broader consequences of models. Carey (1989) articulated some interesting ideas about the potentially enormous consequences of transmission and ritual models of communication proc-

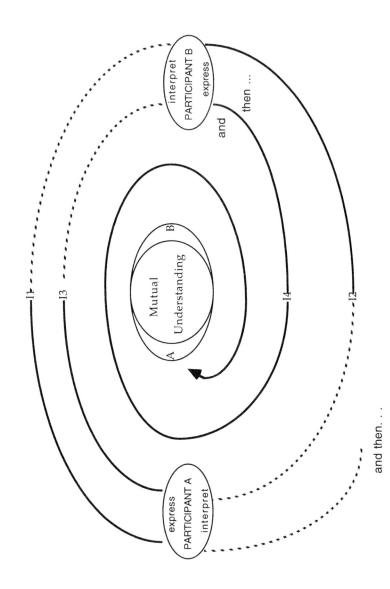

FIG. 3.4. The convergence model of communication (from Kincaid & Schramm, 1975). Copyright 1975 by the East-West Communication Institute. Used by permission.

esses. Carey's ideas largely emerge from a rather unique synthesis of the disparate ideas of three figures: Dewey, Canadian scholar Harold Innis (Marshall McLuhan's mentor), and English neo-Marxist historian Raymond Williams (see Whitby & Whitby, 1990). At present, society experiences a

> derangement in our models of communication and community. The derangement derives, in turn, from an obsessive commitment to a transmission view of communication and the derivative representation of communication in complementary models of power and anxiety. As a result when we think about society, we are almost always coerced by our traditions as seeing it as a network of power, administration, decision, and control—as a political order. (Carey, 1989, p. 34)

In short, the models of communication that dominate a culture profoundly affect the forms of social (i.e., humanly constructed) reality that people experience. They constitute communication, thereby affecting the very processes they seek to describe. In this light, a ritual model offers a "way in which to rebuild a model of and for communication of some restorative value in reshaping our common culture" (p. 35). Thus, it represents to Carey a means of helping restore what Dewey and other progressives saw as the eclipsed public—of contributing to a genuinely participant democracy.

Carey's ideas, apparently rooted in a rather idealistic (in the philosophical sense) version of pragmatism, are not intended to be a scientific theory. Yet one schooled in empirical research might respond: The pictures are pretty, but where is the evidence? In fact, both transmission and ritual models of communication may prove useful in research. Sometimes communication may best be viewed in transmission terms and at other times as a ritual. Finally, some theorists have argued that ritual forms of media use sometimes have harmful consequences, such as the cultivation of distorted perceptions of reality from TV drama (see chap. 9).

4

Theories of Media Audiences

Why do you sometimes go to a movie, listen to the radio, turn on the TV set, read a newspaper or magazine, or perhaps surf the Internet? You may be seeking, consciously or not, something that will take your mind off of your worries, help pass the time of day, or predict tomorrow's weather. In fact, audiences report various motivations for media use. These sometimes include such things as passing time and learning about things or oneself, as well as for arousal, relaxation, companionship, and because of habit (Greenberg, 1974).

Clearly, communication is more than a process by which one party, the sender, does something to another, the receiver. The media do not merely act, and those exposed to them do not merely react. Rather, like with other things in life, it takes "two to tango."

USES AND GRATIFICATIONS RESEARCH

The uses and gratifications approach to mass communication research (e.g., Rosengren, Wenner, & Palmgreen, 1985) examines what people do with the media. Sometimes this issue is studied separately from and less often alongside of the question of what the media do to people. Such research assumes that audiences are to varying degrees active participants in media use, rather than purely passive or reactive objects. As E. Katz, Blumler, and Gurevitch (1974) defined the approach, it is concerned with:

> (1) the social and psychological origins of (2) needs, which generate (3) expectations of (4) the mass media or other sources which lead to (5) differen-

tial patterns of media exposure (or engagement in other activities), resulting in (6) need gratifications and (7) other consequences, perhaps mostly unintended ones. (p. 20)

Contemporary uses and gratifications research tends to reflect five assumptions, according to Rubin (1993):

(a) Communication behavior such as media use is typically goal-directed or motivated. Such behavior is functional for people; it has consequences for people and societies.

(b) People select and use communication sources and messages to satisfy felt needs or desires. Media use is a means to satisfy wants or interests such as seeking information to reduce uncertainty or to solve personal dilemmas.

(c) Social and psychological factors mediate communication behavior. Behavior is a response to media only as filtered through one's social and psychological circumstances such as the potential for interpersonal interaction, social categories, and personality.

(d) Media compete with other forms of communication for selection, attention, and use. There are definite relationships between media and interpersonal communication for satisfying needs or wants.

(e) People are usually more influential than media in media-person relationships. (p. 98)

One common criticism of this approach has been the inconsistent meanings concerning its fundamental concepts. Usually, however, "concepts such as needs, motives, uses, and gratifications sought are used in an equivalent manner as antecedents to behavior; effects, consequences, gratifications obtained, and outcomes appear as consequents of the behavior" (Rubin, 1994, p. 424).

Historical Background

Uses and gratifications research has existed for more than five decades, at least since Herzog's (1940) study of radio listening motives. E. Katz (1959), who wanted to combine the study of audience effects with studies of popular culture, gave the research its present name. Although media-effects studies have tended to overshadow uses and gratifications research, a substantial literature exists.

Functionalism. Traditional uses and gratifications research generally has reflected the influence of both psychological and sociological functionalism (Carey & Kreiling, 1974; E. Katz, 1979). Functional analysis is largely "concerned with examining those consequences of social phenomena which affect the normal operation, adaptation, or adjustment of a given system: individuals, subgroups, social and cultural systems" (C.R. Wright, 1960, p. 606). A key concept often is *homeostasis*, which refers to a harmonizing of parts in the interest of system maintenance. Clearly, the mass media represent one part of society that may help individuals and societies adapt.

In this light, scholars have identified a number of social functions of mass communication. In one of the earliest pieces on the subject, Lasswell (1948) listed three. First, the media survey the environment, pointing out threats and opportunities for individuals and societies. For instance, news media may warn people of an impending hurricane or snow storm. Second, they correlate the parts of society as it responds to the environment. For example, news media may editorialize about and interpret the news of the day for their audiences. Third, the media help transmit the cultural heritage from one generation to the next. For example, political debates, such as those on television shows such as CNN's *Crossfire*, may help socialize children to the world of politics. C.R. Wright (1960) added a fourth function, entertainment, which "refers to communication primarily intended to amuse people irrespective of any instrumental effects it may have" (p. 609). Obviously, this would include much of the content of radio and TV, as well as sections of newspapers such as crossword puzzles and comics. These distinctions at times have guided researchers interested in developing typologies of media gratifications.

C.R. Wright (1960) also developed the notions of *manifest* and *latent function* and *dysfunction*. A manifest function is intended, whereas a latent function is not. A dysfunction harms the welfare of a society or its members. For example, medical news about disease symptoms may save lives by allowing victims to recognize early symptoms and seek medical help. Yet it might also contribute to imagined illnesses in hypochondriacs, perhaps creating so much anxiety that some people avoid seeing doctors even when necessary. The first example represents a manifest function and the second a latent dysfunction.

Psychological and sociological versions of functionalism appear to have surprisingly separate histories. For example, most discussions in books (e.g., Owens & Wagner, 1992) and social-science encyclopedias (e.g., Cancian, 1968; Lundin, 1987; Maryanski & Turner, 1991) are largely limited to only one version. Nonetheless, the two versions clearly have common ancestors, such as Charles Darwin, and they sometimes share certain features, such as the concept of homeostasis. However, the essentially apolitical psychological functionalism finds its roots in progressive Darwinists such as Dewey, but the much more politically controversial sociological functionalism is sometimes directly linked (e.g., by Maryanksi

& Turner, 1991) to conservative 19th-century Darwinists such as philosopher Herbert Spencer.

Principles of psychological functionalism largely restate traditional pragmatist conceptions of social science. Not surprisingly, Dewey (1896) and James (1890/1907) were among its earliest proponents. Functionalists believe that psychology should focus primarily on mental operations and processes, especially as these contribute in a Darwinian sense to an organism's environmental adaptation, rather than on the structures of the mind (Wagner & Owens, 1992). Perception and action are not separate domains; rather, the "mind and behavior act in concert as a system to accomplish adaptive tasks" (Wagner & Owens, 1992, p. 11). By helping to solve practical problems, research in psychology should represent a form of such concerted activity. Despite this, functionalism is not atheoretical. Instead, "basic *theoretical understanding* can produce the precise and general understanding of nature that can allow us to predict and control it in nonobvious ways" (p. 11). Such a description of psychological functionalism is both standard and in some sense covers most of the field today.

Sociological versions of functionalism tend to generate more controversy. These functionalists view society as an organism that, like an individual, must adapt to its environment. They typically focus on how the parts of society work together to help it adjust and survive. As a result, many critics (e.g., Mills, 1959) see them as focused on how social systems maintain themselves rather than on how they change. In effect, critics charge that the social function of functional analysis is to help maintain the status quo and hinder progress. Not surprisingly, researchers who employ sociological functionalism (e.g., Mendelsohn, 1974) often vigorously dispute this. Nonetheless, such charges have long given sociological functionalism a distinctly unfashionable reputation in certain politically correct quarters.

Today, uses and gratifications research may reflect certain rather narrow functionalist emphases less than in the past. For example, many contemporary models do not focus primarily on the gratifications obtained (i.e., consequences) from media use (see Palmgreen, Wenner, & Rosengren, 1985). Nonetheless, as the section on expectancy-value theory makes clear, broadly defined forms of psychological functionalism continue to influence research.

Phases of Research. By the 1970s, three distinct phases of uses and gratifications research had occurred (Blumler & E. Katz, 1974). A series of descriptive studies appeared during the 1940s. For example, Berelson (1949) examined what people felt they missed when a strike kept them from receiving a newspaper. During the 1950s and 1960s, researchers attempted to measure variables linked to media consumption. For instance, E.E. Maccoby (1954) assessed the impact of frustration on how much TV children watch. During this period, however, media scholars tended to focus on other topics, such as the role of attitudes and predispositions in limiting media effects (Swanson, 1992).

By the late 1960s and early 1970s, uses and gratifications research experienced a renewal as researchers searched for alternatives to the limited-effects tradition (Swanson, 1992). In this light, some scholars attempted to explain how audience motivations connected with other aspects of communication. For example, Peled and E. Katz (1974) reported evidence that gratification seeking intervenes between media content and audience response, sometimes yielding effects not predictable from manifest content alone. In a study of media functions in Israel during the 1973 war, they concluded that "televised information served not only the need to know but also the need for relief from tension and for a feeling of social connectedness" (p. 66).

More Recent Developments

Audience Activity.   The concept of an active audience has long been central to uses and gratifications research. Scholars have sometimes used it in an effort to explain why mass communication appeared to have only limited effects. Presumably, active engagement with the media made people resistant to persuasion. Researchers today recognize that audience activity may enhance effects as well. For example, more active engagement with TV news may make people more susceptible to its influence. In addition, researchers today tend to treat audiences as variably, rather than absolutely, active (Rubin, 1993). As commonly used, audience activity

> postulates a voluntaristic and selective orientation by audiences toward the communication process. In brief, it suggests that media use is motivated by needs and goals that are defined by audience members themselves, and that active participation in the communication process may facilitate, limit, or otherwise influence the gratifications and effects associated with exposure. (Levy & Windahl, 1985, p. 110)

Levy and Windahl (1984, 1985) proposed a typology of audience activity along two dimensions. First, *preactivity* occurs before, *duractivity* during, and *postactivity* after exposure. Second, each of these may involve selectivity, involvement, and utility orientations. *Selectivity* refers to "nonrandom selection of one or more behavioral, perceptual, or cognitive media-related activities" (Levy & Windahl, 1985, p. 112). Selective exposure seeking, an individual's decisions about what content to watch or read based on anticipated gratifications, exemplifies preactivity selectivity. As such, the definition is broader than the use of selective exposure in persuasion research (see chap. 7). In persuasion, selective exposure usually refers to someone's tendency to seek information that is congruent with his or her attitudes. *Involvement* refers to "first, the degree to which an audience member perceives a connection between him or herself and mass media content; and second, the degree to which the individual interacts psychologically with a medium or its messages" (Levy & Windahl, 1985, p. 112). Attention to a message represents one form of duractivity involvement. *Utility* refers to the use of media by individuals "for manifold social and psychological purposes" (Levy & Windahl, 1985, p. 112). For instance, after reading a newspaper, a person may discuss what he or she has read with others—a postactivity utility, according to Levy and Windahl. Some researchers use somewhat different categorizations of activity, however. For example, Rubin and Perse (1987a) defined *involvement* rather broadly as participation with media messages. In this light, talking about messages exemplifies a form of it.

Variations in such activities are often assumed to result in part from audience motives or gratifications sought, as well as attitudes toward a medium or its contents, such as perceived realism and news affinity (i.e., how much importance someone attaches to the news). An important empirically based distinction exists between instrumental and ritualized motives and use. Instrumental media use involves relatively active exposure to specific types of material. "It is marked by using a medium's content for information utility reasons, and affinity with and perceived realism of that content" (Rubin & Perse, 1987b, p. 59). Instrumental use "entails selectivity, intentionality, and involvement of media consumers" (Conway & Rubin, 1991, p. 444). Ritualized use concerns the medium more than its content. It is "associated with diffuse motives (e.g., pass time, habit, relaxation) and more exposure to and affinity with the medium" (Rubin & Perse, 1987b, p. 59). For example, one might turn on the TV to learn about tomorrow's weather, a form of instrumental use, or simply because one is accustomed to doing so to relax. An instrumental orientation occurs frequently with exposure to news and other informational contents. Ritualized media use often involves entertainment contents.

Psychological and Sociological Origins of Media Motivations. During recent years, both psychological and sociological factors have been linked to motivations or gratifications sought. Motives are often depicted as expressions of needs. In a correlational study, Conway and Rubin (1991) tested various theories concerning the psychological antecedents of motives. The results were mixed. For example, the study examined tension-reduction theory—the idea that people "seek to reduce arousal in their lives and pursue experiences to reduce negative tension" (p. 448). As hypothesized, higher levels of reported anxiety predicted an increase in certain ritualized motives, such as use of TV for escape or to pass time. In contrast, an expected association between increased authoritarianism, presumably indicating an enhanced need for cognitive consistency in a person's perceptions, and greater information-viewing motivation did not emerge. On the whole, available studies indicate that psychological attributes commonly correlate with media motivations, but in ways that often await clarification (Swanson, 1992).

Apparently, psychological and sociological influences are intertwined. For example, TV is an important source of escape among older persons who are alone and dissatisfied with their present life (Rubin & Rubin, 1982). Donohew, Palmgreen, and Rayburn (1987) examined the relations among a person's lifestyle, psychological need for arousal, media use, and gratifications seeking. Presumably, people with different lifestyles feel most comfortable at different arousal levels. "Those with high levels will tend to expose themselves to more novel, varied, or even threatening sources of stimulation, whereas those with low arousal needs will tend to turn toward that which is more routine for them" (p. 257). The researchers found coherent patterns involving several lifestyle types. For example, outgoing activists and energetic doers who find life interesting tended to have heavy needs for stimulation and to exhibit heavy use of print media. Such people displayed very low levels of gratification seeking from cable TV perhaps because they have little time for it. Thus, needs, such as for activation, "may permeate and energize entire lifestyles, leading people to engage in various pursuits and activities which, in turn, generate more immediate needs for media-related gratifications" (p. 273). Therefore, "the roots of media use are far deeper than most previous investigations have indicated" (p. 274), the authors concluded.

Gratifications Sought and Obtained.   Clearly, media use may or may not prove satisfying. For example, someone may watch a dramatic program in hopes of temporarily forgetting about everyday financial problems, yet experience discomfort after encountering a character who is going through similar difficulties. Early research, however, tended to overlook the distinction between gratifications sought and obtained. Subsequent work (e.g., Palmgreen, Wenner, & Rayburn, 1980) has found correlations, but also clear differences, between the two. "These results indicated that gratification-seeking is not a self-fulfilling prophecy; that is media content is not a blank screen onto which audiences project whatever gratifications they hope to find" (Swanson, 1992, p. 310). Much of this research leaves out forms of activity, such as attention, which presumably intervene between gratifications sought and obtained (Levy & Windahl, 1985).

Palmgreen and Rayburn (1979) developed a discrepancy model, focused on the differences between gratifications sought and obtained, to predict media use. Based on the theoretical idea that repetition of a stimulus influences a response only if reinforcement occurs, they hypothesized that smaller discrepancies will correlate with greater exposure. As expected, such differences helped discriminate viewers of public TV from nonviewers and predicted amounts of viewing among persons who made their own choices about what to watch. Separate indicators of gratifications sought and obtained, however, also predict media use (Wenner, 1986). Thus, both what a person obtains from media content and its comparison to what the person anticipated may be important.

Expectancy-Value Theory. Of course, uses and gratifications is an approach to research; it is not in any sense a theory. In fact, much early research was essentially atheoretical. Only in relatively recent years have explicit theories appeared. During the past 20 years, a fourth phase — concerned with formal uses and gratifications theory building and testing — has appeared (Palmgreen et al., 1985). Research concerning expectancy-value theory exemplifies this tendency.

In general, expectancy-value theories assume that at least some of people's behaviors or attitudes result from both their beliefs concerning the likely consequences of behavior or the attributes of an object and from their feelings toward those consequences or attributes (Palmgreen & Rayburn, 1982). Because they deal with the adaptation of an organism to its environment, they clearly fall within functionalist psychology.

Expectancy-value explanations pertaining to media use involve, at least implicitly, the concept of purposive behavior, which has existed in psychology for most of the century. In that field, purposive behavior is most associated with the work of the psychologist Edward Chase Tolman (1932). Tolman's work consisted of the application of pragmatist ideas within the then-dominant behaviorist version of psychology (Pepper, 1934). Fundamentally, Tolman assumed that "the elements of a purposive act — stimuli, responses, and goals — cannot be understood except as they are functionally bound together in a single complex whole" (L.D. Smith, 1986, pp. 97–98). Tolman believed in studying what he termed *molar behavior*, rather than breaking behavior down into its molecular elements, such as physiology.

Tolman (1932) defined *purposiveness*, whether in humans or animals, as docility. An organism learns to deal with its environment through a process of trial and error. To Tolman, purposes and expectancies act as intervening variables between environmental stimuli and a person's observable response. Tolman characterized both learned behavior generally and science specifically as consisting of efforts to attain distal goals by pursuing experiential strands. His ideas assume that a person's environment is a kind of metaphorical spider web branching out in all directions and leading to either desirable or undesirable consequences (L.D. Smith, 1986). In short, a person forms symbolic hypotheses about the unknown as a means of attempting to deal with aspects of the environment. In a uses and gratification framework, these unknowns obviously involve the content and consequences of a person's media-related choices. Thus,

> the concept of audience expectations concerning the characteristics of the media and potential gratifications to be obtained is essential to the uses and gratifications assumption of an active audience. If audience members are to select from among various media and nonmedia alternatives according to their needs, they must have some perceptions of the alternatives most likely to meet those needs. (Palmgreen et al., 1985, pp. 21–22)

Palmgreen and Rayburn (1982, 1985) took a contemporary variant of expectancy-value theory — that of Fishbein and Ajzen (1975) in the field of persuasion (see chap. 7). They modified and applied it to the study of media uses and gratifications. The basic model is as follows:

$$\text{Exposure}_x = w_1\left(\sum_{i=1}^{n} GS_i\right) + w_2(A_x), \tag{1}$$

> where X is some medium, program, or content type, GS_i is a generalized orientation, tendency or motive to seek various gratifications from X (and GS_i is the ith gratification sought from X), A_x is attitude toward X, and w_1 and w_2 are empirically derived weights (see Palmgreen & Rayburn, 1982, pp. 567–568). For example, a person is likely to listen to operatic broadcasts to the degree that her attitude toward them is positive and she is motivated to seek various gratifications from them. (Babrow & Swanson, 1988, p. 2)

In turn, the gratifications a person seeks presumably emerge from judgments about expectancy and value:

$$GS_i = b_i e_i. \tag{2}$$

GS_i = the ith gratification sought from some media object, X (some medium, program, content type, etc.);

b_i = the belief (subjective probability) that X possesses some attribute or that a behavior related to X will have a particular outcome; and

e_i = the affective evaluation of the particular attribute or outcome. (Palmgreen & Rayburn, 1985, p. 63)

Thus, a belief multiplied by an evaluation helps determine a gratification sought. For example, assume that a person places great value on keeping up with current events. If the person believes that TV news does a good job of providing such information, he or she should tend to report watching such news to learn about current events. Empirical evidence (Palmgreen & Rayburn, 1982) has supported this with reference to numerous individual gratifications possible from watching TV news. These included finding out about government officials and making up one's mind about important issues.

Palmgreen and Rayburn also summed the various belief-evaluation products in an attempt to predict a generalized tendency to seek gratifications from a source. According to them,

$$\sum_{i=1}^{n} GS_i = \sum_{i=1}^{n} b_i e_i. \tag{3}$$

Thus, one's overall tendency to seek gratification from a source should result, in substantial part, from the combined weight of one's beliefs and evaluations concerning the individual attributes of the source. Consider the extent to which someone believes that TV news helps one find out about government officials, make up one's mind about important issues, and so on. These should combine with the value that a person places on each of these to influence the person's tendency to seek gratification from such news. Palmgreen and Rayburn (1982) found evidence suggesting that the summated belief-evaluation products, or expectancies, have a direct impact on a person's overall tendency to seek gratification from such news. In turn, the latter seems to affect exposure to the source. Other analyses (Palmgreen & Rayburn, 1985) were consistent with the process model pictured in Fig. 4.1. Following gratification seeking comes media consumption, which should reflect not only exposure, but "the meaning assigned by the respondent to content, structural, or contextual elements" (Rayburn & Palmgreen, 1984, p. 559). In turn, consumption affects perceived gratifications obtained. The latter then feed back to influence beliefs, but not evaluations.

For the sake of simplicity, assume that only one type of expectancy comes into play in a viewing situation. A person may turn to a local TV station for news, rather than an out-of-town station, because the person wants local information concerning tomorrow's weather. This gratification sought arises from a belief that the person will learn about tomorrow's local weather. Perhaps this is valuable information (an evaluation) because the person has tickets to attend a community baseball game the next day. Thus, the degree to which the person seeks the gratification depends on his or her degree of belief that the information will be available multiplied by the value he or she attaches to it. After watching the

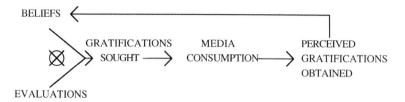

FIG 4.1.   An expectancy-value model (from Palmgreen & Rayburn, 1985).
Copyright 1985 by Sage Publications, Inc. Reprinted by permission of Sage
Publications, Inc.

weather, the person will develop a perception (i.e., gratification obtained)
about the information learned. This may affect the person's beliefs about
the source, but should not influence his or her evaluations about the usefulness of weather information.

Finally, expectancy values also should affect a person's attitude, A, toward an object or behavior (Palmgreen & Rayburn, 1982).

$$A = \sum_{i=1}^{n} b_i e_i. \tag{4}$$

Separately from gratification seeking, attitude should predict exposure.
As hypothesized, expectancy values correlated strongly with attitudes, as
represented by satisfaction with TV news. Satisfaction, however, was unrelated to exposure to such news (Palmgreen & Rayburn, 1982), contrary
to Eq. (1). Thus, the theory did not receive unqualified support.

In an extension of the Palmgreen–Rayburn research, Babrow and
Swanson (1988) relied on a more complete version of the Fishbein–Ajzen
theory. They examined attitudes toward watching TV news, rather than
satisfaction with such news. Babrow and Swanson questioned whether
satisfaction and attitude are the same thing. Beyond this, they argued that
someone who has a positive attitude toward a news show might not feel
the same about watching it. Perhaps the program would interfere with an
evening meal. In their analyses, the researchers also added a measure of
intention to watch news. The Fishbein–Ajzen theory assumes that behavioral intentions will intervene between attitudes and behavior.

As expected, attitudes related significantly, but sometimes only mar-
ginally so, with behavioral intentions. In turn, intentions strongly predicted reported news exposure. Thus, attitudes may have an indirect
influence on exposure. Therefore, including attitudes and behavioral intentions in analyses, in addition to gratification seeking, improved prediction of a person's news exposure.

Beyond this, Babrow and Swanson assessed the extent to which expectancy values and gratification seeking are distinguishable. They found ev-

idence that expectancy-value judgments may affect behavioral intention and news exposure only indirectly — through their influence on attitudes. In contrast, gratification seeking appeared to have both direct and indirect impacts on intent and news exposure. Hence, Babrow and Swanson (1988) concluded that expectancy values and gratifications sought "are highly related but distinctly different judgments" (p. 1). They also speculated that two may influence each other, rather than expectancy values only unidirectionally affecting the gratification seeking as previously assumed. "For example, a viewer may want to avoid some consequence, such as being bored by a situation comedy, and the desire to avoid boredom may lead a pessimistic viewer to overestimate the probability that the show will be boring" (p. 3).

Audience Involvement. Expectancy values clearly are rather weak predictors of exposure. Perhaps they primarily influence aspects of instrumental audience activity, rather than the more ritualistic sheer exposure. Thus, "the explanatory power of expectancy-value inquiry might increase if the analysis focused less on exposure and more on activity measures as outcomes of attitudes and gratifications sought" (Rubin & Perse, 1987b, p. 77).

Involvement is one widely examined form of audience activity. Researchers have used a number of quite different variables to represent it. These influence communication processes in dissimilar ways (Salmon, 1986). Mass communication researchers tend to use the term rather broadly. In persuasion research (see chap. 7), for example, involvement has only an information orientation (Perse, 1990). A focus on a message source, for instance, is considered low in involvement. Because emotions require less effort than cognition, they are not considered as indicators of it either (Perse, 1990). In media studies, involvement may pertain to any aspect of a message, such as emotional reactions to a dramatic plot (Perse, 1990).

Rubin (1993) used *preinvolvement* to refer to antecedents of media use, including motives and attitudes toward a medium, such as perceived realism. In contrast, *participant involvement* refers to "cognitive, affective, and behavioral participation during, and because of, media exposure" (Rubin & Perse, 1987a, p. 247). In some research, audience responses such as thinking or talking media messages represent the cognitive and behavioral dimensions of participant involvement, respectively (Rubin & Perse, 1987a). Attention represents another form of cognitive involvement.

In one study, Rubin and Perse (1987b) found links among instrumental motives, such as watching TV news for information; increased perceived realism of news; more news affinity; and enhanced forms of activity, such as behavioral intentions and watching to discuss the news with others. In expectancy-value terms, perceived realism represents a belief and affinity an evaluation. "The consequence of this viewing pattern is not sheer news exposure, but an active orientation toward the news program that is manifested in viewing intention and involvement" (p. 76). They also found relationships among ritualized motives such as viewing to pass time and increased distractions, such as doing housework and preparing food, while viewing. Such distractions represent negative indicators of involvement. In these cases, less evident links exist among motives and attitudes, and TV becomes somewhat akin to radio listening. Rubin and Perse (1987b) proposed a temporal sequence, rooted in motives and attitudes, of the links among gratification seeking and activity. First, motives affect viewing attitudes such as perceived realism and news affinity. In a sense, this places gratification seeking ahead of expectancy-value components. Such attitudes, in turn, influence viewing intention, which leads to selective exposure. Exposure then leads to attention to contents and, through it, to other forms of involvement, such as discussing news. Finally, the latter would feed back through attitudes to influence future gratifications sought.

Other involvement research has focused on *parasocial interaction* (Horton & Wohl, 1956)—a form of affective participation. It refers to the feelings of audiences toward characters or personalities, such as those on TV. "Encouraged by conversational manner, interpersonal style, and media production techniques, viewers may react interpersonally to television personae and feel they 'know' the characters the way they know their friends" (Rubin & Perse, 1987a, p. 248). Parasocial involvement can include "seeking guidance from a media persona, seeing media personalities as friends, imagining being part of a favorite program's social world, and desiring to meet media performers" (Rubin, Perse, & Powell, 1985, pp. 156–157). Affiliation theories, which describe people as altruistic and cohesive, may explain why it occurs. These stress "that aspect of human motivation that drives the person to establish with other people connections that are characterized by mutual helpfulness and reciprocated positive affect" (McGuire, 1974, p. 188).

In one study, Rubin and Perse (1987a) examined parasocial and other forms of involvement among soap opera audiences. For example, increases in the extent to which people reported watching soap operas to interact socially with others correlated with enhanced levels of thinking and talking about programs. Similarly, perceiving the programming as realistic predicted greater parasocial interaction with characters. Once again, an instrumental orientation predicted enhanced forms of involvement. Thus, contrary to assumptions that media contents readily affect passive viewers, some more involved forms of media use appear to magnify exposure outcomes (Rubin, 1993).

The Internet. According to Ruggiero (2000), computer-mediated communication is reviving the significance of uses and gratifications research. Researchers need to expand its current models to include such things as interactivity and hypertextuality, he argued. In fact, recent research has begun exploring people's use of the Internet. Ferguson and Perse (2000) explored usage of the World Wide Web (WWW) among college students. They found that students often tended to surf for entertainment, to pass time, and to relax. Information uses appeared to be of lesser importance. This suggests that the Web in some ways offers a functional alternative to TV, they reported. In an exploratory study of Internet use in general (i.e., for e-mail as well as the WWW), Papacharissi and Rubin (2000) found five primary motives. The most salient was information seeking, followed by entertainment, convenience, passing time, and interpersonal utility. They also reported evidence for an Internet-related distinction between instrumental and ritualized use. As they put it,

> it appears that those who were more mobile, economically secure, satisfied with life, comfortable with approaching others in an interpersonal context, and who felt valued in their interpersonal encounters preferred the more instrumental Internet uses, such as information seeking. Those who were less satisfied and who felt less valued in their face-to-face communication used the Internet as a functional alternative to interpersonal communication, or to fill time. (p. 192)

Relationships With Traditional Effects Research. Research also has continued to join uses and gratifications with more traditional areas of effects research. The concept of transaction provides one way to combine uses and gratifications with effects research. The idea that communication involves a transactional process has appeared repeatedly (e.g., Bauer, 1963, 1964; McLeod & Becker, 1974; Self, 1974; Toch & MacLean, 1962). As articulated by Dewey and Bentley (1949) and adopted into perceptual psychology, transactionism treated the individual and environment as interdependent entities. "The individual is a creative agent in his perception of the external world, and the environment is a creative agent in shaping an individual's perceptions" (Kilpatrick, 1988, p. 229). A parallel exists between the role of human activity in perception and that often assumed by research concerning uses and gratifications (Wenner, 1985). For example, the notion of selective perception (see chap. 6) posits that different people may perceive the same objects somewhat differently. As Dewey and Bentley (1949) put it, transactional observation "sees man-in-action, not as something radically set over against an environing world, not yet as something merely acting 'in' a world, but as action *of* and *in* the world in which the man belongs as an integral constituent" (p. 52). Some scholars equate transactional and functional psychology (Kurtz, 1990).

Researchers have used the transaction concept within the uses and gratifications framework. McLeod and Becker (1974) used it in an effort to synthesize the perhaps equally flawed, but antithetical, powerful- and limited-effects models of media influence (see chap. 1). The former exaggerated the impact of media content, they argued. The latter, however, depicted the audience as so selective and active that people can get any effect they desire from any message, making content irrelevant. The researchers examined the political-communication consequences of both the orientations of an individual person, with measures of gratifications sought and of media avoidances, and of his or her communication environment, with indicators of specific forms of media exposure. They found evidence that media exposure and gratifications separately affected political dependent variables, such as a person's interest in an electoral campaign.

Wenner (1985) related the concept of transaction specifically to Dewey and Bentley's work. He described a process in which gratifications sought, modified by the content and context of exposure, potentially result in a perception of gratifications obtained. To Wenner (1985), these components combine transactionally — rather like the taste resulting from ingredients of a peanut butter and jelly sandwich. Consistent with aspects of the research concerning expectancy-value theory and involvement, Wenner advocated development of variables such as media consumption and duractivity as a means of explaining relationships between gratifications sought and those obtained. Ultimately, such factors may transact to produce effects, defined rather broadly as changes in individuals, groups, and societies.

Some researchers have stressed the concept of *media orientations* in including gratification seeking in effects analysis (McLeod & McDonald, 1985). This refers not only to gratification seeking, but to factors "such as attitudes toward the medium and message, dependency on the medium for gratifications, and the quantity and quality of attention paid to the content" (Swanson, 1992, p. 315). In short, a variety of orientations may combine with a person's exposure to media contents to produce effects.

Instrumental and ritualized media orientations sometimes may influence the degree or presence of media effects. Garramone (1984) found evidence that people's motivation to learn information about issues from political advertisements, an instrumental motivation, correlated positively with issue knowledge. Greater cultivation effects (see chap. 9), which concern people's perceptions of the world and fears of victimization, may occur among soap opera viewers with instrumental, rather than ritualized, motives (see J. Kim & Rubin, 1997; Perse, 1986; but see also Carveth & Alexander, 1985).

MEDIA SYSTEM DEPENDENCY THEORY

Similarities exist between traditional uses and gratifications approaches and aspects of media system dependency theory (Ball-Rokeach, Rokeach, & Grube, 1984). To a degree, each depicts audiences as variably active and involved. To an extent, theorists in each domain sometimes predict that forms of audience activity will enhance media effects. In some ways, dependency theory has a more specific focus, however (Grant, Guthrie, & Ball-Rokeach, 1991). For example, a central question to the former is, "Where do I go to gratify my needs?" (Grant et al., 1991, p. 780). An important question to the latter is, "Why do I go to this medium to fulfill this goal?" (Grant et al., 1991, p. 780).

In addition, the media system dependency framework considers interrelationships among media, audiences or individuals, and society. It is an ecological approach in that it

> focuses on relationships between small, medium, and large systems and their components. An ecological theory views society as an organic structure; it examines how parts of micro (little) and macro (big) social systems are related to each other and then attempts to explain the behavior of the parts in terms of these relationships. The media system is assumed to be an important part of the social fabric of modern society, and it is seen to have relationships with individuals, groups, organizations, and other social systems. (DeFleur & Ball-Rokeach, 1989, pp. 302–303)

As originally formulated, the media dependency approach attempted to help explain

> complex relationships between large sets of interacting variables that are only crudely designated by the terms "media," "audiences," and "society." It is through taking these sets of variables into account individually, interactively, and systematically that a more adequate understanding of mass communications effects can be gained. (Ball-Rokeach & DeFleur, 1976, p. 5)

When she began working on these ideas, Ball-Rokeach (1998) said she was as unsatisfied as were uses and gratifications theorists with mechanical effects models that assumed passive audiences. "However, the move to an active individual who employs interpretative powers to override the influence of creators of media texts was not the kind of active individual that I saw around me" (p. 9). Instead, she saw people who experienced ambiguity linked to structural alienation and conflict that they could not control directly. Ball-Rokeach (1998) provided a detailed comparison and contrast of the two approaches.

At the heart of the model is the concept of *dependency* – the idea that "the satisfaction of needs or the attainment of goals by one party is contingent upon the resources of another party" (Ball-Rokeach & DeFleur, 1976, p. 6). Two sociological conditions should influence the degree of audience media dependency. First, as societies increase in complexity, the media theoretically tend to perform a greater number of unique functions. Many of these functions differ according to how central they are to society or to groups of its members. "For example, providing sports coverage to politically active groups is probably a less central function than providing them with information about national economic or political decisions that strongly affect their lives" (Ball-Rokeach & DeFleur, 1976, pp. 16–17). Hypothetically, then, as the number and centrality of functions that a medium serves increases, so will a society's dependency on it. Second, a relatively high degree of conflict and change will affect dependency by making existing social frameworks unsatisfactory for people to cope with life.

> People's dependence on media information resources is intensified during such periods. This is a joint consequence of the reduced adequacy of their established social arrangements and the media's capacity to acquire and transmit information that facilitates reconstruction of arrangements (p. 7)

During the stability of the 1950s, for example, limited media effects, as many researchers thought, may have occurred. During the 1930s and 1960s, however, perhaps social turmoil enhanced media influence. Not only does this dependence lead to greater media effects, according to the model, but it may in turn either directly or indirectly (because it increases effects) alter society and the media as well. For example, news coverage of massive protests may contribute to increased conflict in society and thus to the passage of laws designed to change media operations (Ball-Rokeach & DeFleur, 1976). Figure 4.2 illustrates the model.

More recent formulations have focused on dependencies of individual people, rather than those of mass audiences. "It is the individual, rather than the audience, who has ongoing dependency relations with the media system" (Ball-Rokeach et al., 1984, p. 5). The type and intensity of such dependencies arise out of interacting clusters of sociological and psychological variables, according to the theory. These consist of

> *structural factors*—the pattern of the media's interdependent relations with political, economic, and other systems; *contextual factors*—the nature of the social environment within which individuals and social groups act, particularly the extent to which the social environment is threatening, predictable, and interpretable; *media factors*—the nature and quality of the media system's activities in constructing, and defining the utility of, its messages; *interpersonal network factors*—the ways in which interpersonal networks shape individuals' media-relevant expectations and motivations; and, finally, *individual factors*—the individual's goals that may be served by media use. (Ball-Rokeach et al., 1984, pp. 3–4)

Thus, dependency basically originates outside of an individual's media use. This concept differs from a dependency notion in some uses and grat-

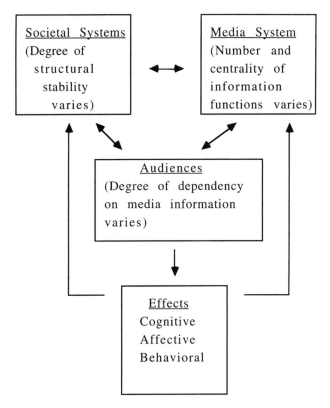

FIG. 4.2.   The media dependency model (from Ball-Rokeach & DeFleur, 1976). Copyright 1976 by Sage Publications, Inc. Reprinted by permission of Sage Publications, Inc.

ifications research that comes about as a consequence of media use (Rosengren & Windahl, 1989). In the latter case, someone "gets used to a certain medium and its content and thereby becomes 'addicted' to it" (p. 81). Such dependency thus represents a kind of media effect.

Theoretically, individuals exhibit three types of media dependencies (Ball-Rokeach et al., 1984). The first type is understanding dependency. This includes a need for both self- and social understanding. A person may acquire knowledge about his or her values, for example, and how they compare with those of others. Second is a need for orientation, which has both action and interaction components. People can use the media as guides about how to behave, both on their own and with reference to others. Finally, people develop play dependencies, both for solitary and social activities. For instance, someone may enjoy watching a dramatic TV program alone. However, watching a movie together might facilitate a couple's romantic relationship.

Accordingly, as media dependency increases, people tend to select messages that they expect to find useful. They also pay higher levels of attention to them. Finally, they experience greater levels of affect toward the message and its senders and engage in more postexposure communication than do the less dependent. For these reasons, media impact on human cognition, affect, and behavior should tend to increase (Ball-Rokeach et al., 1984).

A major test of the influence of media dependencies among individuals occurred in 1979 (Ball-Rokeach et al., 1984). In the study, researchers combined media dependency theory with a belief system theory from social psychology. Researchers produced a 30-minute TV show, *The Great American Values Test*. It was designed to promote antiracist, antisexist, and pro-environmental values, attitudes, and behaviors among viewers. Television personalities Ed Asner and Sandy Hill were featured. The program discussed results of opinion polls involving the U.S. public. For instance, Asner pointed out that Americans ranked freedom 3rd and equality 12th among 18 values, suggesting that most Americans are more interested in their own freedom than in that of others.

The program thus encouraged viewers to examine their own values and attitudes for consistency, both internally and with ideal self-conceptions. Researchers expected this to create either self-dissatisfaction or self-satisfaction with existing values and attitudes. If dissatisfaction occurred, people would be likely to change their belief systems and associated behaviors. Those experiencing satisfaction should try to extend and enhance the favorable affective state. In either case, the program could have lasting influence on people's values and behavior.

In 1979, all three commercial channels in Tri-Cities, Washington, simultaneously carried the show. Prior to this, advertisements intended to appeal to self- and social understanding goals of those high in TV dependency appeared in the local media and in *TV Guide*. The program was not shown in Yakima, Washington, which served as a control. Respondents in the two communities were randomly selected from telephone directories. As expected, Tri-Cities viewers who watched the program tended to be higher in social understanding and self-understanding dependency than those who did not. Results also indicate that those who watched the program without interruption contributed significantly more money 2 or 3 months later to solicitations for such causes than did people in Yakima, Tri-Cities residents who did not watch, or those whose viewing was interrupted by incidents such as telephone calls. Uninterrupted viewers also attached more significance to values such as freedom and equality and expressed more positive attitudes concerning the values and solicitations.

Beyond this, uninterrupted viewers who were high in overall TV dependency responded more favorably, according to these criteria, than did other uninterrupted viewers. The authors' conclusion was notable, if somewhat controversial. According to them, "a single 30-minute exposure to a TV program designed to conform to certain theoretical considerations can significantly affect the beliefs and behaviors of large numbers of people for at least several weeks or months subsequently" (Ball-Rokeach et al., 1984, p. xiv).

The authors suggested a self-education theory of media influence to explain their findings. Unlike the assumptions behind most advertising of passive uncritical audiences, the theory depicts people as selecting self-relevant information from their media environments. "Active agents who depend upon the media system to attain their self-understanding and social understanding goals are likely to expose themselves to media messages that are anticipated to serve such dependencies" (Ball-Rokeach et al., 1984, p. 160). Such people then consider appropriate information reflexively, sometimes resulting in media effects. The theory thus represents a humanistic, educational alternative to traditional persuasion theories (see chap. 7), according to its authors. Even so, this research could help further evil or self-serving purposes, such as those of a Hitler or someone attempting to convince teenagers to purchase speedy cars (Ball-Rokeach et al., 1984). The authors nonetheless reported it "because the suppression of scientific data seems to us and to colleagues with whom we raised this issue to pose an even greater danger" (Ball-Rokeach et al., 1984, p. 172).

ENTERTAINMENT THEORY

Some researchers (e.g., Zillmann, 1985) have questioned the introspective indicators employed in uses and gratifications research. Despite recent progress in validating such self-report data (Rubin, 1994), people simply may not always know the real determinants of their behavior (Zillmann & Bryant, 1994), perhaps especially in situations involving ritualized orientations. In addition, many human choices about media use sometimes may occur rather impulsively, without conscious deliberation (Zillmann & Bryant, 1994).

Such reservations underlie substantial components of entertainment theory. This research is related to, but for such reasons somewhat distinct from, uses and gratifications research. It often has examined why mediated comedy, drama, horror, or sports events entertain audiences (see Zillmann & Bryant, 1994). Of course, most of the contents of electronic media are meant to do this (Zillmann & Bryant, 1994). Beyond this, substantial portions of print media content—including comics, crossword puzzles, and horoscopes—are also designed to amuse or divert, and thereby to attract, audiences.

Media critics often describe these emphases as harmful to audience members who otherwise might spend more time with educational materials, for instance. Yet research indicates that entertainment contents can have some positive effects. For example, one study concerned the TV program preferences of viewers who experienced experimentally manipulated boredom or stress (Bryant & Zillmann, 1984). As expected, based on an optimal arousal theory, bored persons generally watched exciting rather than relaxing programs. Evidently, they rather successfully sought to alleviate their condition. Stressed persons, however, chose similar amounts of exciting and relaxing shows. Apparently, either type of show can reduce tension, in different ways, possibly for different people. Exciting programs may distract some people from thinking about the source of their stress, whereas a relaxing show may soothe the anxiety felt by others (Bryant & Zillmann, 1984). Additional evidence from the study indicated that some persons managed to identify why they made such choices. This suggests that "subjects make intelligent program choices—mostly intuitively, but sometimes following comprehension of the circumstances—when using television exposure as a means for alleviating boredom and stress" (Bryant & Zillmann, 1984, p. 20).

Similarly, Meadowcroft and Zillmann (1987) found that premenstrual and menstrual women were more likely than other women to select comedy entertainment. Apparently, the women selectively chose comedy to overcome the depression and irritability associated with these conditions, as predicted by a theory of affect-dependent stimulus arrangement. According to this learning theory, program selection initially is random but becomes purposive based on previously experienced relief. Perhaps education about these and similar studies could help media consumers deal more effectively with stressful and other uncomfortable psychological or physiological states.

CONSEQUENCES OF AUDIENCE RESEARCH

Rather obviously, for better or for worse, audience research can help media industries attract audiences to their fares. Perhaps the most important potential consequence of much audience research is its contribution to helping understand the relationship of people to media. As Swanson (1992) said of uses and gratifications research, "audiences are not impotent in the face of all-powerful media but rather are active, endeavoring to use media content to serve their own purposes and interests" (p. 306). Some critics, however, see uses and gratifications research as " 'pollyanish,' in that it tends to view media consumption exclusively in positive terms" and find that it "tends to ignore the overall negative effects of media on the culture" (Heath & Bryant, 1992, p. 288). Nonetheless, such research cannot entirely absolve mass media of responsibility for their impact, in part, because they often especially affect those who make more active use of them. In the language of chemistry, such research suggests at most that effects are like *compounds* formed from *elements*, including people's media orientations and media contents.

In this light, audience research may help place media-effects evidence in perspective. For example, harmful behaviors linked to TV violence may occur in the context of larger sociocultural values. Such values probably contribute both to the amount of mediated violence available and whatever popularity it has among audiences. Thus, TV may have increased U.S. homicide rates (see chap. 10), but it perhaps did so by acting as a mediating variable between the cultural environment and human behavior. In short, TV violence may be a proximate contributor to homicide, but the cultural or social antecedents of such content are likely to be distal contributors. Only future research linking the causes of human desires to watch media violence with such media effects can better establish this point.

Beyond this, Mendelsohn (1974) is almost alone in addressing the possible social consequences of uses and gratifications research. In many ways, his 27-year-old discussion still applies. Of course, media contents generate advertising revenues to the extent that they attract large audiences and sometimes the right kinds of audiences as well. Broadcast ratings and print media circulation estimates therefore frequently determine what survives in the competitive marketplace. At times, these also allow the media industries to claim that they merely provide what audiences want — statements that at worst help them evade responsibility for certain social effects of their products. On reflection, arguments that the media merely offer what people want are somewhat fallacious. For example, ratings only reflect people's choices among available content, not necessarily what audiences actually desire (Mendelsohn, 1974).

According to Mendelsohn, uses and gratifications work could enhance existing transactions involving communicators and their audiences. In this regard, Mendelsohn drew a distinction between elitist conceptions of human needs, which some media critics often emphasize, and desires — what audiences really want from the media. "Policy recommendations flowing from subjectively determined audience needs generally are one-sided, undemocratic, and insensitive to the actualities of media audiences' expectations and behaviors" (Mendelsohn, 1974, p. 304). In addition, the concept of needs can help confer legitimacy to highly questionable media content, as when gossip columns are said to meet an assumed need to know on the part of the public (Mendelsohn, 1974). Studying people's wants and desires, as well as their expectations of the media, seems more democratic. In particular, Mendelsohn advocated the use of research to examine the media-related desires of specific subgroups, such as working-class Americans. For example, the development of *Sesame Street* relied on elaborately detailed research into the needs and expectations of targeted child audiences (see chap. 6). In their attempts to cater to mass audiences, the media usually tend to overlook substantial subpopulations, Mendelsohn argued.

Researchers who would describe the media-related wants and expectations of the public face an enormous, but not impossible, task (Mendelsohn, 1974). To do so would require a protracted dialogue and debate involving members of the public who would have to give serious thought to their concerns and the issues involved. In addition, realistic alternatives must be presented to the public, which should receive an opportunity to experience some of the alternatives, such as different technological systems of news delivery. As Mendelsohn (1974) said, "All too often public wants and expectations focus on what has been rather than on what might be" (p. 308).

The alternatives to use of such research, according to Mendelsohn, include basing content decisions on elitist critics who want the media to provide the public with what the critics (but not necessarily everyone else) believe is needed, or leaving the judgments to practitioners and entrepreneurs, who often rely on exposure measures such as TV ratings. Mendelsohn's ideas have yet to take hold fully within the communication industries. Nonetheless, technological change, such as the fact that audiences sometimes have hundreds of TV channels to choose from, are helping to bring at least some of his ideas to fruition by forcing more attention to audience subpopulations.

5

Media Ownership and Theories of Media Content

Legislative and public debates in the United States often display one narrow focus: They treat the current ownership system of mass communication as a given. For example, popular commentators and politicians argue about the effects of media violence and possible regulatory responses, usually without questioning the commercial nature of U.S. TV. The debates concerning the 1996 Telecommunications Act illustrate this tendency. It updated the 1934 Communications Act, placing it among the most important federal laws of that decade. According to critics, its purpose "is to deregulate all communication industries and to permit the market, not public policy, to determine the course of the information highway and the communications system" (McChesney, 1997, p. 42). In Congress, discussion ranged from the position of Newt Gingrich to that of then-Vice President Al Gore. Gingrich equated profitability and public service, and Gore said markets can solve public concerns once corporate profitability is assured (McChesney, 1997). This focus has existed since the failure of the broadcast reform movement during the 1930s. That movement attempted to ensure the dominance of nonprofit radio. McChesney (1993) provided a detailed historical account.

PATTERNS AND THEORIES OF MEDIA OWNERSHIP

Of course, in the United States, the mass media operate almost entirely as for-profit businesses. The few exceptions largely involve public radio and television, which attract rather small audiences. This is not true everywhere, however. In the United Kingdom, license fees fund the government-chartered, nonprofit British Broadcasting Corporation. It carries no

93

advertising, and its radio and TV operations attract large audiences. Created during the 1920s, it operated as a monopoly until the 1950s. Today, British TV features numerous commercial alternatives. These include the ITV, regional stations, and (of course) numerous satellite sources, including some from the United States. Canada has a similar system, as does much of Europe.

In media research as well, researchers often treat the nature of the present media system as a constant, rather than as a potentially fruitful variable. In part, this occurs because at times they explore whatever questions others wish to fund. For example, what if the original vision of radio as an educational medium had panned out? Field forefather Paul Lazarsfeld might have conducted "field experiments in which alternative types of educational programming were evaluated" (E.M. Rogers, 1992, p. 470). This is not to denigrate the competence or worth of existing research. Ignoring ownership structures is not a sign of good science, however, critics charge. In addition, it narrows its potential applications and benefits as well. As Sterling (2000) put it, "the real answers to most of the everyday expressions of concern about or praise for media lie with the owners and managers of American print, film, and electronic media companies" (p. xv).

Such tendencies have long existed in other social research. Shortly after World War II, a series of articles in *Commentary* magazine by prominent scholars discussed the current state of social science. A number made similar statements. Bell (1947) said that industrial sociologists tend to operate only as technicians, dealing with problems as defined by management. They do not examine how factory methods might be changed to "best stimulate the spontaneity and freedom of the worker" (p. 87). Glazer (1946) questioned the propriety of social scientists who attempted to promote the harmonious operation of internship camps during World War II for Japanese Americans. Dewey (1947) attempted to get at the roots of these concerns. According to him, "The common element is a troubled awareness of a narrowness, a restraint, a constriction imposed upon the social sciences by their present 'frame of reference,' i.e. the axioms, terms, and boundaries under which they function today" (p. 378). This "tends to give scientific warrant, barring minor changes, to the *status quo*" (p. 379; italics original).

Four "Theories" of the Press

For decades, many scholars have characterized existing media systems according to a fourfold typology in which ownership plays an important role. These so-called *four theories of the press* (Siebert, Peterson, & Schramm, 1956) are not empirical scientific theories. Rather, they are normative ideas that are also meant to describe existing systems. They apply to all forms of mass communication, not just to print. The articulation of these ideas is not without critics (e.g., W.E. Berry et al., 1995; Picard, 1985).

The two most basic types are the authoritarian and libertarian systems. In the former, media may be owned either privately or publicly. Historically, this may be the most common form. In it, the media exist to advance government policies. Criticism of state policies tends to be forbidden. Authoritarians usually argue that elites are uniquely competent and the masses are lacking. Often governments employ formal censorship to control the media. In other cases, the state merely denies a publication access to its monopolized newsprint supply. Many different philosophical ideas, including Plato's realism and Hegel's organicism, can be associated with such a model. In contrast, the ideas of nominalists John Locke and John Stuart Mill purportedly underlie libertarian theory (but see W.E. Berry et al., 1995). These systems feature private ownership and typically limit controls largely to marketplace mechanisms. Only limited legal regulation occurs. The purpose of mass media is to inform, but they also exist to entertain and sell products. Libertarians tend to assume that average people can make intelligent decisions from among what they find in a marketplace of ideas, to borrow a famous phrase from U.S. Supreme Court Justice Oliver Wendell Holmes.

The totalitarian and social responsibility models are variants of the two main types. Totalitarian media systems largely exist only in communist societies and represent an extreme form of authoritarianism. In them, forms of mass communication are owned publicly, yet the ruling Communist Party and not the state typically controls them. Marx, Lenin, and similar figures provided the philosophical rationale. The media exist to promote the socialist system and the existing party dictatorship. They may carry some criticism of tactics, but party objectives usually are sacrosanct.

Karl Marx, whose ideas remain influential among some of those studying patterns of ownership, actually said little about mass communication (Siebert, Peterson, & Schramm, 1956). According to Marxist ideas, the ruling class, defined by its ownership of the means of production, controls and owns the press in capitalist societies. Therefore, media have effects that reinforce capitalism. Ordinary and working class people never will have reasonable access to them. Legalities such as the U.S. First Amendment do not "defend the working reporter's expression from control by the publisher or station owner and their surrogates" (W.E. Berry et al., 1995, p. 145). In Marxist societies, the media typically have attempted to promote the objectives of a Communist Party hierarchy.

The social responsibility model represents an attempt to update the libertarian theory in light of changes in media ownership, such as increased concentration. The Commission on Freedom of the Press (1947) formalized it. The basic idea is that freedom carries with it responsibility. To remain in private hands, the media should meet societal expectations in a number of areas, such as providing a forum for a plurality of views concerning public affairs. If not, the government steps in. Social responsibility theory has certain affinities with the civic-journalism movement (see chap. 1).

Of course, certain cultural and historical contexts may influence the ways scholars see media systems. According to W.E. Berry et al. (1995), the Siebert, Peterson, and Schramm book describing the four theories was "driven by an agenda rooted in the context of its composition, specifically the cold war-era global expansion of the U.S. model of privately owned for-profit media" (pp. 7–8). The work "defines the four theories from within one of the four theories—classical liberalism" (p. 21). Only in that model is political world "divided into individuals versus society or the state. By contrast, postmodern notions of community or polity deny the salience of the individual versus society opposition" (p. 21).

Partly in contrast to the four-theories theorists, Altschull (1984) argued that those who finance the press, including but often not limited to its owner, rather inevitably affect its content. This takes place under all media systems, he alleged, to varying degrees. "The press is the piper, and the tune the piper plays is composed by those who pay the piper" (p. 254). He discerned four different patterns, although pure examples are rare, exceptions exist, and overlapping occurs. With official control, such things as state decrees and rules control the press. News media may be state enterprises, such as in communist societies. Under commercial control, the views of advertisers and their allies, usually including owners and publishers, determine content. Much of the U.S. media today probably fall in this category to a considerable extent. A financing entity such as a political party or religious organization controls content in the interest pattern. Examples occurred shortly after the founding of the United States and in political house organs today. Finally, with informal patterns, media content reflects the goals of individuals who supply money.

As an alternative to libertarian, Marxist, and even Altschullian explanations of U.S. mass media, Akhavan-Majid and Wolf (1991) articulated the *elite power group* description. According to it, a number of features characterize U.S. media today. These include growing concentration and conglomeration, links to other power elites, and ability to exercise selfish control on government even as it controls them. None of these is consistent with libertarianism. In contrast, Altschull and Marxists see media as tools of the powerful, rather than as a power group themselves. In my view, the elite power group notion probably provides the best available description of U.S. media today.

Conglomerate Control

In much of the world today, several dozen conglomerates own much existing communication media. Many, but not all, of these largely specialize in media. They may have horizontal integration by possessing holdings in diverse areas. These may include books, magazines, sound recording, newspapers, radio, and TV. Often they have forms of vertical integration. For instance, they may own companies devoted to content, such as TV production companies, and those that distribute, such as networks and stations. They also may possess a variety of nonmedia entities, such as theme parks or industrial manufacturers.

With some types of mass communication, a single firm dominates. These monopolies include cable TV franchises and many daily newspapers, which often represent the only detailed source of news and efficient advertising in local markets (Gomery, 2000). In other instances, a handful of firms dominates, creating an oligopoly. Examples occur with the book publishing, broadcast TV, and film industries (Gomery, 2000). The magazine industry exemplifies monopolistic competition; it features "a marketplace where there are many sellers, but for any specific product (or service) there are but a few competing products" (p. 519). Other areas may be in transition. The Internet perhaps is moving from open to monopolistic competition (Gomery, 2000).

A look at a couple of the largest media conglomerates may provide a sense of perspective. Before its recent acquisition by America Online, Time Warner ranked 45th among U.S. corporations in the *Fortune* 500 and had 1999 annual revenues exceeding $27 billion. It publishes books via Little, Brown & Co. and Time-Life Books. It also puts out numerous magazines, such as *People*, *Sports Illustrated*, and *Time*. Time Warner owns Cable News Network, Home Box Office, Turner Entertainment, Warner Brothers, the Atlanta Braves, and the Warner Music Group. Disney, with 1999 sales in excess of $23 billion, is almost as large. It owns ABC, A&E, the Disney Channel, and most of ESPN. The Disney empire also includes books, *Discover* magazine, daily newspapers, TV and movie production and distribution entities, music, sports teams, and theme parks and resorts.

The largest media companies also include Australia's News Corp., with 2000 sales of $14 billion; Germany's Bertelsmann, with 1999 sales of $13.7 billion; and Viacom, with 1999 sales of $12.85 billion. In addition, some giant media-related firms belong to much larger industrial corporations. For example, General Electric, with 1999 sales of more than $110 billion, owns NBC. Below these first-level companies are numerous second-tier media firms, with more than $1 billion in annual business. Among them is the largest newspaper publisher, Gannett. Its 1999 sales totaled more than $5.2

billion. These conglomerates do not always exhibit patterns of competition assumed by idealizations of the marketplace. Instead they frequently own stock in each other, engage in joint ventures, and share members of their boards of directors. In some ways, tendencies toward ownership concentration seem to be increasing in part due to the 1996 U.S. telecommunications law and the more general global deregulatory zeitgeist.

Any attempt to describe the current situation quickly becomes history. For example, during early 2001, the world saw the more than $100 billion purchase of Time Warner, the world's largest media company, by America Online, its largest Internet provider. This amounted to the biggest merger in U.S. corporate history. In the newspaper industry the previous year, the Tribune Co. purchased the Times Mirror Co. for some $8 billion. This deal alone exceeded the previous annual record of merger-and-acquisition value for the entire U.S. newspaper industry. In August 2000, the largest newspaper chain, Gannett, completed the $2.6 billion purchase of Central Newspapers, publishers of *The Arizona Republic* of Phoenix and *The Indianapolis Star*. The deal was the second largest in U.S. newspaper history. That July, Gannett also acquired 19 small dailies from Thomson Corp. of Canada. To some, this at times resembled a rather out-of-control corporate Pac-Man game.

During the 1990s, a global media system increasingly supplemented and today threatens to overshadow national markets. During the 1980s, the United States lost some of its traditional global dominance as the owner and producer of mass communications. Articles in Hirsch (1992) address this globalization of mass media ownership. Today many large media conglomerates remain U.S. based, but others operate out of Europe, Asia, and Latin America. Whether based in the United States or abroad, these often have become increasingly involved in the global markets. Between 1990 and 1996, for example, the non-U.S. share of revenues for Disney and Time Warner grew from 15% to 30% (McChesney, 1997). Of course, this took place along with the growth of the global economy, presumably stimulated in part by advertising among transnational firms. The reasons for changes in competition and concentration are not secret. Companies need to enhance profits to survive.

Yet certain complaints may be a bit misleading. A measure reflecting the market share of players indicates that the "media industry remains one of the most competitive major industries in U.S. commerce" (Compaine, 2000a, p. 562). According to indicators such as revenue accounted for by the top 50 companies, rather little change in media concentration occurred between 1986 and 1997 (Compaine, 2000a). This applies to the industries as a whole. However, individual sectors, such as newspapers, have experienced increased concentration (Compaine, 2000a). Also a lack of competition within information industries may pose more of a threat than in other sectors of the economy if it hampers the workings of a marketplace of ideas.

In addition, the Internet may help counter present tendencies toward concentration. It provides a channel for a virtually unlimited number of journalists. Critics such as McChesney (1997) are more than skeptical, pointing to existing and increasing corporate control of the web. Nonetheless, a second coming of competitive, serious journalism could restrain those who might like to emulate the acquisitiveness of Al Neuharth, self-described S.O.B. (see Neuharth, 1989) and former Gannett chairman. Such would-be tycoons someday may gaze lustily at a corporate Pac-Man screen, only to find that thousands of little online piranhas have slowly gelded their financial virility. Events beginning during January 1998 perhaps provided a glimpse of such a future. At that time, an obscure freelance writer placed a story on his web site. It pointed out that *Newsweek* had held back the evidence it had of the then-publicly unknown Bill Clinton–Monica Lewinsky *fin de siècle*. The rest, as they say, is history and herstory. Clinton was impeached, *Monica's Story* became a flash-in-the-pan bestselling book, and the number of daily visitors to Matt Drudge's site soon exceeded the weekly circulation of *Time*. Presumably, advertisers notice such things.

Some Additional Possible Consequences of Media Ownership Patterns

Without question, existing studies of media ownership have their weaknesses. For one thing, they sometimes reflect rather dogmatic ideologies often of the Left. Perhaps their implicit political worldview simply makes them sound a bit strident to more centrist ears. They also sometimes rely on simplistic assumptions that the ownership structure of media organizations somehow determines their effects on individuals and society. This perhaps is a bit reminiscent of effects researchers' evident fondness for treating existing commercial mass media as empirical constants. The arbitrary isolation of the social sciences from the humanities, and the somewhat related separation of the empirical from the critical, among scholars may contribute to both tendencies.

Probably the safest conclusion is that circumstances can lend support to a variety of views. The extent to which one suffers the consequences of media concentration depends on one's goals. Someone looking for detailed news from a local community may find fewer sources than a few decades ago. Yet a person looking for national or world news will find hundreds of newspapers with Internet sites from which to choose.

Hypotheses abound about the possible effect of ownership patterns on media products. For example, Croteau and Hoynes (2000) suggested that integrated conglomerates may favor material that facilitates synergy. Synergy involves "the dynamic where components of a company work to-gether to produce benefits that would be impossible for a single, sepa-rately operated unit of the company" (p. 46). Thus, horizontal integration may encourage book publishers to judge prospective titles based on mo-tion pictures potential (Croteau & Hoynes, 2000). In addition, conglomer-ation perhaps has boosted the emphasis on profitability among newspa-pers and TV news outlets, leading to more efforts to entertain and fewer to inform (Croteau & Hoynes, 2000).

An especially often heard prediction is that competition, especially by separately owned news organizations, improves content by enhancing di-versity. For example, among newspapers "competition should pump up the adrenaline of the newsroom as well as demand that publishers devote greater resources to the quality and content of the 'product'" (Compaine, 2000b, p. 43). In fact, however, research has found relatively little evidence of such content effects (Compaine, 2000b; Entman, 1989; Sterling, 2000). Thus, the problem may be more potential than actual. A uniformity of po-litical coverage, for example, might not occur until some politically evan-gelistic chain acquires a preponderant number of media outlets. In addi-tion, greater content diversity need not always mean better content. Instead, it may involve "more low brow shows, trash journalism, pander-ing politics to go along with opportunities for finding more thoughtful and quality outlets for analysis, entertainment and information. Diversity cuts all ways" (Compaine, 2000a, p. 578).

Corporate ownership may have subtle effects on content diversity, in that it tends to exclude certain topics from the news (Croteau & Hoynes, 2000). "There is no way of proving the connection, but the media's focus on the shortcomings of government, rather than of the private sector, seems consistent with the interests of the corporate media owners" (p. 50). During the early 20th century, the most prominent journalists included muckrakers who documented abuses by private business. During the late 20th century, the most notable journalism, such as the Watergate exposes, tended to target the public sector. Even if such claims are true, the Internet makes it easy for individuals to read material from a variety of periodicals that are more than critical of private business. These range from relatively mainstream outlets such as *The Nation* to publications of small leftist groups, such as *The People*, *Revolutionary Worker*, and so on.

What about the relationship between ownership patterns and media ef-fects on audiences? Even if empirical evidence sometimes seems lacking, existing forms of ownership may diminish the prospects of participatory democracy. According to McChesney (1997), such democracy works best when significant disparities in wealth among citizens are absent, when peo-ple display senses of community and interdependence, and when an effec-tive system of political communication engages them. The current U.S. media system undermines all three, he argued. It "encourages a weak political culture that makes depoliticization, apathy and selfishness rational choices for the citizenry, and it permits the business and commercial interests that actually rule U.S. society to have inordinate influence over media content" (p. 7). In this light, chapter 9 discusses evidence that TV entertainment programming diminishes audiences' civic engagement. That chapter also looks at evidence that exposure to newspaper readership and televised public-affairs fare increases such engagement. Therefore, if U.S. broadcast media had developed as educational rather than commercial enterprises, democracy might have benefited. The civic-journalism movement (see chap. 1) nonetheless has often attempted to build participatory democracy, some would say naively, within the framework of the current media system.

According to McChesney (1997), need for profit fuels markets, which cannot address externalities—unintended consequences that have no impact on earnings. Public acquisition of political information is a positive externality, and the effects of media violence on audiences represent negative ones (McChesney, 1997). "In a democratic society, these externalities cannot be ignored. They must be discussed and debated in the political sphere, with efforts made to emphasize the positive and discourage the negative ones" (pp. 46–47).

THEORIES OF MEDIA CONTENT

Media content often seems to be a lightning rod for criticism. For example, many people like to complain about the amount of sex and violence on TV or in the movies. In addition, political partisans commonly accuse journalists of favoring the other side. Historically, many mass communication studies have examined the content of the mass media using a technique known as *content analysis*. Berelson (1952) defined *content analysis* as "a research technique for the objective, systematic, and quantitative description of the manifest content of communication" (p. 18). Generally, content analyses concern only the manifest or surface content of communication because only this content can be studied "objectively." They are objective in the sense that a researcher must describe precisely how he or she has done a study, allowing other investigators to replicate it. The term *systematic* means that a researcher may not select only those pieces of content that support a hypothesis, but must rely on all that is relevant. Finally, the technique is quantitative—a requirement that distinguishes it from merely reading something and recording one's impressions. Some researchers nonetheless use forms of qualitative content analysis in an attempt to examine the deeper meaning found in messages. Such studies, however, are not replicable and run the risk of revealing more about the mind-set of the researcher than about the content.

Researchers conducting a content analysis follow carefully specified rules to categorize content. For example, a researcher who examines coverage of a presidential campaign may simply measure, in column inches, how much space a newspaper devotes to the various candidates. The categories pertain to the candidates. Someone who studies how much attention network news telecasts devote to different regions of the world uses categories concerning these regions. A key feature of these categories is their reliability. Good content analysts define their categories carefully and provide evidence that another researcher could repeat their procedures with similar results. Studies that report no reliability evidence should be treated with skepticism.

Quantitative content analyses allow researchers to study many allegations and research questions concerning the mass media. For example, one can assess whether TV drama has become more violent in recent years. One can also study whether Western news agencies present distorted or incomplete pictures of developing countries or whether a news medium is providing equal amounts of coverage to all candidates involved in a political campaign. Most studies of media content assume that the content has some meaningful effect on media audiences. Without assumptions of media effects, justifying why content is important often becomes difficult if not impossible. Why should anybody care how much violence occurs on TV programs unless exposure to it affects audiences? Only if media content influences the way audiences respond to it with a degree of predictability can it address the ultimately important effects questions. Of course, content does not always equal response. For this reason, studies of media content may suggest answers to effects questions, but they are not sufficient, in and of themselves, to answer them. In many cases, analyses of media content provide important contextual information for media-effects research. If research shows that exposure to mediated violence contributes to aggression in young people (see chap. 10), tracking how much violence appears on the tube certainly seems worthwhile.

During recent decades, content analysis has had its ups and downs in influence in media studies. In a sense, it is both the easiest and most difficult research approach available to researchers. Data concerning media content generally are *unobtrusive*, meaning that researchers do not have to worry about their presence affecting the behavior of subjects. Demand characteristics, for instance, are not an issue. In addition, many content studies are descriptive, meaning that researchers do not have to worry about the sophisticated designs and statistical procedures used when one focuses on complex issues of cause and effect (see chap. 2). Yet a great deal of time and patience is frequently necessary. The work is time-consuming, often tedious, and can even take a real toll on one's eyesight.

Perhaps the greatest shortcoming of many content-analytic studies, and the reason the technique at times has fallen out of favor among researchers, is the large number of descriptive studies conducted. These frequently concern issues of content, such as how much violence is on TV and to what extent situation comedies present stereotypical images of ethnic minorities or the aged. It is relatively easy, but perhaps ultimately not very useful, to count and categorize media content unless one attempts to predict or explain why the observed patterns occur.

This chapter emphasizes studies that contain at least potential theoretical relevance on the assumption that research that seeks both empirical generalization and theory most likely will help the human race meaningfully adjust to its environment. That is to say, studies that treat variations in media content explicitly as a dependent variable, linked to independent variables such as characteristics of gatekeepers and outside influences on media organizations (Shoemaker & Reese, 1991), are especially useful. For example, only theory is likely to provide people interested in influencing media content with an effective tool for action.

General Influences on Media Content

What appears in the mass media results from many different influences, ranging from the creative impulses of drama writers and journalists to the regulatory actions of government. The routines developed within media organizations and the broader cultures of ideology within which they operate are also important. In the first book of its kind, journalism scholars Shoemaker and Reese (1991) examined theory and evidence concerning influences on media content. They presented a model illustrating five broad categories of influence: individual media workers, media routines, media organizations, nonmedia individuals and organizations, and ideology. The categories are arranged hierarchically; each class evidently is affected by those that encircle it. Ideology, for instance, theoretically constrains all other categories. The authors discussed a number of empirical generalizations about each category of influence as part of a larger theory of content. The focus of the book tended more toward news than entertainment content in part due to the availability of news research.

The first general influence — characteristics and prior experiences of individual workers — evidently does not affect news directly. Indirect effects may occur, however, if these influence workers' professional or personal attitudes, Shoemaker and Reese concluded. This calls into doubt claims that the liberal political beliefs of many journalists, or efforts to staff newsrooms with a more diverse group of workers, will change a medium's performance. Routines, the established ways in which media workers do

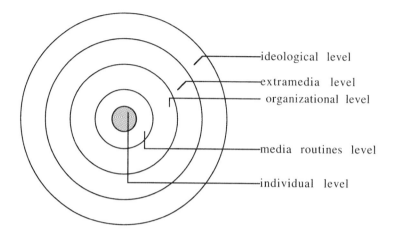

FIG. 5.1.   Hierarchical model of influences on media content (from Shoemaker & Reese, 1996). Copyright 1996, 1991 by Longman Publishers USA.
Reprinted by permission of Addison-Wesley Educational Publishers, Inc.

their jobs, influence content by defining, for instance, news as events
rather than as issues and by standardizing the roles of individual media
workers. Organizational-level influences constrain workers and routines
by giving owners the ability to set policy, for example. Extra media forces
affect content when government regulates it or interest groups create advertiser pressure. Finally, ideology influences news content by such
things as defining certain political groups as outside of the mainstream
and thereby causing them to receive especially unfavorable coverage
(Shoemaker & Reese, 1991). The ideology dominant in a society may also
mandate certain ownership structures, thereby also affecting content. Figure 5.1 illustrates the model.

The "Representativeness" of Media Content

Some research concerns how media content differs from the "real" world.
In fact, contents often differ predictably from statistical indicators of reality. For example, news does not consist of a random selection of occurrences. Rather, certain events have characteristics, such as negative implications for an audience, that tend to attract attention. The need of
commercial mass media to attract audiences, and therefore advertising
revenues, doubtlessly explains some of this discrepancy. For instance, a
TV show that dramatized a mundane, random sample of events in life
would not attract viewers except perhaps in a society in which the medium was a novelty. Hegemony theory (Sallach, 1974) offers another explanation as to why the content of the mass media differs from "reality."

According to it, the mass media tend to reflect the ideological interests of those with power in a society. Thus, they carry content that helps perpetuate the status quo, often distorting reality, according to these theorists.

However, one should carefully consider the philosophical implications of comparing features of media content with the "real" world. All philosophers do not even agree whether an objective world exists independently of human perception, although most assume the presence of such a world. At the very least, however, human mental and sensory apparatuses limit knowledge of the "real" world. In contextualist terms (see appendix), all knowledge comes from the transaction of the knower and the known. One can never know what qualities an event or object has outside of perception. Thus, when examining the extent to which media content provides an unrepresentative picture of the world, one must recognize the very real limits on human abilities to describe an objective, external reality.

In fact, many scholars today see reality as socially constructed (P. Berger & Luckmann, 1966). According to this notion, one can view any social event from any number of perspectives, rendering ideas about journalistic accuracy or bias a bit problematic (see Davis & Robinson, 1989). Journalistic and other ideas become true to the extent that they prove socially useful and are accepted by others (Davis & Robinson, 1989; Tuchman, 1978). This amounts to a perceptual analogue of the underdetermination thesis of science (see chap. 1). Such arguments may help tone down both the hubris of journalists reared in concepts of objectivity and that of media critics who criticize them.

Yet the idea that news is socially constructed may require one qualification. This position, often known as *constructivism* or *constructionism*, may exaggerate the role of the knower while ignoring or minimizing constraints imposed by the known. Some constructivism has its roots in philosophical idealism, which maintains that "*the external world does not exist independently of its being perceived*" (Hunt, 1991, p. 242; italics original). It thus differs somewhat from pragmatism, which assumes that "if there were no minds there would still be a world of physical objects with various knowable properties" (Almeder, 1986, p. 81).

The Nature of News

To borrow a phrase from William James, news concerns the *specious present* — a fact that influences all of its other characteristics (Park, 1940). In other words, it is "a very perishable commodity. News remains news only until it has reached the persons for whom it has 'news interest.' Once published and its significance recognized, what was news becomes history" (p. 676).

Many studies have demonstrated that content of news differs in important ways from statistical indicators of reality. For example, Combs and

Slovic (1979) studied newspaper causes of death. They found that deaths from rare events such as homicides and accidents receive much more attention than do more frequently occurring deaths from diseases such as cancer. In general, the amount of coverage given to particular causes of death did not relate closely to their statistical frequency. According to the researchers, one likely reason for this is a desire to sell newspapers; perhaps people like to read about dramatic causes of death. Such coverage may also result from the fact that people are better able to protect themselves from unusual than from more common causes of death (Combs & Slovic, 1979).

Some researchers have attempted to construct theoretical explanations about the nature of news and its relation to reality. Galtung and Ruge (1965) developed one such theory. It is controversial in large part because of the authors' assumption that "reality" is somewhat irrelevant to studies of news content. The theory explicitly concerns international news. Much of it might apply, with a few slight modifications, to domestic news as well. Although research has only partly supported it, it probably remains the most useful available theory of news content.

Galtung and Ruge began with the assumption that a person involved in the news-selection process (i.e., a gatekeeper) is like a radio listener scanning the air waves in search of a station. Whether the scanner picks up a signal depends on characteristics of the signal, such as whether it is strong enough to hear. Psychological and cultural considerations program the scanner to pick up signals with certain characteristics. According to their theory, certain events contain features or news factors that increase the probability that they will become news. These presumably come into play at every step of the news-selection process. That is to say, they will influence whether a reporter decides to write about a story, how much play the reporter's medium will give to the story, whether wire services and other media pick it up, and even to what extent audiences attend to it. Galtung and Ruge suggested that at least 12 factors exist. The first 8 are assumed to apply in all cultures:

1. *Frequency* means that the event occurs within an appropriate time period. Generally speaking, very slowly occurring events tend to be ignored; the media tend to favor the quick and dramatic.
2. *Threshold* means either that the event is large enough in magnitude to receive attention or that its size increases sufficiently to call attention to it.
3. *Unambiguity* refers to events that are clearly meaningful or interpretable.
4. *Cultural proximity* or *relevance* concerns events that occur in a similar culture to that of an audience or that are otherwise relevant to it.
5. *Consonance* means that the event was expected or desired.

6. *Unexpectedness* means that the event was unexpected or scarce.
7. *Continuity* occurs to the extent that the event has been defined previously as news.
8. *Composition* refers to whether the overall news environment is favorable for an event (e.g., whether other competing news can crowd it out).

The last four news factors presumably apply primarily within Western cultures, which tend to emphasize elitism and individualism:

9. To the extent that an event concerns *elite nations*, it tends to be selected as news.
10. To the extent that an event concerns *elite people*, it tends to become news.
11. If the event can be *personified* (i.e., linked to actions of specific people), it tends to become news.
12. Events with *negative* consequences tend to be selected as news.

From these news factors, Galtung and Ruge derived a series of hypotheses. These include the *additivity hypothesis,* which states that the more of these factors an event embodies, the more likely that it will become news. They also derived the *complementarity hypothesis,* which predicts that if an event is low on one factor, it will have to be high on another to become newsworthy. This hypothesis can apply only if news media have selection criteria that are not restricted to events with the maximum score on all factors.

Researchers have examined the theory in various ways. In their original paper, Galtung and Ruge (1965) tested the complementarity hypothesis by examining whether news items that do not satisfy one factor tend to score high on others (i.e., whether a negative correlation exists between two news factors for a given body of news content). Thus, stories involving culturally distant nations tend to be especially negative. They analyzed how Norwegian newspapers covered political crises occurring during the early 1960s in the Congo, Cuba, and Cyprus and found support for their complementarity hypothesis with several combinations of factors.

In examining this hypothesis, they made no attempt to deal with an external, objective reality. Their theory assumes that, because of the impact of news factors, the content of news tends to differ from what really happened. Nonetheless, Galtung and Ruge maintained that researchers generally cannot determine what really happened. Sociologist Rosengren (1974) took issue with this. He maintained that researchers often do have such information, such as data about parliamentary elections. In addition, he argued that if research finds negative correlations between news factors, it could simply reflect what occurs in reality, rather than the effect of the news factors. For instance, negative events simply may occur more frequently in nonelite nations than in elite ones.

Galtung's (1974) response was interesting. He basically argued that "what really happened" is often unknowable, although perhaps not with such things as parliamentary elections. Beyond this, such data are largely irrelevant to the theory, he claimed. News tends to consist of unexpected events, he noted, which means that reporters normally do not have much of an external baseline on which to rely. A reporter covering a strike, for instance, has no way of knowing ahead of time how long the strike will last and how many lost work days it will involve (i.e., what its objective threshold score is). The only baseline with which to compare the amount of coverage, say, of one strike with another will become available only after the fact. Finally, Rosengren's model assumes that events occur, that news media select items from among them, and the media image results, Galtung argued. Instead, "*there is an image, and that image is imposed on reality*. The result is biased, but it is usually not very meaningful to ask what the correct image would be" (Galtung, 1974, p. 159; italics original). Thus, the media image may tend to correspond to the complementarity hypothesis because of the assumptions of the theory regardless of reality.

Such statements may seem startling especially to journalism students who have internalized the professional concept of news objectivity, but they do contain at least a kernel of truth. The external world (assuming that it actually exists) apparently is an incredibly complicated place of blooming, buzzing confusion. Limitations in human mental facilities and sensory organs seriously hamper anyone's ability to describe it. Reporters who describe news events certainly are no exception, although professional experience and training perhaps help matters somewhat.

Regardless of where one stands on this debate, the Galtung–Ruge theory remains important. Since the 1960s, mass communication researchers have often used it to study the flow of news between and among countries. Some of the studies have used the extra media data advocated by Rosengren, whereas others have not. To a substantial extent, research (e.g., Kariel & Rosenvall, 1984; McCracken, 1987) has supported many aspects of the theory.

Setting the Media Agenda

The Galtung–Ruge theory concerns media coverage of events. In a sense, it is a theory concerning influences on the media agenda. Often, however, the term *media agenda* refers to issues rather than to individual events. Researchers usually define the media agenda as consisting of a hierarchical

ranking of issues according to the amount and prominence of news coverage. Although a not entirely visible line separates the two, events tend to
be more narrowly conceived. Some researchers (see the discussion in E.M.
Rogers & Dearing, 1988) see events as temporally and spatially limited occurrences and issues as arising from the cumulative news coverage of patterns of associated events. For example, the cocaine-related death during
1986 of basketball star Len Bias — an event — evidently contributed to rais-
ing the drug issue on the media agenda. Substantial evidence exists (see
chap. 9) that the degree of emphasis that news media give to issues (e.g.,
unemployment or world trade) affects not only public perceptions of issue
import, but the beliefs and actions of public officials. Thus, an obviously
important question, often vocalized throughout modern history, concerns
the extent to which news stories emphasize objectively important issues.
In Lippmann's (1922) terms (see chap. 9), to what extent does the
pseudoenvironment of news reflect the "real" world? Subject to the previously discussed limitations about external reality, the answer seems clear:
sometimes to a considerable extent, but perhaps more often not. Behr and
Iyengar (1985) found that TV news substantially reflected changes in real-
world indicators of energy issues, inflation, and unemployment. For example, as inflation worsened during the 1970s, TV news focused on it. Yet
the declining severity of the U.S. drug abuse problem, as indicated by use
among the young, did not match its ascending position on the media
agenda during the early and mid-1980s (Shoemaker, 1989).

Nonetheless, the agenda of policymakers often seems to influence the media agenda (see the review in E.M. Rogers & Dearing, 1988). For instance,
Walker (1977) reported that the initiatives of legislators concerning occupational and traffic safety led to increased media attention to these issues. In
fact, news sources may be far more important in general than are journalists
in setting the news agenda (D. Berkowitz, 1992). D. Berkowitz explained this
with a role theory. Journalists and sources "generally define their relationships according to socially prescribed expectations" (p. 92). Notions of objectivity and journalistic work practices encourage news people to favor material from legitimated sources, often policymakers, he suggested.

Message System Analysis

The fictional nature of most drama on TV means that one has to be even
more circumspect than with news about comparing its content with indicators of reality. By definition, TV fiction does not purport to mirror the
"real world," although some theorists argue that it reflects an ideology
that promotes the interests of the powerful. For many years, Gerbner and
his associates have monitored the content of network drama during
prime-time and weekend daytime TV. They have examined programs

such as serials, comedies, cartoons, and motion pictures. Much of their work attempts to identify ways in which the world of TV differs from the "real" world. It (e.g., Gerbner, Gross, Morgan, & Signorielli, 1980) has demonstrated the overrepresentation of people with law enforcement occupations and the heavy amounts of crime and violence.

Their explanation as to why these differences occur meshes commercial considerations with something very much like hegemony theory. Television "is an agency of the established order and as such serves primarily to reinforce—not subvert—conventional values, beliefs, and behaviors" (Gerbner, Gross, Signorielli, Morgan, & Jackson-Beeck, 1979, p. 180). Presumably its need to attract the largest possible audience at the smallest possible cost requires programming that depicts a world differing in important ways from reality.

The most famous feature of these content analyses is their Violence Index. They defined *violence* as "the overt expression of physical force (with or without a weapon, against self or others) compelling action against one's will on pain of being hurt and/or killed or threatened to be so victimized as part of the plot" (Gerbner, Gross, Morgan, & Signorielli, 1980, p. 11). The researchers typically take a sample of 1 week of network programming, including both prime-time drama and weekend children's daytime drama. They construct the index by weighting and combining five components: the percent of characters involved in a killing, the percentage of characters involved in any violence, the percent of programs that contain violence, the number of incidents of violence per program, and the number of violent incidents per hour. The resulting index allows comparison of violent activity on TV during different time periods. Such data also allow researchers to compare the world of TV with statistical indicators of the "real" world and conclude that TV is much more violent, as well as suggesting hypotheses for effects research (see chap. 9). Perhaps especially when combined with effects research, examinations of the relationship of media content and reality "do not imply a dichotomy between media and reality but, on the contrary, make media parts and shapers of reality" (Gerbner, 1986, p. 268).

Related research has examined media representations of various ethnic and sociodemographic groups. Clearly, TV has often underrepresented the elderly in comparison with the actual population (Gerbner, Gross, Signorielli, & Morgan, 1980). Beyond this, stereotypes pertaining to ethnic groups, the elderly and women have often appeared (Gerbner, Gross, Signorielli, & Morgan, 1980; Signorielli, 1985). For example, females in MTV advertising appear in more skimpy clothing than do men and are more likely to promote products designed to improve one's appearance (Signorielli, McLeod, & Healy, 1994). Thus, the ads "preserve and perpetuate stereotypes about women" (p. 100).

The Future: Content-and-Effects Studies

Because media content usually contains little import unless effects occur, an integration of content studies more explicitly into the effects paradigm can increase the import of the former (Shoemaker & Reese, 1991). To some extent, this has occurred. For example, studies of the impact of media violence frequently refer to evidence of the amounts of violence on TV.

Beyond this, future researchers perhaps need to consider the relationship of content to effects in much more detail than in the past, according to Shoemaker and Reese. They argued that theory development in mass communication has reached a plateau. Effects theories tend to come from sociology and psychology and ignore media content and the variables that influence it. Nonetheless, fully comprehending the effects of media violence requires understanding how and why the media depict violence and how it varies across different programs and time periods.

Shoemaker and Reese suggested a number of ways that future researchers can integrate the theories of content with those of effects. For example, one might look at differences in the extent to which the violence in various shows affects audience. Perhaps producers and writers at different production companies tend to have different values, which result in a variety of contextual presentations of violence with different effects on people.

Consequences of Content Research

Besides serving as a starting point for effects studies, analyses of media content may serve as an important indicator of culture in a society. Some research has studied media content precisely for this purpose (see the review in Shoemaker & Reese, 1991). In addition, content studies can help assess how well the media are living up to their social obligations. For instance, researchers have examined to what extent U.S. citizens have an opportunity to choose from a variety of competing viewpoints concerning current events. This is important almost regardless of the effects of the content. Findings of serious inadequacies in the diversity of viewpoints available could suggest that laws are needed to open up access to media channels.

Theories of media content may also prove especially useful to public relations practitioners because their employers or clients often judge them by the amount of favorable news coverage they generate. In many instances, they are rewarded without formal evidence as to whether their work had any impact on the public. In addition, educating media consumers about the nature of media contents may help them recognize important distinctions between it and other forms of reality that they encounter. Perhaps such education might contribute to more appropriate perceptions of the reality (Potter, 1988) found within media contents.

Of perhaps the most importance to society, a refocusing of effects research to more explicitly include media content, and especially theories about content, may prove extremely useful in the application of effects studies. First, some of the inconsistent results of effects studies, such as those concerning violence and sexuality in the media (see chap. 10), almost surely result from a lack of researcher attention to significant content differences. Analyses of the content patterns of TV violence can point out important ways previously ignored by effects studies, in which violence varies across networks or program genres. What aspects of the context of media violence contribute to harmful effects qualities? What contextual aspects render violence harmless or at least less harmful? B.J. Wilson et al. (1998) summarized existing evidence concerning these issues. For example, perhaps TV violence that is glorified or otherwise rewarded will produce more long-term, as well as short-term, aggressive behavior in children than violence that is not, as social learning theory suggests. Perhaps video depictions of sexual intercourse that depict degradation of women are much more likely to result in aggressive reactions by males against females than films that avoid such degradation, as feminist theory suggests. Careful analyses of the components of content that potentially contribute to different effects may provide more coherent research than is now available.

Second, because constitutional protections make it difficult to regulate media content per se, critics may have more success in dealing with some of its more specific features. For instance, convincing broadcasters to reduce glorified violence may prove much easier than convincing them to reduce violence more generally. Third, effective action may require explaining why different forms of content occur. To convince programmers to reduce glorified violence, one may need to understand why some law enforcement dramas on TV tend to glamorize violence, whereas others emphasize its negative consequences. Perhaps certain writers falsely assume that glorification boosts program ratings. Pointing this out might help persuade broadcasters to avoid such programs.

Finally, of course, interest groups and others wishing to affect the content of the media often act according to implicit theories that treat content as a dependent variable. For example, an interest group may try to convince the media to carry more information designed to promote positive objectives (e.g., how to avoid AIDS) or less presumably harmful content (e.g., TV violence). To accomplish its goals, it may attempt to exert pressure through advertisers or even directly on gatekeepers (see Turow, 1984). To the extent that influences on media content are understood, people who wish to influence media will have guides for effective action. The current level of theory development seems rather rudimentary, but could ultimately lead to a much more refined (and hence useful) body of knowledge.

For example, Shoemaker and Reese (1991) presented a number of hypotheses about extra media influences on content as part of their more general theory. These include ideas that advertisers affect content and that interest group criticism of news coverage tends to increase both media self-censorship and efforts at governmental control. Activists interested in influencing media content probably already are likely to make such assumptions. A more elaborated body of empirically supported theory, dealing perhaps with contingencies in the processes and interactions among causal factors, might help these groups much more. For example, such a theory could help explain the conditions under which interest group picketing changes media performance directly without depending on pressure from government or advertisers. It also might identify situations in which such pressure enhances or diminishes the influence from advertisers or government.

Of course, how useful action to influence media content is to society in general depends in large part on the motives of activists and how justified their assumptions about media effects turn out to be. An unscrupulous news source could use knowledge about how a newspaper works to plant an inaccurate or misleading story, damaging a political candidate, perhaps by contacting a reporter near deadline to minimize the chances that the information will be checked. Employees of news organizations, in turn, could only protect themselves by awareness of the assumptions behind such practices. One group may believe falsely that increased media attention to safe sex practices will influence the behavior of those most at risk for AIDS, such as intravenous drug users. Thus, a useful theory of media content may help accomplish the immediate goal, enhanced media coverage, but not the ultimate, socially beneficial goal. Conceivably, an organization could use a content theory to reduce TV violence, yet ultimately harm society if lowering violence has no effect on crime and only deprives people of enjoyable entertainment. Once more, concerns about media content often depend critically on media effects.

6

The Cognitive Effects
of Mass Communication

Until the 1970s, researchers tended to neglect the cognitive impact of mass communication, focusing instead on media influence on attitudes and behavior. Today, the available literature reflects more balance. *Cognition* refers rather broadly to interlinked human mental processes such as attention, knowledge, memory, and perception. It involves "the activity of knowing: the acquisition, organization, and use of knowledge" (Neisser, 1976, p. 1). The dramatic growth of information-processing psychology exemplifies contemporary interest in the subject. Today, this work has influenced other areas of psychology, including that portion dealing with communication. Media researchers have also used more sociological approaches to examine cognitive effects, such as people's learning of public affairs information.

PSYCHOLOGY, COGNITION, AND MASS COMMUNICATION

The interface between media studies and psychology has long represented a fertile meeting point for each (see chap. 1). The relationship today is not without its tensions, however. For example, cognitive psychologists often examine people's processing of simple, isolated stimuli such as individual letters. Communication scholars usually work with more complex, realistic manipulations, such as news stories or TV programs. As a result, psychologists worry whether communication scholars borrow concepts correctly and apply sufficient experimental controls; communication researchers point to the artificial nature of much research and ask: "Aren't psychological experiments often, well, intellectually arid?" (Reeves & Anderson, 1991, p. 597). Underlying these tensions may be mechanistic versus more contextualist world views (see appendix).

When behaviorism dominated psychology during the early and mid-20th century, the study of human mental processes received relatively little attention. Since the 1950s, however, cognitive psychology has become one of the most important parts of the field. In terms of the appendix, it tends to exemplify mechanistic or, less commonly, pragmatist worldviews. The mechanistic influence shows up in work that represents human information processing with flow charts and in theories designed to describe the isolated components of cognition without regard to their broader functions. Those working from a mechanistic perspective study human behavior in an effort to form inferences about the *black box* of the mind. Many researchers assume, metaphorically or literally, that the mind is a computer. According to Gillespie (1992): "mechanistic psychologists assume that the mind, taken as a physical entity, operates like a machine behind closed doors. Predefined, reality is composed of basic elements that interact in such a way that mental activity can be controlled and predicted" (pp. 46–47). Obviously, the computer age has contributed to such work.

Such work is rooted in the associationism of philosophers such as Hume. Associationism provides a relatively simple interpretation of human learning and cognition. "Complex ideas can be reduced to connected simple ideas, and the content of these simple ideas is ultimately rooted in sense impressions. Thus, meaning is generated by the external environment" (Gillespie, 1992, p. 30). Information-processing psychologists usually assume, however, that people actively process information. Hence, the term *neoassociationism* more accurately describes their theories.

Historically, mechanistic researchers have focused on small parts of mental machinery, such as the hypothetically separate sensory, short-term, and permanent memory stores. They have assumed that one can disassemble a machine and examine its individual parts without altering their nature. Ultimately, after describing the pieces experimentally, they often attempt to reassemble the parts into more global theories. By the mid-1970s, a number of experiments (e.g., Bransford & Franks, 1971; Jenkins, 1974; Johansson, 1973) identified shortcomings of mechanistic frameworks, contributing to interest in pragmatist approaches. Today, contextualism is especially evident in work examining the ways that interrelated cognitive processes relate to actual events, instead of attempting merely to isolate the structures of the mind. "It brings the mind out from behind closet doors and into social spaces where meanings can be shared and constructed" (Gillespie, 1992, p. 47). Ecological psychology (e.g., Gibson, 1979; Neisser, 1976), which stresses the mental processes that humans use to deal with real events, largely reflects this approach. According to Neisser (1976), "studies of human memory using lists of nonsense syllables have not been helpful in explaining school learning or everyday remembering" (p. 33).

Thus, studies using "real-world" stimuli, such as memory of mediated messages, seem relatively coherent with pragmatism (see Hoffman & Nead, 1983). Today, mechanistic ideas appear frequently in communication, but researchers often use them to explain the processes or consequences of realistic events, such as watching TV or reading a newspaper. In this light, Fig. 6.1 contains Thorson's (1989) model, which concerns how people process TV commercials and programs. In Fig. 6.1, broken arrows represent information flows that occur automatically, and the solid arrows flows require conscious control by viewers. Only the lower portions of the "machinery" are conscious.

The rectangles in Fig. 6.1 are permanent memory stores. These include goal specification, which represents a person's reasons for viewing TV,

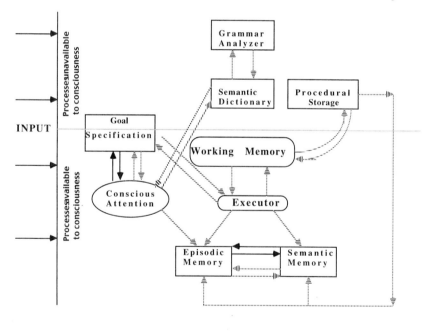

FIG. 6.1.   Thorson's model of commercial information processing (from Thorson, 1989). Copyright 1989 by Sage Publications, Inc. Reprinted by permission of Sage Publications, Inc.

such as to relax. This is depicted as only partly conscious, consistent with contemporary ideas about media audiences (see chap. 4). The semantic dictionary and grammar analyzer store such things as word meanings and sentence structure. People usually recognize words such as TV and the structure of a compound sentence unconsciously. Similarly unconscious is the procedural store, which contains associations, such as that between the smell of a type of perfume and a woman's face, from events in one's past. Episodic and semantic memory are more consciously available. Episodic memory includes a person's memories of events, such as what happened last Christmas. Semantic memory consists of facts and concepts, such as the name of the state that one resides in, abstracted from particular temporal occurrences.

The ovals represent processing mechanisms that coordinate the stores. Conscious attention is "nonautomatic, effortful processing of input" (Thorson, 1989, p. 402). The executor is the conscious control mechanism. It "activates materials from episodic and semantic memory and directs conscious attentional focus" (p. 402). Working memory is an impermanent, limited capacity store. It is "the blackboard upon which the executor is able to keep track of information, combine it, and operate on it" (p. 402).

Attention

Some communication researchers have thought of attention as "focused sensory and cognitive effort that limits attention to other activities" (Perse, 1990, p. 679). As such, it relates closely to, and represents a necessary component of, audience involvement (see chap. 4). Attention may often enhance the impact of mediated messages (Chaffee & Schleuder, 1986). Communication researchers have measured it relying on people's self-reports, observing people for signs of it, or using physiological measures (Chaffee & Schleuder, 1986).

Psychologists have been a bit reluctant to define the concept explicitly (Johnston & Dark, 1986). Neisser's (1976) equation of attention with picking apples rather closely matches the way media researchers apply the concept. "Organisms are active: they do some things and leave others undone. To pick one apple from a tree you need not filter out all the others; you just don't pick them" (pp. 84–85).

Selective Perception

The contributions of the environment and the organism to human perception may be inseparable, like the way hydrogen and oxygen form water. Much research has focused on selective perception—the tendencies of different people to perceive the same objects and events quite differently.

Neisser (1976) treated attention synonymously with perception. Some researchers have attempted to separate the two, reserving perception to refer to audience interpretations of an attended to stimulus. As such, selective perception is a form of selective duractivity (see chap. 4). Many selective perception studies, however, do not separate interpretation from attentive involvement or retention.

Work within transactional psychology (see chap. 4) provides evidence for selective perception. On November 23, 1951, the Princeton University football team hosted Dartmouth in the final game of the season for each school. Of special significance was the fact that the game was the last for one Princeton senior, Dick Kazmaier, an All-American. Early in the game, the star had to leave the field with a broken nose. Later, a Dartmouth player left with a broken leg, and a large number of penalties and outbursts of temper marked the contest.

Student newspapers at the two schools reacted rather differently to the unusual bitterness displayed in the game. The *Daily Princetonian* (cited in Hastorf & Cantril, 1954) reported a few days later:

> This observer has never seen quite such a disgusting exhibition of so-called "sport." Both teams were guilty but the blame must be laid primarily on Dartmouth's doorstep. Princeton, obviously the better team, had no reason to rough up Dartmouth. Looking at the situation rationally, we don't see why the Indians should make a deliberate attempt to cripple Dick Kazmaier or any other Princeton player. The Dartmouth psychology, however, is not rational itself. (p. 129)

In contrast, the *Dartmouth* (cited in Hastorf & Cantril, 1954) reported:

> However, the Dartmouth-Princeton game set the stage for the other type of dirty football. A type which may be termed as an unjustifiable accusation.
>
> Dick Kazmaier was injured early in the game. Kazmaier was the star, an All-American. Other stars have been injured before, but Kazmaier had been built to represent a Princeton idol. When an idol is hurt there is only one recourse—the tag of dirty football. So what did the Tiger Coach Charley Caldwell do? He announced to the world that the Big Green had been out to extinguish the Princeton star. His purpose was achieved.
>
> After this incident, Caldwell instilled the old see-what-they-did-go-get-them attitude into his players. His talk got results. Gene Howard and Jim Miller were both injured. Both had dropped back to pass, had passed, and were standing unprotected in the backfield. Result: one bad leg and one leg broken. (p. 129)

Following the football game, Hastorf and Cantril (1954) showed a film of the game to students at the two schools. Princeton students reported seeing twice as many infractions by Dartmouth players as among those from Princeton. In addition, on the average, Dartmouth students counted only half as many infractions committed by their team as did the Princeton students. According to the researchers,

> the data here indicate that there is no such "thing" as a "game" existing "out there" in its own right which people merely "observe." The "game" exists for a person and is experienced by him only in so far as certain happenings have significances in terms of his purpose. (p. 133)

More recent research has provided additional support for selective perception. For example, one study examined the impact of preexisting views toward capital punishment on the way both opponents and proponents interpreted reports of studies concerning its deterrent value. Exposure to clearly contradictory evidence polarized preexisting attitudes among each group, as people accepted information supporting their presuppositions and criticized that which opposed it (Lord, Ross, & Lepper, 1979). Perhaps this research helps explain the often intense controversies among researchers about the evidence concerning many important questions in the social sciences.

Vallone, Ross, and Lepper (1985) documented what they termed the *hostile media phenomenon*—the tendency of those partisan to an issue to view media coverage as biased against their side. Both pro-Israeli and pro-Arab university students at a U.S. university viewed TV news coverage of the Israeli move into West Beirut in 1982. Afterward each group reported that the coverage contained more negative than positive references to their side. In addition, as an individual's knowledge of the crisis increased, so did his or her perceptions of bias against the person's side. The authors concluded that the findings reflected not just unreasoning desires for preferential treatment, but the operation of more fundamental principles of perception.

The consequences of selective perception are perhaps rather obvious. In their perceptual activities, even human beings with perfect vision may often resemble the legendary blind men who examined an elephant. Anyone who attempts to discuss controversial issues neutrally or to mediate between conflicting groups may experience great amounts of controversy or difficulty. Their tasks are much more challenging than they might be if human perception really involved just a simple, passive mirroring or picturing of an antecedent reality. News people who are criticized from partisans on both sides of an issue might take comfort in this research because it suggests their work may in some sense approach objectivity. However, the evidence presents a warning to mass communicators that their audiences often may not perceive messages the same way as they do or as they intend. Therefore, media messages may not have the consequences intended. In short, the environment often appears to constrain but under-determine human perception.

Inference

How likely is a person to die in an accident, such as an automobile or air-plane crash? In comparison, what are the chances that a disease, such as cancer or a stroke, will produce the death? Unless you have knowledge of statistical data concerning frequency of deaths, you probably will answer the question by relying on an inductive inference based on specific deaths of which you are aware.

Tversky and Kahneman's (1973, 1974) work concerning people's use of judgmental heuristics provides the basis for much of what is understood about human inference. Psychologists have defined *heuristics* as rule-of-thumb techniques that help find, but do not always lead to, correct answers in problem solving. They have distinguished heuristics from algo-rithms—the more tedious methods that inevitably produce a correct an-swer (J.R. Anderson, 1980).

One particularly important heuristic is availability, "in which people assess the frequency of a class or the probability of an event by the ease with which instances or occurrences come to mind" (Tversky & Kahne-man, 1974, p. 1127). Tversky and Kahneman cited the example of people judging the probability of a heart attack for middle-aged persons by the frequency in which their middle-aged acquaintances have suffered heart attacks. Biases occur with such judgments if the rate of heart attacks among acquaintances differs from the rate in the population as a whole. Experiments (Tversky & Kahneman, 1973) indicate that frequencies of classes and events covary with their availability, but biasing factors also influence judgment.

One rather obvious source of such bias might be news, which by defini-tion does not consist of a description of a random sample of events in the world (see chap. 5). Combs and Slovic (1979) tested availability theory in a mass communication context. They found a substantial positive correla-tion between how often newspapers reported various causes of death and people's inferences concerning the frequency of such deaths. This finding withstood controls for actual frequencies of different forms of death. Ac-cording to Tversky and Kahneman (1971), even social scientists trained in statistical inference often make unjustified leaps of judgment. Yet educa-tion about probability techniques apparently can help people make more appropriate judgments (Gebotys & Claxton-Oldfield, 1989). Biased infer-ences may not be intrinsic to humans. Instead, they may result from "a lack of understanding concerning the rules of probability calculus" (Ge-botys & Claxton-Oldfield, 1989, p. 239).

Memory

Historically, cognitive psychologists have described human memory as consisting of several components. Stimuli were thought to flow from sensory to short-term or working memory and sometimes on to the presumably permanent, long-term memory. Some researchers have relied on neoassociationist ideas that treat long-term memory "as a collection of networks, with each network consisting of units or nodes that represent substantive elements of thought, feelings, and so forth, linked through associative pathways" (Jo & Berkowitz, 1994, p. 45). From these, scholars concerned with media effects have adopted the notion of *priming*. This idea "maintains that the presentation of a certain stimulus having a particular meaning 'primes' other semantically related concepts, thus heightening the likelihood that thoughts with much the same meaning as the presentation stimulus will come to mind" (Jo & Berkowitz, 1994, p. 46). In this way, exposure to media violence could activate aggressive thoughts, increasing the chances that a person will behave antisocially at least in the short run.

Some empirical evidence suggests that memory stores may not be neatly separable, however. As a result, the levels-of-processing perspective (Lockhardt & Craik, 1990) has focused on memory procedures rather than structures. According to it, the way someone processes information greatly influences the likelihood that the person will remember it later. For example, describing a film as based on history rather than as fictional may yield deeper audience processing, improving retention of its contents (Perry, Howard, & Zillmann 1992).

Today, some media researchers (e.g., Graber, 1988) use the concept of *schemata* (the singular is schema) to represent memory. " 'Schema' refers to an active organisation of past reactions, or of past experiences, which must always be supposed to be operating in any well-adapted organic response" (Bartlett, 1932, p. 201). In Neisser's (1976) words, schemata "prepare the perceiver to accept certain kinds of information rather than others and thus control the activity of looking" (p. 20). For example, Meadowcroft and Reeves (1989) used the concept of *story schema*, "abstractions of prototypical story parts and how they are related (e.g., setting, beginning, focal problem, problem resolution, etc.)" (p. 356). They found that advanced schematic skills resulted in increased memory of the central contents of a TV program.

LEARNING FROM THE MEDIA

In mass communication research, one of the most studied cognitive dependent variables is public affairs knowledge. A democracy is premised on the informed participation of the citizenry. Of course, the news media potentially play a major role in this. How well, and under what conditions, do people seem to acquire information from the various mass media? Research designed to answer these questions sometimes reflects a clear influence from both sociology and cognitive psychology.

Television Versus Print Versus the Internet

It is sometimes asserted that the important effects of the mass media today are limited largely to TV. Polls taken of the general public often have indicated that a clear majority of the U.S. population identifies TV as its primary source of news (Robinson & Levy, 1986). Yet how meaningful these responses are remains debatable. Do people really know where they acquire public affairs information? For instance, more direct evidence suggests that it is actually from the print media, rather than electronic media, that adults primarily acquire public affairs information. Children, however, may remember TV contents better (Gunter, Furnham, & Griffiths, 2000).

This conclusion for adults comes primarily from cross-sectional studies that correlate an individual's self-reported exposure (e.g., time spent with or days per week viewed) to various news media with his or her ability to answer simple current events questions, such as identifying one's mayor or congressional representative (D.F. Roberts & Bachen, 1981; Robinson & Levy, 1986). Such studies tend to show a marked positive association between exposure to print media (i.e., newspapers and newsmagazines) and knowledge of public affairs. Increased exposure to TV news often relates at best weakly, if at all, with increases in such knowledge. Self-reported dependency on TV for news may even covary negatively with knowledge (Becker & Whitney, 1980).

This evidence suggests sober implications for the future of U.S. democracy. Since the end of World War II, TV news has grown phenomenally, and usage of the print media has declined. Despite evidence that older persons use more print media than do younger persons (D.F. Roberts & Bachen, 1981), there can be no assurance that as today's young grow older they will increase their use of print media.

Thus, the possibility exists that because of TV news, voters ignorant of exactly for whom they are casting ballots will decide many future elections. Society may see many more examples along the lines of what occurred in Illinois during 1986. In that state, candidates belonging to the extreme right-wing political organization of Lyndon LaRouche won the Democratic primary nominations for lieutenant governor and secretary of state. Evidently, voters reacted favorably to their advocacy of mandatory AIDS testing for the entire population and other extreme measures without knowing what the candidates really represented. In the end, the candidates lost the general election, after the Democratic nominee for governor refused to run on the ballot with them. His refusal created widespread press attention, but helped ensure the reelection of his Republican opponent.

D.F. Roberts and Bachen (1981) reviewed a number of theoretical ideas that may help explain the evident superiority of the print media in facilitating adult learning. One relates to actual media content. Unlike many newspapers, TV news often has a show business aspect to it—featuring a focus on exciting visuals that may be of only peripheral import. Second, because of the ubiquity of textbooks, the schools may train people to acquire information from print rather than electronic media. Finally, people may process print information more deeply and actively than they do broadcast information. In contrast, children may learn better from television because pictures "serve as conceptual pegs, to which narrative content is hooked during learning and from which it can be retrieved on recall trials" (Gunter, Furnham, & Griffiths, 2000, p. 111). This is consistent with Paivio's (1971) dual coding hypothesis—the idea that separate representational mental systems exist for verbal and nonverbal information.

In fact, research pertinent to the processing explanation for adults suggests that the idea that people learn little from TV news may be overstated. Because exposure to print news requires more mental effort than does exposure to TV, comparisons of the impact of exposure per se may not be appropriate (Chaffee & Schleuder, 1986). Instead, attention perhaps should be taken into account. Using panel data that included measures of both media exposure and attention to news, Chaffee and Schleuder reported little evidence that people who pay attention learn more public affairs information from print than from TV.

> To answer a question about "reading" a newspaper is simultaneously to report on one's exposure *and* attention (although it provides no guarantee that the reader is being attentive to public affairs news). The same does not hold for television use, however. One can "watch" a TV news program simply because it is on, without it particularly engaging the mind in any serious sense. (p. 104)

Of course, people who watch TV news without paying much attention to it may still learn little. In Neisser's terms, the TV is only one apple in a larger perceptual tree. How often do you turn on local TV news to watch the weather and realize later that you have no idea what the forecast predicted?

The growth of the Internet may be complicating things. Recent multiday experimental research using college student participants indicated that online newspapers less effectively inform people about public affairs than do conventional ones. Tewksbury and Althaus (2000) found that online readers of the *New York Times* recalled fewer public affairs stories than did participants assigned to read the traditional version. Yet online readers recalled more business and technology items. These findings arose from differences in self-selected exposure to various items, resulting from different cues for story salience in the two versions of the paper. "As the online version presents fewer cues about the importance of events, it appears that people are more willing to use their own interests as the guiding criterion," the authors concluded (p. 472). In another experiment, Sundar (2000) found that multimedia additions to news web sites hamper people's memory of story contents.

Overall, an elitist interpretation seems possible. Perhaps the problem is not the public's preference for one medium rather than another, but the fact that substantial segments of U.S. society lack the motivation or even the basic communication skills to become informed citizens. These people may remain forever ignorant of the public affairs knowledge needed to participate effectively in society. Perhaps the proliferation of new communication technology and information resources will forever disadvantage many, leaving future democracy even more than today in the hands of an informed oligarchy.

The Knowledge Gap

In 1988, a brochure signed by the U.S. surgeon general about AIDS was mailed to every household in the country. The mailing cost the U.S. government an estimated $17 million. It was designed to inform the general public about what practices do and do not contribute to the spread of the feared disease. A serious question at that time involved whether the mailing really could accomplish anything. Despite the original appearance of the disease in the United States within the homosexual community, by the late 1980s, intravenous (IV) drug users (and their often heterosexual partners) increasingly accounted for its spread. Whether such a mailing could reach those really at risk seemed doubtful. IV drug users frequently do not have regular mailing addresses. Perhaps the primary effect of the mailing was to inform the already largely informed without reaching the people whom health care experts thought needed the information the most. It is even likely that many IV drug users, whose idea of long-term concerns extends only to tomorrow's fix, perceived the information as irrelevant to their lives.

An old question in mass communication research is the extent to which introducing information into a social system, by mediated and other channels, can reach the uninformed. In fact, strong evidence suggests that sometimes such information primarily reaches only the already informed. Such studies concern a sociological, rather than psychological, effect of the mass media. The key independent variable is the availability of information within a community or other social system, rather than an individual's exposure to the mass media. During the late 1940s, researchers attempted to use mass media to inform citizens in Cincinnati about the United Nations (UN; Star & Hughes, 1950). At that time, the UN was just a few years old and under Western domination. Traditional U.S. isolationists opposed involvement in it. In Cincinnati, the media (including newspapers and radio) were inundated with educational messages about the body. Before and after the campaign, researchers assessed the degree to which the public had acquired the desired information. Evidence suggested that only well-educated individuals, younger persons, and males — those individuals already likely to be relatively knowledgeable on the subject — really learned anything. In other words, the campaign missed the very persons that it was most designed to reach. Based on this and other evidence, about 20 years later three researchers at the University of Minnesota formulated the influential knowledge-gap hypothesis:

> As the infusion of mass media information into a social system increases, segments of the population with higher socioeconomic status tend to acquire this information at a faster rate than the lower status segments, so that the gap in knowledge between these segments tends to increase rather than decrease. (Tichenor, Donohue, & Olien, 1970, pp. 159–160)

The concept of socioeconomic status (SES), widely used in sociology, refers to an individual's social class. Operationally, three highly intercorrelated indicators are often used to represent it: education, income, and occupational status. In the knowledge-gap literature, education alone is generally used. The knowledge-gap hypothesis relates closely to studies of news diffusion (e.g, Deutschmann & Danielson, 1960), which deal with patterns inherent in public awareness of important events. The knowledge-gap researchers approached their subject from the perspective of systems theory, "looking at society and the communities making it up as either systems or components of systems" (Tankard, 1990a, p. 262). Systems theory may reflect the organismic worldview (see appendix) or an integrative form of contextualism. In communication terms, according to Windahl and Signitzer (1992), systems theory

> focuses on the *transaction* nature of communication, going beyond mere interaction between senders and receivers. Transaction implies mutual causality among the parts of the system, that is, interdependency. Constantly shifting roles of senders and receivers and their simultaneous reciprocal responses characterize this approach. (p. 85)

The hypothesis has rather profound consequences for the role of information media in a democratic society. Relatively educated persons generally are more knowledgeable about public affairs than are the less educated (see Gaziano, 1983). Thus, to the extent that news media really only make the already wealthy wealthier, in terms of information, they do not serve the role that many democratic theorists envision. To participate effectively in politics and as a citizen, one needs to be informed. In this sense, information is a vital commodity in modern society — as important as money. Democratic ideals, of course, call for a pluralistic society in which all have at least an equal chance to participate effectively.

There are two operational versions of the hypothesis (Tichenor et al., 1970). First, well-educated persons, as time passes, should acquire knowledge pertaining to a highly publicized topic more rapidly than will less educated persons. That is to say, when a major news event occurs, such as the Iraqi invasion of Kuwait, well-educated people will learn details (such as an ability to name the capital and leader of Iraq) more rapidly than will other people. If researchers administered a questionnaire about Iraq both before and after the invasion, they should find greater increases between the two time points among the highly educated. Second, the cross-sectional association between education and knowledge should be greater for highly publicized topics (i.e., those with more information available about them) than for less publicized issues. For example, assume that a researcher administered a questionnaire in late 1990 about Iraq and Albania. He or she would expect to find greater differences between persons of high and low levels of education in knowledge of Iraq, a highly publicized topic, than of Albania, which was receiving much less media attention.

Many early studies yielded evidence that suggested the knowledge-gap hypothesis. For instance, Samuelson (1960; cited in Tichenor et al., 1970) examined cross-sectional differences in two nearby communities in public affairs knowledge. In one community, a strike had shut down a daily newspaper for about 1 week, presumably not allowing residents time to establish alternative sources for news. In the second, another daily continued to publish as usual. Unlike most such studies, this one assessed the impact of a reduction of information availability in a community. Because less mediated information was available in the strike community, one should observe a smaller difference among educational groups. In the no-strike community, college-educated persons correctly answered an average of about 1 (out of 11) public affairs questions more than did those with a high school education. In the strike community, the difference was less than one half a question.

If the knowledge-gap hypothesis described an inevitable law of social existence, it would suggest that, in the words of its authors, "the mass media seem to have a function similar to that of other institutions: that of reinforcing or increasing existing inequities" (Tichenor et al., 1970, p. 170). There is, of course, no implication that the lesser educated will become less knowledgeable as a result of media publicity. On the other hand, their relative deprivation will increase. Obviously, it amounts to an extremely negative statement about the pragmatic ability of the mass media to help enfranchise the uninformed and could provide ammunition to those who advocate an elitist rather than participatory form of democracy (see chap. 9).

In fact, a number of subsequent studies have shown that under certain conditions knowledge gaps narrow. For example, much early research concerned knowledge of national or even international issues. When local issues are studied, different patterns often emerge. Donohue, Tichenor, and Olien (1975) found that with issues of local concern in 16 Minnesota communities, heavier media coverage of an issue tended to accompany smaller education-related knowledge gaps. These issues included regional planning, mercury pollution, and a dispute over how to finance a sewage disposal plant. Thus, increasing media coverage clearly does not inevitably enhance the relative deprivation of the less informed. A key variable may be the intensity of an issue within a community (Donohue, Olien, & Tichenor, 1987).

Beyond this, Ettema and Kline (1977) discussed various individual-level explanations for knowledge-gap phenomena. First, according to a deficit hypothesis, increased media coverage may primarily benefit the relatively educated because of that group's greater communication competence. Less educated people simply may possess deficiencies in basic skills (e.g., reading) needed to acquire such information. Second, a difference interpretation assumes that people with different levels of education have varied motivational levels to acquire public affairs information, which does not have the same relevance to everyone. Finally, ceiling effects, which occur when someone already has information on a topic, making additional learning impossible, may explain some knowledge-gap phenomena.

An important point, according to Ettema and Kline, is that if skill deficits alone account for knowledge gaps, any increase in information availability should primarily benefit the well educated, except in cases in which ceiling effects occur (when the educated already have the knowledge). That this is not the case implies that the motivational/functional explanation has at least some empirical validity. Genova and Greenberg (1979) also found evidence consistent with the difference interpretation. They found that a person's degree of social interest in a news event predicted knowledge of it, especially with more complex factual domains. Social interest pertains to a topic's perceived utility for one's social milieu. Their work also offered some support for the idea that continuing news coverage of a topic eventually would close such interest-related gaps. In discussing this news–interest–knowledge–gain model, Genova and Greenberg suggested that few issues would receive enough ongoing coverage for this to happen, however.

Exceptions may occur during political campaigns. In an effort to explain inconsistent knowledge-gap phenomena relative to electoral races, Moore (1987) suggested a diverging diffusion curves model. Diffusion of information often follows a flattened "S" curve. Only small groups of people initially learn something, then a surge occurs, after which learning trails off. In Moore's model, separate "S" curves apply to the highly educated and to the less educated. In it,

> both groups enjoy about the same level of information at the beginning of the time period, but the higher-educated voters are hypothesized to learn at a faster rate than the lower-educated voters. At the end of the time period, the lower-educated voters are hypothesized to have caught up with the knowledge level of the higher-educated voters. (p. 195)

Thus, whether knowledge gaps appear to widen or narrow during election campaigns may depend on both the length of races and the time points at which measurement occurs. This suggests that researchers pay attention to amounts of time between primary and general elections (Moore, 1987). Lengthy campaigns may result in more equitable knowledge levels among voters.

Identification of evermore contextual boundaries to knowledge-gap phenomena (as reviewed in Viswanath & Finnegan, 1996) remains among the most salient outcomes of continuing research. Clearly, large numbers of variables, involving both societal structure (e.g., community homogeneity) and audience psychology, may affect whether gaps narrow, widen, or even occur. For example, whether individual-level factors mitigate the impact of SES on knowledge gaps may depend on circumstances (Viswanath & Finnegan, 1996). Of course, the original hypothesis posited an empirical contingency. As documented boundaries pile up to the hypothesis, along with qualifications to these contingencies, researchers who seek broad generalization instead may find frustration. They may feel that they have entered, in Cronbach's (1975) words, "a hall of mirrors that extends to infinity" (p. 119).

Consequences

Much research into the effects of mass communication on public affairs knowledge seems to assume that knowledge is important per se, without reference to its relationship with behavior. Most studies fail to examine any relationship between the two. As Viswanath and Finnegan (1996) put it, knowledge-gap research "is driven by values and insights related to power and its growth and distribution in society" (p. 214). Researchers commonly assume that public affairs knowledge is a commodity as important as money to effective participation in democratic self-governance. This tendency sometimes causes more behaviorally oriented researchers to criticize such work as incomplete on the assumption that what people do with what they know is what really matters.

The relationship between knowledge and behavior is complex and not always a matter of the former ultimately affecting the latter. For example, cognitive dissonance theory (see chap. 7) predicts that behavior may precede knowledge because a person making a choice may seek information that helps rationalize the choice. Not surprisingly, people often do not behave in ways predictable by knowledge levels, according to available evidence (Hornik, 1989). A classic example is cigarette smokers, who often choose to continue even when they know the health risks. Available theories tend to stress the influence of additional factors on the knowledge–behavior relation, ranging from the psychological characteristics of individuals to social influences to the structural characteristics of communities (see Hornik, 1989). For example, Chaffee and Roser (1986) predicted that involved people — those who care a good deal about their health — tend to behave in ways consistent with what they know about good health. They found evidence that cognitive involvement, as indicated by high levels of processing of health information, contributed to consistency. Yet perceiving oneself as at risk for health problems, perhaps an extremely high form of affective involvement, was associated with reduced knowledge–behavior correspondence.

Of course, knowledge usually is not an end in itself, but a means to other things. Sometimes arguments that knowledge should lead to certain behavioral patterns often contain a strand of elitism, however. That is to say, such statements sometimes reflect a concern not only that people have the knowledge to make decisions for themselves, but that they use it to act intelligently in the eyes of someone else. Yet such criticisms perhaps ignore the fact that the goal of much mass communication, especially of news, is to provide people with information that allows them to make their own choices. For example, journalists covering a political race are generally paid to make information about the candidates available, rather than worry about which candidate wins.

Yet whether knowledge is important per se or whether its primary importance lies in an assumed link with behavior may depend on circumstance. Consider the following question: Would the previously discussed example involving the LaRouche candidates in Illinois be as worrisome if the public by and large had understood who the candidates were? Probably not, except perhaps for residents of that state. However, to what extent should a campaign about AIDS attempt to change sexual behavior, as well as make people aware of the risks inherent in such behavior? Perhaps behavior and knowledge are equally important if only because dangerous sexual behaviors affect everyone due to the financial burden on society created by the AIDS epidemic.

MEDIATED COMMUNICATION AND ACADEMIC ACHIEVEMENT

Does TV Hinder Academic Achievement in Children?

For decades now, a malaise of mediocrity has characterized the U.S. education system. Perhaps a report by the National Commission on Excellence in Education, named by then-U.S. Education Secretary Terrel H. Bell, best exemplified this. Following an 18-month study, the commission warned: "Our nation is at risk. The educational foundations of our society are being eroded by a rising tide of mediocrity that threatens our future as a nation and a people" ("Final Report," 1983, p. 36).

Commentators blamed the problem on many factors: the growth of a *pander or perish* philosophy as educators lowered the expectations they make of students, the breakdown of the traditional family, general social permissiveness, and (inevitably) TV. In fact, all of the other alleged causes of the decline may have resulted from TV, according to certain arguments. For example, growing up with the medium might make students unreceptive to traditional forms of instruction, forcing teachers to soften their curricula, perhaps by relying less on the printed word. Certain contents of TV might somehow subvert traditional family values, disrupting the lives of children and their ability to perform at school.

Hornik (1981) summarized typical arguments:

> Television takes up so much of our children's time (and our own). How can it *not* be related to what children learn and do at school? Television lacks intellectual substance—SAT's decline; television presents staccato segments—classroom attention spans shorten; television provides no-effort entertainment—kindergartners are tougher to handle. The relationship of television to schooling outcomes is so logical, so blatant. (p. 193)

In fact, allegations that exposure to mediated communication harms academic performance long predate TV. Earlier concern focused on the purported impacts of watching movies and the reading of comics or even of fiction books (Morgan & Gross, 1980). In 1879, for example, a Miss M.A. Bean presented a paper to a Boston conference. The paper (quoted in Morgan & Gross, 1980) contained the following assertion—one that seems ironic in light of common claims today that TV is harmful because it takes time away from reading:

> What other result can be expected when three-fourths of our pupils average a library book per day, which they claim to read through? What wonder that we have yet to learn of the boy or girl who can devour half a dozen books per week and yet retain rank number one on the school record. . . . It is easy

to see that this mental process, repeated day after day, is not going to produce a generation of thinkers or workers but rather of thoughtless dreamers. (p. 130)

In fact, early research (e.g., Himmelweit, Oppenheim, & Vance, 1958; Schramm, Lyle, & Parker, 1961) suggested watching the tube had little effect on school performance. Admittedly, this research predated today's conditions, when children typically spend much more time (between 25 and 30 hours per week) with the medium (Hornick, 1981). In addition, for more than a decade after most U.S. households acquired TV, student performance on certain standardized examinations, such as the Scholastic Aptitude Test (SAT), improved. Beginning about 1965, however, these scores started declining substantially, helping to rekindle concerns about TV. The scores finally leveled off about 1980 (Gaddy, 1986). One partial explanation for this pattern, of course, focuses on the fact that a larger percentage of the population began taking the tests, deflating average scores.

Nonetheless, theorists have suggested a variety of mechanisms by which TV might hamper the intellectual abilities and academic performance of students. Hornik (1981) identified two broad classes: displacement hypotheses and development of an intolerance for the pace of schooling hypotheses. The former "argue that time spent watching television diverts a student away from school-helping activities such as reading, homework, sleeping, or active problem solving in interaction with a 'live' environment" (p. 194). According to the latter, television "provides no-effort entertainment; it is fast moving, full of attention-grabbing gimmicks, interrupted by commercials, and has an easily turned channel selector" (p. 194). As a result, students expect "snappily paced entertainment and are quick to 'change the channel,' that is, to turn their attention away from their studies if instruction is inadequately entertaining" (p. 194).

To date, the evidence remains only mildly convincing that TV viewing, in general, has a socially significant, negative impact on student abilities or performance. Evidence is mixed concerning the displacement idea, and research has often left the difficult-to-test intolerance hypothesis unaddressed (Hornik, 1981). Frequently, children or adolescents who are heavy viewers also tend to perform relatively poorly at school or in reading achievement (Gaddy, 1986; Gortmaker, Salter, Walker, & Dietz, 1990; Morgan & Gross, 1980; Potter, 1987; Ritchie, Price, & Roberts, 1987). Possibly, however, this pattern primarily results from the influence of extraneous variables. For instance, less intelligent children tend to both watch a lot of television and perform poorly in academics (Corteen & Williams, 1986; Morgan & Gross, 1980). When researchers control for the impact of third variables, the data suggest perhaps a modest reduction of reading ability and possibly no effect at all on general school performance (see the discussions in Hornick, 1981; Potter, 1987). Of course, intelligence might be an effect as well as a cause of TV viewing. If so, some of these studies may be overly conservative in their conclusions.

Some of the best evidence concerning the impact of TV comes from longitudinal research. Corteen and Williams (1986) examined whether reading skills among children in a Canadian community declined after TV became available for the first time in the community during the early 1970s. They used much the same design as that employed to study the impact of TV on aggressive behavior in the same community (see Joy et al., 1986). The research yielded scattered evidence that the presence of the medium hindered the development of reading skills perhaps by displacing activities such as pleasure reading that might speed up its development.

Unfortunately, measures of the children's intelligence, arguably a crucial control, were sometimes not available. In addition, a series of panel studies attempted to link TV exposure to subsequent changes in either a child's reading skills (Ritchie et al., 1987) or performance at school (Gaddy, 1986; Gortmaker et al., 1990). Such studies controlled for any reverse impact of these dependent variables on TV viewing. They also eliminated effects of third variables, such as intelligence, prior to initial measurement. All found little or no relationship between viewing and subsequent performance or skills among students at grade levels ranging from elementary to high school. The studies employed basically the same techniques used in longitudinal panel research that assesses the impact of TV violence (see Huesmann & Eron, 1986c; Milavsky et al., 1982). The panel technique is a conservative one that might tend to understate the impact of TV, however.

In addition, TV still may hinder achievement significantly in very specific contexts. For one thing, experimental evidence suggests that students who attempt to study with the TV on, a common phenomenon, experience difficulty recalling what they have read (Armstrong, Boiarsky, & Mares, 1991). Evidently, this occurs when the combination of TV and reading exceeds human information-processing capacities. In addition, watching more than 30 hours of TV per week may interfere rather seriously with performance at school, via time displacement, according to cross-sectional correlations (Potter, 1987). Finally, although research thus far has failed to show a clear and socially significant general harm, it even more clearly has failed to demonstrate any generally beneficial effect of watching TV either (Gaddy, 1986).

Based on these studies, parents might choose to exercise caution about how much time they allow their children to spend with TV, especially in light of far more compelling evidence from other domains, such as the impact of TV violence. Perhaps future research, using much more sophisticated approaches than in the past, will someday document the impressionistic claim that watching TV hinders academic attainment in socially significant ways.

Can TV Improve Academic Achievement and Cognitive Development? The *Sesame Street* and *Blue's Clues* Experience

For the most part, research has failed to show especially striking negative or positive educative effects of general TV viewing. Nonetheless, clear evidence exists that TV can be educational for children, especially if programs are designed with their interests in mind.

Beginning with the fall of 1969, millions of children in the United States and other countries grew up watching TV characters such as Oscar the Grouch, Big Bird, Kermit the Frog, and the Cookie Monster. These characters appeared on *Sesame Street*, a Children's Television Workshop (CTW) program designed not merely to entertain, but to help prepare preschool children for formal education. In particular, those responsible for the show hoped to reach disadvantaged children, such as those in the inner cities, thereby acting as a sort of televised Head Start program, albeit one designed for all children (Lesser, 1974). As of 1993, about 11 million households in the United States saw the show, which also was televised in 38 other countries.

In the wake of its popularity, researchers at the Educational Testing Service (ETS) assessed how effective *Sesame Street* was. In general, it succeeded in teaching certain basic intellectual skills to children from a broad variety of backgrounds (see Lesser, 1974). The learning appeared most marked, however, in instances in which researchers encouraged children and their parents to watch the show (T.D. Cook & Conner, 1976). Theoretically, this is not surprising, given the well-established learning theory principle concerning the positive effects of reinforcement. Yet how much benefit occurred in the absence of encouragement perhaps was less clear (T.D. Cook & Conner, 1976). Therefore, perhaps parental encouragement for children to watch such programs is in order.

Research has continued concerning the program and its coproductions in other countries. By the start of the new century, more than 1,000 studies existed. Following a review of these, Fisch, Truglio, and Cole (1999) reported wide-ranging evidence of positive effects, in some cases persisting as long as the high school years. Most involve enhanced academic skills, but evidence also exists of short-term impacts on social behaviors, such as reduced aggression.

In related work, researchers examined the effects of watching *Blue's Clues*. The Nickelodeon program was created "with a mission to empower, challenge, and build the self-esteem of preschoolers, all the while making them laugh" (D.R. Anderson et al., 2000, p. 180). It has often led the ratings among preschoolers as well. Its content is based on learning theory, as well as comments from outside advisers and from the target audience. The show features a live character, Steve, and his animated puppy, Blue. The puppy leaves paw prints on objects that serve as clues to problems that the children are encouraged to help solve.

In a series of studies, D.R. Anderson et al. found evidence that the program does attain its mission. For example, one field experiment comparing regular watchers to demographically similar children who did not get the program provided evidence that viewing enhanced cognitive development. Other research found that by encouraging interaction, seeing the program seems to change the way kids watch other TV programs. Such research nicely supplements evidence that prosocial content contributes to altruistic behavior in children (Paik, 1995).

7

Generally Intended Mass Media Effects: Attitude Change and Persuasion

By any standard, the concept of *persuasion* has long evoked sinister images. People remember the invectives of Nazi propagandist Joseph Goebbels and exaggerated stories of the brainwashing of U.S. troops more than 40 years ago by their Chinese and North Korean captors. Yet persuasion refers to a variety of activities, some designed to accomplish good for society and some not. Tremendous percentages of the contents of today's mass media are designed to *persuade* — a concept that can be defined as attempting to change people's attitudes and behaviors through the written or spoken word. Viewed in this light, the vast majority of space in newspapers and magazines, and substantial portions of electronic media contents, involve efforts at persuasion. These include advertisements, editorials, press releases, and other persuasive arguments reported as part of news stories.

In general, how effective the media are at persuasion remains open to substantial doubt. Decades ago, Bauer (1964) wrote of the "obstinate audience," which is highly resistant to persuasive messages. Research concerning the impact of commercial advertising may exemplify this. For example, McGuire (1986a) argued that research has failed to demonstrate that advertisers generally get their money's worth. Following a literature review, McGuire argued that existing studies have failed to demonstrate especially large effects. Such studies include both econometric ones, which often use advertising expenditures to predict brand shares, and research that looks at the impact of advertising on individual persons. Professional propagandists have often attempted to exaggerate their power, however (V. Key, 1967).

Future work might demonstrate important effects perhaps by documenting that ads which explain only a few percent of the variation in whether those exposed bought a product nonetheless increased sales markedly. Nonetheless, available evidence suggests only modest effects. Perhaps the most important lesson from decades of research is that persuasion is a complex process, more often than not defying attempts at generalization. Certainly, the persuasion stimulus does not simply determine the audience response.

INTRODUCTION TO ATTITUDES

Audience attitudes traditionally are a key dependent variable in mass communication research. Typically, researchers have seen them as the most easily measured indicator of persuasion. Some attitude change research, however, such as that involving sexually explicit materials (see chap. 10), concerns unintended effects. Conventionally, researchers view attitudes as intervening variables between communication and behavior. That is to say, communication affects attitudes, which in turn influence audience behavior in a presumably predictable manner. In fact, empirical research has often failed to justify any assumption that people inevitably behave in ways consistent with their attitudes, although the two frequently tend to covary, at least modestly (McGuire, 1986c). Nonetheless, more recent research (Kim & Hunter, 1993a, 1993b) suggests that severe problems with methods may have obscured a generally strong relationship.

Various definitions of *attitude* have been proposed. In the simplest sense, an attitude is "a response locating an object of thought along some dimension of judgment" (McGuire, 1986c, p. 114) or simply a summary evaluation of an object. In more behaviorist terms, sometimes it is seen as a generalized intent to behave in a certain way toward an object or as a form of behavior in its own right. More elaborate definitions depict attitudes as consisting of three separate components, perhaps echoing Descartes' mechanism (see Cronen, 1995). The first part is a cognitive element, consisting of what a person knows about an object. Researchers sometimes measure this with checklists, in which a person indicates which adjectives describe the object. Next is the affective, or feeling, component. This is the heart of the concept, and researchers often measure this with *feeling thermometer* scales. Finally, there is a conative component, referring to behavioral intentions. Researchers can assess this by merely asking how a person believes he or she would act in a given situation. Traditionally, many researchers have assumed that a message will affect the three components sequentially. First, a person gains awareness of the object and its features. Then he or she forms or alters his or her attitude based on these impressions. Finally, the person forms or alters behavioral intentions. The concept does not usually cover actual behavior other than that involved in responding to a questionnaire.

Furthermore, any strict separation of these three components, however useful for research purposes, may be distortive. These elements are often interwoven among themselves, and among related attitudes, in an elaborate tapestry. To at least a modest degree, the components of attitudes are apt to influence each other reciprocally, as well as attitudes toward affected objects. In effect, people possess not single attitudes, but interlinked systems of attitudes (see McGuire, 1986c, 1989). That is to say, a person's attitude toward a Ford automobile, for example, is apt to consist of an interwoven batch of thoughts, feelings, and behavioral intents toward the Ford, not in isolation, but relative to each other and to other objects. These other objects could include not only other automobiles that a person might buy, but also objects (e.g., a European vacation, a stock mutual fund) that a person might have to sacrifice to buy a new Ford. When researchers measure attitudes, they often treat them as if the objects they refer to are isolated from one another in people's minds. Such practices may be useful simplifications, but they also can be distortive.

Attitude is often contrasted with a number of related ideas in various ways. An opinion, for example, commonly is considered narrower than an attitude. Sometimes it refers merely to an expression of an attitude. A value often concerns something broader than an attitude. For instance, an opinion might refer to what a person expresses concerning a proposal to require parental consent for minors to obtain abortions. An attitude might refer to the person's general feelings about legalized abortion, which in turn might reflect broader values about the origins or sanctity of human life or a woman's right to control her body. The concept of emotion includes the affective component of an attitude, but also refers to extremely transitory human reactions. Attitudes are often assumed to have an element of temporal stability to them, although some theorists (e.g., Petty, Wegener, Fabrigar, Priester, & Cacioppo, 1993) treat this distinction as relative. Persuasion research tends to assume that verbal communication is the major source of human attitude formation and change. Nonetheless, other factors, including nonverbal communication and direct experience with an object, may also affect attitudes (McGuire, 1973a).

McGUIRE'S MODEL OF PERSUASION RESEARCH

Building on previous work by psychologist Hovland (see chap. 1), McGuire (1973a) presented an influential linear model of persuasion. His model (see Fig. 7.1) provides a useful framework to later examine specific

	Source	Message	Channel	Receiver	Destination
Presentation					
Attention					
Comprehension					
Yielding					
Retention					
Overt behavior					

FIG. 7.1. McGuire's model of persuasion (from McGuire, 1973). Copyright 1973 by Houghton Mifflin. Reprinted by permission of Houghton Mifflin.

theories and hypotheses (for a somewhat expanded version, see McGuire, 1985). In verbal communication, McGuire listed five classes of independent variables: characteristics of the source, message, channel, receiver, and destination. Source characteristics include communicator credibility. Message variables include use of fear appeals and types of misleading arguments. Channel variables include whether the message is presented live or via TV or newspapers. Audience characteristics include receivers' personality characteristics and prior opinions concerning a subject. Finally, destination variables concern the target of a message, including factors that may lead people to resist persuasion.

McGuire also listed six classes of dependent variables in a linear sequence that persuasion is presumed to follow in most instances. A message is presented, and the receiver attends to it, comprehends it, yields to it (attitude change or formation occurs), retains the altered attitude, and ultimately acts in accordance with it. A fundamental assumption seems to be that no one stage can be skipped or the entire process breaks down. For example, if a person ignores (i.e., fails to attend to) a message, no intended behavioral effect can occur. Of course, persuasion does not always follow this invariant sequence. In some cases, people may yield to messages before they understand them (e.g., if the message comes from an especially admired source). Like all models, McGuire's simplifies communication. Nonetheless, it also helps demonstrate its complexity. A potentially infinite number of theories and hypotheses can fit into any cell of Fig. 7.1. For example, a researcher can test a variety of hypotheses (and theories) concerning the impact of specific source factors such as credibility.

This model can help clarify why persuasive messages may not have the powerful effects often assumed. For them to be effective, many different things must happen. If a commercial appears on TV, audiences must attend to it. That is, they cannot run to the kitchen for a snack, visit the bathroom, press the mute button, or turn to another channel. They must also understand the message and then adjust their attitudes accordingly. Finally, they have to recall the message at an appropriate later time and behave accordingly. If any of these does not happen, persuasion may not occur. For example, one humorous ad on TV depicted a group of guys who show up in drag at a bar that has a ladies' night special on the advertised brand. To be effective, the ad must not only hold the attention of audiences, but it also must be something that people remember and act on when they purchase beer. Quite likely, many people who enjoyed the commercial will buy other brands on the basis of personal preference or prices. If you were at the grocery and you saw an advertised special for another brand, would you pay more simply because you enjoyed an ad?

TYPES OF PERSUASION THEORIES

At different times in modern history, different theoretical approaches have moved in and out of favor in the social sciences. For example, behaviorism — the idea that scientists should only study observable behavior — dominated substantial portions of social science during much of the first half of the century. More recently, social science fields have become much more eclectic as information-processing and other cognitive approaches have attained considerable influence. One should keep in mind that none of these approaches is inherently right or wrong. Rather, all may prove useful in different contexts in unraveling the complexities of persuasion. McGuire (1973a) provided an influential categorization of types of persuasion theories.

One general type is the learning theory, which assumes that persuasion is largely a function of knowledge acquisition. These theories, rooted in behaviorism, tend to ignore or downplay yielding. One of the best known learning theories concerns classical conditioning, which involves an unconditioned stimulus (US), an unconditioned response (UR), and a conditioned stimulus (CS). The most famous illustration of classical conditioning comes from the work of Russian physiologist Ivan Pavlov, who presented a dog with meat powder. Of course, biology causes a dog to salivate (the UR) in the presence of meat powder (a US). Pavlov rang a bell when providing meat powder to the dog, and eventually the bell alone (the CS) produced salivation. Conditioning occurred when the dog associated the bell with the meat powder because of the repeated pairing of these stimuli. Today, the use of sex in advertising often seems to represent an attempt to use principles of classical conditioning. For example, a car maker may use an ad depicting a young woman in a bikini alongside a sports car. Eventually, the advertisers seem to assume that men will pair the two psychologically so that the car alone will produce salivation.

Operant or instrumental conditioning is another form of learning theory. Associated with the behaviorist psychologist B.F. Skinner, this type of theory stresses the use of punishment and rewards as a learning mechanism. Given a particular stimulus, one type of response may result in punishment, making the response less likely to occur in the future. Another type may result in reward, making it more likely to occur again. For example, a baseball fan may turn on the TV to watch a favorite team. If the team wins, the fan is rewarded and is likely to respond with greater enthusiasm the next time a game is shown. Many researchers who study operant conditioning do so to modify human behavior in socially desirable ways, such as increasing the effectiveness of education. Thus, the influence of contextualism on their work is unmistakable (see S.C. Hayes, Hayes, & Reese, 1988).

In general, these learning theories stress environmental stimuli, suggesting that human behavior results primarily from factors outside of the human being. There is also an often implicit and not entirely justifiable assumption that communication variables that affect learning will also influence attitudes (McGuire, 1973a). Nonetheless, these theories have their value. Operant conditioning principles help explain why communicators often have trouble persuading people. For example, a voter may have cast ballots for victorious political candidates in the past and come to regret it when the victors failed to keep campaign pledges. As a result, the voter may tend to react negatively to news coverage and advertising concerning political campaigns.

Information-processing theories, according to McGuire, attempt to take a broader view of the persuasion process. They view human beings as rational, linear processors of incoming stimuli. McGuire's model in Fig. 7.1 reflects such a perspective. Included within these theories are influences from certain others, such as learning theory. They are consistent with people rationally making voting decisions based on a careful evaluation of political issues in the news, for example. Thus, the perspective tends to ignore a possible ego-defensive, irrational function of attitudes.

Thus, functional theories (e.g., D. Katz, 1960; Kelman, 1958), which examine people's motivations for having their attitudes, provide a necessary and supplementary perspective. These theories may view human beings as heavily nonrational. D. Katz (1960) listed four functions that attitudes may serve for people. The first of these is an adjustment or utilitarian function: "a recognition of the fact that people strive to maximize the rewards in their external environment and to minimize the penalties" (p. 170). For example, a student who has trouble with mathematics may develop a negative attitude toward the subject and avoid courses in the area. Second, attitudes can serve an ego-defensive function. In D. Katz's terms, these are "mechanisms by which the individual protects his ego from his own unacceptable impulses and from the knowledge of threatening forces from without, and the methods by which he reduces his anxieties created by such problems" (p. 172). Freudians would refer to these attitudes as *defense mechanisms*. Unlike the first type, these attitudes are formed by conflict within the person without any direct reference to the attitudinal object. For instance, a person with an inferiority complex may develop bigoted attitudes toward members of a different ethnic group merely to bolster his or her ego. Third, attitudes may serve value-expressive goals. These attitudes express a person's central values and the sort of person he or she conceives him or herself to be (D. Katz, 1960). A person may take pride in being a conservative and react negatively to a newspaper editorial advocating gun control. Finally, some attitudes serve a knowledge function as a means of making sense of the blooming, buzzing confusion (in William James' terms) of life. For instance, some people may like a broadcast drama because it helps them make sense of the world (Herzog, 1944). Although researchers have not universally agreed with D. Katz's system of categorization, the study of attitude functions has clear applications for persuasive communicators. Some research (Shavitt, 1990) suggests that advertisements are more effective if they address the type of functional needs that a promoted product serves. For example, coffee may serve primarily a utilitarian function, and an ad could emphasize this (Shavitt, 1990). In general, these theories of persuasion are rooted in psychological functionalism, as are learning and conflict-resolving theories, to a degree (see Manis & Landman, 1992; Wagner & Owens, 1992).

During the 1960s, conflict-resolving theories dominated much sociopsychological research. The models of Heider and Newcomb (see chap. 3) reflect this perspective, as does Leon Festinger's theory of cognitive dissonance, discussed later in this chapter. These theories view people as likely to adjust their attitudes and behaviors to accommodate demands such as self-interest, communication, or pressures from others.

During the 1970s and 1980s, categorizing theories were very much in vogue. These (e.g., Brewer & Nakamura, 1984) rely heavily on closely related terms such as *prototypes*, *schemata*, and *scripts*. These ideas refer to cognitive representations of generic concepts (e.g., politician), including the attributes making up the concept (a large ego, a desire to hold public office, and an inordinate willingness to tell people what they want to hear instead of the truth) and the relationships among the attributes. When a person receives new information (e.g., learns of the existence of a political candidate who is frank), he or she is likely to file it away into existing categories, changing them only slightly. According to these theories, persuasion involves shifting a person's perception of what stimulus he or she is evaluating. For instance, a political candidate (e.g., a Ross Perot, John Silber, or Clayton Williams) may be so outspoken during a TV debate that a person changes his or her perception of the candidate as a politician, maybe putting the candidate into a new category of *antipolitician*.

SOURCE EFFECTS

The impact of the credibility of a communicator is one of the most heavily researched factors. Research suggests that source credibility actually consists of several components, the most important of which are often termed *expertness* and *trustworthiness* (G.R. Miller, 1987). In the real world, these factors may be largely independent of one another. For instance, it is easy to think of instances in which experts — such as politicians — are not trustworthy. Unfortunately, a lot of research does not attempt to separate their impact. Nonetheless, much research suggests that high-credibility sources are often the more persuasive (McGuire, 1973a). Presumably, many people have had unpleasant learning experiences with people who are inexpert or untrustworthy.

Evidently, however, one important exception can occur. In a groundbreaking study, Hovland and Weiss (1951–1952) examined the effect of source credibility as time passed. The researchers presented subjects with magazine articles intended to vary in source credibility. For example, the source for a message about the impact of TV on motion picture attendance was either *Fortune* magazine or a gossip columnist. The source for an article about nuclear submarines was an influential U.S. nuclear physicist, J. Robert Oppenheimer, or *Pravda*.

Immediately after exposure to the message, credibility seemed to have its greatest impact. A month later, the differences were narrowed. In fact, respondents in the high-credibility condition demonstrated decreased agreement with a message as a function of time, whereas those in a low-credibility condition showed increased agreement. This latter phenomenon has become known as a *sleeper effect*. Researchers have assumed that it may result from people's gradual tendencies to forget a source or disassociate it from the message. The practical implications of this are potentially enormous. It suggests that, in the long run, messages from even obviously dishonest people may be quite effective, at least in changing attitudes. It raises the possibility of pernicious communication effects reminiscent of the 1920's fears about propaganda (see chap. 1). One theoretical interpretation of it even predicts that a low-credibility source eventually will be the most effective.

Nonetheless, subsequent research has often failed to replicate the sleeper effect (see M. Allen & Stiff, 1989). Instead, a complicated picture has emerged involving three different theoretical models (M. Allen & Stiff, 1989). Figures 7.2, 7.3, and 7.4 depict the three.

M. Allen and Stiff did a meta analysis of 20 sleeper effect experiments. Only five supported the first of these, the traditional model (M. Allen & Stiff, 1989). It assumes that attitude change results from separate audience assessments of the content of a message and of source credibility. In the high-credibility condition, audience attention to the source distracts it from learning details of the message, beyond an impression of the source's general position and his or her credibility. As time passes and the audience forgets about the source, attitude change disappears. In the low-credibility condition, however, the source does not distract the audience

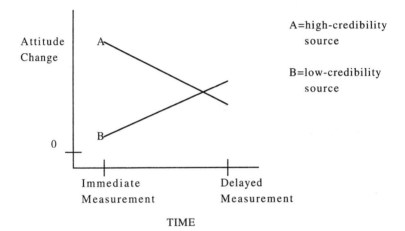

FIG. 7.2.   The traditional sleeper-effect model.

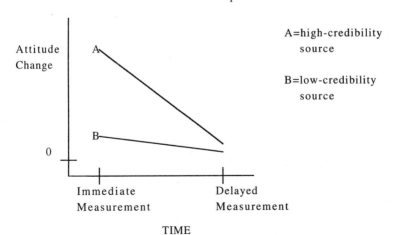

FIG. 7.3.   The forgetting sleeper-effect model.

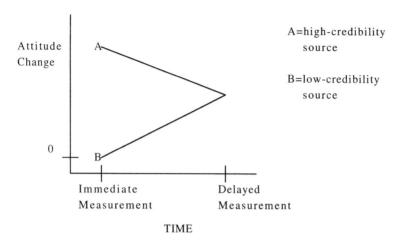

FIG. 7.4.   The disassociation sleeper-effect model.

from the details of the message. With time, people retain details of the message but forget the source. Thus, attitude change will tend to increase. Ultimately, because of information recalled, the low credibility source will be the most effective. No evidence exists, however, that low credibility enhances message retention over time (Hovland & Weiss, 1951–1952); if anything, it may retard it (Perry et al., 1992).

Ten of the 20 experiments were consistent with the forgetting model, in which attitude change declines with time in both groups (M. Allen & Stiff, 1989). This model assumes that the high-credibility source will initially produce the most attitude change, but that people gradually forget the message and ultimately revert to their original attitude. It assumes that persuasion is the result of simple reinforcement, which high credibility only enhances for a short time (M. Allen & Stiff, 1989). Thus, any advantage of high credibility wears off. In these cases, attitude change linked to a low-credibility source diminishes at a slower rate. This model is based on a type of learning theory. It is contrary to the original idea of a sleeper effect because time never results in evidence of enhanced effectiveness. Nonetheless, some sources have termed it the *relative sleeper effect*.

Only five experiments could properly examine the disassociation model, which reflects the information-processing view of persuasion (M. Allen & Stiff, 1989). Four of these supported it. As it turns out, a researcher can only measure the impact of disassociation if the low-credibility message has no initial effect. Hence, an attitude pretest must be used. In many ways, this model resembles the traditional model. It does not assume, however, that high credibility distracts people from the details of a message. As time goes by, people gradually disassociate the source from the message, which lowers attitude change if a source is high in credibility and raises it if a source is low. The low-credibility message should never be more effective. Unfortunately, in one case it was, and results in the other four contained similar, but not significant, results. Contrary to the model, the five experiments together suggested that, after a delay, the low-credibility source may result in the most attitude change (M. Allen & Stiff, 1989).

At bottom, M. Allen and Stiff concluded that some sort of sleeper effect exists, but that no single model clearly fits all the data. Thus, the effect of source credibility as time passes remains uncertain (M. Allen & Stiff, 1989). Unfortunately, no one has specified adequately under what conditions the various patterns occur.

Part of the confusion may be because researchers have often not kept sleeper effect subjects in an information vacuum about a topic. Studies used in the meta-analysis relied on time intervals ranging from 1 to 6 weeks between presentation of a message and the delayed measurement of attitude change (M. Allen & Stiff, 1989). During this interim, people may receive additional information or hear other arguments about an issue, which obviously could influence their attitudes.

For example, contaminating communication theoretically could make a conventional sleeper effect falsely resemble the forgetting model. A study may use as a message a strong pitch on TV concerning the safety benefits of a late model vehicle. The source could be either a representative of a respected consumer organization or a used car salesperson (a stereotypically untrustworthy source). Research subjects might later recall details in the message and evaluate the car favorably (without regard to the source) until a highly publicized car accident produced by a mechanical failure killed a celebrity. This information, of course, would likely lower attitude change, regardless of the credibility condition, falsely supporting the forgetting model in subsequent attitudinal measurement.

In a series of experiments not cited in the meta-analysis, Pratkanis, Leippe, Greenwald, and Baumgardner (1988) found evidence that sleeper effects only happen if the discounting cue (i.e., credibility manipulation) occurs after the message. Most of their studies used a design that allowed them to study sleeper effects within the temporal confines of a single, informationally rich laboratory setting. This should eliminate problems with uncontrolled contamination. Their findings led them to offer a differential decay interpretation of sleeper effects. If a person encounters the message prior to learning information about the source, he or she will not tend to counterargue while reading the message. As a result, both the message and cue will be stored separately in memory, and each should have a strong initial persuasive impact. With a low-credibility source, these tend to offset each other. The impact of the cue should decay more rapidly than, and independently of, that of the message because the order of presentation inhibits memory of the cue. This resembles a primacy effect. According to this, the first presented of two contradictory messages will prove most influential after a time delay (see N. Miller & Campbell, 1959). The net effect of differential decay is to produce the absolute sleeper effect pattern.

MESSAGE EFFECTS

Fear Appeals

Appeals to fear often appear in the mass media. Televangelists warn viewers of eternal damnation, politicians predict the dire consequences of passing or not passing a trade agreement, and editorial writers caution members of the baby boom generation not to count on social security for their retirement. Clearly, many communicators assume that scaring audiences will change their attitudes and behavior.

If someone wanted to design a film to promote safe sex practices as a way to avoid AIDS, how much would the person want to attempt to frighten an audience? Imagine he or she needed to choose one of three messages. The first consists of statistics about the impact of condom use on the rather low likelihood of contracting the disease from a single sexual encounter with a randomly selected person. The second consists of an oral description of the ravages that the disease produces. The final message contains film of people dying painfully from AIDS-related complications. Which might prove the most effective?

These messages presumably differ in the levels of fear they will produce. The first has a low fear appeal, the second contains a moderate appeal, and the final message is high in fear appeal. Unfortunately, they differ in other ways as well, such as in their vividness and perhaps credibility. Nonetheless, if the person relied on available theory, he or she could find a reason to choose any of the three messages. Boster and Mongeau (1984) reviewed competing theoretical explanations, which generally assume that enhanced fear appeals lead to greater perceived fear in audiences. Where the explanations tend to differ concerns the impact of perceived fear on attitudes and behavior.

The person might choose the high fear appeal message on the assumption that perceived fear is an unpleasant drive, producing attitude or behavioral change aimed at its reduction (Boster & Mongeau, 1984). He or she might choose the low fear appeal message on the assumption that low levels of perceived fear diminish the likelihood that audiences will attempt to deny or minimize the threat (Boster & Mongeau, 1984). Both of these involve conflict-resolving mechanisms. Yet a moderate appeal might be chosen because, as McGuire's (1973a) information-processing ideas suggest, the communicator wants enough perceived fear to change attitudes and behavior, but not enough to interfere with attention to or comprehension of the message. Finally, the person might choose different messages depending on the audience. A high fear appeal might be preferred for those low in anxiety about the topic and a low fear appeal for anxious persons. This might produce enough perceived fear in each group to change attitudes and behavior without interfering with attention or understanding.

As most theories suggest, a meta-analysis of 25 fear appeal studies indicates that increasing fear appeals in a message enhances perceived fear among audiences (Boster & Mongeau, 1984). Nonetheless, the average correlation between these ($r = .36$) also suggests that manipulations of fear are not overwhelmingly effective. For one thing, researchers may have difficulty altering the fear appeal of a message without also changing other aspects of it. Perhaps because of this, research usually does not show powerful effects. On the whole, enhanced fear tends to result in more message-consistent attitude change, to a small extent, and to increased behavioral compliance, to an even smaller extent (Boster & Mongeau, 1984). Although this would seem to support something like the drive-reduction idea, the existence of numerous exceptions to the general pattern render it and other available theoretical positions inadequate (Boster & Mongeau, 1984). Interestingly, evidence indicates that lower fear messages may be more effective with the highly anxious (Boster & Mongeau, 1984). Thus, high fear appeals are apparently the most effective except perhaps with the very anxious.

Whether experimental results generalize to the real world is always problematic. In a fear-appeal experiment, the researcher controls a person's exposure (and perhaps also his or her attention) to a message. Under normal circumstances, people can control these for themselves. In some circumstances, they may tend to avoid exposure or attending to high fear-inducing messages, perhaps causing messages with medium levels to be the most effective in naturalistic settings (see the later discussion of selectivity processes). Thus, experimental studies may minimize factors that could eliminate strong fear appeal effects in the "real" world.

Rather ironically, the most influential fear appeal theory during the past couple of decades downplays the role of emotional fear in favor of cognitions. In an effort to identify crucial components of fear appeals, R.W. Rogers (1975) articulated an expectancy-value approach (see chap. 4) — his protection motivation theory. "The proposed formulation asserts that attitude change is not mediated by or a result of an emotional state of fear, but rather is a function of the amount of protective motivation aroused by the cognitive appraisal processes" (R.W. Rogers, 1975, p. 100).

According to the original version, such appeals may contain three key components. These include the degree of noxiousness of the depicted event, the likelihood of the event occurring unless preventive behavior takes place, and the odds that an available response might prevent the problem. The theory links each of these to several cognitive processes: a person's appraised severity of the event, his or her expectancy of exposure, and the person's belief in efficacy of the response. In turn, these cognitive motivations mediate the impact of the fear appeal components by creating protection motivation. According to Rogers, this variable in turn "arouses, sustains, and directs activity" (p. 98).

The cognitive components multiply to produce attitude change, according to Rogers' theory. Thus, the effect of one on protection motivation and change in behavioral intent depends on the others. If any equals zero, no protection motivation should arise. With the AIDS example, no protection motivation would arise if a person did not care whether he or she got the disease, considered him or herself immune, or believed that condom usage would do nothing to prevent exposure. Subsequent to its original articulation, the theory has been modified to apply to areas other than fear appeals (see the summary of the theory and meta-analysis of its not insubstantial evidentiary basis in Floyd, Prentice-Dunn, & Rogers, 2000).

Partly in response to R.W. Rogers and others with similar ideas, Witte (1992, 1994) attempted to put "the fear back into fear appeals," to borrow a phrase from the title of her 1992 article. Her extended parallel process model, which extends work by Rogers and others, endeavors to explain why fear appeals at times fail and in other instances succeed.

According to Witte (1992), three central constructs are fear, threat, and efficacy. *Fear* "is a negatively-valenced emotion, accompanied by a high level of arousal, and is elicited by a threat that is perceived to be significant and personally relevant" (p. 331). *Threat* "is an external stimulus variable (e.g., an environmental or message cue) that exists whether a person knows it or not" (p. 331). Messages with fear appeals often contain information about the severity of the threat and a person's *susceptibility*. These may lead to *perceived severity* — "an individual's beliefs about the seriousness of the threat" (p. 332), and *perceived susceptibility* — "an individual's beliefs about his or her chances of experiencing the threat" (p. 332), among those encountering the message. Information about efficacy in the message may lead to two forms of perceived efficacy. These include *perceived response efficacy*, involving "thoughts or cognitions about the effectiveness of the message's recommendations in deterring the threat" (Witte, 1994, p. 114), and *perceived self efficacy*, "an individual's beliefs about his or her ability to perform the advocated response to avert the threat" (p. 114).

According to Witte's theory, a person encountering a typical fear appeal, with information about threat and efficacy, may make two appraisals. First, he or she will consider the degree of threat. Fear results when threat is perceived as moderate or high. The person then considers the efficacy of the advised response. If the threat is seen as low, however, no additional response occurs. With the AIDS example, the person might perceive a substantial threat, yet feel empowered to eliminate the danger through his or her behavior.

Danger control processes follow appraisals of significant threat and efficacy. In such cases, people "are motivated to control the danger (protection motivation) by thinking of strategies to avert the threat (adaptive outcomes). When danger control processes are dominating, *individuals respond to the danger, not to their fear*" (Witte, 1992, p. 338; italics original). In short, someone may practice abstinence or safer sex instead of worrying. Yet if a person perceives substantial threat but little efficacy, fear control processes result. "When fear control processes are dominating, *individuals respond to their fear, not to the danger*" (p. 338; italics original). In short, a person deals with his or her fear perhaps by maladaptively denying the threat. A person with an extensive history of unprotected sexual contact may convince him or herself that AIDS is spread by drug abuse, not sex.

Nonetheless, fear may indirectly affect adaptive, danger control processes. If appraised cognitively, it may contribute to a person's desire to process a message. "That is, thinking about the threatening message may first contribute to the experience of fear, and experiencing fear may then cause a person to upgrade his or her estimates of the threat" (p. 338). Finally, individual differences among people, and not just the message, influence perceptions of a message, such as threat and efficacy. Witte (1994) reported numerous, mostly successful, tests of her model.

Deceptive Communication

Consider the following sentence:

> Taking Eradicold Pills as directed will get you through a whole winter without colds.

Now read two more sentences:

> Get through a whole winter without colds. Take Eradicold Pills as directed.

Do the two sentences express equivalent messages?

One concern about persuasion focuses on deception, which can occur with varying degrees of explicitness. For example, an advertisement can use clearly false information to create a false belief or it can imply more than is stated. Obviously, the first sentence exemplifies the former. Of course, nothing prevents colds with certainty. The last two sentences contain a more subtle message. The statements are not deceptive on the surface because the advertiser has not linked them directly. Nonetheless, many in the audience will, according to experimental research using these and similar claims (Harris, 1977). A large number of studies document the tendency of people to remember implications in such statements as having been stated (see Harris, 1989). Existing enforcement of deceptive advertising often focuses on clearly false advertising claims. Thus, perhaps implied deception should be the most worrisome. Such claims are not clearly legal, but regulators have not been especially forceful in dealing with them (Harris, 1989).

Persuasive communicators may use a number of other techniques meant to induce miscomprehension (Harris, 1989). These include such devices as hedges ("Circle Orange Juice may help prevent the flu"), implied comparisons ("You'll get more with Bore"), and implied slurs on the competition ("When you don't want to wait for a taxi, call Blue Cab"). Obviously, people might interpret the first claim as a factual statement, and they might use claims in the last two to compare Bore with other political candidates and Blue Cab with its competitors. Unfortunately, training people to avoid making such inferences has proved difficult (Harris, 1989). Harris' research is consistent with theory in cognitive psychology (e.g., Bransford, Barclay, & Franks, 1972) that depicts human memory as reconstructing sentences based on inferences made during initial processing of them and under the influence of someone's background knowledge. The question of to what extent these inferences contribute to behavior remains open, however.

Message Repetition

Chances are, readers can think of instances in which they believe that repeated exposure to a message or object has enhanced their liking of it and instances in which they have grown weary of it, with repetition. For example, my favorite music video at one time was "Adios Mexico" by the Texas Tornados, a song evidently describing a rock star's romantic experiences during his first visit to the country. At first, I found the video rather bizarre and unappealing, assuming (incorrectly) that it described a visit to a red-light district, perhaps by a Texan truck driver. The singer, the late Doug Sahm of the old Sir Douglas Quintet, danced around on stage in a performance distorted by psychedelic visual effects, and TV made the words difficult to understand. Yet the video has an exuberant quality to it that greatly appealed to me by the third or fourth time I saw it probably because it reminded me of the way I feel when I enter (but not when I leave) Mexico. Yet I came to detest an advertisement for a Ray Stevens music video that I also saw repeatedly on Country Music Television. I changed the channel or pressed the mute button on the remote control whenever it appeared.

Several hundred studies have examined the affective impact of repeated exposure to a stimulus, such as a message or object. Psychologist Zajonc's (1968) monograph, which indicated parsimoniously that familiarity with a stimulus resulting from simple exposure enhances people's liking of it, contains the most famous of this research. This issue contains considerable practical import for mass communication. If repetition ensured favorable reaction to a message, advertisers could merely attempt to get people to see a message as often as possible. Beyond this, it might suggest a mechanism by which TV could help reduce hostility among ethnic groups by exposing people to those from other cultures.

Bornstein (1989a) reviewed 208 subsequent experiments. Following a meta-analysis, he concluded that this exposure–affect hypothesis receives support except in certain contexts. Children seem to prefer novelty to familiarity, and boredom may counteract the effect of repeated exposure especially with simple stimuli. Bornstein (1989a) argued that evolutionary theory may help explain these patterns. Perhaps people who prefer the safely familiar instead of the dangerously unknown tend to survive longer and produce more offspring. However, children may benefit from seeking novelty, which helps them learn about the world. Unlike adults, they have parents to protect them from danger. Similarly, after repeated exposure to some message, boredom may set in if the stimulus has never proved itself as either dangerous or positively reinforcing. This is adaptive if a person then turns to a safe, positively reinforcing stimulus. Thus, those contingent relationships suggest limits to the effectiveness of mediated persuasion.

Subliminal Persuasion

Communication scholars have long scoffed, evidently with good reason, at the idea that Madison Avenue manipulates its audiences with subliminal advertising. This idea refers to "embedding material in print, audio, or video messages so faintly that they are not consciously perceived" (M. Rogers & Smith, 1993, p. 10). The current idea of subliminal persuasion has been around for several decades. During the 1950s, muckraker Vance Packard (1957) introduced the idea of a subthreshold effect. A New Jersey marketing researcher, James Vicary, claimed to have used the technique to increase concession sales at a movie (M. Rogers & Smith, 1993). More recently, the subliminal seduction books of W. Key (1972) have sold millions of copies.

Although evidence indicates that limited effects of subliminal phenomena can occur in laboratory settings, almost certainly advertisers could not make effective use of them (see the reviews in Perloff, 1993; M. Rogers &

Smith, 1993; but also see Bornstein, 1989b, for a qualified, but more pessimistic, conclusion). At worst, such subliminal effects may reflect the impact of repeated exposure to a product. Research has not supported the effectiveness of quickly flashed suggestions to drink a soft drink or buy popcorn (Bornstein, 1989b).

Persuasion appears difficult enough even when people are aware of a message. Yet contemporary models of human information processing (see chap. 6) depict some cognitive activity as occurring unconsciously, and reasons exist why subliminal stimuli might enhance persuasion (Bornstein, 1989b). Unconsciously processed messages could circumvent people's learned defenses against unpopular or untrustworthy sources, for instance. Beyond this, people who are unaware of the effects of such stimuli on their behavior might create after-the-fact rationalizations, which could reinforce such behavior in the future.

Nonetheless, other factors tend to offset such advantages (Bornstein, 1989b). Television sets, for example, may not even be able to present stimuli at short enough intervals for subliminal persuasion to occur. Beyond this, only a blurred distinction exists between subliminal and some other forms of persuasion. An ad may combine a tobacco product with a scene depicting youthful, attractive people enjoying it. Thus, a receiver who is aware of the message might fail to connect the ad to its influence on him or her (Bornstein, 1989b).

On the contrary, by and large the public has a somewhat different idea. Survey research from several areas of the United States indicates that most people have heard of subliminal advertising, most believe that advertisers use it, and most believe that it has an effect (M. Rogers & Smith, 1993). Interestingly, the more education a person has, the more likely he or she will believe that subliminal advertising works (M. Rogers & Smith, 1993). Perhaps the blame for this lies in part with educators who are ignorant about research or are more interested in entertaining their students than in teaching them. A tendency of people to selectively base their judgments on case histories rather than statistical information (S.E. Taylor & Thompson, 1982) may also contribute.

CHANNEL EFFECTS

Before designing a message to warn people about AIDS, a communicator might like to know which medium will most effectively deliver it to the public. In mass communication research, channel or modality factors usually refer to the comparative persuasive advantages of different media or to comparisons between the impact of mediated and interpersonal communication. In the AIDS example, perhaps a video message would prove more effective than a written one possibly due to an assumption about the greater vividness of the former.

Relatively few studies have examined the persuasive advantages of different media. S.E. Taylor and Thompson (1982) reviewed a number of these. They found only weak evidence that videotaped messages sometimes have more impact than do written or audio ones — an effect that may only occur if both highly credible sources and simple messages are used. Television may enhance the positive characteristics of credible sources. Written formats may permit more opportunity for a person to digest difficult messages (Chaiken & Eagly, 1976). In addition, most studies have failed to find any persuasive difference between face-to-face and mediated messages or any real benefit for vivid messages (S.E. Taylor & Thompson, 1982). That no general disadvantage may exist for mediated messages somewhat contradicts early evidence concerning the greater persuasiveness of opinion leaders than of media sources (see chap. 1).

Chaiken and Eagly (1983) tied modality effects to the heuristic-systematic model of persuasion (discussed later in this chapter). Basically, this model presumes that persuasion occurs in two ways. Heuristic processes occur when people do little detailed processing of the message, but often base judgments on cues such as a source's identity. With systematic persuasion, people focus primarily on argumentation. The memorial advantage of written formats for difficult messages "is one indicator of the greater attention to message content that accompanies systematic processing" (Chaiken & Eagly, 1983, p. 254). Given this, Chaiken and Eagly hypothesized that broadcast formats should lead respondents to "predicate their opinions primarily on their reactions to the communicator and less on their reactions to message content" (p. 243). Yet those who receive written messages, which contain less salient communicator cues, "should show a greater tendency to predicate their opinions on their evaluation of message content" (p. 243). Two experiments, involving both audio, video, and written modalities as well as likable versus unlikable experimenters, were conducted (Chaiken & Eagly, 1983). Results were largely as anticipated. The likability of the communicator affected persuasion only with the audio or video formats. As expected, respondents exposed to a likable source were most persuaded by audio or video. Written messages proved most persuasive with an unlikable source, who evidently detracted from message arguments in audio and video formats. Their findings imply that "only highly contingent and tentative advice might be given to those interested in choosing a maximally persuasive medium for conveying a particular message" (p. 255).

Clearly, more research is needed into medium effects. Students should keep in mind that the meta-analyses and literature reviews dealing with other persuasion phenomena generally lump together studies using mediated and live stimuli. Therefore, to the extent that evidence of differential effects emerges, some of their conclusions may require qualification for scholars and students who are concerned primarily with the persuasive impact of mass communication. This will be especially true to the extent that channel variables interact with other factors. For example, source credibility may have more effect with video than written messages (see Petty & Cacioppo, 1986)

AUDIENCE EFFECTS

Cognitive Dissonance Theory and Selectivity Mechanisms

> The individual has a stock of old opinions already, but he meets a new experience that puts them to a strain. Somebody contradicts them; or in a reflective moment he discovers that they contradict each other; or he hears of facts with which they are incompatible; or desires arise in him which they cease to satisfy. The result is an inward trouble to which his mind till then had been a stranger, and from which he seeks to escape by modifying his previous mass of opinions. He saves as much of it as he can, for in this matter of belief we are all extreme conservatives. So, he tries to change first this opinion, and then that (for they resist change very variously), until at last some new idea comes up which he can graft upon the ancient stock with a minimum of disturbance of the latter, some idea that mediates between the stock and the new experience and runs them into one another most felicitously and expediently. (James, 1907/1975, pp. 59–60)

In his classic limited effects argument (see chap. 1), Klapper (1960) implicated forms of selective exposure as handmaidens of reinforcement and circumventors of media influence. The theory of cognitive dissonance provides a rationale as to why selective exposure may occur. Festinger articulated the original version. With roots in Gestalt psychology, the psychological functionalism of William James and others, and subsequent balance models of social psychology (see chap. 3), it became one of the most influential in social psychology during the 1960s. Even today, debate continues about its usefulness. As a balance theory, cognitive dissonance theory assumes that people have difficulty tolerating discrepancy. Unlike the previously discussed models, dissonance theory allows discrepancy to exist purely within an individual without reference to another person.

The basic elements of the theory consist of an individual's cognitions and the relationships between or among them. Cognitions can be dissonant (logically opposed), consonant (consistent), or irrelevant to one another. For example, consider a person who supports a political candidate.

If the person also believes that the candidate lacks integrity, the two cognitions are dissonant. If the voter approves of the candidate's stand on abortion, the cognitions are consonant. Finally, the person's belief that eating raw oysters poses a health risk would probably be irrelevant to support of the candidate.

Critical to the theory is the idea that a person will feel pressure to reduce uncomfortable dissonance. Such pressure could lead to changes in either cognitions or behavior. Hence, the theory involves the functionalist idea of homeostasis (see chap. 4). Dissonance can lead to a variety of behavioral effects. If the voter experiences a moderate level of dissonance because of the integrity issue, he or she might avoid news reports concerning it — a type of selective avoidance. In addition, he or she might seek news articles that favorably depict the candidate's integrity. This phenomenon is a form of selective exposure. At very high levels of dissonance, however, a different selectivity mechanism might occur. Because selective information perhaps could not reduce dissonance, a person actually might seek contradictory information, forcing him or her to change one of the cognitions causing the problem (Festinger, 1957). Thus, the person might try to learn about the candidate's integrity as a way of changing his or her voting intention. Such behavior involves preactive selectivity (see chap. 4).

Research conducted during the 1950s and 1960s, however, suggests that these mechanisms (especially avoidance) do not occur especially frequently. As a result, McGuire (1973a) termed this selective avoidance idea "the most excessive extrapolation beyond the data so far offered by communication theorists" (p. 240). Yet subsequent research using better controls perhaps provides a bit more support for such selective exposure. Following a literature review, Cotton (1986) concluded that dissonance-motivated selective exposure does appear to exist, although how often it occurs outside of experimental settings, and whether such selective avoidance takes place, remain a bit debatable.

Forms of selective attention and selective retention also could occur. Perhaps if people's attitudes often do not influence their exposure to consistent and inconsistent messages, they nonetheless may attend to or retain supportive information to a greater extent than nonsupportive information. Selective attention represents both durative selectivity and involvement, whereas selective retention is a form of postactive selectivity (see chap. 4).

A meta-analysis by J.V. Roberts (1985) indicated that people's attitudes weakly, but distinctly, influence the extent to which they retain message contents. Especially at delayed intervals, people tend to remember more if contents are supportive of their attitudes. This suggests that reconstructive processes (such as message rehearsal), rather than an attention mechanism, produce the differences. In general, the evidence supporting these forms of selective exposure, attention, and retention perhaps is weaker than that supporting the more general phenomenon of selective perception (see chap. 6).

Individual Differences and Persuasion

Does a person's susceptibility to media influence vary from context to context? Are some people in general more easily persuaded than are others? In short, is persuasibility a state or trait? What characteristics of people render them more easily influenced by messages than are others? Researchers have long expressed interest in these questions, but the answers are quite complex.

Early evidence concerning the impact of personality and other traits, such as self-esteem or even intelligence, on persuasion tended to yield conflicting results. In an effort to reconcile these, McGuire (1968) developed an information-processing theory based on six postulates. The theory suggests that the effects of mediated persuasion are somewhat limited and variable.

The first, or mediational principle, posits that a personality characteristic affects persuasion through all six steps indicated in his model (see Fig. 7.1). For example, a researcher studying the impact of self-esteem should take into account its impact on attention and comprehension of a message, rather than just on yielding or behavior. Second, the combinatory principle suggests that the impact of personality on these mediating steps often varies. For example, low self-esteem may interfere with comprehension of a message, but increase yielding.

Third, the situational-weighting principle focuses on the varying import of the various steps across situations. For instance, an extremely simple message may minimize the negative impact of self-esteem on comprehension, making its impact on yielding even stronger. The fourth, confounded-variable principle, indicates that people with one personality trait tend to have others, which may relate differently to persuasion. For example, intelligence may be positively correlated with high anxiety, which reduces the positive impact of the former on message comprehension. Fifth, the interaction principle suggests that the impact of personal factors likely vary depending on source and message characteristics (as with the previously discussed interaction involving esteem and message difficulty). Finally, the compensation principle states that a characteristic that makes an individual open to influence in certain ways will tend to make him or her resist persuasion in other ways. For instance, high intelligence may increase a person's comprehension of a message, but decrease yielding because it facilitates counterarguing. At bottom, McGuire's theory suggests that there are no general principles to the impact of individual differences on persuasion. It clearly implies that mediated efforts at persuasion affect different people to a different extent and perhaps in different ways.

Often McGuire's assumptions (if true) should create a nonlinear relationship between a personal characteristic and persuasion. For example, people with low esteem may have trouble comprehending a message perhaps because their unhappiness distracts them. Yet if they understand a message, they may yield readily because of a lack of confidence in their own judgments. People with high esteem may both understand and resist the message. Hence, people of moderate self-esteem should be the most easily influenced because all steps in the model occur to at least a moderate extent.

During subsequent years, efforts to test the theory ironically yielded inconsistent results, according to standard literature reviews, which relied on small subsets of the available research (see Rhodes & Wood, 1992). In a much more comprehensive examination, Rhodes and Wood (1992) used meta-analysis to assess the impact of self-esteem and intelligence as predicted by McGuire's theory. Exactly as expected, they found that moderate levels of self-esteem enhanced persuasion. Insufficient data existed to examine any curvilinear impact of intelligence. Rather, persons of low intelligence seemed generally more persuadable than persons of high intelligence (Rhodes & Wood, 1992).

Message Discrepancy

Assume that a person was given time on public access TV to prepare a message in favor of more restrictive abortion laws, and the person knew the potential audience tended to favor the prochoice position. What type of message would he or she use? Would the person be more effective if he or she argued that abortion should remain legal in cases of rape, incest, or if pregnancy threatened a mother's life, but should not be permitted as an after-the-fact form of birth control? Would an argument categorically equating abortion with murder prove more effective?

A type of categorizing theory may help answer this question. Social judgment or assimilation contrast theory (M. Sherif & Sherif, 1967) suggests that the person should consider how central the abortion issue is to the values of the audience. It predicts that, in many instances, a curvilinear relationship exists between message discrepancy and attitude change. The theory assumes that people assimilate messages that fall within their latitude of acceptance or latitude of noncommitment. In other words, people tend to minimize differences between their own beliefs and positions that others advocate as long as the discrepancy is mild. As part of the process of assimilation, a person may change his or her own attitude at least somewhat. Yet the theory predicts that people will contrast arguments that fall within their latitude of rejection. This is a process in which a person exaggerates the discrepancy of messages that advocate positions quite different from his or her own. In such cases, a boomerang effect theoretically may occur, shifting attitudes in the opposite direction of an argument.

The theory contains an important qualifying condition, however. To the extent that an issue is ego involving to an individual, the person's latitude of rejection should increase and the person should exhibit less tolerance for discrepancy. It is important to keep in mind that such ego involvement tends to vary from person to person. Johnson and Eagly (1989) termed this *value-relevant involvement* because it refers "to the psychological state that is created by the activation of attitudes that are linked to important values" (p. 290). The ultimate prediction is that highly involving messages, in this sense, produce less attitude change than less involving messages. This idea is consistent with the work of Klapper (1960). He identified ego-involved attitudes as one factor likely to limit media effects perhaps by stimulating mediators such as selective perception.

Research has provided only partial support for social judgment theory. McGuire (1973a) concluded that the tendency of extreme argument to produce attitude change is more convincing than occasional findings that discrepancy inhibits persuasion. Boomerang effects may occur only rarely (M.A. Hamilton, Hunter, & Boster, 1993). However, a meta-analysis largely confirmed the idea that value-relevant involvement inhibits attitude change (Johnson & Eagly, 1989), although the causal mechanisms remain unclear. Despite whatever shortcomings it has, social judgment theory does emphasize the need to take into account what members of an audience already believe. Deciding whether to take an extreme or moderate position on abortion might depend on the person's assumptions as to whether the opinions of the audience mostly resulted from deeply held values, perhaps pertaining to a woman's right to privacy. If so, highly discrepant arguments might not work.

DESTINATION VARIABLES

During much of 1993, news reports focused on controversy concerning the proposed North American Free Trade Agreement (NAFTA). NAFTA links Canada, Mexico, and the United States into a common trading bloc, with most tariffs applied to goods traded among these countries gradually eliminated. Prior to its approval, former independent presidential candidate Ross Perot used fear appeals in an attempt to increase public resistance to NAFTA. Perot claimed that the agreement would result in a giant sucking sound, as industry moved to Mexico to take advantage of lax environmental law enforcement and low wages. This could increase serious unemployment problems then present in the U.S. economy.

Treaty proponents accused Perot of using techniques akin to those criticized by students of propaganda early in the century (see chap. 1). For example, Perot quoted a statement by a former U.S. labor secretary that the treaty would cost more than 100,000 jobs in this country. He did not mention that she simultaneously estimated that the treaty would lead to a net creation of U.S. jobs (Nomani & Carroll, 1993). Instead of acting in anticipation of Perot's efforts, the Clinton administration waited several months to react. By this time, Perot evidently had substantially influenced mass opinion about the treaty and increased the pressure on Congress to oppose it. Clinton prevailed only after he made a number of expensive deals with uncommitted legislators. What if he had acted more preemptively?

Destination variables concern the target of a message and what sort of response is urged (McGuire, 1973a). Perhaps the most significant research concerning destination variables involves factors that may increase the resistance to persuasion among members of audiences. As a possible counter to manipulative uses of persuasion research, this research is of obvious potential value to society (McGuire, 1973a). The sleeper effect research reviewed earlier also represents a kind of destination variable because it involves a comparison between short- and long- attitude change (McGuire, 1973a).

Researchers (McGuire, 1962; McGuire & Papageorgis, 1961; Papageorgis & McGuire, 1961) developed an *inoculation theory* concerning resistance to persuasion. This approach combined information depicting an upcoming persuasive attempt as a threat to a person's attitudes along with explicit refutation of arguments contained in the message. In this sense, this approach represents an antecedent of the elaboration likelihood model (ELM; see the following discussion), which also emphasizes counterargumentation. Results indicate that not only did the inoculation bolster resistance to arguments it mentioned, but it also increased resistance to other arguments. This might occur because, in addition to weakening the credibility of refuted arguments, immunization may produce a sense of threat and thereby stimulate receiver defenses. More recently, inoculation theory has been applied, with at least modest success, in an effort to reduce the effectiveness of comparative ads (Pfau, 1992). Consistent with defense stimulation, the theory may work only with relatively involving products. Getting people worked up about low-priced products such as soft drinks or detergents might prove quite difficult (Pfau, 1992).

THE ELABORATION LIKELIHOOD MODEL

According to McGuire's model, an earlier variable, such as comprehension, is necessary but not sufficient to produce a later one, such as yielding. Steps also may occur independently of one another, however. For example, someone who encounters a message "might get the information all wrong (scoring zero on a knowledge test) but think about it in a manner that produces the intended change" in attitudes (Petty & Priester, 1994, p. 97).

Thus, building on McGuire's work, psychologists Richard Petty and John Cacioppo focused specifically on attitude formation and change. Their ELM emphasizes the way audiences process messages. It attempts to provide "a fairly general framework for organizing, categorizing, and understanding the basic processes underlying the effectiveness of persuasive communication" (Petty & Cacioppo, 1986, p. 125). The theory is quite complex, and only certain of its major features are discussed.

The ELM posits two general types of message processing, which actually represent ends of a continuum (Petty & Cacioppo, 1986). *Central processing* occurs when audiences elaborate messages. In other words, people draw on their prior experience and knowledge to scrutinize arguments carefully. In an effort to determine a message's merit, people actively generate favorable and/or unfavorable thoughts about it. Such processing requires both motivated and able audiences. Yet "it is neither adaptive nor possible for people to exert considerable mental effort in thinking about all of the media communications to which they are exposed" (Petty & Priester, 1994, p. 101). With *peripheral processing*, audiences form or change attitudes in a variety of ways. They may simply engage in less message elaboration—a quantitative difference (Petty & Wegener, 1999). However, qualitative differences may occur. For example, attitude change may occur, in the absence of consideration of the merits of message arguments, via identification with a message source (Petty & Wegener, 1999). Finally, attitudes linked to central processing tend to persist longer, predict behavior better, and be more resistant to change, according to their theory.

One important motivational variable is the audience's degree of involvement—a concept that subsumes various things in different research contexts (Salmon, 1986). In persuasion, Johnson and Eagly (1989) defined it as "a motivational state induced by an association between an activated attitude and the self-concept" (p. 305). The ELM may concern only outcome-relevant involvement, whether an issue affects a person's ability to achieve desirable outcomes (Johnson & Eagly, 1989). Unlike social judgment theory, in which value involvement inhibits attitude change, outcome-relevant involvement can either reduce or promote it (Johnson & Eagly, 1989). Other variables that may increase motivation include one's personal responsibility for evaluating an issue and a person's need to understand the world (Petty & Cacioppo, 1986).

Involvement in the ELM is linked to the perceived personal relevance of a message. For example, Petty and Cacioppo (1979, Experiment 2) presented undergraduate students with an editorial advocating a requirement that undergraduates pass comprehensive examinations in their major before receiving a degree. In high-involvement conditions, the message concerned the students' institution, rather than another school. Involvement enhanced attitude change resulting from compelling messages and retarded it with specious ones. Beyond this, high-involvement students engaged in more counterarguing and had fewer favorable thoughts from weak messages than from strong ones. Message quality did not affect these two variables in low-involvement conditions.

Central processing also requires an ability to elaborate. Some research indicates that distraction can inhibit central processing, thereby enhancing the impact of weak messages and inhibiting that of strong ones (see Petty & Cacioppo, 1986; Petty & Priester, 1994). Repeated exposure to a message, however, can improve processing, increasing the influence of compelling arguments and reducing that of spurious ones (Petty & Cacioppo, 1986).

According to the ELM, a source or message characteristic, such as attractiveness, may influence persons who engage in peripheral processing by acting as a simple cue (Petty & Cacioppo, 1986). However, it can also serve as an issue-relevant argument for central processors. "For example, if a spokesperson for a beauty product says that 'if you use this product, you will look like me,' the source's physical attractiveness serves as relevant information for evaluating the effectiveness of the product" (Petty & Priester, 1994, pp. 106–106). Among those whose processing falls halfway between the central and peripheral extremes, it may influence how much processing occurs. For example, an attractive or highly credible source may increase people's processing, enhancing agreement with strong messages and diminishing it with weak ones (Petty & Cacioppo, 1986). In addition, processing of messages can be either objective or biased. In many circumstances, someone just wants information. In others, such as those addressed by certain balance models, people may want to adopt the position of a liked source (Petty & Wegener, 1999). Bias can exert effects with both central and peripheral processing.

The theory attempts to integrate many earlier ones. For example, the information-processing and reasoned-action theories presumably apply to central, and certain conditioning and balance theories to peripheral, processing. Because of its scope, some scholars may have viewed it as a bit imperialistic. The ELM has become a lightning rod, both for praise and criticism. Some critics have argued that it is vague, incoherent, not falsifiable, and/or inconsistent with available evidence (see M. Allen & Reynolds, 1993; M.A. Hamilton et al., 1993; Mongeau & Stiff, 1993; but see also the response by Petty et al., 1993). Inevitably, research will lead to its continued modification and perhaps eventual abandonment. Nonetheless, its present status qualifies the ELM as a leading, but by no means the ultimate or definitive, theory of persuasion.

COMPETITORS WITH THE ELM

The best known rival of the ELM is the rather similar heuristic-systematic model (see Chen & Chaiken, 1999; Eagly & Chaiken, 1993). It "delineates two basic modes by which perceivers may determine their attitudes and other social judgments" (Chen & Chaiken, 1999, p. 74). The first of these is *systematic processing*, akin to central processing in the ELM. It "entails a relatively analytic and comprehensive treatment of judgment-relevant information. Judgments formed on the basis of systematic processing are thus responsive to the actual content of this information" (p. 74). They require both the ability and capacity to process messages. Thus, systematic processing tends not to occur when people lack knowledge about a subject or encounter time pressure. *Heuristic processing* resembles peripheral processing in the ELM. It "entails the activation and application of judgmental rules or 'heuristics' that, like other knowledge structures, are presumed to be learned and stored in memory" (p. 74). Examples of heuristics include notions that experts can be trusted and consensus opinions are bound to be true. Heuristic judgments make minimal cognitive demands.

HSM theorists assume that a least-effort principle partly guides people who possess only limited cognitive resources (Chen & Chaiken, 1999). Yet other motivations also occur. Thus, "the heuristic-systematic model incorporates least-effort notions into its *sufficiency principle*, which maintains that perceivers attempt to strike a balance between minimizing cognitive effort on the one hand and satisfying their current motivational concerns on the other" (p. 74; italics original). It assumes cognitive effort occurs until perceivers' actual confidence in, for example, the accuracy of judgment matches their goals. Goals may involve such things as the accuracy of judgment, the desire to have attitudes matching one's material interests, or a need for attitudes that promote one's social hopes. Despite their similarity, the HSM and ELM differ in certain ways (e.g., Chen & Chaiken, 1999). For example, the two HSM routes can occur simultaneously.

In contrast with these dual-route models, the *unimodel* of Kruglanski and E.P. Thompson (1999) posits only a single route for persuasion phenomena. Dual routes involve "functionally equivalent types of evidence from which persuasive conclusions may be drawn" (p. 83) and are unnecessary, they argued. According to the unimodel, persuasion amounts to but one form of judgment formation. It is "a process during which beliefs are formed on the basis of appropriate evidence" (p. 89). In turn, evidence consists of information or data that apply in forming a conclusion. The unimodel retains some of the features of dual models, however, such as the idea that differences in motivational and cognitive abilities affect the degree to which elaboration occurs.

As a somewhat simplified example, Kruglanski and Thompson (1999) discussed an environmental expert who wants to prohibit freon because it helps diminish the Earth's ozone layer. To one who already favors banning anything that harms the ozone layer, this may seem persuasive evidence of the need to outlaw freon. "Such orderly and logical processing of a message argument from evidence to conclusion has been typically considered the hallmark of persuasion by the systematic or central route" (p. 90). In contrast, another person might not necessarily believe in banning anything that diminishes the ozone layer. Instead, the second person might believe in the validity of experts' opinions. To this person, the knowledge that the environmental expert is in fact an expert might validate the notion of banning freon. According to Kruglanski and E.P. Thompson,

> Such reliance on source attributes (such as expertise) has been typically regarded as characteristic of persuasion via the peripheral or the heuristic route. Yet from our unimodel's perspective, the two persuasion types share a fundamental similarity in that both are mediated by an if-then, or syllogistic, reasoning leading from evidence to conclusion. (p. 90)

Kruglanski and Thompson (1999) presented several experiments testing, and largely supporting, their unimodal. For example, prior tests of dual-route models have tended to rely on both very brief expertness cues and lengthy messages. The unimodel authors (1999, Study 1) presented evidence that the length and complexity of a text, rather than whether it serves as an expertness cue or message argument, affects its influence on people with different degrees of involvement. College students read about a proposal to institute a requirement that graduating seniors pass an exit examination concerning their major. To vary involvement, students were told the exam either would or would not apply to them. They also read a resume designed to manipulate the expertness of the source of a message they examined in support of the test proposal. With both a lengthy message and detailed and complex expertise information, the expert source proved more persuasive to the highly involved than did the inexpert one. Expertise did not significantly affect the less involved.

Not surprisingly, proponents of dual models took issue with the unimodel. For example, Petty, Wheeler, and Bizer (1999) claimed that the unimodel authors misunderstood some aspects of the ELM, which can accommodate the empirical findings presented in support of the unimodel. For instance, "nonmessage variables (like source expertise or one's mood) can have impact under either the central or peripheral routes" (p. 158). In addition, the fact that qualitative differences can occur in the activities of central and peripheral processors suggests a need for two routes, they argue. "If the only differences involved in persuasion were quantitative ones, then one might simply speak of one persuasion process that operated in varying degrees" (Petty & Wegener, 1999, p. 48). For another example, HSM advocates Chen and Chaiken (1999) claimed that "the distinctions that dual-process theories draw between processing modes allow a level of predictive specificity whose value seems to outweigh that of the presumed parsimony offered by a single process approach" (p. 82).

At bottom, its authors (1999) claimed that the unimodel "abounds with implications for real-world persuasion contexts that expand the range of tools in the communicator's kits and lend increased flexibility to their endeavors" (p. 106). At first glance, one seems to contain obvious interest to advertisers, who often attempt to persuade the apathetic. The unimodel "affords the possibility of effective persuasion via message arguments when the recipient's processing motivation is low, providing that such messages are appropriately terse and easily understood" (p. 106). In short, advertisers need not rely only on such things as source credibility cues and heuristics. Those who fear the possible consequences of persuasion research (see the discussion at the end of the chapter) might begin to worry that the unimodel will evolve into a kind of psychological unabomb!

Advertiser interest depends on whether behavior, as well as attitudes, is so influenced. According to the unimodel, attitude-behavioral links depend on "the depth or extent of processing, rather than the type of information processed" (p. 106). Whether less motivated people process simple message arguments deeply enough to change their behavior seems questionable. Additionally, ELM researchers may dispute the idea that their model would not predict effects of simple messages among the less motivated. In general, questions arise about the extent to which the ELM, HSM, and unimodel differ—not in their presumptions, but in their empirical consequences. With apologies to William James for slightly altering his famous phrase, a difference that does not make much difference perhaps is not much of a difference.

THE RELATIONSHIP OF ATTITUDES
AND BEHAVIOR

Of course, the importance of media effects on attitudes may depend on some link between attitudes and behavior. McGuire (1986c) described the often reported low correlation between attitudes and behaviors as a scandal of social psychology. Indeed, it is not difficult to think of anecdotal instances in which people behave contrary to their expressed attitudes. In news reports, we learn about the fundamentalist minister who visited prostitutes, for example. Yet we often think of such instances as exceptions to general rules.

For many years, some evidence suggested that anecdotal exceptions to general rules may even be the rule. LaPiere (1934) traveled with a Chinese couple and stopped at about 200 hotels and restaurants. Only one place refused service to the couple. LaPiere later wrote each of the establishments asking whether they served Chinese guests. More than 90% indicated that they did not. Although the LaPiere study contained a number of problems that perhaps render it meaningless (C.A. Kiesler, Collins, & Miller, 1969), it hardly stood alone in pointing to a lack of correspondence between attitudes and behaviors. Wicker (1969) reviewed several dozen investigations of these relationships. He concluded that "it is considerably more likely that attitudes will be unrelated or only slightly related to overt behaviors than that attitudes will be closely related to actions" (p. 65). By this time, some investigators were suggesting abandoning the concept of attitude. Today, much evidence suggests that attitudes do predict, and presumably influence, behavior to some extent. Typically, researchers take one of three positions on the subject (Kim & Hunter, 1993a).

Attitudes Are Behavior

Behaviorists tend to treat attitudes either as forms of behavior (e.g., Bandura, 1969) or as purely cognitive phenomena, without consequences for behavior. One way to treat an attitude as behavior is to equate it with an opinion or expressed attitude.

In Some Contexts

Other research stresses moderating variables. According to it, attitudes may be either largely irrelevant to behavior or strongly predictive depending on circumstances. For example, the extent to which a person has direct experience with an object, rather than encountering it indirectly (e.g., via the mass media), evidently increases predictability (Fazio & Roskos-Ewoldsen 1994). Advertising, for example, often concerns products or issues of more importance to persuaders than persuadees. According to the ELM, receivers may process such messages peripherally and exhibit low attitude–behavior correspondence.

The ELM concerns the processes of attitude formation and change. Beyond this, two influential theories specifically focus on the mechanisms by which attitudes guide behavior. The first of these — the theory of reasoned action (Ajzen & Fishbein, 1980) — is perhaps as much a theory of strong attitudinal influence as a contingent model. The theory applies to instances in which action is deliberative, involving a calculation of its potential costs and benefits, and under a person's volitional control. It also assumes that people carefully consider how others will view what they do. According to it, a person's beliefs about the likely consequences of a behavior and his or her affective response to these perceived consequences contribute to the person's attitude toward the behavior. In turn, both the attitude and his or her perceptions of social norms concerning the behavior affect the person's behavioral intention. Finally, the behavioral intentions should influence behavior strongly. Therefore, attitudes may not influence behavior if they are contrary to social norms. To date, empirical work has provided reasonably strong support for the theory (see the discussion in Perloff, 1993).

The second theory is a functional process model proposed by Fazio and his colleagues (e.g., Fazio, Powell, & Herr, 1983). It does not assume that a person must actively think about an attitude if it is to affect behavior. "When someone sees a cockroach he or she probably does not consider the beliefs about how unsanitary cockroaches are, nor is he or she likely to reason out what other people think of smashing the cockroach" (Fazio & Roskos-Ewoldsen, 1994, p. 84). Instead, to guide behavior, an attitude must be accessible when a person encounters an object to which it pertains. Accessible attitudes tend to help people simplify and deal with their environment. If accessed, the attitude tends to cause a person to perceive the object selectively (see chap. 6) in ways consistent with the attitude. The perceptions will affect behavior. Thus, one should expect that the more readily one can recall an attitude from memory, the more impact it will have on the way a person behaves. Much research also supports this (e.g., Fazio, Powell, & Williams, 1989). For example, it suggests that advertising may work only if it contributes to attitudes that are both favorable and easily accessible if someone encounters the product.

These two theories are not necessarily inconsistent. Perhaps the theory of reasoned action applies more if behavior has especially important consequences and deliberation occurs. With more spontaneous acts, the process model of Fazio and others may be pertinent (Fazio, 1990; Fazio & Roskos-Ewoldsen, 1994). In short, the former may apply only when people have both the motivation, perhaps based on fear of making an invalid judgment, and the opportunity to make careful judgments. In this sense, the two theories have an obvious parallel with the central and peripheral routes of attitude formation and change of the ELM (Fazio, 1990; but see also Petty & Wegener, 1999).

Thus, someone who wants to spend $20,000 on a new car might weigh information carefully from sources such as consumer publications or opinion leaders, as well as his or her perceptions of social norms. Hence, an advertisement that depicts an automobile as socially desirable might have some limited influence on behavior, as suggested by the Ajzen–Fishbein model. Attitude accessibility, perhaps enhanced by a catchy jingle in an ad, may affect what toothpaste the person buys during a weekly supermarket visit.

Attitudes Strongly Relate to Behavior

Proponents of this view tend to argue that severe conceptual weaknesses and problems with methods exist in earlier research, which often suggests only a modest correspondence between the two. Although perhaps only a minority of researchers take this position at present, some impressive evidence supports it.

Two researchers (Kim & Hunter, 1993a) proclaimed that *"Relevant attitudes strongly predict volitional behavior"* (p. 132; italics original) following a meta-analysis of previous research. Kim and Hunter examined 138 studies with a combined sample of more than 90,000 participants. They selected only research that met several criteria. The selected studies had to attempt to predict behavior from attitudes (e.g., rather than vice versa), had to rely on previously unpublished data, and could not measure attitudes only with behavioral intentions (rather than affective or cognitive indicators) or personality traits. In addition, the research had to focus on forms of behavior under people's volitional control, as suggested by the theory of reasoned action. This criterion eliminated certain of Fazio's studies. Research also had to provide enough information to allow the calculation of a correlation (see chap. 2) between attitudes and behavior.

Kim and Hunter then attempted to correct the correlations for weaknesses in the research, such as measurement and sampling error. They did so by estimating the size of the coefficients if these problems did not exist. The adjusted correlations indicate that attitudes predict volitional behavior with an extremely high degree of accuracy ($r = .79$), by social science standards. In addition, predictability increased to the extent that the attitudinal measures contained relevance, or correspondence between elements of the attitude and of the behavior, such as a common target. Finally, these patterns generally remained similar across a wide variety of topics, such as consumer behavior and family planning. Obviously, this calls into doubt certain situational interpretations of the attitude–behavior relationship. For example, situational variables may well affect the size of the attitude–behavior relationship, but seldom do they eliminate correspondence among large numbers of people. Of course, substantial correlations do not demonstrate that human beings never behave in ways contrary or unrelated to their attitudes, but they do suggest that such patterns are distinctly atypical. Ultimately, then, this study may help resolve one of the most vexing controversies facing social scientists.

In a follow-up meta-analysis, Kim and Hunter (1993b) examined the extent to which behavioral intentions influence volitional behavior and mediate the attitude–behavior relationship. This research relied on 92 previous studies, with a sample size of more than 10,000. They found evidence consistent with the idea that behavioral intent is an even stronger predictor of behavior than is the evaluative component of an attitude. Evidence also supported the commonly assumed idea — as in the theory of reasoned action — that the evaluative component affects intent, which in turn influences behavior.

The meta-analyses have obvious implications for persuasion research concerning attitudes. Beyond this, they may suggest something important about other media effects as well. For example, researchers examining the impact of sexual materials (see chap. 10) have often used attitudinal responses such as behavioral intentions. Ethical and legal considerations prevent them from studying sexual battery. Evidence that attitudes and intentions effectively predict behavior could enhance the significance of such research.

MEDIATED PERSUASION AND CHILDREN

The previously discussed research focuses on the general impact of persuasion. For the most part, it describes effects on adults, such as college students who serve as subjects in communication experiments. Today, however, special concerns exist about children, who are presumably more susceptible. These concerns especially apply to the impact of advertising. Research into the impact of advertising on children has often used forms of cognitive developmental theory. In short, a child's mental capacities and his or her life experiences contribute to different types of integrated cognitive functioning at different ages. According to Wackman and Wartella (1977), these

> posit that children develop gradually through a series of stages which are differentiated qualitatively in terms of the types of cognitive structures present. The development process is dependent upon maturation, but it also depends on the child's experience, since the child is an active agent who tries to cope with his environment and, in this process, develops new structures and new organizations. (p. 205)

Thus, as they mature, children do not merely develop more cognitive capabilities, but they develop qualitatively different capacities. The work of Swiss child psychologist Jean Piaget is the best known and most developed form of this theory. Piaget's theory describes the different forms that a child's cognition takes at different levels of maturity. From about ages 2 to 7, a child is in a *preoperational stage*, marked (among other features) by an inability to take the point of view of others (Wackman & Wartella, 1977). This should make it difficult for children to appreciate the intent behind advertising. From about ages 7 to 12, the child is in the *concrete-operational stage*, marked by more sophisticated cognitive abilities.

Prior to the late 1960s, relatively few people expressed such concern. During the 1960s, however, the networks moved most of their children's offerings together on Saturday mornings and increased the amounts of advertising well beyond that found with other shows (Kunkel & Roberts, 1991). In particular, aggressive ads directed at children, who might not understand that adults were trying to manipulate them, often accompanied the shows (Kunkel & Roberts, 1991). As one ad executive put it: "Sooner or later you must look through kids' goggles, see things as they see them, appeal to them through their childish emotions and meet them on their own ground" (Mahaney, 1969, p. 18; cited in Kunkel & Roberts, 1991, p. 57).

In 1970, the Federal Communications Commission (FCC) startled the broadcasting industries when it agreed to seriously consider a petition from a public interest advocacy group, Action for Children's Television (ACT). The group proposed that all TV stations be required to carry educational programs directed at children, and that all children's programs not contain commercial sponsorship. Although the policies proposed by ACT obviously never came to pass, in 1974 the FCC adopted guidelines limiting the amount of advertising permitted on programs for children and requiring the separation of all ads directed at children from adjacent shows (Kunkel, 1991). This prohibited use of characters in ads that accompany programs in which the characters appear. This is called *host selling*. It also proscribed program-length commercials (B.J. Wilson & Weiss, 1992). Not satisfied, ACT went to the Federal Trade Commission (FTC), which had the authority to regulate unfair advertising. In 1978, the FTC proposed banning or restricting all children's TV commercials because of the assumption that any ad directed at people too young to understand its intent is deceptive (Kunkel & Roberts, 1991). Following lobbying by opponents, in 1980 Congress passed a bill removing the FTC's ability to restrict unfair ads (Kunkel & Roberts, 1991).

In the early 1980s, after the Reagan administration took office, the federal government pursued a deregulatory agenda. In 1984, the FCC removed its ban on program-length commercials, although the prohibition of host selling remained. It also ended all limits on the amounts of permitted commercials. In 1982, the National Association of Broadcasters (NAB) code, which included self-regulations pertaining to children's ads, was rescinded in response to a government antitrust suit. This left only minimal self-regulation from within the advertising and broadcasting industries (Kunkel, 1992). Nonetheless, concerns did not die. In 1990, Congress passed the Children's Television Act of 1990, which once again restricts the amount of advertising accompanying children's programs (Kunkel, 1991).

What does the research say about children and advertising, and what impact has it had on policy? Today, children typically see at least 20,000 commercials a year and perhaps substantially more. Nonetheless, perhaps the most important question involves not whether commercials influence children, but whether they do so because the young do not understand the nature of ads (D.F. Roberts & Bachen, 1981). Consistent with Piaget's ideas, most studies seem to indicate that children do not become fully aware of the intent behind advertising until they reach about age 7 or 8 (D.F. Roberts, 1983). Additional evidence exists that children who do not recognize the persuasive intent of ads are more easily influenced by them than are others (Kunkel & Roberts, 1991). This often means that ads affect younger children more than older ones (see Kunkel & Roberts, 1991).

Yet apparently ads sometimes affect children in secondary school to a greater extent than they do those in primary grades, and they do so in ways that McGuire's (previously discussed) compensation and confounded-variable principles might explain. Perhaps primary school children tend to pay less attention to ads and comprehend their contents less than do older children, sometimes more than counteracting the influence of the younger group's greater naiveté (McGuire, 1986b). Fortunately, research indicates that adolescents, especially those who are knowledgeable about tactics, are rather skeptical toward advertising (Boush, Friestad, & Rose, 1994). Nonetheless, any influence at all on those who do not understand the nature of advertising remains a source of special concern. It is sometimes argued that persuasive messages targeted at those who do not understand them are deceptive regardless of their contents. Fortunately, evidence exists that instructing young children about the TV industry can markedly improve their understanding of the intent of ads (D.F. Roberts & Bachen, 1981).

Despite the sometimes clear implications of these findings for policy, the history of regulatory attempts indicates that research does not have a dominant influence. Instead, policy largely results from the competition among those with different values and from the political consequences of those values (Kunkel & Roberts, 1991). Thus, the historical debate about regulation of children's advertising once more seems to illustrate the limited effects of mass communication research on public policy.

CONSEQUENCES OF PERSUASION RESEARCH

The social scientific study of media persuasion can present scholars with an ethical dilemma. At worst, it sometimes helps educated people manipulate others in ways that benefit the former at the expense of the latter. Thus, persuasion research at times may exemplify, to borrow a phrase from Rorty (1982), the "dark side of the social sciences" (p. 204). Such statements can implicate research that helps improve the effectiveness of manipulative propaganda, including media contents such as commercial advertising and political speeches. In this light, Glazer (1946) discussed exploitative uses of social science. Glazer's speculative comments illustrate a perhaps natural reaction to the threat of a self-centered technocratic elite:

> The manipulation of human beings has a much longer history than the science of human relations. That science can now make it more efficient. But to use it in this way involves us in an unhappy paradox; for science historically has been, and from its nature should be, the way to break the power of manipulation, the dominance of one group over another. . . . The answer of the problem of the democratically uncontrolled expert and the conscienceless manipulator is easy to state and almost impossible to realize; when people know as much as experts, there will no longer be need of them; when the manipulated know as much as the manipulators, then the manipulators will lose their power. The "knowing" that people need is of a special kind: it is thinking scientifically and understanding some of the important results of scientific thinking. (p. 86)

In short, if only propagandists are knowledgeable about research, it can potentially improve their effectiveness. However, if only their targets are aware of it, research may help them resist such attempts, as well as perhaps even turn the tables on their would-be oppressors. If both groups are similarly aware, persuasion research might lose much of its value for either side, according to the logic of Glazer's arguments.

In effect, scholars might integrate the scientific study of persuasion into a modern version of propaganda analysis (see chap. 1), which could help protect audiences. Public education about persuasion and propaganda then might help ensure that when persuasion occurs, it is more likely to be transactive, with each party giving to get, and less manipulative. This could build on people's implicit ideas or theories about how persuasion works (Roskos-Ewoldsen, 1997). Modern persuasion theories and models, such as the ELM, typically contain no explicit place for what audiences know about persuasion, nor have researchers focused much on the impact of audience knowledge about tactics such as fear appeals (Friestad & Wright, 1994; but see Roskos-Ewoldsen, 1997).

Despite this, drawing a line between victimizers and victims in human affairs can be a bit arbitrary at times. Virtually all human beings regularly try to persuade others via communication. In addition, as McGuire (1985) noted, "persuasion is the worst possible mode of social mobilization and conflict resolution—except for all the others" (p. 235). Nonetheless, research probably tends to benefit the powerful rather more than it does the less fortunate, although much of it is available to the public via scholarly journals. Persuasive communicators, rather than members of their audiences, are often more likely to study it. In addition, advertising, marketing, and public relations agencies often conduct research, the results of which remain proprietary.

Persuasion research has obvious potential consequences for persons in the communication industries. It provides guidance and an indication as to the effectiveness of the source of their livelihood — paid advertising. If advertisers were to take seriously any suggestion that they are wasting their money and stop, mass communication industries might change radically.

Many forms of media persuasion receive First Amendment protection. Legally, however, commercial advertising is not protected speech. Consumers have recourse to a wide variety of remedies for false or misleading ads, ranging from enforcement of criminal statutes in some states to administrative procedures of the FTC. Of course, sometimes advertisers still employ misleading or otherwise unethical practices, and drawing the line between these and robust advocacy can be difficult. The content of ads often suggests that the industry is trying to get away with as much as it can. Especially in these instances, media consumers need to understand research findings that may contribute to the effectiveness of such practices as a way to counteract them.

Education about persuasion techniques, especially unethical ones, thus has a place in the curricula of universities and public schools as part of general consumer education. The ELM, with its emphasis on counterarguing and careful processing of persuasive messages, might help educators in this task. Yet education can also more effectively inform the public about various popular myths about the industry, such as the effectiveness of subliminal advertising, that poor teaching in the schools now may help create or maintain.

Some of the probable consequences of persuasion research make it easier to sympathize with those (e.g., Carey, 1989) who want the field of media studies to abandon its traditional emphasis on effects no matter how unrealistic such arguments may sound. Yet to terminate the academic study of persuasion would leave future research in the hands of proprietary interests, such as advertising and marketing agencies. Academic research at least makes it possible to help level the playing field by disseminating research to the public via education and other means. Even publicly available knowledge about persuasion also carries with it the risk that the unscrupulous, but not their potential victims, will use it.

Of course, the import of these considerations increases if future work overcomes the shortcomings of today's persuasion studies. At present, no one can be quite certain whether the present impotence results from inherent difficulties within the processes of persuasion or from severe shortcomings with the research that purports to gauge their effectiveness. Things may be much as they appear, and persuading people may be difficult at best. Or, research may contain so many flaws that it fails to detect effective persuasion. In this light, one prominent scholar a while back made a rather striking prediction about the future.

According to James Beniger (whose comments appeared in Bogart, 1987), accumulating research in cognitive science suggests that many previous findings, often based on standard survey questionnaires, may largely result from artifactual contaminants such as question order and syntax. His comments are interesting because they anticipate that scientific progress someday will overcome much of the present difficulties both in persuasion and research used to assess it. Perhaps the previously discussed meta-analytic studies of the attitude–behavior relationship represent a notable step in this direction. When one considers the possible consequences of such progress, Beniger's predictions perhaps are rather troubling as well.

> Our collective capacity to influence public opinion and behavior will grow more rationalized, gradually forsaking art in the name of science. We can expect greater efforts to educate students and consumers about the newly understood mechanics of attitudinal and behavioral change, with a corresponding increase in interest in governmental regulation of advertising, market research, and public relations activities. (p. S174)

Should scientific progress continue, persuasion researchers eventually will have much more trouble than at present dodging the ethical and moral consequences of their work. Many of people's worst fears about the field may gradually become more true as manipulators use basic scientific work to overcome people's natural and social defenses against persuasion. After all, future Slobodan Milosevics and drug peddlers — as well as charitable organizations and toothpaste manufacturers — might take effective advantage of research. In this light, a then perhaps premature warning made following the atomic bombings of Japan may seem more reasonable: "It is not too early for the social scientists to begin to ask themselves some of the questions that the atom physicists are now desperately asking themselves, perhaps a little late" (Glazer, 1946, p. 86).

Kaplan (1964) may be right when he argued that the world cannot turn its back on knowledge:

> There are many by whom behavioral science is hated and feared as making possible the manipulation of man, adding to the rule of force the new dimensions of brainwashing and engineered consent. I think it is true that knowledge is power, and that power over the mind may confront us with greater problems and dangers even than the power over the atom. . . . But

the knowledge which confronts us with dangers by the same token presents us with opportunities. It may be that we will learn enough, or perhaps that we already know enough, to destroy ourselves; but if we turn our backs on knowledge, forgo the opportunity to ward off the danger, we are as if dead already. There is no guarantee that the true and the good go always hand in hand, but it is man's estate to reach out to both. (p. 410)

8

Communication Campaigns

On January 1, 1994, armed peasants occupied several towns and small cities in Chiapas, the southernmost state in Mexico. The activity occurred on the very day that the North American Free Trade Agreement (NAFTA), which the Mexican government hoped would help modernize the national economy, took effect. The guerrillas called themselves the Zapatista Army of National Liberation, after Emiliano Zapata, the legendary commander of an army of peasant Indians during the Mexican Revolution about 80 years earlier. Within days, government military forces regained control of the towns, following fighting that cost more than 100 people their lives.

The insurgents intended to overthrow the Mexican government—in their words, to end the government's abuse of the Indian population in one of the country's poorest and least industrialized states. Some of them proclaimed building socialism, along Cuban lines, as a goal. Knowledgeable observers, however, viewed the rebellion (like Zapata's own) largely as an attempt to resist modernity, which threatened the traditional culture and values of some local people. The revolt coincided with NAFTA taking effect, and some rebels carried anti-NAFTA banners, clearly suggesting such a conclusion.

These incidents perhaps explicate the difficult moral issues and problems inherent in programs that would use mass communication to stimulate modernization of the Third World or promote other forms of social engineering. Who should control the communication or modernization process and decide what forms it should take? Who stands to benefit from it? Who may be hurt by it? What right, in general, do technocratic elites have to try to impose their values on others? Apparently, many of the Indians of Chiapas did not want to become linked to the modern, Western world. Perhaps they believed that such development would benefit those in the larger cities while increasingly turning rural areas into colonies, much as the modernizing First World earlier had colonized much of the Third World. Perhaps they feared that modernization would offer them little beyond a more degraded environment. What right did their government have to disrupt their lives by imposing development on them?

Communication campaigns take many forms, often involving the mass media and usually reflecting rather obvious values. Sometimes these values seem extremely difficult to challenge. Examples of campaigns abound in modern life. The Centers for Disease Control and Prevention (CDC) in Atlanta tries to disseminate information about AIDS to the public. A Third World government uses a series of radio messages to instruct people about modern contraception in hopes of reducing birth rates. The Clinton administration tried to convince the public that a crisis existed in U.S. health care as a means to bring pressure on Congress to approve its proposals. Advertisers and public relations practitioners place interrelated sets of messages in the media in an effort to sell a product or improve mass opinion about a client.

Some campaigns purportedly involve only information without any persuasive intent. Yet this distinction sometimes proves overdrawn. For instance, can anyone really believe the CDC would make the effort it has to inform the public about AIDS unless those behind the effort assumed that doing so might change human behavior and thereby slow the spread of the disease?

According to E.M. Rogers and Storey (1987), a communication campaign must contain at least four components: "(1) a campaign intends to generate specific outcomes or effects (2) in a relatively large number of individuals, (3) usually within a specified period of time and (4) through an organized set of communication activities" (p. 821). Campaigns generally exemplify persuasion in action; they try to use knowledge about persuasion, most of which comes from laboratory settings, in accomplishing "real-world" goals (Perloff, 1993).

The study of campaigns has a long history. Contemporary scholars (e.g., Perloff, 1993) have identified three eras differentiated by variations in assumptions of campaign effectiveness. During the first period, research suggested that campaigns have minimal effects. Such work included Lazarsfeld's study of the impact of political campaigns during 1940 (see the discussion of Lazarsfeld et al., 1968, chap. 1). It also included an effort in Cincinnati a few years later to inform the public about, and build support for, the UN (see the discussion of Star & Hughes, 1950, chap. 6).

Despite these early failures, researchers realized that campaigns could attain success if they used appropriate strategies (Perloff, 1993). The work of Mendelsohn (1973), in which researchers collaborated with communication practitioners, began the second period — during the 1960s and 1970s. Perhaps best exemplifying this second era is the work of the Stanford Heart Disease Prevention program (A.J. Meyer, Nash, McAlister, Maccoby, & Farquhar, 1980). In three California towns, researchers identified four groups of persons with above average risks of developing heart disease. Three of the groups were exposed to a mass media campaign designed to increase knowledge of risk factors and modify contributing behaviors such as smoking. One of these groups also received face-to-face forms of instruction based on social learning principles such as modeling. The fourth group received no treatment and served as a control group. Results indicate that a media campaign can lower the risk of heart disease especially if interpersonal communication supplements it. Finally, and subsequently, researchers perhaps took a more realistic view, realizing that campaigns can have at least moderate effects if they focus on initial outcomes that have rather significant consequences later.

> Now more attention is given to the intermediate or indirect effects of communication that may cumulatively contribute to the sorts of major attitude changes or overt behavior changes that earlier campaigns sought and that contemporary campaign planners would still like to generate. (E.M. Rogers & Storey, 1987, p. 831)

THE DIFFUSION OF INNOVATIONS

Communication campaigns often center around the diffusion of innovations, the study of which has roots in many different academic fields, including anthropology, communication, education, and rural sociology (E.M. Rogers, 1983, 1995). As defined by E.M. Rogers (1995), *diffusion* refers to a "process by which an innovation is communicated through certain channels over time among the members of a social system" (p. 5). It refers both to planned and spontaneous processes. It often results in *social change*, "the process by which alteration occurs in the structure and function of a social system" (p. 6). An *innovation* "is an idea, practice, or object that is perceived as new by an individual or other unit of adoption" (p. 11). Thus, research might study human adoption of innovations such as agricultural techniques, food products, or safer sex practices. This newness may refer to the knowledge, opinions toward the object, or a decision to adopt it.

Central concepts in Rogers' definition of *diffusion* include channels, time, and a social system. A *channel* refers to "the means by which messages get from one individual to another" (E.M. Rogers, 1995, p. 18). These may be especially rapid and efficient if they involve mass media. In addition, however, people highly depend on the opinions of those like them who have adopted the innovation, suggesting that a combination of interpersonal and mediated messages will prove optimal. Thus, successful communication is much more likely with high levels of homophily. This is "the degree to which two or more individuals who interact are similar in certain attributes, such as belief, education, social status, and the like" (pp. 18-19). In typical diffusion situations, however, heterophily occurs. For instance, the technical competence of change agents often means they do not speak in ways that are familiar to those they wish to reach. This obviously can help make them ineffective. For example, E.M. Rogers (1995) discussed the failure of an effort to convince residents of a Peruvian village to boil water. The change agent tried unnecessarily to explain the germ theory of disease, which hampered diffusion. For instance, one housewife wondered, "How do microbes survive in water that would drown people? Are they fish? If germs are so small that they cannot be seen or felt, how can they hurt a grown person?" (p. 4).

Time is an important part of diffusion study. When successful, an innovation diffusion presumably tends to follow a five-step temporal process. It begins with knowledge—when a person or organization learns about the innovation. Next, opinion formation occurs, followed by a decision whether to adopt. Next, implementation may occur. Finally, confirmation may take place, perhaps reinforcing the initial decision. For example, someone during the early 1950s may have learned about TV from a friend at work. The person may have formed a favorable opinion about the entertainment material available relative to the costs of buying a receiver. After the purchase, the person might or might not have found TV rewarding.

Time also plays a key role in classifying adopters according to their *innovativeness*—the relative speed with which they adopt. E.M. Rogers (1995) identified five types: innovators, early adopters, early majority, late majority, and laggards. Typically, if one plots the numbers of adopters against time, a curve appears that looks a little like a much-flattened S.

> At first, only a few individuals adopt the innovation in each time period (such as a year or a month, for example); these are the innovators. But soon the diffusion curve begins to climb, as more and more individuals adopt in each succeeding time period. Eventually, the trajectory of adoption begins to level off, as fewer and fewer individuals remain who have not yet adopted the innovation. (p. 23)

This certainly was the case with TV. By 1950, only about 10% of U.S. households had obtained the medium. Then the rate of acquisition speeded up drastically. By 1960, about 90% had it, and a much slower rate of increase followed (see Centerwall, 1989).

A *social system* consists of "a set of interrelated units that are engaged in joint problem-solving to accomplish a common goal" (p. 23). The system often affects the processes of diffusion in any number of ways. For example, in the Peruvian water boiling example, social norms helped prevent diffusion. Hot foods traditionally are linked with disease; thus, boiling makes water only acceptable for sick persons. Other examples include people who will not eat pork, sacred cows, or whole rice (E.M. Rogers, 1995). The system may also determine whether innovation decisions occur collectively or among individuals.

Finally, consequences occur. These involve changes in individuals and/or social systems. According to Rogers, they may be desirable or not and anticipated or unanticipated. Many diffusion campaigns, such as the Stanford heart disease program, result in beneficial campaigns with anticipated consequences. Notorious exceptions exist, however. For example, at one time, multinational corporations used advertising (and the results of diffusion research) to promote bottle feeding of Third World babies. Because poor families lack such things as pure water and the ability to clean bottles, bottle feeding contributes to large numbers of infant deaths (E.M. Rogers, 1995). In response, governments have banned such ads, and diffusion scholars have refocused on promoting safer breastfeeding.

In recent diffusion work, E.M. Rogers (1995) stressed convergence rather than linear models of communication (see chap. 3). As he put it, "A linear conception of human communication may accurately describe certain communication acts or events involved in diffusion, such as when a change agent seeks to persuade a client" (p. 6). Yet a "client may come to the change agent with a problem, and the innovation is recommended as a possible solution to this need. The change agent-client interaction may continue through several cycles, as a process of information exchange" (p. 6).

MASS MEDIA AND NATIONAL DEVELOPMENT

This section primarily focuses on what is arguably the most important potential issue in the entire media effects area — the mass media and national development. It concerns the ability of the mass media to facilitate or hinder what Schramm (1964) called the *terrible ascent* of developing countries toward modernization. Researchers and governments have frequently employed communication campaigns in these efforts. The potential consequences of such work obviously affect the vast majority of the world's population, which lives within the so-called *Third World*, in the impoverished countries of Africa, Asia, and Latin America. They also may touch everyone else. No one knows how much of the turmoil in the world today, and the constant threats it generates to those who live in developed countries, would disappear if developing countries really did develop, at least in ways compatible with the wishes of their people.

Some striking patterns emerge if one examines data concerning the amount of mass media in a country and its level of development. The presence of mass media, as indicated by such things as per capita availability of radio receivers or newspapers, historically has correlated substantially and positively with indicators of a country's development, such as its per capita income or gross national product (Rummel, 1972). Such correlations suggest that mass communication is a meaningful indicator of development.

In part because of such data, many scholars have argued that mass communication tends to promote development, which they often conceived not only in economic terms, as per capita wealth, but also in political terms, as political stability or democracy. Positive theories (Wells, 1972) address that this may happen. One can think of reasons that almost any form of media content might promote modernization. Entertainment media may show the purported advantages of life in developed countries to traditional peoples, thereby promoting a necessary desire for change. Persuasive media may act as a sort of agricultural extension service and facilitate diffusion of innovations. They may provide information about, and convince people to use, new agricultural, medical, or birth control techniques. Information media might inform citizens about public affairs, thereby promoting political participation and democracy. Yet neutral theories depict media availability as an effect, rather than a cause, of modernity (Wells, 1972). Development efforts that exclude a role for the media implicitly assume this. Finally, negative theories predict that media will hinder development (Wells, 1972). For example, by depicting the wealth and culture of the West, mass communication may create unrealistic expectations. When economics frustrates these hopes, social chaos may follow. Rising expectations may turn into rising frustration. The turmoil in Iran during the late 1970s, culminating in the Islamic revolution, and that in Poland during the early 1980s, eventually contributing to the overthrow of communism, perhaps represent anecdotal illustrations of this.

During the 1950s and 1960s, the positive theories seemed especially promising despite evidence from other contexts that communication campaigns had little effect. For a time during the 1960s, such hopes appeared justified. In many developing nations, the presence of media grew along with development indicators such as literacy rates (E.M. Rogers, 1976). By 1970, however, it became evident that something was wrong (Stevenson, 1988). In subsequent years, the gaps between rich and poor nations often grew, and the term *developing* assumed the status of a euphemism. Instead of modernity, visitors to the Third World often encountered "urban slum dwellers watching American television programs through a jerry-built line to the TV set" (Stevenson, 1988, p. 29).

The Early Hopes

During the spring of 1950, the poverty-stricken little Turkish village of Balgat remained almost untouched by the modern world despite that it lay only 5 miles or so south of Ankara—a major city (Lerner, 1958). Balgat consisted of only about 50 buildings, and no road even linked it to Ankara. Few of the villagers actually made the difficult, 5-hour journey to visit the big city. In addition, the village chief owned the only radio receiver in town, and few residents were given the privilege of listening to it. Most lived as they had for hundreds of years.

By 1954, stunning changes had occurred. A road now linked it to Ankara, and plentiful buses only took 20 minutes or so to go back and forth. The village now contained about 500 buildings, at least 100 radio receivers, electricity, and a new pipe that soon would bring purified water. Most of the men, traditionally small farmers, now worked for much higher wages in Ankara, and much of the food came from outside the village. Balgat, which the elderly chief still ruled, would soon be incorporated into Greater Ankara. In short, Balgat had more or less joined the modern world.

Sociologist Daniel Lerner (1958) described these changes as descriptive of the process by which modernization comes to traditional societies. The key, in Lerner's mind, was the concept of *empathy*—the ability of a person to see him or herself in another person's situation. Lerner believed that for modernization to occur, traditional people must encounter the modern world and picture themselves as part of it. They may encounter modernity directly or via the mass media. According to Lerner, mass communication has the potential to act as "mobility multipliers" and greatly speed up the transition of traditional societies. Change in the individual, the "man in the mirror" of Michael Jackson's song, must precede social change. The idea that individual change is a prerequisite for social reform may involve an implicit philosophical assumption of mind–body dualism (see Hook 1939/1995), which pragmatists generally reject (see appendix).

More specifically, Lerner believed that modernization begins with urbanization. To live in a city requires that one become literate to function. Literacy, in turn, leads to what Lerner termed *media participation*. Once people have these, they discover "the tingle of wondering 'what will happen next'—the tingle which sounds the knell of traditional society, of routinized lifeways in which everyone knew what would happen next because it had to follow what came before" (p. 62). Finally, media participation contributes to affluence, political stability, and democratic government.

Lerner's book appeared in the context of the 35-year-long cold war between the West and the Soviet Union. Each side waged many battles for the hearts and minds of those in the Third World, which included many newly independent countries, especially in Africa and Asia. The U.S. government feared the example of the Soviet Union, which had risen in a few decades from an insignificant Euro-Asian backwater to a military and political (if not yet economic) superpower. Despite its destruction of millions of innocent (and some not-so-innocent) lives, Stalinism appeared to have modernized the country with unprecedented speed. To a degree, many media and development efforts served as a weapon in broader U.S. attempts to present the Third World with an alternate road to rapid development.

During the late 1950s and early 1960s, the UN promoted the possibility of using mediated communication to stimulate development. At the time, Western nations still tended to dominate its agenda. In 1962, the Unesco General Conference authorized a major study concerning the practicalities of media development. Wilbur Schramm (1964) of Stanford University conducted the study, which was published under the title *Mass Media and National Development*.

Schramm's study focused less on political stability or democracy as an outcome of development than on economics. The study presented evidence of the lack of communication links within developing countries and between those and the First World. He advocated the all-around expansion of media in developing countries, arguing that "mass communication, if used adequately and well, can indeed make a substantial contribution to national economic and social development" (Schramm, 1964, p. 252). He concluded:

> But we must remember that the full power of mass communication has never been used, in any developing country, to push economic and social development forward. This is the really exciting question: how much could we increase the present rate of development, how much could we smooth out the difficulties of the "terrible ascent," how much further could we make our resources go, how much more could we contribute to the growth of informed, participating citizens in the new nations, if we were to put the resources of modern communication skillfully and fully behind economic and social development? This is the challenge of the evidence presented here. (p. 271)

The "Passing" of the Dominant Paradigm

When Schramm's book appeared, many social scientists thought they understood the role of communication in development (E.M. Rogers, 1976). Less than a decade later, that understanding seemed largely illusory. By the 1970s, traditional efforts to stimulate development via the media had failed. In this environment, E.M. Rogers (1976), originally a proponent of the Lerner–Schramm position, proposed a rather drastic modification. He began by redefining *development* as more than economic growth. To Rogers, the time of the dominant paradigm had passed. In its wake, development would mean a widely participatory process of social change in a society, intended to bring about both social and material advancement (including greater equality, freedom, and other valued qualities) for the majority of the people through their gaining greater control over their environment. (p. 225)

The old Lerner–Schramm approach tended to be largely top–down; it involved efforts by government officials or other elites to persuade the masses. The new approach, based on examples in such disparate societies as China, Tanzania, and Taiwan, focused on local initiatives. People in villages and other communities should promote development from the bottom–up by deciding what forms it should take for them. In response to local requests, communication media could provide information about problems and possibilities inherent in different forms of development and concerning the experiences of other local groups (E.M. Rogers, 1976).

During the same time period, scholars took a number of more extreme positions, reflecting the influence of critical scholarship. Beltran (1976) argued that by using Western models rooted in sociological functionalism and psychological theories that stressed the culpability of individuals for underdevelopment, the Lerner–Schramm approach ignored social structures in the developing world. He rather iconoclastically hoped to see emerge from "a sociology of nonadjustment and a psychology of nonconformity, a communicology of liberation which should help shape the new Latin America that most of its 300 million human beings want and deserve" (p. 129). Others took even more radical positions. Modern forms of communication, according to Schiller (1976), subjugate the developing world, keeping its peoples away from true development, presumably based on some sort of socialist model, and promote the interests of capitalist elites.

More Recent Developments

Currently, pluralism characterizes the current state of development research (E.M. Rogers, 1989). Its goals are generally much more modest; its scholars include many more people from the developing world, and researchers are relatively open to a wide variety of methods and theoretical approaches. Despite Rogers' proclamation of its passing during the 1970s, the Lerner–Schramm approach remains a viable option for some efforts (E.M. Rogers, 1989). Indeed, the radical alternatives to it have not necessarily proved more useful. As Stevenson (1988) said:

In Tanzania, Mozambique, and the dozen or so other Third World countries that had consciously mobilized mass media to create a future envisioned by the radical theory of development, communication development projects looked pretty much like they did in countries still subscribing to the Lerner-Schramm argument. And whether the goal of development was economic growth of the 1960s or the "authentic" Third World development of the 1970s, the result was about the same. (p. 118)

Yet for all their evident failures, studies of communication and development have had some limited successes. For example, the presence of telephones, a previously overlooked factor, clearly contributes to economic growth (Stevenson, 1988). The media also seem to have some limited utility, at least as education tools (Stevenson, 1988). Possibly, new forms of communication technology will prove even more effective in promoting growth (E.M. Rogers, 1989).

The current pluralistic environment of development research seems especially congenial to pragmatism. Jacobson (1993) argued that the emphasis pragmatism places on the values inherent in science can help mend the present divisions between so-called *objective academic researchers*, such as those who follow the old Lerner–Schramm mold, and *participatory researchers*, who follow revisionist models in an effort "to foster self-reliance in local peoples by helping them conduct their own learning and their own research" (p. 215). By viewing development communication as a practical discipline (Craig, 1989), inquiry can help local people improve their lives and contribute to general scholarly knowledge, Jacobson argued.

In any case, one interesting possibility remains. Perhaps the difficulties with using the media to promote development result not so much from shortcomings in the Lerner–Schramm ideas, but from the conditions of their application. Mass communication may represent a necessary, but not sufficient, condition for modernity. Perhaps other factors inhibiting development, such as government corruption or rapid birth rates, caused the failures of earlier efforts. For example, essentially geometric increases in the populations of many Third World nations may have made modernization impossible. This was caused by neutralizing economic growth with more mouths to feed and creating or helping maintain plentiful, and therefore cheap, sources of labor. In this light, students might consider the following question: To what extent might economic productivity in the United States suffer without modern communications?

The Social Capital Thesis

In 1970, Italy created new regional governments that received much of the authority formerly held by its central government. Political scientist Robert Putnam (1993) tried to explain why, during subsequent decades, some regional governments both succeeded in their responsibilities (e.g., pertaining to agriculture and health) and helped bring prosperity to their regions and why others failed. He found evidence that the roots lay in cultural patterns going back centuries. Putnam's interpretation at times echoed the ideas of realist critics of ethical nominalism (see chap. 1 and appendix), such as Charles Peirce (quoted in Lewis & R.L. Smith, 1980):

> The gospel of Christ says that progress comes from every individual merging his individuality in sympathy with his neighbors. On the other side, the conviction of the nineteenth century is that progress takes place by virtue of every individual's striving for himself with all his might and trampling his neighbor under foot whenever he gets a chance to do so. This may accurately be called the Gospel of Greed. (p. 257)

Putnam focused in large part on a few key concepts. The idea of *social capital* has appeared in social science repeatedly (e.g., Coleman, 1988) during the past century. Researchers often treat it as a characteristic of both individuals and collectivities, such as states. To Putnam (1995), it refers to "features of social life — networks, norms, and trust — that enable participants to act together more effectively to pursue shared objectives" (pp. 664-665). It includes both *social trust* and *civic engagement*, forms of involvement in one's community, whether political or nonpolitical.

According to Putnam (1993), parts of northern Italy (e.g., Emilia-Romagna) have these in abundance. He described them as prerequisites to good government and prosperity. In areas of southern Italy (e.g., Calabria), in contrast, he found highly individualized culture. There people often seek special favors from political figures, and top-down communication patterns dominate. Perhaps not coincidentally, sections of northern Italy today belong to the postmodern world, whereas regions of southern Italy (e.g., Sicily) remain in the Third World. As Putnam (1993) noted, "the North-South gap in Italy, and the range of theories that have been offered to account for it, mirror the broader debate about development in the Third World" (p. 159).

Consistent with positive theories of media and development, newspaper reading in Italy predicted increased engagement. However, Putnam's (1995, 2000) more recent work depicted TV and related media as often hampering U.S. civic engagement and social capital (see chap. 9).

In its emphasis on individual behavior, rather than social structures, Putnam's culturalist interpretation seems a little reminiscent of Lerner. In fact, much of the criticism of his Italian study came from those in the structuralist school of political science. For example, Tarrow (1996) argued that a civic-capacity deficit is "a by-product of politics, state building, and social structure" (p. 396). If so, "policy makers who attack the lack of social capital by encouraging association would be attacking the symptoms and not the causes of the problem" (p. 396). Jackman and Miller (1996) reanalyzed Putnam's data and critiqued his methods. They reported finding "little evidence to indicate a systematic relationship between political culture and political and economic performance" (p. 632). They questioned the way culturalists measure key variables and called for scholars to redo interpretations in more institutional terms.

THE IMPACT OF ADVERTISING AND
COUNTERADVERTISING CAMPAIGNS: TOBACCO
AND ALCOHOL

In the 1920s, the American Tobacco Company launched an advertising campaign designed to market Lucky Strike cigarettes to women. For some 40 years prior, smoking had primarily been a male pastime, but its popularity among women was increasing. The campaign theme was "Reach for a Lucky instead of a sweet." It obviously tried to exploit female fears of weight gain. In 5 years, Lucky Strike sales almost tripled (Pierce & Gilpin, 1995). Tobacco has been so commercially successful that today it kills perhaps 400,000 people in the United States each year. Despite decades of warnings from health authorities, its products remain the leading cause of preventable death.

Tobacco manufacturers spend an estimated $6 billion annually in advertising their products to the U.S. public (Strasburger & Donnerstein, 1999). Despite industry claims that ads only lure existing smokers from one brand to another, promotional activities clearly appear to attract new smokers (Pierce, Choi, Gilpin, Farkas, & Berry, 1998; Pierce & Gilpin, 1995). Such activities include media advertising and product giveaways.

Frequently, they affect those below the age of legal consumption. Of course, the most notorious evidence of effects on the young occurred with the R.J. Reynolds "Joe Camel" campaign. Even young children demonstrated high levels of recognition of the cigarette-puffing corporate icon (see the review in Pollay et al., 1996). Longitudinal evidence from the mid-1990s links tobacco promotions to an estimated 34% of smoking experimentation among California adolescents (Pierce et al., 1998). Nationwide, about 700,000 adolescents per year may be so affected. McGuire's model of persuasion, in which exposure to a message may lead to understanding and development of a cognitive or affective response, guided this research. As hypothesized, Pierce et al. found greater experimentation among those with more receptivity to promotions. Elsewhere, comparisons of correlations between amounts of brand advertising and product choice for different age groups suggest that tobacco ads affect adolescents more strongly than they do adults (Pollay et al., 1996). Teens' sense of invulnerability may contribute.

Yet advertising may also help prevent tobacco consumption. In 1988, California passed Proposition 99, which increased tobacco taxes and provided funds for a statewide, multimedia antismoking campaign. The campaign targeted adult smokers, pregnant women, ethnic minorities, and children. It stressed the consequences of second-hand smoke and contained material aggressively attacking the tobacco industry. Less confrontational efforts also took place in certain other states, such as Arizona and Massachusetts. Based on comparisons of campaign costs and cigarette consumption in the two states, Goldman and Glantz (1998) estimated that the California media effort was seven times more cost-effective than was the Massachusetts program. Following comments from respondents in discussion groups, they identified the antiindustry and second-hand smoke messages as especially effective. This rather problematically assumes, however, that perceptions of effects are meaningful indicators of effects. Hu, Sung, and Keeler (1995) provided a more modest interpretation of the California media campaign. They found that it reduced smoking, but somewhat less so than did the tax increase.

In any case, funds spent on tobacco marketing apparently continue to massively outweigh those spent to unsell smoking (Elliott, 1999). This raises one especially horrifying possibility about the net consequences of campaign research. By making promotions more efficient, applications of communication and psychological inquiries could contribute to larger numbers of needless human tobacco-related deaths than they prevent. For example, they could help bring about the predicted deaths during adulthood of 300 million of the children and adolescents in the world today from tobacco use (Deen, 1999). Many of these are expected to occur in developing countries, which tobacco companies today are targeting (Deen, 1999). Perhaps a global treaty to ban all promotions of tobacco products is the only appropriate response to the likelihood that tobacco marketers take advantage of existing research. At present, however, no real evidence illustrates such influences of theory and research.

In contrast, the $2 billion spent annually on U.S. alcohol advertising represents a much smaller, but by no means negligible, potential danger. Alcohol appears to cause about 100,000 U.S. deaths annually. Light to moderate consumption may lower risks of heart attacks and strokes, however, preventing an unknown numbers of deaths. Among the young, ads appear to increase consumption only modestly (see the review in Strasburger & Donnerstein, 1999). Even so, longitudinal data from 17 developed countries suggest that bans on alcohol advertising substantially lower motor vehicle fatalities (Saffer, 1991). This research was based on a consumer demand theory, which treats advertising as a determinant of taste.

9

Mass Communication, Public Opinion, and Civic Engagement

Obviously, elites of one sort or another rule much of the world. It is difficult to see how this situation could change in the foreseeable future. Nonetheless, elites often have to take into account the desires of both the masses and of publics, groups of interested persons. As V.O. Key (1967) said, even a tyranny "needs the ungrudging support of substantial numbers of its people" (p. 3). As British politician James Bryce (1981) wrote of public opinion processes around the turn of the century: "In some countries, the leaders count for, say, three-fourths of the product, and the mass for one-fourth only. In others these propositions are reversed" (p. 8).

Philosophers and other writers have often disagreed about how much say the masses should have, even in a democracy. Classical democratic political theory viewed humankind as essentially rational and able to choose wisely from a marketplace of ideas. In the United States, press freedom represents an attempt to help ensure such a marketplace. By the early 20th century, however, the Industrial Revolution had created an increasingly differentiated, complex society. Whatever the earlier merit of democratic theory, many writers believed that direct self-governance had become impossible.

At that time, one debate produced some remarkable insights – ideas that still influence media research. Journalist Walter Lippmann (1925) apparently believed in just enough democracy to keep the elites from abusing the masses, whose judgment he questioned. Instead of directly governing themselves, Lippmann largely thought that the masses should only hold leaders and experts accountable after the fact via the voting booth. Philosopher John Dewey reacted sharply to Lippmann's views. "The world has suffered more from leaders and authorities than from the masses," Dewey (1927/1946, p. 208) asserted.

The Lippmann–Dewey debate reflected a natural tension among early 20th-century progressive intellectuals. It revolved around values, the perceived consequences of relying on mass judgment, and assumptions about the potential ability of communication to promote participatory democracy. In fact, scholars today do not always recognize that the two men expressed a surprising number of rather similar ideas. For example, each recognized that modernization rendered democracy impotent, and each (in somewhat different ways) hoped *experts* could help improve things. Lippmann, a former student of William James, viewed human intelligence as a guide to action. Unfortunately, according to Lippmann, the masses had to rely on frequently inaccurate or at best incomplete impressions based largely on the content of newspapers. In addition, he felt that most people simply were too busy with other things to bother with the minutiae of public policy. At bottom, Lippmann (1925) argued that "when public opinion attempts to govern directly it is either a failure or a tyranny. It is not able to master the problem intellectually, nor to deal with it except by wholesale impact" (pp. 70–71).

Lippmann (1922) introduced to popular culture and social science the now famous concept of the *stereotype*, previously used to refer to a printer's mold. As used by Lippmann, it described the necessarily simplified (and sometimes distorted) impressions presented to and absorbed by the masses via the media and the wider culture. A stereotype can be viewed as a type of hypothesis about the world that may help people deal with the blooming, buzzing confusion of life (in James' terms). In Lippmann's (1922) words, the basic problem involved:

> the insertion between man and his environment of a pseudo-environment. To the pseudo-environment his behavior is a response. But because it *is* behavior, the consequences, if they are acts, operate not in the pseudo-environment where the behavior is stimulated, but in the real environment where action eventuates. (p. 15)

In his 1922 book, *Public Opinion,* Lippmann argued that the newspaper failed to inform people adequately. As a result, Lippmann advocated "the formation of independent cadres of social scientists working in quasi-public bureaucracies (the Bureau of Standards was his model) using the latest statistical procedures to produce veridical representations of reality" (Carey, 1989, p. 81). In his much more polemical *The Phantom Public,* Lippmann (1925) went further, calling for an approach that "economizes the attention of men as members of the public, and asks them to do as little as possible in matters where they can do nothing very well" (p. 199). He seemed to more or less give up on the possibility of effective governance based on knowledgeable mass opinion. What he did, according to V. Key (1967), was destroy a straw man—the idea that " 'the public' could be regarded as an omnicompetent and omniscient collectivity equipped to decide the affairs of state" (p. 5). Key doubted whether "these beliefs had ever been held save in the autointoxication of political oratory directed to the average man" (p. 5).

Dewey, however, apparently saw Lippmann's ideas as threatening to destroy the better in the name of the best. In response, Dewey (1927/1946) largely acknowledged the accuracy of many of Lippmann's insights about what *is*, but he sharply disputed Lippmann concerning what *might be*. "The essential need is the improvement of the methods and conditions of debate, discussion and persuasion" (p. 208). For example, Dewey advocated improved journalistic techniques, along the lines of what today is called *interpretive reporting*, in which news consists both of descriptions of events and the historical and developmental contexts in which they occur. He also criticized the influence of the profit motive. According to Dewey, "the assembling and reporting of news would be a very different thing if the genuine interests of reporters were permitted to work freely" (p. 182). To Dewey, experts should perfect processes of inquiry and disseminate (via the news) their conclusions, not execute policy. Until such things occur, "we have no way of telling how apt for judgment of social policies the existing intelligence of the masses may be. It would certainly go much further than at present" (p. 209). At bottom, Dewey tended to see Lippmann as depicting journalists and their audiences as political spectators (Carey, 1989).

At least on the surface, time has not been kind to certain of the arguments of Dewey and other participatory democrats. Considerable research evidence now supports Lippmann's attack on the classical democrats' notion of well-founded opinion among the masses (V. Price & Roberts, 1987). In addition, interpretive reporting has become something of an ideal within the field of journalism, although in practice modern news products continue to fall far short of Dewey's hopes. For example, news reports today frequently consist of isolated and sensational catastrophes artificially removed from their contexts. Possibly, like Lippmann, modern research rather effectively describes what is without pointing meaningfully to what might be. Perhaps part of the problem remains the inability of participatory democrats to provide effective blueprints for change. Nonetheless, the civic journalism movement (see chap. 1) represents an attempt to create Deweyan participatory democracy. In short, the empirical and normative questions remain. Is it possible for social inquiry to help move society at least vaguely in the direction of Dewey's ideals? Would such movement in fact be desirable?

MASS COMMUNICATION AND PUBLIC OPINION

What Is Public Opinion?

In research, the concept of *public opinion* sometimes refers to a kind of sociological equivalent of the attitude. Thus, many scholars implicitly assume a sort of operationist and nominalist stance by measuring it as an aggregation of the attitudes of isolated individuals. To them, public opinion becomes whatever polls measure or, more honestly, as "what opinion polls try to measure" (Converse, 1987, p. S14). Dramatic improvements in polling have been made in recent decades, aided by developments in opinion measurement, probability sampling techniques, and the almost universal presence of telephones in U.S. households. Some imperfections, such as tendencies to underrepresent members of certain social groups, nonetheless remain. In addition, of course, some opinion polls are of higher quality than are others, in part, because they take more advantage of such improvements.

Although overlap exists between most conceptions of public opinion and the results of polls, the two are by no means identical. Opinions expressed in polls are sometimes considered public if they concern public affairs, perhaps excluding those concerning certain marketing phenomena, for instance. Beyond this, some polls are designed to predict behavior, rather than describe mass opinions. For example, polls play various roles in election campaigns. These include informing candidates about issues of concern for and opinions of potential voters, as well as identifying effective arguments (Crespi, 1989). Many such polls are judged, however, by their ability to forecast elections (P. Meyer, 1991). In this, they encounter special problems—beyond those of describing a snapshot of opinion. For example, Crespi discussed the predictive accuracy of 423 preelection polls mostly from the early 1980s. He found a 5.7 percentage point average difference between polling results and the vote a winning candidate received. Factors not present in opinion polling, such as difficulties in predicting who will vote and people who change their minds between interviews and elections, contribute.

If all polls do not always attempt to describe opinions, neither do all conceptions of public opinion involve polls. Instead, public opinion takes on very different meanings, each arguably useful for specific research purposes in different contexts (see the discussion in V. Price, 1992). Of course, scholars usually use the term to refer to some sort of public judgment ideally based on rational and informed deliberation and/or discussion. They often presume that this plays a critical role (in both senses of the term) in limiting the behavior of those with political and/or economic power. Obviously, the topic involves two separate terms. The concept of *public* may refer to either the masses or one or more groups of persons who are interested in or otherwise involved with an issue. Blumer's (1946) definition reflected the latter conception. To him, a public consists of a group of people who face an issue, are divided about how to deal with it, and discuss the issue.

In this light, one can conceptualize opinion as a *process* or *product*, as forms of political discussion that contribute to a consensus about issues within groups or as what the isolated masses think about a subject, or even as both. Some conceptualizations reflect an influence of philosophical realism. For example, a number of early pragmatists

> viewed the individual self, including attitudes and opinions, as a social entity formed through communication and social action. Public opinion was likewise thought to be a product of interactive influences, formed with "the larger mind," shaped by — but by no means reducible to — the many individual expressions that enter public discussion. (V. Price & Roberts, 1987, p. 782)

This rather metaphysical, and philosophically realist, concept preceded, but did not guide, the development of modern polling techniques. The latter obviously tend to rely on the operationist conception of opinion as a product. It has its critics. After noting that officials, not the public, make most decisions, V. Key (1967) suggested that depicting the public as a kind of organic entity may be "of more poetic than practical utility" (p. 9).

Nonetheless, the perception that actual public opinion processes are difficult to reduce to numbers persists. Some scholars have even argued that easily countable phenomena do not count when it comes to public opinion. Blumer, a disciple of pragmatist philosopher/social psychologist George H. Mead, made perhaps the best known of these arguments. To him (Blumer, 1948), polling had little or nothing to do with public opinion, although it could help predict election outcomes. Instead, public opinion involved things that policymakers consider when they act, such as the positions advocated by interest groups with different amounts of power. In a special issue of *Public Opinion Quarterly* that celebrated its 50th birthday, guest editor Eleanor Singer (1987) responded sharply to Blumer's criticism of opinion surveys:

> Blumer was wrong. However partial, misleading, or inconclusive the polls may be as indicators of public opinion, they are better than anything else we've got. With them, . . . we can measure all the things Blumer thought we should. Without them, attempts to sound public opinion are subject to error — not necessarily greater error than polls, but immeasurable error. There lies the crucial difference. (p. S1)

Perhaps some middle ground exists. For instance, with deliberative polls, researchers assemble a scientific sample of persons and have them discuss issues among themselves (McCombs & Reynolds, 1999). Changes in the distribution of opinion can then be noted. One example occurred with the National Issues Convention in Austin, Texas, during 1996. A national sample of participants came to town, appeared on PBS, and questioned national politicians.

Progress certainly has occurred in studying the processes of opinion. Nonetheless, were he alive today, Blumer likely would not agree that modern measurement techniques capture the concept. Yet today's polls represent a component, although not the whole, of Blumer's concept of public opinion (Salmon & Glasser, 1995). For example, political decision makers are by no means immune from their influence—a point more explicitly recognized in V. Key's (1967) definition. Public opinion "may simply be taken to mean those opinions held by private persons which governments find it prudent to heed" (p. 14). Thus, indications might be found in polls and many other sources. These include letters and phone calls from citizens to government officials, talk radio discussions, editorials and letters in newspapers, petitions, activities by lobbyists and pressure groups, and election returns. Any of these potentially influences government. Of course, governmental activities, including public relations, may also influence such opinion. At bottom, government sometimes responds to such public opinion, sometimes leads it, and sometimes largely ignores it (V. Key, 1967).

Politicians and laypersons who rely on opinion polls may encounter additional difficulties. For example, newspaper reports of polls tend to ignore certain shortcomings (see M.M. Miller & Hurd, 1982). For example, some newspapers do not point out that the reported accuracy of polls based on samples of 400 or 500 people tends to fall dramatically when responses within demographic subgroups, such as ethnic minorities, are reported. In Lippmann's terms, polls rather easily can become part of an inaccurate pseudoenvironment about mass opinion that policymakers and citizens both may use to form political judgments.

Yet defenders maintain that polls promote participatory democracy, giving a voice to an otherwise silent majority that has no affiliation with activist special interest groups. Such groups, and politically involved individuals, may exert influence on government far in excess of their numbers. For example, poll pioneer George Gallup "promoted the habit of thinking of a poll as a continuous referendum by which majority will could be made known" (P. Meyer, 1991, p. 240). Meyer termed this the *referendum model* of public opinion and warned that it is much too simple for the modern world. For example, interest groups may be necessary to protect minorities against majority tyranny. In any case, evidence exists (e.g., Page & Shapiro, 1983) that poll results often predict what public officials will do.

Other writers today see public opinion as something that only appears in unusual circumstances, as when a salient political issue develops (see the discussion in V. Price & Roberts, 1987). They question to what extent the masses really make meaningful judgments about issues in ordinary circumstances. This is by no means a new concern. Because of traditional forms of news dissemination, Dewey (1927/1946) saw public opinion as "intermittent" — as something that "appears only in crises" (p. 178). To Dewey, "only continuous inquiry, continuous in the sense of being connected as well as persistent, can provide the material of enduring opinion about public matters" (p. 178). In this tradition, today many scholars continue to debate the extent to which modern polls really measure public opinion, instead of often tapping meaningless *psuedoopinions* (see the discussion in V. Price & Roberts, 1987). Accordingly, V. Price and Roberts argued that public opinion:

> may be conceptualized largely as communication between political actors who are restlessly pursuing public recognition and support for their views and members of the interested public who are trying to understand the issue and decide whom to support. (p. 807)

Even less conventionally, some theorists today (see the following discussion about the ideas of Noelle–Neumann) view public opinion as nothing more than how people behave in public, which may sometimes have even less than do poll results with what people really think.

Perhaps calling the results of polls mass, rather than public, opinion would help settle these issues (V. Price & Roberts, 1987). Of course, the results of most polls are largely descriptive, in the sense that they attempt to describe what the masses think often without really attempting to explain why. This chapter primarily concerns whatever role the media play in influencing mass and public opinion. Therefore, it examines four contemporary, but distinct, theoretical approaches: cultivation, the spiral of silence, agenda setting, and discursive public opinion processes. Since the late 1960s, scholars have conducted a great deal of research within the first three areas. Each purports to rebut, in various ways, the limited-effects model of mass communication (see chap. 1), and each focuses on cognitive processing of messages to an extent (V. Price, 1988). All provide "modified mass society models of atomized individuals at the mercy of centralized media" (Beniger, 1987, p. S51). In part because of this, scholars who emphasize the role of audience activity (see chap. 4) sometimes criticize cultivation research. Much less research pertaining to the recently articulated fourth approach exists. Nonetheless, it goes much farther into a possible new paradigm for the study of public opinion centered around processes and social contexts (Beniger, 1987; V. Price, 1988).

Media Cultivation of Social Reality: George Gerbner and the Mainstreaming of Critical Research

As Dewey (1916) put it, communication and commonality represent the keys to human community. Given this, what kind of community may TV be helping to create or maintain? Gerbner, Bell Atlantic professor of telecommunication at Temple University, does not give an especially encouraging answer. He is largely responsible for spectacularly influential, yet heavily criticized, research into the impact of media on the perceptions and opinion of the masses. Both contextualism (Gerbner, 1986) and traditional critical theory (see chap. 1) influenced his work. Unlike many other opinion researchers, Gerbner examines the impact of TV drama rather than of news. An examination of some details of his life is perhaps necessary to understand his work.

Today, Gerbner may be the most visible mass communication theorist, both among communication scholars and others. He is well known to scientists in traditional academic areas such as psychology and sociology, to policymakers in Washington, DC, and to those who work within the industry. His research combines studies into the institutional production of TV messages, content analyses concerning the extent to which the world of TV drama accurately reflects the "real" world, and effects research into TV's cultivation of basic attitudinal assumptions in its audience. It has generated much publicity in the popular press and controversy within academia. The research contains elements of both European critical and U.S. empirical research. In recent years, scholars have called for increased dialogue between the two schools. One of Gerbner's major contributions has been to introduce concepts influenced by European critical scholarship into the mainstream of effects study.

His background is natural for such a role. Gerbner was born in Budapest, Hungary, in 1919. The son of a teacher, he won a national literary prize and published a book of poetry while still a teenager. In 1939, at age 19, he left Hungary to avoid being drafted into the military services of a country that supported the Nazis. After living briefly in Italy, France, and Mexico, he came to the United States, became a U.S. citizen, and enlisted as a private in the U.S. Army. The Office of Strategic Services (OSS), the World War II predecessor of the Central Intelligence Agency (CIA), recruited him. As the war ended, he hunted war criminals in Hungary, personally jailing the first Nazi prime minister of the country. His OSS experience may help account for the vaguely conspiratorial tinge sometimes evident in his theorizing.

After the war, Gerbner returned to California. In 1951, he received his master's degree in communication in education from the University of Southern California (USC). His graduate studies led him toward the newly evolving academic discipline of mass communication. From 1951 to 1952, he worked as a research associate for the cinema department at USC and collaborated with Adorno in studies of the psychodynamics of TV drama. Adorno also left Europe to avoid the Nazis. Especially known for his research into the authoritarian personality, he was one of the critical scholars from the Frankfurt School of Sociology in Germany to influence the communications field. From 1952 to 1956, Gerbner was an instructor at El Camino College and taught reading development and the social aspects of mass communication. He continued his graduate work and received his doctorate from USC in 1955. A journal article based on his dissertation illustrates an early critical, scientific stance. The field of communication "has no value orientation for making much sense of its findings in terms of urgently needed judgments," Gerbner (1956, p. 171) wrote, at a time when mainstream scholars believed widely in the value-free myth of logical empiricist inquiry. "Vigorous search for a technique and value-oriented theoretical structure appears to be the major need in the progress toward a science of communication" (p. 171).

In 1956, Gerbner became an assistant professor at the Institute of Communications Research at the University of Illinois. He taught social aspects of mass communication along with mass communication and popular culture. Perhaps his biggest break came in 1964, when he was hired as dean and professor at the Annenberg School at Pennsylvania. The school provided the base for Gerbner's research efforts for decades. Founded in 1959 by Walter Annenberg, it receives a majority of its operating budget from a publishing firm owned by the Annenberg family.

By the late 1960s, Gerbner had started his most important scholarly endeavor—the cultural indicators project. This eventually consisted of three elements. The first, institutional process analysis, investigates the formation of policies concerning the flow of media messages. It has remained somewhat undeveloped because funding is difficult to obtain. Grants from the Surgeon General's Scientific Advisory Board on Television and Social Behavior, the National Institute of Mental Health, the White House Office of Telecommunications Policy, and the American Medical Association have fueled other aspects of the project. The second, message system analysis (see chap. 5), involves the content analysis of TV programming. By 1972, he was ready to begin his cultivation analysis—the effects portion of this trilogy that is of primary concern here.

Gerbner is concerned with the impact of TV drama, which he sees as the primary enculturation agent in U.S. society (Gerbner, Gross, Morgan, & Signorielli, 1982). Watching TV is seen as equivalent to a religious ritual. The TV set is turned on for about 7 hours per day in the average household. Gerbner claimed that most people watch it according to routinized schedules regardless of available programming. Unlike many other theorists, Gerbner focused not on short-term behavioral changes produced by specific programming, but on the presumably long-term attitudinal and cognitive impact of rather habitual exposure.

Gerbner's research assumes that the implicit messages within TV drama are relatively uniform regardless of specific programs, different networks, and time. Since 1969, he and his associates have gathered content data concerning thousands of programs and characters to bolster this assumption and to identify important ways in which televised "reality" differs from "reality" per se. For example, characters in TV drama are involved in violence much more often than are people in "real" life (Gerbner et al., 1982).

Content data led to specific predictions about cultivation effects. For example, the level of violence on TV might cause heavy viewers to overstate the extent of crime in actual life. Exploring this early, global (i.e., across-the-board) version of the cultivation hypothesis was a primary concern of Gerbner and his associates during the 1970s. In 1973, he began editing the *Journal of Communication*, which provided a publication outlet for a great deal of critical research, including that of the cultural indicators project.

Like many empirical theorists, Gerbner views mass communication as performing something of a reinforcement function in society. Such reinforcement, however, is anything but the benign version described by limited-effects scholars (D.F. Roberts & Maccoby, 1985). Instead, he described TV as important because it cultivates in its audiences fundamental assumptions and attitudes, which perpetuate the status quo. For example, perhaps TV's impact on viewer conceptions of violence in society is significant because such conceptions might make the public more receptive to legislation that diminishes civil liberties. In this light, scholars have distinguished first-order from second-order cultivation effects. First-order effects are linked directly to manifest TV content. Thus, they involve such things as someone's estimates about the frequency of crime in society or the numbers of elderly people in the general population. Second-order cultivation includes perceptions less directly tied to content. They include values, opinions toward political issues, and fear of crime.

After some early research efforts yielded evidence consistent with cultivation, the need for theoretical refinement became apparent. By 1980, Gerbner and his associates supplemented the global cultivation hypothesis with the related concepts of *mainstreaming* and *resonance*. Mainstreaming occurs when the average responses on an attitude or perceptual measure for members of different demographic groups are more similar among heavy TV users than among light viewers. For example, African Americans and Whites who are heavy viewers may express similar perceptions about crime levels in society. Among light viewers, however,

Afrcan Americans may have perceptions that are very different from those of Whites. Mainstreaming is seen as a process in which general programming cancels out or overrides the impact of other factors, at least in part. Yet resonance takes place when specific issues have a particularly marked relevance to and impact on members of a specific group. As a result, the average responses for different groups become more varied among heavy viewers. For instance, programs that feature African Americans as victims of criminal violence may affect the latter's perceptions of crime much more than it does perceptions among Whites. Although these patterns are described as exceptions to the general trend of global cultivation (Gerbner, Gross, Morgan, & Signorielli, 1981), the mainstreaming concept in particular has been the focus of much Annenberg research since the early 1980s (e.g., Gerbner et al., 1982). It may occur more frequently with second-order than first-order cultivation (R.P. Hawkins & Pingree, 1990).

The mainstreaming idea has some fascinating implications. One often hears anecdotal claims that the cultures in different regions of the United States are becoming more alike. Morgan (1986) investigated whether TV viewing appears to contribute to a greater uniformity of political perceptions among people in different sections of the country. He found correlational evidence of this. For instance, among heavy viewers, the percentages of people in the conservative South Atlantic states and in more liberal New England who identified themselves as liberals were much more similar (about 28%) than among light viewers (about 24% in the South Atlantic area vs. 42% in New England). Heavy TV viewing perhaps canceled out the influence of local culture on political self-designations. Such evidence is contrary to the idea that the "rural isolated hinterlands were to be drenched in the cosmopolitan, liberal, sophisticated values of the urban elite" (p. 136). Instead, the "center of gravity of the television mainstream appears to be firmly located in the greater Southeastern U.S." (p. 136).

Assumptions about the reasons for the mainstreaming phenomenon reveal an often implicit conspiratorial edge. Survey research indicates that self-designated liberals, moderates, and conservatives who are light viewers of TV generally show marked differences on attitudes toward political issues. Such differences occur with reference to open housing, free speech for deviate groups, and federal spending on health and welfare, for example (Gerbner et al., 1982). Among heavy viewers, political self-designation typically has much less association with attitudes. Heavy viewers tend to take the conservative or moderate stands on social issues, such as free speech, and more liberal positions on economic issues, such as health spending. According to researchers, the economic basis of TV, resting on mass consumption of advertised items, "would seem to dictate an economically popular and even populist stance" (Gerbner et al., 1982, p. 123).

However, the need to attract audiences at the lowest cost possible "means striving for the broadest and most conventional appeals" and "presenting divergent or deviant images as mostly to be shunned, feared, or suppressed" (p. 105). These needs presumably lead to TV messages cultivating social moderation or conservatism and economic liberalism in audiences. The research also indicates that heavy viewers from lower class backgrounds are much more likely than light viewers to see themselves as middle class. The researchers concluded that the TV experience may represent "an especially powerful deterrent to working-class consciousness" (p. 110). A Marxist could take this as evidence that TV creates a false consciousness in the masses, deflecting them from their historical mission as supporters of socialism.

At a certain point, one wonders exactly what the cultivation researchers are suggesting about those responsible for TV messages. No one would seriously argue that network and corporate executives get together weekly for lunch to discuss how best to brainwash the masses. In fact, the theory seems to assume that the symbolic content of TV drama represents a logical, and perhaps inevitable, outgrowth of a commercial mass medium operating within a capitalist economy.

Gerbner's status and visibility really took off during the 1980s, but the decade did not begin entirely auspiciously. In *Communication Research*, one of the most influential publications in the field, sociologist Hirsch (1980, 1981) published a widely cited critique of cultivation theory and the methods used to test it. Hirsch's criticisms appeared to reflect the skepticism that traditional logical empiricists feel about the rigor of critically influenced research. Hirsch's multipronged critique included a claim that much of the evidence for cultivation effects disappears when appropriate statistical controls are used. Hirsch (1981) also argued that concepts such as resonance and mainstreaming could explain virtually all possible research findings. In effect, Hirsch argued that the cultivation hypothesis is not falsifiable (see chap. 2). If true, such a claim could damage the scientific status of cultivation theory.

Certain changes within the mass communication field during the 1980s probably helped enhance Gerbner's stature. Increasing dissatisfaction with mechanistic and logical empiricist approaches to research has been evident within traditional social scientific fields at least since the early 1970s. Such unrest perhaps arose a bit later within communications, but during the 1980s it was unmistakable. The field saw a supplementation of traditional research into media effects with a variety of different approaches, including increasing numbers of analyses of media content and studies of media control structures. In such an atmosphere, the influence of Gerbner could not help but increase. Yet the presence of Gerbner's research as a model probably has intensified the field's eclecticism.

What can be said then about the current status and future influence of Gerbner's cultivation hypothesis? Much of the evidence supporting the cultivation hypothesis involves cross-sectional correlations, and doubts exist about the extent to which experimentation is appropriate. Cultivation presumably requires substantial amounts of time to develop, during which experimental control and observation of human behavior is virtually impossible. One of the most premature and perhaps naive conclusions that one could draw is that cultivation effects are necessarily and inherently all-powerful. The statistical association of TV exposure with audience perceptions is quite modest according to a recent meta-analysis (Morgan & Shanahan, 1997). Yet its proponents (e.g., Morgan & Signorielli, 1990) argued that a small shift "in the cultivation of common perspectives may alter the cultural climate and upset the balance of social and political decision without necessarily changing observable behavior" (p. 20).

One can only guess what influence Gerbner's cultivation research will have on future generations of mass communication theorists. It seems likely, however, that the general thrust of his theoretical ideas will outlive many of the specifics — a tendency apparent historically with many social scientific theories. Hirsch's (1981) claim that concepts such as resonance and mainstreaming can account for any research finding seems overstated. Nonetheless, others (T.D. Cook, Kendzierski, & Thomas, 1983) wrote of the need to develop a model that predicts a priori when different cultivation phenomena will occur. Additional explanation of the processes involved in cultivation may be a prerequisite for improved prediction. It may seem strange to psychologize a theoretical approach that has some of its roots in European, realist macrosociology, but such a model may have to come from psychology (see e.g., Potter, 1991).

Unfortunately, Gerbner and his colleagues have written little about the cognitive phenomena involved in cultivation phenomena. Work that draws on modern cognitive psychology to develop long-term, information-processing explanations of mainstreaming and other cultivation phenomena may be necessary to improve the predictive utility and scientific value of this theory (see R.P. Hawkins & Pingree, 1990). In fact, the entire field of opinion research seems to be moving in this direction (Beniger, 1987; V. Price, 1988). According to Potter (1993), scholars need to go beyond examining whether a cultivation effect occurs and make more effort to explain why and how they occur. Lacking "evidence for psychological processes, the cultivation hypotheses stands on a tenuous foundation" (R.P. Hawkins & Pingree, 1990, p. 36). Thus, third variables and reverse causation might explain some of the findings. Perhaps "viewers with certain beliefs about the real world choose to watch television *because* they see those same beliefs portrayed there" (Potter, 1993, p. 585).

Clearly, much remains to be learned about psychological mechanisms. For example, R.P. Hawkins, Pingree, and Adler (1987) studied whether perceptions about the world of TV intervene between viewing and first-order effects. No support emerged for this idea. No relationship appeared between a person's amount of TV exposure and, say, his or her estimate of the odds that a typical character will be involved in violence. This calls into doubt the idea that people construct first-order responses in the relatively rational, structured ways posited by learning theory (Shrum & O'Guinn, 1993).

They also examined the idea that first-order effects mediate between TV exposure and second-order cultivation. People may form impressions of the characteristics of the world rather directly from TV content. Inferences derived from such impressions might in turn affect opinions and values. Research failed to support this notion, however. This evidence of the independence of these two effects suggests that they perhaps occur in different ways (R.P. Hawkins & Pingree, 1990). Possibly, first-order effects, as might show up with people's estimates of the frequency of crime, result when people combine and summarize separate memory traces of different events on TV fairly automatically (R.P. Hawkins & Pingree, 1990). This is consistent with some evidence (M. Shapiro, 1991). Questions can be raised as to whether such activity occurs only in response to researcher questioning, however (R.P. Hawkins & Pingree, 1990). However, second-order beliefs, such as on opinions concerning civil liberties issues, might result when viewers identify TV events as implying certain beliefs (R.P. Hawkins & Pingree, 1990). Perhaps these are a part of culture, making them potential beliefs for everyone. Then while watching TV, "an experienced event 'fits' or 'activates' an already existing idea" (R.P. Hawkins & Pingree, 1990, p. 46). Most researchers apparently accept that second-order cultivation is likely to influence real-world behavior (R.P. Hawkins & Pingree, 1990). Nonetheless, researchers have done very little with whatever link exists between cultivated perception and human behavior. In theory, cultivation is part of a much larger cultural process that inhibits progressive change, a way by which societal elites and a capitalist culture manipulate the masses.

Research concerning psychological mechanisms underlying cultivation and related phenomena continues. M. Shapiro (1991) examined the idea that people make first-order judgments by retrieving relevant information, which they weigh and balance for veracity, from their memory of events. He reported some support for this model. Mares (1996) found experimental evidence that people's tendency to incorrectly remember events from TV drama as from news programs markedly contributed to TV-biased reality judgments.

In a promising line of research, Shrum (1996) and Shrum and O'Guinn (1993) empirically linked the availability heuristic (see chap. 6) to first-order effects. According to availability, "people assess the frequency of a class or the probability of an event by the ease with which instances or occurrences come to mind" (Tversky & Kahneman, 1974, p. 1127). Availability processes are seen as less rational than those hypothesized by learning theory.

For example, according to evidence (Shrum, 1996), soap operas contain numerous depictions of doctors and lawyers. Heavy soap-opera viewers in turn perceive greater frequencies in the U.S. workforce for these occupational groups than do light viewers. Consistent with availability, these images presumably are more accessible in the memories of heavy viewers. As a result, heavy viewers estimate occupational frequencies more quickly than do light viewers. In turn, different response speeds help explain the two groups' different frequency estimates for occupational groups (Shrum, 1996). Thus, accessibility, "the ease with which information is retrieved" from memory (Shrum & O'Guinn, 1993, p. 440), seems to explain why at least some cultivation phenomena occur. This is similar to the accessibility literature pertaining to attitudes and behavior (see chap. 7).

Criticisms of cultivation research continue. For example, some evidence (J. Kim & Rubin, 1997; Perse, 1986) indicates that, contrary to certain cultivation assumptions, more active, less ritualized TV use may enhance both first- and second-order effects. In addition, some results may reflect little more than the wording of questionnaire items (A.M. Rubin, Perse, & Taylor, 1988). Finally, to what extent the supposed uniformity of TV messages remains, as cable technology increasingly permits viewers to select from hundreds of stations, is debatable. Yet, cultivation researchers argue, such developments "have been accompanied by *decreased* diversity in ownership and greater concentration and commercialization of production and control, with little evident diversification in programming" (Morgan & Shanahan, 1997, p. 7).

The Spiral of Silence

Interestingly, right-wing critics of TV content often make arguments about the impact of the medium that in some ways resemble those of cultivation researchers. For instance, former Vice President Dan Quayle's famous, or notorious, criticism of a TV depiction of single mothers rested on assumptions that TV legitimized harmful, alternative lifestyles. In the present era of alleged *political correctness*, media researchers did not exactly knock one another over to study Quayle's allegations (but see Morgan, Leggett, & Shanahan, 1999, for evidence that Quayle was not entirely wrong). However, scholars have vigorously examined the work of a German communication theorist, Noelle-Neumann, whose ideas may help explain why what some call *political correctness* exists and how the media may promote it.

Noelle-Neumann (1974, 1977, 1979) developed an influential theory concerning the role of communication (including forms of mass communication) in influencing public opinion. Her theory is known by one of the key image-evoking phrases in her writing — the *spiral of silence*. At bottom, Noelle-Neumann is interested in explaining how powerful media effects might occur. It emerged out of the social milieu of post-World War II Germany and from a wide variety of other influences (see the discussion in Beniger, 1987), including conformity theory (e.g., Asch, 1952) in social psychology and the *social self* concept of early pragmatists.

During the 1990s, Noelle-Neumann's work became especially controversial in ways that have nothing to do with the formal, quantitative data bearing on it. First, Bogart (1991) discussed her purported participation in Nazi-related activities during Hitler's rule. Later Simpson (1996) suggested that her theoretical work echoes views she developed during that era. According to Simpson, it reveals much more about the theorist, "her times, and the origins of her published ideas than it does about public opinion as such" (p. 151). Noelle-Neumann (1992) vigorously denied that she was or is anti-Semitic or belonged to the Nazi party. In response to Simpson, Kepplinger (1997) accused him of violating "fundamental principles of scientific argumentation" (p. 115). For instance, Simpson replaced science with politics, Kepplinger charged, by focusing on the mentality of the scientist, rather than on the empirical merits of the theory. Whatever the truth about the Noelle-Neumann and the Nazi era, in a world in which data underdetermine theory, one's background potentially conditions how one interprets evidence. Thus, information about personal history and political beliefs may shed light on a scholar's work.

In some ways, her theory even resembles Gerbner's cultivation idea. Both tend to emphasize the not-so-benign reinforcement function of the mass media, and both assume that media content is rather uniform. Unlike Gerbner, however, whose ideas have roots in the political left, Noelle-Neumann has long been associated with the Christian Democratic Party — a sort of German equivalent of the U.S. Republicans. Whereas cultivation research implicitly depicts the masses as at the mercy of the mediated right, Noelle-Neumann evidently sees leftist media interests as the culpable manipulator.

In her theory, Noelle-Neumann begins with a peculiarly behavioral, and evidently novel, definition of public opinion. This idea has its roots in the 18th and 19th centuries with writers such as Locke and Hume (both early positivists), as well as Rousseau and Madison. Public opinion, according to Noelle-Neumann, refers to pressure to conform and the range of opinions and behaviors that one can express in public without fear of sanction.

To Noelle-Neumann, public opinion arises from the interaction (or per-haps transaction) of the individual with his or her social environment. In her theory, public opinion pertains not only to governmental affairs, but to pressures on individuals to conform in various ways, such as shoveling snow from their sidewalks in winter or avoiding certain hairstyles. Per-haps most important, it contributes to consensus in society, according to her theory. Without it, society presumably would have a more difficult time functioning. One can view her concept of public opinion as an adap-tive mechanism by which even relatively libertarian societies control dis-sent and maintain coherence as a functioning metaphorical organism.

At the roots of Noelle-Neumann's theory is the idea that people have a profound fear of isolation (i.e., they possess great fear of separation from their social environment and also doubt their own judgment). Most peo-ple, it is assumed, would rather act contrary to their judgment than risk isolation. Because of this, people possess a metaphorical quasistatistical organ, which they use to determine, especially in changing circumstances, when different types of public expression risk isolation. Thus, they moni-tor the climate of opinion—what they believe others think or will think at some future time. People then contrast this climate with their own private opinion—what they really think privately. For example, one may have strong feelings about a sensitive issue such as legalized abortion or prefer-ential treatment for women and minorities in the workplace. If someone senses that most of those at work disagree, the person is likely to voice the popular opinion, in that context, or at least keep silent. Even more impor-tant than the current climate of opinion, according to Noelle-Neumann, is its perceived future state. Persons holding a minority position on an issue may feel that their position is gaining in popularity, encouraging them to express it in public. These persons may be more vocal than a silent major-ity that feels that the popularity of its ideas is declining.

The mass media may affect people's conceptions of the present or fu-ture climate of opinion. People may read poll results or news interviews with activists, for example. Noelle-Neumann described the content of mass media as often reflecting consonance, or high levels of agreement, on many issues. This idea is similar to the cultivation researchers' claims that TV drama contains a high degree of uniformity in the implicit messages that it presents to audiences.

Ultimately, people can only rely on public expression, rather than what others really think, for their perception of the opinion climate. A kind of snowballing effect occurs. Those with one position feel that their strength is gaining and they become increasingly vocal. Others hear these argu-ments, adjust their perceptions of the opinion climate accordingly, and be-come more likely to express the chic opinion. Thus, expression reflecting one side comes to dominate public discussion, whereas public airings of opposed arguments decline or spiral into silence. Nonetheless, Noelle-Neumann's evidence indicates that this process is not absolute. Often a very committed hard core of believers, which public opinion will not silence, exists.

Thus, public opinion is often very dynamic, at least when examined for substantial time periods. One can easily think of anecdotal examples to illustrate this. For example, few students taking mass communication courses, at least in many major state universities, during the early 1970s expressed much sympathy with the Republican Party. This, of course, was the time of the Vietnam conflict and Watergate, and pro-Republicans perhaps faced social ostracism. By the mid-1980s, however, such students favored the Republicans in much greater numbers, at least in public.

A possible weakness in her theory concerns the relationship between public and private behavior. Voting—a very private act—is the primary way in which ordinary citizens participate in the political process. Hence, behavioral public opinion may not influence it greatly unless the public behavior of others markedly influences one's private opinions.

In many ways, her theory seems to have some disturbing implications. For one thing, it suggests that legal guarantees, such as those found in the First Amendment, may not ensure freedom of expression. Some civil libertarians have argued that economic considerations, such as the need to limit one's expression to keep a job, prevent true freedom of speech. Some civil libertarians have even argued that a guaranteed minimum income for every member of society is necessary to protect freedom of speech. If Noelle-Neumann is right, even this is insufficient. In a sense, perhaps only wealthy hermits may have "true" freedom of expression, but often they lack much of an audience.

Since the theory appeared in the 1970s, other researchers (e.g., Gonzenbach, 1992; Salmon & Neuwirth, 1990) have provided somewhat qualified support to many of Noelle-Neumann's ideas and research findings. Nonetheless, a suspicion remains that the theory may apply primarily in highly regimented societies like the one it was developed in or that non-German researchers may have experienced difficulty in testing it appropriately. Based on a literature review, Salmon and Mou (1992) concluded:

> With few exceptions, researchers outside of Germany have not found much in the way of consistent empirical support for several of the model's pivotal assumptions and claims. They have found what might be characterized as a "modest" degree of reluctance, rather than consuming fear, about publicly expressing a minority opinion on most issues. (p. 150)

More recently, a meta-analysis of available survey evidence concerning aspects of the theory (Glynn, Hayes, & Shanahan, 1997) found only a small relationship between someone's willingness to express an opinion and the extent to which the person believes others share the opinion. The authors speculated that experiments looking at actual expression—as opposed to surveys querying respondents' willingness to talk—might yield stronger evidence.

If taken to an extreme, Noelle-Neumann's theory describes what might happen if, in J. Campbell's (1995) words, "a group is able to fuse its members into social automata" (p. 68). This could involve entirely submerging the creative, individualistic element of the human self, the "I" within the part, the "me," that reflects the influence of group norms (see chap. 1). Social nominalists will find in it a recipe for what they fear most—the obliteration of individuality.

In contrast, a healthy community might balance the ethical influence of both parts of the self and of nominalism and realism more generally (see chap. 1, appendix; cf. Lewis & Smith, 1980). This might encourage criticism by "individuals firmly rooted in the life of their community who see there problems and possibilities of resolution and who try to bring this perspective before the public" (J. Campbell, 1995, p. 62). In this light, social control is by no means inherently bad. Thus, John Dewey attached particular importance to positive freedom to make "the best of oneself as a social being and not merely the negative freedom from external restraint or compulsion" (Westbrook, 1991, pp. 37–38).

Agenda Setting

By the early 1970s, the field of mass communication research was ready for a major shakeup (Kosicki, 1993). Dozens of years of research into the persuasive impact of the media on attitudes and behavior had failed to connect the media decisively to either (Kosicki, 1993). The still-entrenched limited-effects generalization left researchers frustrated, and many seemed to feel that only different approaches and questions offered the possibility of demonstrating the socially significant media effects suggested by anecdotal evidence and intuition.

One day during the 1960s, Maxwell McCombs was sitting with colleagues from UCLA in a Los Angeles bar (E.M. Rogers, Dearing, & Bregman, 1993). Their conversation concerned that day's issue of a newspaper, why the paper emphasized some stories rather than others, and what consequences these choices might have for readers. In a nearby bookstore, McCombs bought a book, one that he had encountered earlier as a graduate student, written by political scientist Bernard C. Cohen (1963). The book concerned the relationship between news media and governmental foreign policies. In it, Cohen made one now famous, if somewhat impressionistic, statement. The press "may not be successful much of the time in telling people what to think, but it is stunningly successful in telling its readers what to think about" (p. 13). On that day, the modern study of news agenda setting began to take shape.

This idea—that the news media define the importance of issues or events (i.e., the agenda) for their audiences—has become one of the most influential in modern mass communication research according to citations and the more than 200 published studies concerning it (E.M. Rogers et al., 1993). Agenda setting can be seen as a gatekeeping process, resulting in an inevitably incomplete picture of reality, or as a surveillance function of media for society in which public problems dictate media and audience attention (Carter et al., 1992).

The idea actually goes back to early in the century to the work of writers such as Lippmann (1922). It generally concerns mass opinion (as measured by polls) about the import of different issues, rather than the specific positions people take on the issues. Variations on the simple theme continue to abound in the research literature. These include studies concerning how the media agenda, the emphasis the press places on some issues rather than others, is set (see chap. 5); the extent that the media and audience agendas reflect other indicators of the import of issues and events (e.g., Combs & Slovic, 1979); and the actual cognitive mechanisms underlying agenda setting among individuals (e.g., Iyengar & Kinder, 1987). Other research has related the press agenda (e.g., Pritchard, 1986) and the mass agenda (e.g., Pritchard, Dilts, & Berkowitz, 1987) to the agendas of public officials such as prosecutors (e.g., to changes in the perceptions and related actions by the latter).

During the late 1960s, McCombs and Shaw, both by then part of the journalism faculty at the University of North Carolina, obtained a small research grant from the NAB to conduct research concerning Cohen's idea (Tankard, 1990b). The original empirical study (McCombs & Shaw, 1972) was based on the 1968 presidential campaign. During the campaign, researchers questioned 100 undecided voters in Chapel Hill, North Carolina, about what they considered the key issues. They used undecided voters to maximize the possibility of observing evidence of large media effects. They also collected content-analytic data about what issues the news media serving the community emphasized. The research relied on the level of analysis of the issue—correlations were calculated between the amount of emphasis given to 15 issues (e.g., law and order, foreign policy) in the news and by their respondents. Extremely large relationships emerged. For instance, the correlation between the degree of emphasis that an issue received in major news items and aggregate judgment about it among respondents was .967.

Such correlations are virtually unheard in typical social-scientific research, which usually uses individual people as a level of analysis. Scholars using aggregate data commonly do find relatively large relationships, although not often of the size reported in the study. Of course, these correlations did not prove the existence of an all-powerful agenda-setting effect, but they were consistent with such an effect. Perhaps some third factor—such as the inherent import of issues—affected the agendas of both the media and undecided voters. Perhaps news gatekeepers simply intuited public perceptions and provided what the audiences wanted. Actually, the authors initially experienced some difficulty in finding an outlet for their research. The Theory and Methodology division of the Association for Education in Journalism (as these were called then) rejected an initial paper reporting the results possibly because the research seemed a bit unorthodox (Tankard, 1990b). Despite such alleged shortcomings, the work was finally published by the *Public Opinion Quarterly*. A massive reaction, as indicated by the numbers of subsequent studies and patterns of citation (see E.M. Rogers et al., 1993), followed. Evidently, researchers found that the piece contained both fresh ideas and a possible key to resolving the seemingly eternal conundrum between intuition about media effects and actual empirical evidence.

Subsequent research employing more controlled designs has indicated that the media influence on audience agendas, using both individuals and aggregates as levels of analysis, is marked and substantively important. In one experiment, Iyengar, Peters, and Kinder (1982) demonstrated that manipulations of issue salience affect which problems both individuals and groups attach importance to. For example, viewers whose experimentally manipulated TV news programs contained substantial numbers of stories proclaiming the vulnerability of U.S. defense capabilities grew more concerned about the issue, as indicated by individual change scores. Using the unit of analysis of the issue, defense went from ranking sixth out of eight issues in importance to ranking second among those in the experimental group. The issue ranking remained stable among those within a control group during the 6-day course of the study (Iyengar et al., 1982). Behr and Iyengar (1985) used nonexperimental longitudinal data. They found evidence that naturally occurring TV news coverage influenced aggregate public concerns about issues. For instance, after a lead story on CBS TV news aired during the 1970s about energy, an average of about 1.25% more of the public named the topic as the most important problem (Behr & Iyengar, 1985).

E.M. Rogers and Dearing (1988) reviewed the main lessons learned during the previous 15 years. They used the term *public agenda* to refer to what has been previously called the *mass agenda* in this chapter.

(1) The mass media influence the public agenda. This proposition, implied by the Cohen (1963) metaphor, has been generally supported by evidence

from most public agenda-setting investigations, which cover a very wide range of agenda items, types of publics, and points in time.

(2) An understanding of media agenda-setting is a necessary prerequisite to comprehending how the mass media agenda influences the public agenda.

(3) The public agenda, once set by, or reflected by, the media agenda, influences the policy agenda of elite decision makers, and , in some cases, policy implementation.

(4) The media agenda seems to have direct, sometimes strong, influence upon the policy agenda of elite decision makers, and, in some cases, policy implementation. (pp. 579–580)

Since the mid-1980s, research has extended agenda setting in various ways. Experiments by Iyengar and Kinder (1987) and others indicate that a related priming phenomenon can occur. This occurs when audiences use issues emphasized in the news to form broader judgments. "By calling attention to some matters while ignoring others, television news influences the standards by which governments, presidents, policies, and candidates for public office are judged" (p. 63). Scholars have often assumed that priming results from the accessibility of cognitions or attitudes concerning issues. Priming theory "views people as the victims of the architecture of their minds . . . not by conscious *choice*, but merely because information about the issue appears automatically and effortlessly in consciousness" (J.M. Miller & Krosnick, 2000, p. 302; italics original). Perhaps education and conscious deliberation might counteract this tendency.

However, some recent work disputes the existence of accessibility in priming. J.M. Miller and Krosnick (2000, Experiment 2) manipulated whether students saw TV news stories concerning issues such as pollution or crime. The manipulations evidently increased issue accessibility, but the latter did not affect the issues influencing their evaluation of President Clinton's performance. When it appeared, priming occurred only among politically knowledgeable people who rated news trustworthiness as high and who also used news to make inferences about issue import. Therefore,

People who evidence priming appear not to be unknowing victims of a powerful and manipulative force. Rather, they are political experts who apparently *choose* to rely on a source they trust to help them sort through the wealth of information they have obtained in order to make judgments. (J.M. Miller & Krosnick, 2000, p. 312; italics original)

The import of their finding for the health of democracy depends on whether news media personnel deserve such trust by selecting stories based on news values. In short, are doubters too cynical or are trusters suckers? The authors cautioned, however, that accessibility could still oc-

cur in natural, nonexperimental contexts. Here people may not be as motivated to think rationally. Their findings contradict earlier "real-world"
correlational research that priming occurs mostly among the less knowledgeable (Krosnick & Kinder, 1990) and experimental evidence that priming seems to occur to a similar extent among both the politically skilled
and unskilled (Iyengar & Kinder, 1987). This would seem to suggest treating the Miller and Krosnick findings as tentative. A complicated
correlational relationship among independent variables, perhaps only
dealt with adequately by the 2000 study, might explain the varied results,
however (see J.M. Miller & Krosnick, 2000).

Interestingly, agenda setting rather than accessibility emerged as a mediator of priming (J.M. Miller & Krosnick, 2000, Experiment 1). According
to evidence, "in order for priming to occur, agenda setting must occur
first, and priming sometimes follows" (p. 311). In addition, agenda setting
occurred most strongly among those who trust news and know a lot about
politics. It "implies that, like, priming, agenda setting may be a more
thoughtful, deliberative process than previously thought" (p. 312). Unlike
priming, agenda setting also "occurred among people who were neither
highly trusting nor highly knowledgeable, which suggests that agenda
setting might also occur automatically and with little cognitive effort
among certain citizens" (p. 312). Beyond this, priming may have an especially important influence on people's voting decisions. Of course, in a
spectatorial rather than participatory democracy, most people's involvement in politics at most largely involves casting ballots every so often to decide what gang of rascals to turn the government over to.

At bottom, clear evidence exists today that the media not only tell what
people what to think about, but that what people think about influences
what they think. D. Weaver (1991) took this notion even further. His research showed significant relationships not only between the salience of
the federal budget deficit in the media and the directions of opinion people held about the deficit, but between media salience and political behavior. As salience grew, people became more likely to sign petitions, attend
meetings, and write letters concerning the deficit.

The potential consequences of agenda setting and related forms of research for society are probably rather obvious. Because of the phenomenon,
the media may help build a degree of consensus among the public and
policymakers about what issues are most important. The evidence that the
mass agenda influences that of policymakers perhaps may seem hopeful
for democracy as well. In short, an agenda "is a familiar tool for collective
behavior, for a community to think together about matters of shared consequence" (Carter et al., 1992, p. 869). Yet it is clear that the news agenda does
not always reflect the import of issues, as indicated by objective indicators
(see chap. 5). In this sense, it clearly confirms certain of Lippmann's fears

during the early 20th century. Thus, to avoid becoming overly concerned with trivia, news consumers need to be educated about and understand the agenda-setting effect and related phenomena. News personnel also need to consider this consequence of their work. Too often, inappropriate emphases in the news may contribute to a failure among media audiences to recognize, and base their judgments on, issues that ultimately will matter to them. Here the role of theory may be especially important. "We need to understand agenda setting well enough to suggest what the media might do that would improve the public's capability to think together about its common problems" (Carter et al., 1992, p. 870).

Today, then, agenda setting may represent one of the more important consequences of mass communication. Whether this will remain so in the future, as technological innovation continues, is debatable. Conceivably, as interactive forms of news delivery replace traditional forms such as printed newspapers, people could increasingly set their own agenda, rendering contemporary concerns about the influence of media agendas largely moot.

Public Opinion as a Discursive Process

Perhaps Noelle-Neumann exaggerated the influence of pressures toward conformity. Instead, as Blumer thought, the processes of public opinion may arise more from a lack of agreement within a public with reference to a conflictual issue (V. Price & Allen, 1990).

The discursive processes approach draws on a rather eclectic mixture of earlier work, including cognitive psychology (see chap. 6), the early pragmatists' concept of public opinion, Lippmann's writings, and the study of small groups and intergroup communication. It rests on the idea that "public opinion arises out of a communicative response to changing circumstances — circumstances that dictate a need for collective action" (V. Price, 1988, p. 662). Hence, researchers "seek theories to explain an information-processing phenomenon that is both social (*public*) and cognitive (*opinion*)" (V. Price, 1988, p. 660).

Mass communication is central to such work. In theory, mass media "allow coordinated mass attention, thought, and expression across a large and heterogeneous group to the brought to bear upon a shared problem of issue" and thereby "allow for the transformation of the mass (as a group of disconnected individuals) into an organizing, structured public" (V. Price, 1988, p. 665). According to social identification theory, the organization of public opinion occurs in three steps. First, the media can provide people with information about what groups are involved with an issue, causing them to "perceive themselves and others in relation to the issue primarily as members of groups" (V. Price, 1988, p. 672). Second, "by depicting how those groups are responding to the issue, media reports can indicate the normative group opinions people may adopt" (V. Price, 1988, p. 672). In effect, people learn the stereotypical features, often in an exaggerated way, of various groups as they pertain to the issue. Finally, "people impute their group's perceived opinion norm to themselves and become more likely to express this exaggerated norm" (V. Price, 1988, p. 672). Therefore, news reports can lead people to respond to issues in terms of group identities, contributing to the emergence of a public as time passes.

One study (V. Price, 1989) yielded experimental evidence that is largely consistent with this model. College students majoring in hard science or engineering fields and in humanities or social-scientific fields received news articles portraying student opinion about a university plan to increase curricular requirements. If the article pictured opinion as split, both groups of majors tended to oppose the plan. Yet when the news portrayed a split along the lines of type of major, students tended to express opinions consistent with their own group.

GENERAL CONSEQUENCES OF PUBLIC OPINION RESEARCH

Many of the same social issues that arise with persuasion research in general also apply to studies of public opinion — a topic that is of particular concern to practitioners of public relations. Unlike advertising, public relations attempts to influence the perceptions of various publics, rather than sell products. Also unlike advertising, it does not underwrite the costs of news gathering and dissemination (although its practitioners sometimes do aid as well as try to manipulate such processes). Perhaps even more than in the past, the influence of those who would manipulate the pseudoenvironment of the public is troubling. Modern techniques designed to influence opinion continue to appear. More than a decade ago, Singer (1987) expressed a probably prescient concern:

> Daily polls, instantaneous results, the ability to link opinions with demographics in narrowly defined areas — all these, combined with desktop publishing and interactive systems, make it possible to tailor persuasive messages to microenvironments rather than mass publics. If, as seems likely, even the mass media may have more than minimal effects, there is a real possibility that specialized media, carrying specialized messages, will be more effective still. (p. S1)

The research reviewed here tends, with varying degrees of empirical support, to picture media audiences as subject to a number of different, sometimes less than healthy, opinion processes. Audiences sometimes form distorted impressions of the "real" world from TV drama, they may adjust their public behavior to conform with media-linked perceptions of social correctness, they may (or may not) judge political candidates based on peripheral issues emphasized in TV news, and they often take stands on different issues based on mediated descriptions of positions taken by groups to which they belong. These findings, along with evidence that mass opinion influences the behavior of leaders (e.g., Page & Shapiro, 1983), do not speak entirely well for classic democratic ideals.

Yet the situation may not be hopeless. Existing research may merely illustrate the difficulties inherent in using existing media to solve society's need for mass communication (Carter, 1990). Perhaps researchers can contribute to more meaningful forms of public discourse about issues perhaps by pointing out the problems with common news techniques and by public education about the nature of news and related fields.

Beyond this, researchers might even help devise improved means of mass communication to help create a genuine public—an entity that has no "corporate existence" and "must be constituted" (Carter, 1990, p. 283). Of course, this is a goal of the civic journalism movement (Merritt, 1998) discussed in chapter 1.

Thus, agenda-setting research "might well be seen as a research and development effort on behalf of society—as a project in what might be and not just as a hypothesis about what has been" (Carter et al., 1992, p. 877). Humans "must be able to share thoughts to come to a shared idea, an agreement predicated on mutual understanding. This constructed agreement—this 'public opinion'—can then guide the moves we make together" (Carter, 1990. p. 283). As Blumer (1946) said, "It is only in this way that the public, divided as it is, can come to act as a unit" (p. 192). In short, modern society perhaps suffers from an excess of publics and the lack of a real Public, as Dewey suggested. Perhaps, left by themselves, individual people are incompetent to judge political policies. Competence possibly occurs only when people get together and reach a consensus. Maybe today, even more than during the 1920s, researchers face an essential problem. In Dewey's (1927/1946) words, the world continues to need "the improvement of the methods and conditions of debate, discussion and persuasion" (p. 208).

MASS COMMUNICATION AND CIVIC ENGAGEMENT

Putnam's TV Indictment

In addition to affecting the opinions of rather spectatorial masses, forms of mediated communication may make creation of participatory democracy much more difficult than otherwise. Modern research seems on its way to warranting the following assertion:

> The increase in the number, variety, and cheapness of amusements repre-
> sents a powerful diversion from political concern. The members of an incho-
> ate public have too many ways of enjoyment, as well as of work, to give
> much thought to organization into an effective public. (Dewey, 1927/1946,
> pp. 138–139)

Putnam (1995, 2000) provided evidence that substantial declines in social capital and civic engagement (see chap. 8) occurred in the United
States from the 1960s through the 1990s. These trends seem especially
noteworthy because they occurred as the educational level of the population grew. Education correlates positively and substantially with social
capital and engagement. Putnam's sources include membership records
in bowling leagues and labor unions. He also cited data pertaining to interpersonal trust, membership in the Parent–Teacher Association, frequencies of voting and working on community projects, driver obser-
vance of stop signs, religious participation, and much more. In his famous
bit of poetic license, people today are *bowling alone*; in truth, they often
bowl together, but without joining leagues (Putnam, 2000).

Putnam has devoted much effort to explaining these declines, which often show up primarily among persons born after World War II. As he
(1995) put it, "It is as though the post-war generations were exposed to
some mysterious X-ray that permanently and increasingly rendered them
less likely to connect with the community" (p. 676). After considering suspects such as family instability and economic climates, Putnam (1995) initially indicted, but said he was not ready to convict, TV as the cause. This
meshed with some earlier research. For example, Tan (1977) paid people
not to watch for a week and observed that their social activities increased.
Television might destroy social capital by taking time away from social
activities, by cultivating a distrust of others, as well as in its general childhood socialization effects, Putnam noted. Here, I focus primarily on evidence pertaining to its effects on social capital.

According to Putnam's data, the United States today largely replicates
Italy's north–south social–capital divide (see the discussion in chap. 8).
The states with the most social capital include the Dakotas, Minnesota,
and Vermont. Nevada and many southeastern states rank at the bottom.
His work in a sense echoes Morgan (1986), who found that the TV-
induced mainstream of U.S. political attitudes resembles those typically
found among residents of the South. As a British newsmagazine put it,
Putnam "is too polite to say so, but he clearly feels the whole country is becoming like those American states that are already conspicuously lacking
in social capital, notably Mississippi, Louisiana and other states in the old
Confederacy" ("American Politics," 2000, p. 86).

Critics have challenged Putnam's evidence of declining engagement and trust. Perhaps most prominent was the late Everett C. Ladd, head of the Roper Center for Public Opinion Research. According to Ladd (1999): "Contemporary America hasn't dissipated the country's historic reserve of social capital. We really do have a chance to pass on to succeeding generations a richer supply than any predecessor enjoyed" (p. 156). Ladd's survey evidence, for example, showed rising levels of charitable giving and volunteering. Even if correct, Ladd's arguments might not acquit TV, which still could dampen ongoing social–capital increases.

Similarly, others challenged aspects of the TV indictment. Norris (1996) found an association between more time spent watching TV and less political activity, although some of the findings slipped below significance when controls were applied. He also reported that increased viewing of current-affairs programs covaried with greater activity. In another correlational analysis, Moy, Scheufele, and Holbert (1999) examined Putnam's time-displacement hypothesis. They found evidence that a person's TV viewing reduces his or her civic engagement, but not because of time pressures. Instead, TV use may be "functionally equivalent to group membership" in that it exposes people to previously private activity, "behavior that very closely parallels interpersonal behavior" (p. 39). Similar to other studies, they associated both more newspaper reading and watching TV news with increased engagement. In other correlational analyses, Shah (1998) reported very mixed evidence, and Uslander (1998) found little support for the TV indictment. Clearly, Putnam's ideas are young by social scientific standards. Decades of scientific work, rather than individual studies, will provide their real test.

In a more recent book, Putnam (2000) presented voluminous amounts of data, including some from Roper, bearing on his thesis. In general, he took some of the work of critics such as Ladd into account yet retained a largely intact bowling-alone conclusion. For instance, one controversy involved PTA membership. Ladd (1999) alleged that it has declined as parents merely replaced the PTA with similar groups. Putnam (2000) partially acknowledged this. Even so, parental participation still declined substantially after 1960, Putnam claimed. Only future scholarship will show if his most recent work helps create greater scholarly consensus about his ideas than has existed previously. Some relatively initial positive reviews of the book (e.g., Barber, 2000) suggest that it may.

Putnam (2000) modified his 1995 indictment of TV. He presented additional evidence linking watching with diminished engagement, but also examined the possible impact of program types. Following a simultaneous analysis of numerous variables expected to forecast social participation, he reported that dependence on TV for entertainment is "*the single most consistent predictor* that I have discovered" of someone's civic disengagement (p. 231; italics original). In addition, a person's exposure to types of programming correlated with his or her civic activity, holding constant demographics and total time spent watching the medium. In this way, Putnam found evidence that watching news programs contributes to engagement. In the same way, however, he showed that viewing daytime programs—such as those with game, quiz, and talk formats—relates negatively with engagement. He wrote, "Those program types that are most closely associated with civic isolation constitute a massive and growing share of television programming" (p. 244).

In summary, Putnam (2000) suggested that TV, along with related electronic media such as VCRs, accounts for about 25% of declines in U.S. social capital. Other factors—such as growing financial pressures, suburban growth, and generational change—also contribute, he said. The replacement of the unusually civic World War II generation by baby boomers and Generation X appears especially important. As he put it, "At the very least, television and its electronic cousins are willing accomplices in the civic mystery we have been unraveling, and more likely than not, they are ringleaders" (p. 246).

Unfortunately, much available data leave issues of reverse causation—the idea that civic detachment may lead to television viewing instead of the opposite—unaddressed. As Putnam (2000) put it, "Truly conclusive evidence on this crucial point is not at hand, and given ethical restrictions on human experimentation, it is not likely to be available any time soon" (p. 235). One might expect, for instance, that among lonely, withdrawn persons, TV use represents a functional alternative to interpersonal interaction (see Finn & Gorr, 1988; Perse & Rubin, 1990). Thus, perhaps only an effect of detachment on viewing occurs. A fair amount of work suggests otherwise, however (see Putnam, 2000, for a partial review). For example, along with their other evidence, Moy, Scheufele, and Holbert (1999) reported that a model based on an assumption that civic engagement affects media use did not fit their data beyond chance.

Actually, Putnam (2000) may even understate TV's role a bit. He may not have considered certain indirect ways that TV might diminish social capital. For example, Meyrowitz (1985) theorized (see chap. 11) that TV contributed to the massive movement of U.S. women into the labor force a few decades ago. Increased numbers of working women caused a small part of the decline, Putnam (2000) suggested.

Barber (2000) cogently interpreted Putnam's position: "Television may be social capital's most insidious enemy" (p. 32). Viewers "communicate less, go to church less, volunteer less, attend club meetings less and are less given to comity in their social relations" p. (32). Because it privatizes leisure time, probably clinically addicts audiences (who value it mostly for its low cost), and encourages passivity, TV "reinforces a world of watching rather than doing" (p. 32). In short, Dewey redux.

Also in an apparent response to critics, Putnam (2000) noted that social capital has its dark side. In this light, he discussed two dimensions of it. *Bonding* capital operates within social groups and may at times encourage exclusion of outsiders. In contrast, *bridging* capital works across groups and may foster tolerance. In general, however, Putnam found different benefits from each. "Strong ties with intimate friends may ensure chicken soup when you're sick, but weak ties with distant acquaintances are more likely to produce leads for a new job" (p. 363). Nonetheless, one suspects that when only the former exists, it may tend to replace the rugged individualism of the individual with the perhaps slightly less nominalist rugged individualism of the subgroup or special interest assembly. In contrast, a Peircean social realist would consider a person ethical only if his or her behavior takes into account the future well-being of the entire human community (Lewis & Smith, 1980). Even assemblages such as the Ku Klux Klan, the Peruvian Red Path guerrillas, or a fatty food marketers' association might benefit from bonding capital. Unfortunately, it remains a bit unclear to what extent evidence of media effects applies with these subtypes of social capital.

Putnam (2000) also explored the consequences of declining social capital. These appear to include more crime, poorer public health, shorter life expectancy, and lower educational attainment. Less economic prosperity and weaker and more corrupt democratic practices also may follow. He based his conclusions on both prior research and his own data analyses. In most cases, the causal mechanisms remain a bit unclear, but Putnam discussed many plausible theories. For example, social capital may reduce crime by developing continuity and responsibility in citizens. It may encourage healthy behavior and stimulate the immune system. It promotes parental involvement with the education of their children, and it can help connect people with potential economic partners. In addition, its norms of reciprocity may discourage tax cheating.

In some cases, readers may find Putnam's (2000) conclusions a bit astonishing. For instance, concerning social capital and health, he wrote, "If you smoke and belong to no groups, it's a toss-up statistically whether you should stop smoking or start joining" (p. 331). Beyond this, he noted that public health researchers have concluded that moving from a low to a high social-capital state would be almost as propitious as giving up smoking. In terms of health and other correlates of enhanced social capital, the northern tier states often outperform, and parts of the South all too frequently flounder. These include longer life expectancy, greater children's welfare, better educational performance, and lower rates of both TV viewing among kids and homicide.

To make joining a bit easier and thereby promote good health, should one also turn off Oprah and Ricki, switch on the local news, or read the Sunday paper? If Putnam is right, what can be done? Rather than tell people to "Just say 'No!' " to the TV, he (2000) offered the following challenge to media industries and their audiences:

> *Let us find ways to ensure that by 2010 Americans will spend less time sitting passively alone in front of glowing screens and more time in active connection with our fellow citizens. Let us foster new forms of electronic entertainment and communication that reinforce community engagement rather than forestalling it.* (p. 410; italics original)

Examples might include civic journalism (see chap. 1), which often involves both electronic and print news media, and use of the Internet in ways that enhance social capital, according to Putnam.

The Internet

By 1999, an estimated 62 million people, still only 1% of humanity, used the Internet (Biocca, 2000). Explosive future growth seems inevitable. This has created both concerns and hopes about its implications for future human communities. For example, civic journalist Davis Merritt (1998) discussed "Harold the Rutabaga Man." Harold is a mythical soul who resides in the future and spends his time in online discussions with the handful of others in the world who share his rutabaga obsession. Obviously, Harold is not likely to participate meaningfully in politics. He raises the specter of future human communities that exist only online among those sharing extremely narrow informational fetishes. Yet some scholars argue that the Internet will lead to improved social relationships by freeing people from geographical constraints and isolation due to illness or social stigmata (see the review in Kraut et al., 1998).

Available evidence so far is quite mixed. Some (Kraut et al, 1998; Putnam, 2000; Tewksbury & Althaus, 2000) suggests that Merritt's fears may not be entirely imaginary. For example, Putnam (2000) found that people who rely on the Internet for news tend to display less civic involvement than do others. In one widely publicized study, Kraut et al. (1998) used longitudinal data to study the social and psychological impact of the first year or two of one's usage of the Internet. Greater use correlated with less family communication, declining social circles, and increased depression and loneliness. Effect sizes often appeared modest, however. Two causal mechanisms may explain these patterns, according to Kraut et al. First, perhaps like TV, time with the Internet may simply detract from other social activities. Nonetheless, this explanation seems less than compelling because much Internet use, such as e-mail, is social, according to

Kraut et al. However, the Internet may lead people to substitute weak social ties for stronger ones. Online friends probably will not perform tangi-
ble favors, for example, such as baby-sitting or small loans, they noted.
Putnam (2000) suggested that weak ties enhance bridging social capital,
however, implying that online acquaintances are not necessarily bad. In
any case, to deal with such problems, Kraut et al. suggested such things as
policy initiatives to promote interpersonal communication on the Internet
and the development of technology to enhance the ease with which people, as well as information, can be located.

The Kraut et al. study must be regarded as quite tentative for a couple
of reasons. First, the sample consisted of members of 93 intentionally unrepresentative families: those with teenagers in high school journalism
classes and those in which an adult served on the board of a community
development organization. The researchers wanted participants with
some existing common interests. J.S. Shapiro (1999) claimed that they "in-
advertently selected participants whose social contacts were likely to decline during the course of the study, even without Internet access" (p.
782). This could occur for reasons such as teenagers going off to college. In
addition, cross-sectional research by J.E. Katz and Aspden (1997) found no
differences between Internet users and others on a variety of interpersonal
communication and membership variables following statistical controls.
In fact, these scholars suggested that the Internet is enhancing existing social relationships. In short, somewhat dark clouds have appeared. To
what extent they contain harmful pollution or beneficial rain may not be
quite clear for some time to come.

10

Unintended Effects of Mass Communication: The Impact of Media Violence and Sex

In part because of the sheer volume of evidence now available, researchers looking at the effects of media violence or sexually explicit materials sometimes resemble the legendary blind men who examined an elephant. The men came to many different, contradictory conclusions as they examined different sections of the animal's body. Depending on research questions (e.g., the impact of media violence on young children or adolescents) and sometimes on rather subtle variation in methods used, the findings vary tremendously. In addition, perhaps more so than in other areas of effects research, political (and perhaps religious) agendas often have influenced (if not determined) the specific topics investigated. In particular, changes in the political agenda of U.S. liberalism clearly have been important because most social scientists work in an academic culture dominated by it (see the discussion in L. Berkowitz, 1971). For example, during the 1960s, many liberals viewed sexually explicit materials as a healthy form of rebellion against old-fashioned, Puritanical values. Indeed, U.S. leftists often idolized macho revolutionary heroes such as Argentine revolutionary Che Guevara, and ads for sexual materials provided a significant source of support for countercultural newspapers. Liberals expressed concern about media violence, especially John Wayne-type movies depicting the virtues of U.S. territorial conquest. They nonetheless tended to treat adult sexuality in almost all its forms as politically correct. Early research was quite congenial to this view. Concerns about media sex came primarily from conservatives, some of whom displayed a religious agenda that rather dogmatically considered sexual materials harmful prima facie. By the mid-1970s, the influence of feminism became extremely pronounced in progressive academic circles, and some researchers began pursuing research questions suggested by some of the more radical (and puritanical) feminists. Not surprisingly, as the questions changed, so did the answers.

To say that ideological contexts influence the nature of research is not to say that ideology determines research findings. In fact, at times this is clearly not the case. For instance, no one could fairly allege that all significant researchers into the impact of media violence or sex hold uniformly liberal beliefs. Nonetheless, social scientists in this area (and other particularly controversial areas, such as the effects of school busing) may be especially prone to selective interpretation of research data for unconsciously political purposes. What a blind man thinks about the form of the elephant is not solely the result of his sense of touch. His expectations and previous experiences (and perhaps also his hopes) factor into his perceptions. Only as time passes and a variety of often conflicting political agendas play themselves out and cause researchers to examine different questions can a relatively complete picture emerge. Unfortunately, by that time, the structure of the elephant may have changed significantly. For example, new technological developments, especially forms of virtual reality, promise to add new dimensions to the debate about media sex and violence. For example, computer technology likely will continue to create a variety of participatory forms of simulated sex and violence within the foreseeable future. This doubtlessly will keep some critics happily worried and researchers occupied with all sorts of novel questions for decades to come.

This chapter contains two primary sections. The first deals with the impact of media violence. Reviews (e.g., Grossman & DeGaetano, 1998; B.J. Wilson et al., 1998) often identify three major effects: behavioral aggression, desensitization, and increased fear. The focus here primarily is on the first of these, given the voluminous amounts of evidence bearing on it and the social significance of behavioral phenomena. The second section deals with the impact of sexual media contents on various attitudes and behaviors. Researchers interested in these phenomena often study attitudes because ethical and legal problems prevent them from examining more meaningful behavioral phenomena such as sexual battery. Nonetheless, this chapter also emphasizes effects on behavior—especially its aggressive and criminal forms—as the outcomes of primary interest

THE MOST RESEARCHED ISSUE: THE IMPACT OF TV VIOLENCE

On October 6, 1977, a jury in Miami convicted 15-year-old Ronald Zamora of the first-degree murder of 82-year-old Elinor Haggart. Zamora was also convicted of burglary, possession of a firearm while committing a felony, and robbery. The jury deliberated for only about 2 hours. Despite his age,

Zamora was sentenced as an adult to life in prison. Under Florida law, he is not eligible for parole until he has served at least 25 years.

His defense attorney did not dispute the physical facts of the case. Zamora shot his elderly neighbor after she surprised him and another youth as they robbed her Miami Beach apartment. The issue of the potential causal impact of TV violence, however, was what really made the case noteworthy and newsworthy beyond the Miami area.

Zamora's defense attorney, Ellis Rubin, unsuccessfully argued that the young man was innocent because he suffered from temporary insanity linked to habitual exposure to TV violence. Zamora regularly spent several hours each day watching extremely violent programs on TV. He became especially obsessed with the TV character Kojak and wanted to shave his head in imitation of the TV cop played by actor Telly Savalas. Supposedly years of viewing had left the youth unable to distinguish, when he murdered the woman, between the fantasy world on TV and reality.

The defense suffered a major setback when the judge refused to allow as evidence social-scientific studies suggesting that a causal link exists between exposure to TV violence and aggressive behavior. In addition to psychiatric evidence, the judge would only allow studies that linked specific acts of media violence to specific instances of behavior, and no such studies existed. Without the social-scientific evidence, the defense clearly failed to impress the jury.

Did the novel defense have any basis in truth? Perhaps. Today, the evidence is in many ways much stronger than in 1977 that we live in a more violent or at least aggressive society as a result of the widespread presence of TV violence. The similar conclusions reached by groups such as the American Medical Association, American Psychological Association, the Centers for Disease Control and Prevention, and the National Academy of Science (see the review in B.J. Wilson et al., 1998) indicate substantial scholarly consensus.

The more recent evidence at times is both controversial and somewhat surprising to those familiar with the limited-effects background of communication research. Most dramatically, Centerwall (1992) argued that TV and TV violence contribute to roughly 50% of homicides in the United States. This perhaps involved as much as 10,000 murders in some years. Based on an epidemiological study initially involving comparisons among Canada, South Africa, and the United States, he concluded that roughly 10 to 15 years after TV is introduced into a society, rates of murder are likely to double. Rates of other violent crimes such as rape and injurious assault also tend to double, although the data are less well developed. What has happened, according to Centerwall, is that the first generation raised with TV from infancy has reached the crime-prone years of adolescence and early adulthood. In contrast, TV apparently has much less effect on adolescent or adult aggression (Paik & Comstock, 1994). Due to the potentially extreme social significance of Centerwall's work, it receives especially detailed scrutiny in this chapter.

Exposure by Young People to TV Violence

That very high levels of violence exist on U.S. TV and young people spend huge amounts of time viewing it is virtually beyond dispute. Academic debates exist about just what constitutes violence; but no matter how one defines it, a lot is present on TV (McGuire, 1986a). For example, in 1994, The National Cable Television Association funded studies related to TV violence, such as its presence in contents carried by 23 U.S. broadcast and cable channels. The studies (*National Television Violence Study,* 1997–1998) involved researchers at the Universities of California at Santa Barbara; North Carolina at Chapel Hill; Texas at Austin; and Wisconsin at Madison. Overall, the work found continuing high levels of violence especially on premium cable channels.

What is less clear, however, is why so much violence exists. Research (e.g., Diener & DeFour, 1978) has failed to show that violence enhances program ratings. One possibility is that violence enhances the marketability of U.S. programs abroad. McGuire (1986a) suggested that many producers and writers may lack the talent to create material of real artistic value and tend to use violent content as a substitute. Yet advertisers today are often less interested in overall ratings for programs than in what type of people see a show. One Times Mirror poll indicated that persons under age 30 are more likely than older persons to watch violence on TV (Rosenstiel, 1993). Advertiser desires to sell products to younger adults and adolescents may account for much of the violence on the tube. In this light, J.T. Hamilton (1998) suggested that the advertisers' interest in females between the ages of 18 and 34 helps explain the presence of media violence. He found no evidence that children are targeted, however. This could somewhat distinguish TV from the game, motion picture, and music industries. In 2000, the Federal Trade Commission (FTC) accused these three of using mechanisms such as TV ads to market sexual and violent fare to children.

In any case, children typically see substantial amounts of TV violence. Young people typically watch about 16 or 17 hours of TV weekly, starting as young as age 2, and see thousands of violent acts annually according to some research (Neilsen Media Research, 1998, as cited in Strasburger & Donnerstein, 1999). U.S. youth ages 8 to 18 watch about 3.25 hours daily, and about 65% have sets in their bedrooms (D.F. Roberts, 2000). The National Television Violence Study examined forms of violence that, according to empirical evidence, contain a high risk of teaching aggression to children below age 7. These children may not distinguish fantasy entertainment from reality (B.J. Wilson et al., 1998). Such violence is concentrated in children's programming and child-oriented basic cable (B.J. Wilson et al., 1998).

Theoretical Ideas

Why might TV contribute to aggressive human behavior? A number of theoretical ideas concern the relationship between exposure to mediated violence and viewer aggression. McGuire (1986a) provided a useful typology, and this section in part relies on his categorizations of the theories. Some are *causal* theories, in McGuire's terms. They predict that exposure will influence aggressiveness. Others are *reverse causal* theories, describing reasons that aggressiveness could affect exposure. Within these categories, the theories can be subdivided into *positive* and *negative* theories. Positive theories predict that exposure and aggression correlate positively (i.e., where one is high, so is the other); negative theories predict negative relationships between the two (i.e., where one is high, the other tends to be low). One point to keep in mind is that these theories are not necessarily mutually exclusive. The fact that exposure may enhance aggression in one setting does not mean that aggression cannot also enhance exposure in the same setting or that exposure does not reduce aggression in another setting. All these theories could apply in different contexts.

Figure 10.1 depicts a typology of theories. Quite a large number of the theories are positive and causal (i.e., predict that exposure contributes to enhanced aggressiveness). One of the best known of these is *social learning,*

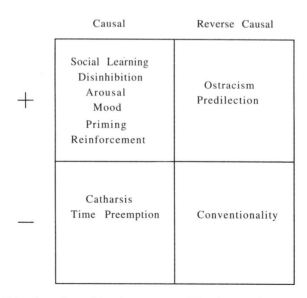

FIG. 10.1.   A typology of theories concerning TV violence and aggression.

or modeling, theory (Bandura, 1973). The theory implies that exposure may affect aggression because children tend to imitate what they see on the screen. This might be especially true if children identify aggressive characters or forms of violence that are rewarded or not punished. For an argument that links social learning theory with pragmatic contextualist philosophy, see Zimmerman (1983). Centerwall (1992) suggested that this mechanism goes a long way toward explaining why TV and TV violence may double homicide rates. Modeling, or imitative behavior, is a useful instinct that helps infant children learn many different forms of behavior needed for normal lives, he said. However, infants do not know what behaviors should be imitated (Centerwall, 1992). Later on, when a person faces severe stress, violence may erupt:

> it is precisely at such moments that adolescents and adults are most likely to revert to their earliest, most visceral sense of what violence is and what its role is in society. Much of this sense will have come from television. (Centerwall, 1992, pp. 3059–3060)

Another, somewhat related, idea is *disinhibition* theory. This suggests that exposure to mediated violence diminishes a person's biological or socially induced inhibitions against aggressive behavior, making future aggression by the person more likely. Human beings perhaps evolved aggressive capacities as a means of adapting to their environment in earlier stages of history, when people lived in hunter–gatherer societies. Today, of course, violence generally is dysfunctional in the modern world. Societies tend to develop cultural mechanisms, and species biological ones, inhibiting such behavior psychologically. Societies may also channel it into relatively acceptable forms such as game hunting. One possible effect of mediated violence is a gradual loss of such restraints against violence directed at other human beings. *Arousal* theory applies mainly to angry or chronically aggressive individuals. It predicts that exposure to mediated violence excites people, multiplying their underlying aggressive tendencies. *Mood* theory predicts that exposure to media violence creates bad moods in viewers, thus increasing their aggressive propensities. According to *priming* theory, exposure to media violence activates aggressive thoughts, increasing the chances that a person will behave antisocially. Beyond this, viewing mediated violence may reinforce one's existing violent tendencies, increasing the likelihood of such behavior.

A retired military psychologist, Lt. Col. Dave Grossman (1998) relied on some of these ideas to make a provocative argument. Human beings do not kill one another naturally, he said; in fact, they have a biologically programmed aversion to doing so. Historical studies indicate that most soldiers in the U.S. Civil War or even World War II would not shoot to kill. Eventually, the military learned to overcome this. As a result of knowledge of such things as classical and operant conditioning, about 90% of U.S. troops in Vietnam shot to kill. When children watch violent TV, it has similar effects, according to Grossman. In addition, such long-term exposure "makes them easy bait for the conditioning effects of violent video games" (Grossman & DeGaetano, 1998, p. 47).

However, some theoretical ideas predict that violence exposure actually reduces human aggression. The *catharsis* notion, which goes back to Aristotle and the ancient Greeks, is associated in its modern form with psychologist Seymour Feshbach (1955). According to this theory, exposure to mediated violence provides an aggressive person with a vicarious means of getting such behavior out of his or her system, thus lessening behavioral aggression. The second idea is even simpler. According to *time-preemption* theory, watching TV (including violence) simply lessens the time a person has available to wreak havoc in the streets.

Reverse causal theories are important because of the possibility that a reciprocal relationship exists between violence exposure and aggression. Each may feed on the other (i.e., exposure may enhance aggressiveness, which leads in turn to additional exposure). McGuire (1986a) mentioned two positive theories. *Predisposition* theory predicts that aggressive people are predisposed to like violence on TV and hence tend to view a lot of it. According to *ostracism* theory, having an aggressive personality causes others to shun a person, leaving the individual with nothing to do but sit home and watch TV with all its violence. *Conventionality* theory is the single idea that is both negative and reverse causal. It predicts that mild-mannered people tend to stay home and watch TV instead of going out and exposing themselves to the dangers in the outside world. Hence, a lack of aggressiveness could actually increase a person's exposure to TV violence in these instances.

Early Evidence

A number of early studies partly focused on the possible impact of media depictions of violence and criminality. Although more recent studies provide far more detailed evidence, early studies contain more than historical interest. They indicate that society has long had evidence that addresses its concerns. Early studies are also the only indicator of effects in earlier times characterized by relatively primitive forms of mass communication. Similar to certain modern studies, these sometimes primarily concerned whether an effect occurs, rather than the theoretical mechanisms producing it.

The Payne Fund Studies.   Research into the effects of mediated crime and violence actually predates, by a couple of decades, the arrival of TV as a popular mass medium. In the late 1920s and early 1930s, the Payne Fund studies assessed the impact of motion pictures, such as then popular gangster films, on young people. In one of the most significant of these studies, Blumer and Hauser (1933) primarily used qualitative techniques such as interviews with heads of penal institutions and life histories of delinquent youth. Such techniques at best are suggestive, rather than indicative, of media effects. They found evidence that exposure to movies played a role in shaping delinquent and criminal behaviors, although criminologists tend to criticize their methods (Lowery & DeFleur, 1983). In interpreting their findings, Blumer and Hauser stressed the roles of learning and imitative behavior, thus foreshadowing modern social learning theory. These and other findings of the Payne Fund studies contributed to forms of self-censorship of controversial topics within the motion picture industry that lasted into the 1960s. For several decades, motion picture themes that glorified criminal behavior and showed it being rewarded, particularly dangerous, according to social learning theory, tended to be absent from the silver screen.

Television and Children. Of course, TV became an established mass medium in much of the developed world by the mid-1950s. Public concern followed about the amounts of violence found on the medium. At that time in the United Kingdom, the Nuffield Foundation sponsored a major study of the impact of TV on the young at the suggestion of the British Broadcasting Corporation (BBC). Eventually, the results were published in a volume entitled *Television and the Child* (Himmelweit et al., 1958). The researchers found that the example set by parental viewing habits was important in influencing how much time children spend with TV. They also found that intelligent children watch the medium a good deal less than do less intelligent children. Based on ratings by teachers and personality inventories of the children, the authors reported finding no more aggressive or delinquent behavior among viewers than among nonviewers (who at that time were still fairly numerous). They did, however, suggest that crime and violence on TV may affect children who are emotionally disturbed (Himmelweit et al., 1958). They also recommended that crime and violence on TV be reduced during times at which children are likely to view the medium.

In the United States, the first major study of the effects of TV was carried out between 1958 and 1960. The findings from its 11 studies appeared in a volume entitled *Television in the Lives of Our Children* (Schramm et al., 1961). Regarding whether TV contributed to violent behavior, results suggest that little delinquent behavior could be traced directly to the medium, but that TV may play a role in some cases. Once again, the authors emphasized the role of parents—especially their ability to provide children with love and security—as a form of protection against harmful effects. Perhaps this research today is most memorable for its frequently quoted conclusion about TV effects:

> For *some* children, under *some* conditions, *some* television is harmful. For *other* children under the same conditions, or for the same children under *other* conditions, it may be beneficial. For *most* children, under *most* conditions, most television is probably neither harmful nor particularly beneficial. (p. 1)

Of course, concerned citizens, politicians, and parents want a simple answer, but this summation is not unlike answers repeatedly suggested by research into many domains of media effects.

The Surgeon General's Report.   The turbulence of the 1960s — in which U.S. rates of many violent crimes essentially doubled and violence took the lives of many prominent leaders — did little to reassure those with concerns about media violence. One political leader, above all, echoed these public concerns — U.S. Senator John Pastore, a Democrat from Rhode Island. Pastore served as chairman of the Senate Commerce Committee's Subcommittee on Communications, which oversees the FCC. Following some prodding by Pastore, the U.S. Surgeon General named a committee in 1969 to study the issue. Perhaps significantly, the Surgeon General's office allowed TV networks and the National Association of Broadcasters (NAB) to eliminate the names of some potential committee members. Even so, the report of the committee, formally known as the Surgeon General's Scientific Advisory Committee on Television and Social Behavior (1972), supported the idea that watching media violence increases the probability of aggressive behavior.

More Recent Evidence

Until relatively recently, the evidence available consisted primarily of cross-sectional correlational studies (in which researchers measured both variables at about the same time) and experiments looking at the short-term impact of mediated violence. In many instances, both tended to suggest that exposure enhances aggression in young people at least in the short run. Most studies show that if exposure to TV violence and aggression are measured at the same time, children who are high in exposure also tend to be high in aggressiveness (Milavsky et al., 1982). Following a meta-analysis of available studies, Wood, Wong, and Chachere (1991) found that experimental manipulations of media violence generally contribute to immediate increases in aggressiveness of children in unconstrained interaction, such as on playgrounds. Of course, the correlational studies do not meet all the criteria for causal inference, and experimental studies (in which researchers control TV exposure) may not represent what happens when children encounter TV violence under normal circumstances. Nonetheless, the two are complementary: Each tends to be strong in ways that the other tends to be weak. Other research has failed to provide evidence for negative causal theories such as catharsis (Goranson, 1970).

The most important issue, however, is not the short-term effects, which may wear off within minutes or hours. It is whether a child's exposure to TV violence contributes to long-term forms of aggression that may increase the likelihood of criminal behavior as he or she reaches adulthood. In this regard, aggression is a relatively stable characteristic as a child matures. To a sometimes amazing extent, by social scientific standards, one can predict how aggressive a child will be (in comparison with others) later from his or her behavior early in life (see the discussion in Huesmann & Eron, 1986b). Perhaps to a lesser extent, childhood aggression predicts the likelihood of adult criminality (see the discussion in Rosenthal, 1986). Nonetheless, directly studying the issue of the cumulative impact of exposure to TV violence during lengthy time periods is difficult and expensive. Obviously, direct experimentation is out of the question because researchers cannot control human TV-related behavior during long periods of time. Fortunately, evidence has become available in the last 20 years or so that provides much more insight into the long-term effects of mediated violence. Researchers have used a variety of innovative methods that examine long-term effects without the artificiality present in true experiments. These have retained some (but by no means all) of the controls present in short-term experimentation.

The NBC Study. During the late 1960s, the National Broadcasting Company (NBC) started an elaborate study into the long-term effects of mediated violence that was designed to answer, once and for all, widespread social concerns. J. Ronald Milavsky, then head of the social research department at NBC, and a team of researchers designed a panel study in which repeated measurements were taken on a sample of respondents during an extended period of time. The results appeared in book form some 15 years later (Milavsky et al., 1982). Respondents initially consisted of some 2,400 children in Grades 3 to 6 and more than 600 boys ages 13 to 19. For each child, the researchers measured exposure to TV violence and aggression as many as six different times during a period of as much as 3 years. They measured exposure by asking children to identify their viewership of 45 different shows during previous weeks. To assess aggression among elementary school children, each child's classmates were asked to identify whether they had seen the child engaging in various aggressive acts. These included pushing and shoving other children. For the adolescent boys, the researchers relied on self-report indicators of aggressiveness. Their basic model—to simplify things with minimal distortion—involved relating initial viewing to later changes in observed aggression.

The results of the NBC study were controversial. After voluminous amounts of analyses, Milavsky and his colleagues concluded that no evidence exists that violence exposure contributes to long-term changes in aggression among young people. Undergraduate students often react by wondering whether the NBC link to the research did not predetermine the authors' conclusions. There is no evidence of this, however. More sophisticated critics (e.g., Kenny, 1984; McGuire, 1986a) reacted by arguing that the data in fact suggested a weak effect. Whether one interprets the results as suggesting a weak effect or none at all depends on some technical issues in data analysis. Nonetheless, it is clear that the NBC study failed to provide evidence of a long-term, powerful effect among youths in the age group studied. As such, it suggests a minimalist answer to social concerns: TV has little or nothing to do with enhanced aggression at least beyond very short-term situations.

The Cross-National Studies.   One criticism of the NBC study was that it "approached the problem from an atheoretical perspective that provided little guidance for selecting appropriate analyses" (Huesmann & Eron, 1986b, p. 7). Huesmann and Eron (1986c) organized a series of theoretically guided studies using similar methods. The measure of aggression included mildly criminal behavior, such as peer reports of a child starting a fight or taking other childrens' possessions without asking.

Huesmann and Eron suggested that one major difference exists between research concerning the impact of media violence and cigarette smoking. According to them, "a physiological model exists to explain how smoking causes cancer, whereas we do not yet have an adequate psychological model to explain the process by which television viewing engenders aggression" (Huesmann & Eron, 1986a, p. 49). An information-processing model concerning how children might learn and recall schemas and strategies for aggressive behavior, and within which a variety of processes such as social learning and disinhibition might occur, guided the work. An attempt was made to identify variables, such as a child's identification with characters, that may explain or enhance any exposure–aggression relationship.

The studies concerned TV violence viewing and aggression in five different countries: Australia, Finland, Israel, Poland, and the United States. The research, conducted by investigators in each of the countries, examined children for 2 years. The children were in the first and third grades at the start of data collection. In most instances, the researchers found evidence that violence viewing contributed to enhanced aggression. Apparent exceptions included Australian children and Israeli children in kibbutzim — a form of collective farm. Beyond this, factors such as identification with TV characters sometimes appeared to contribute as well. Huesmann

(1986) suggested that, during a sensitive time period early in life, children acquire scripts or programs for behavior. Viewing media violence may not only teach such scripts to children, but may serve as a cue for children to recall those they have learned previously.

In some cases, reverse causation also seemed present; aggression predicted future increases in viewing of TV violence. Thus, children may turn to media violence for justification when faced with the consequences of their aggression, such as ostracism by parents or peers. Based on the U.S. data, Huesmann and Eron (1986a) stated a conclusion much different from that of the NBC researchers:

> A plausible model to explain these findings seems to be a multi-process, reciprocal action model, in which violence viewing and aggression mutually facilitate each other, contribute to academic and social failure, and are engendered by such failure. Imitation of specific aggressive acts undoubtedly plays a role, but such imitation may be no more important than the attitude changes TV violence produces, the justification for aggressive behavior TV violence provides, the scripts for aggressive behavior it teaches, the cues for aggressive problem solving it furnishes, or the social and intellectual isolation it encourages. (pp. 78–79)

Such effects nonetheless may not appear strong by social-scientific standards (Huesmann, 1986). Some scholars (e.g., McGuire, 1986a) have suggested that the cross-national and NBC studies similarly suggest the existence of a somewhat weak effect. Nonetheless, they may complement earlier evidence that amount of TV viewing at age 8 predicts the seriousness of crimes committed by age 30 among both U.S. females and males (Eron & Huesmann, 1984).

The CBS–Belson Study.   With funding from CBS, William Belson (1978) investigated the possible contribution of TV violence to acts of serious violence among more than 1,500 teenage boys in the United Kingdom. Using self-report data, he compared boys of above and below average levels of lifetime exposure to TV violence. Following application of numerous controls, those boys with above-average exposure committed serious acts of violence 49% more often during the previous 6 months than did those with below-average exposure. Examples of serious violence included animal abuse, assault, and rape. Belson interpreted this as often resulting from disinhibition and, in some cases, imitation. He also reported no evidence that the most serious violent tendencies caused heavy violence viewing. However, he found evidence of a bidirectional effect involving TV and less serious forms of violence by the boys. Like all research, doubts can be raised about Belson's work—most obviously about the validity of his retrospective measure of violence exposure.

The Canadian Study.   In 1973, TV became available for the first time to a small, but evidently fairly typical, Canadian community. Just prior to this, a field study was designed (Joy et al., 1986). In it, trained coders recorded the amount of physical and verbal aggression during play time for a group of first- and second-grade children in the community and in two matched towns that already had the medium. The measure of physical aggression included mild forms of property and violent crime, such as stealing, hitting, and biting. The two towns with TV in effect served as control groups to eliminate possible confounds, such as any tendency for children to become more aggressive as they mature. Two years later, the behavior of the same children (n = 45) again was observed. In the town that had TV for only 2 years, the average rate of physical aggression per child had more than doubled. It increased from less than one incident every 2 minutes before TV to more than one per minute 2 years later. Verbal aggression was almost twice as high (Joy et al., 1986). Both changes attained significance. In the other two communities, no significant changes were observed. The study did not attempt to identify the theoretical reasons for this. According to the authors, however, a variety of interwoven mechanisms, including social learning and disinhibition, likely contributed to their findings.

However, there was one anomaly. At the start of the study, one might expect that children in the town without TV would display less aggressiveness than would children in the other two communities. This was not the case. Rather, the introduction of TV seemed to make children in the community in which TV was introduced 2 years earlier more aggressive than were children in the other towns. The authors speculated that the introduction of TV somehow disrupted the children's social systems. If so, enhanced aggression might last only long enough for the systems to reestablish themselves (Joy et al., 1986). Another possibility, however, is that something about the community that initially had no TV elevated aggressiveness among the children independently from the presence of the medium.

Thus, the Canadian study took advantage of a situation that is almost impossible to find in the modern, developed world today (i.e., researchers observed the behavior of children both before and after TV came to town). In the United States today, few nonviewers exist, and those are apt to differ from other people in all sort of ways in addition to TV use (see the discussion in Gerbner et al., 1981). Often nonexperimental researchers essentially must compare the behavior of people who spend different, but still substantial, amounts of time watching the medium. Because virtually everyone sees some TV, documenting effects can be especially difficult. The Canadian study thus suggests that effects may be stronger than the previously discussed panel studies imply. In comparison with the panel studies, the study may be especially meaningful because it relied on naturally observed behavior — perhaps a more valid measure than reputational or self-report indicators of aggression.

Studies such as this, and Centerwall's subsequently discussed epidemiological research, examine the impact of the presence of TV, rather than directly looking at TV violence exposure. A question sometimes arises (e.g., Medved, 1999) about the extent to which observed effects result from media violence. For example, Putnam's (2000) work suggests that even nonviolent entertainment TV may detract from existing social ties and thereby contribute to crime, including violence (see chap. 9). Of course, infallible answers are elusive. Nonetheless, vast amounts of experimental evidence implicate violence exposure as contributing to more aggressive behavior than does nonexposure or exposure to other forms of content. In addition, at least in the United States, the correlation between one's TV exposure and exposure to violence is very high (see Milavsky et al., 1982). Finally, Belson (1978) controlled for violence exposure and found no additional effect of TV exposure on serious violence among British youths. This tentatively warrants the assertion (if the reader will forgive a bit of intended redundancy) that violence at least is the predominant cause. Some in the industry may find this somewhat consoling. Evidence that TV in general, as well as violence in particular, contributes to violent crime could lead to especially severe forms of regulation.

The Epidemiological Approach. Based on an epidemiological technique seldom used by media-effects researchers, Centerwall (1989) articulated a kind of maximalist position about the impact of TV and TV violence. He argued that the introduction of the medium may double homicide rates in many cultures. He did the study while employed at the Centers for Disease Control and Prevention and later at the University of Washington.

Centerwall took advantage of a historical anomaly. Because of political differences in South Africa between Afrikaners (who are of Dutch ancestry) and English-speaking Whites, the Afrikaner-dominated government prohibited TV broadcasts until 1975. The Afrikaners felt that South African TV would rely on programming from English-speaking nations such as Great Britain, providing a cultural advantage to persons of English descent. This anomaly allowed Centerwall to compare changes in violent crime rates in South Africa with those of the United States and Canada, in which TV became a popular mass medium during the late 1940s and 1950s.

Results indicate that 10 to 15 years after the introduction of TV, murder rates doubled in Canada and the United States. During the same time period in South Africa, which remained without the medium, murder rates remained comparatively stable. He compared homicide rates among Whites in South Africa and the United States with overall rates in Canada, which had a 97% White population as of the early 1950s. He excluded U.S. and South African Blacks because of the vastly different conditions under which they live. Of course, this research technique, which uses "real-world" data to compare a case population with external control groups, leaves open the possibility that some unaccounted factor other than TV is producing the observed patterns. Centerwall (1989) examined a number of factors that might explain the data. These included changes in the three countries in percentages of the population that are ages 15 to 34 (the most likely people to commit homicide), changes in alcohol consumption, increased urbanization, and variations in economic conditions. None of these variables plausibly explained the results, he argued. However, research can never eliminate all confounding factors.

Because it examined murder rates, rather than indicators such as playground aggression, Centerwall's study appeared to make a strong case supporting people's worst fears about TV violence. Actually, it may be more consistent with earlier research than might appear at first glance. First of all, the time that lasting effects occur perhaps is prior to the onset of adolescence. After that age, exposure to media violence may have relatively little impact on aggressiveness (Paik & Comstock, 1994). Second, earlier long-term research (taken as a whole) seems to suggest at least a modest long-term effect. As Centerwall (1989) pointed out, even if TV only makes everyone slightly more aggressive, it theoretically could double the number of homicides in a society. Homicide is an extreme, and still very rare, form of aggression in the United States. Assume that variations in aggressiveness among humans form a Gaussian normal distribution — the bell-shaped curve that grades in many college courses approximate. Then a slight increase in the aggressiveness of everyone could double the number of people who exceed the homicide threshold at the extreme end of the curve (Centerwall, 1989). Previous studies that demonstrate individual-level effects render the issue of a possible ecological fallacy, which occurs when one falsely generalizes findings from groups to individuals, moot (see the discussion in Centerwall, 1989). In a kind of summary, he (Centerwall, 1996) wrote, "evidence indicates that if, hypothetically, television technology had never been developed, today 10,000 fewer homicides would occur in the United States, 70,000 fewer rapes, and 700,000 fewer injurious assaults" (p. 75).

The findings certainly merit a degree of skepticism. Earlier research linking media coverage of suicides to subsequent increases in suicide rates remains controversial (e.g., see the debate between J.N. Baron & Reiss, 1985, and Phillips & Bollen, 1985) although it is not clear that the objections would apply with Centerwall's research. In addition, an examination of the broader historical context of U.S. homicide trends suggests that claims that TV doubled homicide rates may exaggerate things. For one thing, overall U.S. murder rates (i.e., rates reflecting all ethnic groups) increased greatly during the 1960s, but only to about the same levels that the country experienced during the 1920s and 1930s—before TV was available to the public. Indeed, during the mid-1930s, overall U.S. homicide rates were actually substantially higher than at any point during the 1960s (U.S. Bureau of the Census, 1975). Keep in mind, however, that older data may be less valid than more recent information.

In fact, some researchers have attributed the increases in U.S. crime during the 1960s in large part to the post-World War II male generational cohort reaching the crime-prone years of adolescence and early adulthood (McGuire, 1986a). A historically high U.S. birth rate occurred from the mid-1940s to the early 1960s, roughly coinciding with the years in which the public acquired TV. Critics are likely to object to Centerwall's use of the 15- to 34-year-old age group to examine the impact of the proportion of people of crime-prone ages on murder rates. Centerwall (1989) reported that this proportion remained almost the same in the United States in 1970 as it was in 1950. For 1970, Centerwall lumped together a segment of the large post-World War II baby boom cohort with people born earlier, when substantially lower birth rates occurred.

Nonetheless, it seems unlikely that TV had nothing to do with increased murder rates. According to other evidence, only about 25% of the increase in U.S. homicides from 1950 to 1979 resulted from increased percentages of males ages 18 to 24 in the population (Huesmann & Eron, 1986b). In fact, the U.S. murder rate declined noticeably from 1980 to 1985. From 1985 to 1990, however, it increased by about 20% —back to roughly the 1980 level (U.S. Bureau of the Census 1992). The numbers of males ages 15 to 24 actually declined from 1980 to 1990. In addition, urban rates of arrest (per 100,000) for violent crimes began rising in 1960 disproportionately among youths ages 10 to 14 and somewhat later among older age groups (see Centerwall, 1989). Thus, the size of a population cohort apparently is not the predominant factor.

These data also make it difficult to argue that the levels of drug abuse in U.S. society from the 1960s onward is the major cause. To my knowledge, Centerwall has not discussed this factor. I know of no evidence that drug-related behavior increased first among those ages 10 to 14. The fact that overall rates of violent crime have remained at comparatively high levels since the 1960s, despite a somewhat aging population, also suggests that the large generational cohort cannot explain all of the increase.

During the years after its publication, however, a possible problem with Centerwall's research became evident. According to FBI crime data (USFBI, annual volumes), overall U.S. rates of murder and nonnegligent manslaughter, which FBI statistics combine, dropped substantially. After peaking in 1991, this rate fell by 41.8%—from 9.8 to 5.7 per 100,000 people—through 1999. In 1958, the year White homicide rates started increasing, the overall rate was 4.7. This largely reversed the increase he attributed to TV and TV violence—factors that have not exactly disappeared. Perhaps an unidentified correlate of the presence of medium, rather than TV, has been at work all along.

Yet an examination of additional data indicates that medical technology may account for a chunk of this reversal. Such things as surgical advances and 911 numbers may have turned many potential murders into lesser offenses such as aggravated assault (Grossman, 1998). Grossman estimated that if society still relied on the medical technology from 1940, U.S. homicide rates might be 10 times higher. If everything other than technology remained equal, homicides should decline with time, although improved weapons could offset this somewhat.

In fact, the 1990s apparently did not largely eliminate previous increases in violent crime. Keep in mind, however, that, due in part to underreporting, overall violent crime data are less valid than homicide data (O'Brien, 1985). During that time, overall violent crime decreased much less than did homicide, according to FBI data. From its 1991 peak to 1999, the rate of U.S. violent crime declined by only 30.7%. This FBI violent-crime index includes aggravated assault, forcible rape, homicide, and robbery. It fell from 758.1 to 534.7 per 100,000 (USFBI, annual volumes). The rate remained 4.3 times greater than the 122.1 per 100,000 level of 1958. Improved police productivity during the 1970s and 1980s could account for some of the remaining high levels of overall violent crime without affecting homicide rates (O'Brien, 1996). Even so, technological advances may have held down homicides uniquely. Perhaps factors such as longer criminal sentences, a strong economy, and even legalized abortion caused declines in U.S. crime without negating evidence about TV and TV violence.

Additional evidence that TV increased homicide rates came when Centerwall (1989) tested 11 follow-up hypotheses derived from the theory that introducing TV into a susceptible population increases homicides. All turned out as predicted, although one of six inferential tests employed fell a little short of significance. For example, U.S. African American tended to acquire TV an estimated 5 years later than did Whites, and homicide rates among non-Whites began increasing 4 years later than did rates among Whites (Centerwall, 1989). In another example, the introduction of TV preceded major increases (of at least 52%) in homicide rates in the six countries in which existing longitudinal research indicate that natural exposure to TV contributes to enhanced aggression among individual people (Centerwall, 1989). Examples of such research include Belson's work in England and that of Eron and Huesmann in the United States. He also included data from Canada, Finland, Israel, and Poland. Based on prior research, he (1989) noted that effects may not occur in some cultures, such as Australia. Of course, the contextualist theme of this book also suggests that effects may vary in different cultures and might be entirely absent in some. In testing this hypothesis, Centerwall generally used 3-year averages to control for variability created by small numbers of homicides.

In this light, Zimring and Hawkins (1997) said they had disconfirmed Centerwall's general theory of a causal linkage between TV and lethal violence. For example, they examined data from France, Germany, Italy, and Japan. In none of these countries did a confirming pattern occur they alleged. Zimring and Hawkins provided no evidence that individual-level effects of natural exposure occur in any of these four, however. Without this, doubts arise as to their relevance to Centerwall's theory. In fact, two panel studies of Japanese children failed to link natural exposure to subsequent aggression (see Kodaira, 1998). In Germany, analyses of panel data concerning 11- to 15-year-olds suggest that TV viewing increases reactive (i.e., to provocation) aggression, but apparently not destructive forms (Groebel, 1983). Whether this qualifies Germany for use in assessing Centerwall's theory seems questionable. Given Centerwall's ideas and in the absence of other causal factors, one would not expect to observe a major increase in homicide in a country 10 years or so after the introduction of TV without individual-level effects among children.

In addition, Zimring and Hawkins pointed to evidence that homicide rates fluctuated between 1974 and 1990 in the United States and Canada. Such changes, much smaller than the prior doubling of the rate, may have little bearing on Centerwall's theory, however. He never claimed TV caused all homicide. Finally, they showed that homicides declined in England and Wales after 1978, eventually stabilizing at pre-TV levels. Zimring and Hawkins thus raised doubts about Centerwall's work, especially as it applies in England. Perhaps something other than TV caused murder rates to rise and later fall in England. The decline might result from improved medical technology and/or crime prevention efforts, however. These have no obvious relevance to his theory.

In contrast, during the 1980s and at least through 1993 or 1994, homicide rates for Canada, Finland, Israel, and Poland remained at levels substantially greater than the pre-TV-effect rates cited by Centerwall (1989). This conclusion comes from my calculation of all possible 3-year averages for these periods based on available World Health Organization data (WHO, annual volumes through the most recent, 1996). For no such period did the homicide rate fall to near the pre-effect level for any country. The closest occurred with the relatively volatile Israeli statistics for the 1990 to 1992 period; rates remained about 33% above the pre-effect level. From 1991 to 1993, they rose back to about 53% above the level. In any case, Zimring and Hawkin's anomalies address only pieces of Centerwall's (1989) evidential array. To my knowledge, no one has offered an explanation that competes with TV. Scientists tend to hold onto an incomplete or imperfect explanation until a better one comes along. Nonetheless, such criticism accents possible boundary conditions of his research.

Perhaps especially significant, Centerwall (1989) predicted that White homicide rates in South Africa would double perhaps as early as the late 1980s. At that time, available data from 1983 already showed a 56% increase from 1974, the year preceding the introduction of TV into the country. In fact, this happened according to data available in the early 1990s. The rate climbed by 130% from 1974 to 1987 (Centerwall, 1992). One caveat: To my knowledge, no longitudinal evidence exists as to whether natural TV exposure among individual South Africans contributes to aggression. This lack of evidence possibly results from the long-time absence of TV. It raises an obvious question about the validity of comparisons between South Africa and Canada or the United States. Perhaps Centerwall's (1989) discussion of the cultural and historical similarities among these countries mitigates such concerns, however. Nonetheless, this is probably the shakiest aspect of his work. In part because of this, one cannot discount arguments such as those of Zimring and Hawkins.

In the decade following the 1989 publication of the original study, mass communication scholars (other than textbook authors) appeared to pay only modest amounts of attention to it, as indicated by citation indexes. Perhaps many were unaware of it or tended to dismiss it because the study suggested something almost unthinkable. In this light, D.C. Whitney (2000) said Centerwall had made "goofy claims" (p. 195). In addition, the research used an unfamiliar technique that experimental psychologists, for example, may see as incomparable to their own. Nonetheless, Centerwall (1989) argued in detail that his research met epidemiological criteria for inferring causation from nonexperimental data. In contrast with communication scholars, the medical community appeared to pay close attention. For instance, partly based on Centerwall's work, the American Academy of Pediatrics urged parents to limit children's exposure to 2 hours per day and omit all violence. Until and unless other research refutes it or provides better explanations, society must take him seriously. To not do so risks allowing the perfect to destroy the good.

Even if TV contributes to an increased frequency of criminal homicides, it operates within the context of numerous other causal factors. According to Centerwall (1992), "every violent act is the result of an array of forces coming together—poverty, crime, alcohol and drug abuse, stress—of which childhood exposure to TV is just one" (p. 3061). For this and other reasons, perhaps many potential options are available to help deal with the problem.

Consequences of Violence Research

> Courses of action which put the blame exclusively on a person as if his evil
> will were the sole cause of wrong-doing and those which condone offense
> on account of the share of social conditions in producing bad disposition,
> are equally ways of making an unreal separation of man from his surround-
> ings, mind from the world. Causes for an act always exist, but causes are not
> excuses. Questions of causation are physical, not moral except when they
> concern future consequences. It is as causes of future actions that excuses
> and accusations alike must be considered. (Dewey, 1922/1957, p. 18)

The meaning and import of research concerning TV violence and other
causes of criminal aggression are found partly in the extent to which it can
help reduce antisocial and criminal behavior. By this standard, such research has had less success than one might hope. During the late 1990s,
teenagers committed highly publicized multiple homicides in schools at
places such as West Paducah, Kentucky, Jonesboro, Arkansas, Jackson-
ville, Mississippi, and Littleton, Colorado In doing so, they carved a jag-
ged gash across the U.S. heartland. More than a few commentators alleged
that media violence played a role. Whatever the causes, such events, and
the continuing rates of U.S. violent crime, highlight obvious shortcomings of existing knowledge. The most that one can say to date is that research suggesting harmful media effects may have kept violent crime today from being even worse than it is. Perhaps it has done so by convincing
some parents to limit their children's TV exposure. Research could fail
either because TV has little impact on violent crime rates in the first place
or because of shortcomings in the way (or the extent to which) research is
applied.
   In my opinion, the latter possibility is extremely likely. Some studies do
not support the existence of harmful behavioral effects of TV violence, and
one can always find fault with any single study. Taken as a whole, however, the evidence seems quite convincing (see Paik & Comstock, 1994). A
possible doubt about it still exists, but such doubts seem less and less reasonable as more studies are done (for a contrary opinion, see Freedman,
1992, but also see the response by Huesmann, Eron, Berkowitz, & Chaffee,
1992). In my opinion, the real open question pertains to the magnitude of
the effect—how frequently does it occur and to what extent does it involve
lethal violence? Given my partial agreement with Centerwall, my guess is
that TV contributes to roughly one third of U.S. criminal violence, including homicide. Estimates by others have tended to range from 5% to 15% of
violence (see Strasburger & E. Donnerstein, 1999). Often research has only
attempted to determine whether, rather than to what extent, an effect occurs. This may explain this lack of consensus. In any case, the research is a

first step. Its application (or lack thereof) depends on what ordinary people and society do to protect children.

What about the Ronny Zamoras of the world, as well as the Jonesboro and West Paducah murderers, whose violent behavior may result in part from media violence? Do they deserve to go free if the environment in which they lived contributed to their actions? Social-scientific studies can only suggest the presence of a causal relationship if correlations exist across large numbers of people. It is impossible to link the behavior of a single individual definitively to factors in an individual's particular environment. Thus, there can be no proof of the culpability of TV in individual cases.

Most probably, judges will continue to prohibit defense attorneys from using general social-scientific evidence to plant a seed of doubt in the minds of jurors. If allowed, research evidence could then exonerate virtually any violent criminal. Even if Centerwall's research provides an accurate picture, many homicides still would occur without TV. Perhaps the punishment function of the judicial system has a useful deterrent effect to violent crime, regardless of whether persons convicted truly are (in whole or in part) responsible for their actions.

As with many other debates about media effects, the issue of freedom of expression hovers above arguments about TV violence. Regardless of to what extent media violence is a constitutionally protected form of free expression, many people in the United States would object to government intervention designed to reduce or eliminate it. One must weigh the consequences of legal restriction in terms of its potential not only to set a precedent for restriction of other types of expression that people may find offensive or dangerous, but perhaps also in terms of the reduced pleasure among those who enjoy violent programs (McGuire, 1986a). Imagine the outcry that might occur if the government tried to ban televised football or hockey. Hence, an optimal solution would involve extra legal activities either to reduce TV violence or shield those whose behavior it is most likely to affect.

One possibility would be for the TV industry to reduce violence voluntarily. Centerwall (1992) argued that it is no more realistic to expect TV industries, which are in the business of delivering audiences to advertisers, to do this voluntarily than to expect tobacco companies on their own to reduce crop production. Yet a survey of TV station managers from around the United States found that 74% felt the medium carried too much needless violence (Moca, 1993).

Concerning possible regulation, one excellent history of the policy debate about TV violence (Rowland, 1983) suggested that the complexly contingent results of media violence research in the past have allowed policymakers to appear concerned without forcing them to take real action. Nonetheless, some action has occurred recently. As part of the 1996 Telecommunications Act, Congress required that new sets larger than 12 inches carry v-chips. These devices allow parents to block access to certain TV programs based on ratings codes. Since that time, much controversy has focused on the codes used. For example, in some circumstances, codes may attract children to programming by creating a sense of *forbidden fruit* (Cantor, Harrison, & Krcmar, 1998). See M.E. Price (1998) for detailed discussion about v-chip issues.

Perhaps the v-chip is necessary but not sufficient to encourage parents to monitor the exposure of children in the evidently most vulnerable, preadolescent age groups (Paik & Comstock, 1994). Its effectiveness depends on the actions of both parents and those who can reach parents with information about the potential dangers (e.g., educators, pediatricians, and social workers). Although as many as 80% of U.S. adults believes that TV has a negative impact, most parents do not control the media exposure of their children with any consistency (Strasburger & Donnerstein, 1999).

Education, then, can play an important role. In the author's opinion, education about the possibly harmful consequences of TV violence has a place not only in the curricula of universities, but also in those of junior high and high schools. Society should warn every potential parent in the United States about this evidence and, perhaps more important, inform him and her about how to minimize the potential harm resulting from media violence. Perhaps the consequences of TV violence could even be discussed in elementary schools to make its potential victims aware of the dangers. These topics belong alongside forms of education such as driver training and those concerning the negative consequences of alcohol, illegal drugs, sexual behavior, and tobacco. Such instruction, of course, should be education and not propaganda; it should expose future parents to the diversity of opinion about TV violence and respect their academic freedom to decide for themselves about the problem. Nonetheless, schools should not wait to include the topic on their educational agenda in the hope that absolute proof—an ideal that science never meets—will emerge.

If one accepts Centerwall's conclusions, in some years as many as one fifth as many people in the United States died from homicides linked to TV as died in motor vehicle accidents. This figure excludes the effects of homicide and other crimes of violence on the lives of those who are executed or sentenced to lengthy prison terms after committing it. Although school systems in the United States have done relatively little about educating children regarding TV and its effects, some systems have at least experimented with including critical viewing skills in their curricula (see J.A. Brown, 1991). To the extent that the companies that control mass media are reluctant to gore their own oxen by devoting space and time to the possible behavioral impact of mediated violence, the need for attention to the topic in school increases. Of course, these companies provide such coverage to issues like the harmful effects of illegal drugs.

What about those children who may already be damaged? Evidence suggests that psychological intervention can lower future aggression levels markedly among heavy violence viewers. Efforts to convince such children not to imitate TV violence evidently reduced those displaying above-average aggression several months later from 62% to 38% (Huesmann, Eron, Klein, Brice, & Fischer, 1983; Rosenthal, 1986). To fund such interventions, lawmakers perhaps could tax advertising revenues generated by violent TV programs or at least those that children are likely to see. To do so would be consistent with treating media violence as a form of pollution (see J.T. Hamilton, 1998). This could help reduce its potentially huge negative externalities — "costs that are borne by people other than the individuals involved in production activities" (p. 1). These might include expenses associated with courts, police, and prisons. In addition, the need for security fences, guard dogs, medical care, and so on also might fall. Such a proposed tax would face tough, but probably not hopeless, First Amendment barriers. It also would not address incalculable costs of media violence, such as losses of peace of mind and possible premature death.

Desensitization Effects

In the early morning hours of March 13, 1964, a man grabbed 28-year-old Kitty Genovese as she walked toward her Queens, New York, apartment. He repeatedly stabbed her, left, and returned to stab her again. Neighbors heard screams, but failed to call police until after she died. In a unique way, the case touched the conscience of U.S. residents and even helped inspire a popular topical song, "Outside of a Small Circle of Friends." Some of Genovese's neighbors later said they were afraid or did not want to get involved. An elderly woman who lived in the same building as the victim reported hearing nighttime screaming on many other occasions. Trying to understand this evident lack of empathy requires difficult speculation, but perhaps the woman had become numb to cries by other human beings.

A fairly well-documented effect of exposure to violence involves desensitization. Media audiences, for example, may become acclimatized to aggression and violence to the point that they delay acting if they encounter it in "real" life. Of course, this can contribute to the presence or severity of crime. In an experimental illustration, Drabman and Thomas (1974) exposed half of a group of third- and fifth-grade students to a cowboy film depicting numerous violent events. All children then were told that they were responsible for monitoring the behavior of two younger children. Ultimately, the younger children fought and appeared to destroy property. As hypothesized, the subjects who saw the film took longer to seek adult help.

Fear Effects

Fear can be conceptualized as "an emotional response of negative hedonic tone related to avoidance or escape, due to the perception of real or imagined threat" (Cantor, 1994, p. 221). Perhaps to a surprising degree, children and adults enjoy being frightened by media contents, such as horror movies (Cantor, 1994). Dramatic features such as monsters and seeing others become threatened often frighten audiences. The idea of stimulus generalization suggests that more realistic depictions will increase fright among audiences, and some research supports this (Cantor, 1994). According to the principle, "if a real-life stimulus evokes a particular emotional response, media depicting the same stimulus will evoke a similar though less intense response" (Harrison & Cantor, 1999, p. 99).

A serious question is whether fright reactions result in long-term harm to children. Perhaps partly due to ethical constraints on scholars, research has had problems documenting such harm (Cantor, 1994). Nonetheless, according to self-report data, about 90% of a sample of undergraduates had experienced enduring fright reactions to media (Harrison & Cantor, 1999). These included difficulty eating or sleeping and phobias. A person might develop fear of blood after viewing *Jaws*, for example. Many of the implicated stimuli, such as a killer's breathing, related to violence. Most examples took place in childhood and adolescence. Such effects "are a burden to children trying to cope with fears that are often irrational and unnecessarily intense" (p. 111). At the time of the study, about a quarter of participants reported that such anxiety still existed. At bottom, parents "should be aware of the types of media that may contribute to enduring fright effects in their children" (p. 113). The most enduring impact seemed to occur when young people saw depictions of blood and injury in programs they viewed because persons other than themselves wanted to watch.

Beyond this, cultivation research (see chap. 9) suggests that exposure to TV drama leads viewers to exaggerate the presence of crime and violence in everyday life. It also increases people's fear of becoming crime victims, especially among those living in urbanized, high-crime areas (Gerbner, Gross, Morgan, & Signorielli, 1994). Such effects may do both harm and good. They might diminish support for civil liberties, yet also cause vulnerable people to avoid risk.

THE IMPACT OF SEXUALLY EXPLICIT MATERIALS

In 1977, a 15-year-old boy in Madison, Wisconsin, pleaded *no contest* to the second-degree sexual assault of a 16-year-old girl. The judge in the case, Archie Simonson, released the boy, claiming that the youth had merely "reacted normally" to the climate of sexual permissiveness in the city. The judge cited the presence of sex-oriented businesses and women who wore clothing that all but exposed their breasts and buttocks. Many segments of the community reacted with outrage. Local feminists and other activists mounted a successful recall campaign, and voters elected another candidate in the subsequent election. Nonetheless, the judge's comments echoed commonly heard concerns about the impact of open sexuality, including mediated forms, on the young.

Researchers concerned with the impact of sexual materials face a number of obstacles in addition to those faced by scientists concerned with media violence. Ethical and legal considerations preclude the manipulation of many sexual materials in experiments using minor subjects (presumably the group most susceptible to influence). Correlational researchers attempting to examine whether the availability or legal status of sexual materials appears to influence rates of sex crimes face potentially horrendous validity problems, particularly with the most serious of these crimes. According to statistics, rape is both the most underreported and overreported of serious crimes in the United States (Dershowitz, 1992). That is to say, many (perhaps most) victims do not report the crime, and a large number of claims (in comparison with other serious crimes) turn out to be spurious. This danger probably is much greater than with the research on media violence and homicides. If a homicide occurs, police virtually always will know about it; the only exceptions presumably will occur rarely, as when people simply disappear or an incompetent autopsy is performed. In addition, the law enforcement officials rarely may confuse the crimes of manslaughter and homicide (see Centerwall, 1989). Thus, much of the experimental and nonexperimental evidence is necessarily less conclusive than that concerning media violence.

Nonetheless, concern about the possible harmful effects of sexually explicit materials has been an especially hot topic in mass communication research during recent decades. To a large degree, this reflects their widespread availability in the United States and other parts of the Western world, as well as the centrality of sexuality to adult life. *Sexually explicit materials* can be defined as verbal or pictorial media contents that explicitly describe or depict nudity and/or sexual activity involving humans. Primarily, this section deals with the impact of pictorial (including video), rather than purely verbal, materials.

Many people use connotatively loaded terms such as *erotica* and *pornography* to refer to sexual media contents. Although these words are avoided here, some consideration of the various meanings they carry is useful for those who encounter them elsewhere. Often *erotica* refers to sexually explicit materials that a person approves of or at least does not find especially objectionable. *Pornography*, derived from a Greek word referring to writings about prostitutes, tends to refer to sexual materials that a person disapproves of. In the scientific literature, erotica often refers to any sort of material that causes, or is designed to create, sexual arousal. Pornography sometimes refers to material that is legally obscene (see the discussion of legal regulation later). Some feminist writers (e.g., Steinem, 1980) use the term to refer to material that is both sexually explicit and that degrades women or presents them in dominated roles. In principle, even highly explicit materials need not be pornographic, by these criteria, as long as men and women are presented as equals. Some feminists apparently find the vast majority of sexually materials on the market degrading, however.

Erotic depictions, of course, have existed throughout human history. In the United States, censorship of sexual materials has come and gone at different times. During certain periods, severe forms of legal restraint on sexual materials, even by the standards advocated by today's social conservatives, have occurred. One wave of puritanical activism occurred after the Civil War. During the 1930s, customs officers prevented an actress from bringing James Joyce's novel *Ulysses*, often considered one of the classics of modern literature, into the United States. During the late 1960s and early 1970s, however, many legal restrictions on sexual materials were removed, and the remaining laws tended to emphasize keeping the materials away from children.

Nonetheless, the courts have ruled that legally obscene materials do not enjoy First Amendment protection, making the prospect of government control much more likely than with violent materials. Yet determining what is obscene is not easy. Interestingly, legal guidelines focus on the content, rather than on effects of the content. Clearly, purely violent materials do not qualify, but sexual ones may. The definitive court decision was the 1973 *Miller v. California* ruling of the U.S. Supreme Court. In this case, the court rejected a national standard for obscenity. Instead, it allowed local communities to set certain limits of permissibility. Therefore, what may be obscene in Atlanta may not be in San Francisco or New York. The court ruled that legal obscenity exists only if material meets all of the following criteria (*Miller v. California*, 1973, as cited in Nelson & Teeter, 1973):

(a) whether "the average person, applying contemporary community standards" would find that the work, taken as a whole, appeals to the prurient interest . . .

(b) whether the work depicts of describes, in a patently offensive way, sexual conduct specifically defined by the applicable state law, and

(c) whether the work, taken as a whole, lacks serious literary, artistic, political or scientific value. (p. 428)

Thus, something could depict patently offensive sexual conduct, as legally defined, but remain protected if it contains overall literary value. In effect, the court made the prosecution of obscenity cases quite difficult, but not impossible. The ruling applies to the sale, public exhibition, importation, or transportation across state lines by common carrier of such material. In the privacy of their homes, people retain the right to view even clearly obscene materials. Materials depicting children in sexual activity are the one clear exception. Simple possession of these carries felony penalties according to federal law. Legally, pictures and films of minors engaged in sexual activity are assumed harmful on their face. Children, of course, cannot legally consent to sex.

U.S. mass opinion at times has been rather divided about the legalization of many sexual materials, with older adults, religious evangelicals, and women more likely than others to favor restriction ("Growing Support," 1986). To a degree, many people evidently base their opinions about legal restriction on assumptions of effects (Commission on Obscenity and Pornography, 1970; but also see M.E. Thompson, Chaffee, & Oshagan, 1990). Critics have argued that exposure to these materials has a wide variety of negative consequences. Such purported effects include sexual arousal and promiscuity, behavioral aggression, and negative attitudes toward women.

One of the best established effects of exposure to these materials is also the least surprising. Many studies suggest that, for most people — male or female — exposure to sexual materials is arousing. Whether one considers such arousal good or bad, of course, depends in part on one's values. More interesting is evidence that satiation occurs. With repeated exposure, sexual materials tend to be less arousing, although their effect reintensifies after a period of nonexposure (J.L. Howard, Liptzin, & Reifler, 1973). This suggests that novelty is at least partly responsible for the arousal (McGuire, 1986a). Finally, experimental evidence also indicates that, once users become bored with conventional materials, they may seek out progressively more explicit, deviant, or violent materials (Zillmann & Bryant, 1986b). This suggests that exposure to sexual materials may follow a pattern analogous to use of illegal drugs. Users may begin with relatively harmless stimuli (nonviolent mediated sex or marijuana) and proceed to more harmful materials (violent sex or cocaine). Yet any tendency for consumers to seek more harmful sexual materials may not persist for any substantial time period.

Exposure to Sexual Materials

Surprisingly little is known about people's exposure to sexually explicit materials other than such behavior is quite widespread in modern U.S. society, especially among males. In fact, virtually all adults voluntarily see materials depicting nudity at one time or another, and such exposure usually begins by the high school years (Bryant & Brown, 1989). In addition, even some junior high students report exposure to X-rated films, which suggests that existing attempts to keep materials from adolescents are not especially effective. A number of problems have limited the usefulness of existing research on use of sexual materials. These problems include difficulties in obtaining reliable data due to the sensitive nature of questions asked in surveys and a lack of consistent definitions across studies and time periods, which compounds problems with the external validity of limited samples (Bryant & Brown, 1989).

Media Sex and Viewer Aggression: Theoretical Ideas

Contemporary social-scientific concerns about the impact of sexual materials focus primarily, but not exclusively, on behavioral aggression, including both sexual and generic forms. Many of the same theoretical ideas that concern the impact of media violence apply to mediated sex also. Social learning theory, for example, has several positive, causal implications for the impact of sexually violent content on sexual aggression. If a film depicts a violent rape, a man watching it might expect to enjoy raping someone if he observes a man enjoying it in the film. Similarly, if the victim reacts favorably to rape on film, an observer might consider committing the crime (Check & Malamuth, 1986). In addition, watching a film in which a rapist escapes punishment could remove inhibitions about rape among audience members, perhaps making a real rape more likely.

Other theories concern more generic forms of aggression that may be linked to either violent or nonviolent materials. A type of arousal theory, excitation transfer (Zillmann, 1971), suggests that if a person is predisposed to aggressive behavior, arousal produced by sexual materials may enhance these predispositions. A person may interpret sexual arousal as anger, leading to violence in some circumstances. Another idea predicts that some subjects will react negatively to sexual materials, making generic aggressive behavior more likely. Unlike research on TV violence, a number of feminist theories frequently guide research concerning sexually explicit materials. For example, many feminists view pornography as a phenomenon that both reflects a patriarchal (i.e., male-dominated) society and helps perpetuate it. By presenting women in a submissive role, sexually explicit materials tend to reinforce male dominance, according to some feminists. These writers often see rape, presumably linked to sexual materials, as a particularly vicious expression of this dominance, rather than as a matter of sex. In fact, however, many of these ideas often mesh neatly with conventional empirical social science ideas, such as social learning theory (see Check & Malamuth, 1986).

Negative causal theories also exist. Social learning theory predicts that a violent sexual film could reduce the likelihood of rape if models do not enjoy it or if the rapist encounters punishment (Check & Malamuth, 1986). Similarly, the catharsis notion suggests that people predisposed to sexual aggression may vicariously get it out of their system by the use of sexual materials. Among reverse causal theories, social learning theory predicts that men who are inclined to favor rape may more likely be aroused by sexual materials, with this reinforcement resulting in relatively high levels of exposure (Check & Malamuth, 1986).

Early Research

Ironically, assumptions about harmful effects have led to regulation of sexually explicit materials at various times in U.S. history, but meaningful research largely did not occur until after the removal of many legal restrictions in the late 1960s and early 1970s. By the late 1960s, surprisingly little was available. As part of the Payne Fund studies, Blumer and Hauser (1933) attempted to examine the impact of motion pictures on sexual forms of delinquency in young people. Such behavior could range from consensual, but illicit, sexual relations to gang rape. Because it relied on largely qualitative data obtained from case histories of and interviews with delinquents, this research really could not demonstrate effects. Nonetheless, the authors reported that the limited sexuality then available in motion pictures could contribute to sexual delinquencies among both boys and girls.

However, a number of other early studies in fact suggested that sexually explicit materials do not cause sex crimes and may actually reduce their frequency. In January 1968, President Lyndon Johnson appointed the Commission on Obscenity and Pornography, pursuant to a federal law that declared sexually explicit materials a national concern. Communication scholar Joseph Klapper (see chap. 1), then the director of social research at CBS, was among those named. In 1969, President Richard Nixon named Charles H. Keating, Jr. of Cincinnati to replace another member who had resigned to accept a diplomatic post. Keating later became famous as a result of the savings-and-loan scandals in the United States. In the early 1990s, he was convicted of securities fraud and sentenced to prison. The work of the commission, by Congressional mandate, included studying the impact of sexual materials especially on minors. In particular, the group was to determine whether these materials contribute to criminal and other antisocial behaviors.

In preparing its study, the commission solicited written statements from various organizations, held public hearings, and initiated a program of formal research. In 1970, it issued its report, which contained highly controversial conclusions. Regarding the impact of sexual materials, the members assigned to study effects concluded (Commission on Obscenity and Pornography, 1970):

> If a case is to be made against "pornography" in 1970, it will have to be made on grounds other than demonstrated effects of a damaging personal or social nature. Empirical research designed to clarify the question has found no reliable evidence to date that exposure to explicit sexual materials plays a significant role in the causation of delinquent or criminal sexual behavior among youth or adults. (p. 139)

Needless to say, this conclusion aroused many people. President Nixon denounced it, and commission member Keating also dissented vigorously. Nonetheless, the report has provided those advocating a libertarian approach to sexual materials with a good deal of ammunition during the past couple of decades.

In fact, much of the research available by the early 1970s (including that included in the commission's report) suggested that sexually explicit materials may reduce the incidence of sex offenses. During the 1960s, Denmark became the first country in the world to remove essentially all restriction on the production and distribution of sexually explicit materials. Consistent with a vicarious catharsis mechanism, Kutchinsky (1973) reported that a decrease in the number of sex offenses followed. Nonetheless, other researchers have taken issue with any claim that removal of restriction lowered behavioral sex offenses (see Check & Malamuth, 1986).

Other evidence of the apparent harmlessness of sexual materials came from studies comparing the use of sexually explicit materials among convicted rapists and other sexual offenders with the use of such materials by other men. Findings (e.g., R.F. Cook & Fosen, 1971) suggested that convicted sex offenders generally report less exposure to sexual materials during preadolescence and adolescence than do other men. One possibility is that men who commit sex crimes tend to come from sexually restrictive family backgrounds, which discourages them from exposure to these materials. Nonetheless, some researchers have recently challenged certain of these conclusions as well (see Marshall, 1989).

Early research also examined the impact of sexual materials on sexual behavior. Because of the AIDS crisis, this question today perhaps seems more important than it did two decades ago. If exposure makes people promiscuous or more willing to engage in novel forms of sexual behavior (i.e., anal intercourse) that put one at a high risk for acquiring the HIV virus, such materials could be very damaging. In fact, it appears that exposure only slightly increases, during the short term, the likelihood that someone will engage in forms of sex to which they are already accustomed (Commission on Obscenity and Pornography, 1970).

The Meese Commission

Not surprisingly, many concerned observers and some researchers did not
regard early research, especially that suggesting that sexually explicit materials are harmless, as definitive. Research continued, and by the early and
mid-1980s, evidence existed that exposure to certain sexual materials could
have harmful effects. During the Reagan presidency, another U.S. government commission issued a report largely contradicting the findings of the
Commission on Obscenity and Pornography. At the request of President
Reagan, the Attorney General's Commission on Pornography, better
known as the Meese Commission (after Ed Meese, the attorney general at
the time its report was released), was established in 1985 to study sexual
materials and their impact. Unlike the earlier commission, the Meese Commission did not fund original research, but the intervening years had provided it with a much larger body of research on which to rely. In real dol-
lars, its budget was only one sixteenth the size of that given to the original
commission. The Meese Commission basically reviewed research and gathered testimony from a wide variety of people, including researchers, supposed victims, and performers. In 1986, it issued its report.

The Meese Commission concluded that sexually violent material, including depictions of sado-masochism and rape, contributes to aggressive
behavior against women (*Attorney General's Commission on Pornography*,
1986). The 1970 commission generally did not deal with sexually violent
materials. In light of the evidence about the impact of media violence and
aggressiveness, this conclusion of the Meese Commission is not terribly
surprising. More controversially, the Meese Commission also concluded
that exposure to sexually violent materials can produce antisocial and
possibly unlawful acts of sexual violence against women. For rather obvious ethical reasons, most empirical research has focused on aggression,
but not sexual aggression, as a dependent variable. Hence, the latter conclusion requires an assumption that what causes aggressive behavior also
is likely to cause sexually aggressive behavior. The commission reported
that the amount of violence in sexual materials increased after 1970, but
some researchers (e.g., E. Donnerstein, Linz, & Penrod, 1987) have challenged this judgment.

With somewhat less confidence, the Meese Commission also concluded
that exposure to certain nonviolent materials causes people to perceive
sexual violence as less serious and to develop attitudes that women like to
be forced into sex (attitudes the commission also linked to violent sexual
materials). These nonviolent materials include those depicting degradation, domination, subordination, or humiliation. Largely based on inference rather than research evidence, members also concluded that expo-

sure to degrading materials likely bears some relationship to increased sexual violence and discrimination against women in modern society. Finally, commission members disagreed about whether nonviolent and nondegrading materials, which members described as relatively uncommon, are harmful.

The report of the Meese Commission was no less controversial than that of its predecessor. Predictably, cultural conservatives lauded it, whereas others expressed dismay. The Reverend Jerry Falwell, for instance, called it "a good healthy report that places the United States government clearly in concert with grass roots America," and a civil liberties attorney called the report "little more than prudishness and moralizing masquerading behind social science jargon" (cited in Black & Whitney, 1988, p. 556).

The backgrounds of certain commission members added to the controversy. The chairman was Henry Hudson, a Virginia prosecutor known for vigorously pursuing obscenity cases. Member James C. Dobson, a licensed psychologist and radio program host, later was responsible for the widely publicized film of mass murderer Ted Bundy's claim, shortly before execution, that pornography contributed to his crimes. Critics charged that the Reagan administration had loaded the commission with individuals predisposed to conclude, or who had already concluded, that sexual materials have harmful effects.

In any case, regarding violent sexual materials, a relative unanimity of opinion exists. They have rather clear harmful effects at least for short periods of time. Whether the addition of sex to violent materials constitutes an additional source of harm and whether nonviolent sexual materials are likely to be harmful remain more vigorously debated questions. The evidence today regarding nonviolent sexual materials suggests at least that the conclusion of the 1970 obscenity commission was far too simple. The following discussion focuses on important studies conducted relatively recently, including several that appeared between the publication of the reports of the two U.S. commissions and that appeared to influence the Meese Commission.

Allen, D'Alessio, and Brezgel's (1995) meta-analysis of experimental laboratory research from the 1970s and 1980s is probably the most complete summary available. In part due to ethical concerns, little such work has been done after 1989. Subject to the usual limitations of and concerns about experimentation, they found that exposure to both violent and nonviolent media depictions of sexual activity increase nonsexual aggression in the laboratory. Looking at pictorial nudity apparently reduces such aggression, however. They also found only partial support for social-learning and excitation-transfer theory. Readers may keep these generalizations in mind as individual studies are discussed.

The Effects of Violent Sexual Materials on Aggression

The experimental finding that violent sex increases short-term laboratory aggression by male college students against both males and females is quite robust. Researchers usually measure aggression by a person's willingness to administer electric shocks or noxious noise to another person in a laboratory setting. Of course, such behavior may or may not generalize to sexual or other forms of aggression typically committed in the "real" world, and it may only persist for a short time. One salient finding is that violent sexual materials seem to make males more aggressive with females than with other males. For example, E. Donnerstein (1980) experimentally examined the effect of exposure to an X-rated film depicting a rape on male aggression against females and other males. Subjects who viewed the sexually violent film exhibited increased aggression (as measured by average shock intensities) against females immediately following exposure regardless of whether the female target had angered them previously in comparison with men viewing a film without sex or violence. Aggression against males also increased, but to a much smaller extent. Clearly, an arousal mechanism could account for certain of these findings. Yet aggression against a female who had not angered the male subjects suggested that subjects associated the female target with the rape victim, making "her a stimulus that could elicit aggressive responses" (E. Donnerstein, 1980, p. 276).

A potentially important question is whether the enhanced aggressiveness occurs solely because of the violence or whether the sexual context somehow markedly enhances (or otherwise changes the nature of) the effects of violence. The results of a recent meta-analysis were "inconsistent with the view that violence is the sole culprit" and suggested that "erotica and violent erotica are analogous to violent portrayals in influence" (Paik & Comstock, 1994, p. 537). Not all evidence suggests such a conclusion, however. In an unpublished study, E. Donnerstein, L. Berkowitz, and Linz (1986, as discussed in E. Donnerstein et al., 1987) exposed male college students to a neutral film, an X-rated film, a nonsexual film depicting violence against women, or a violent X-rated film. Those exposed to the violent X-rated film behaved most aggressively of the four groups against a women confederate. The violence-only film produced more aggression than did the nonviolent sexual film, which did not differ in its effects from the neutral film. When viewed alongside the evidence that nonsexual media violence has harmful long-term effects primarily among preadolescents, one can suspect (with some appropriate caution) that these effects will persist only for short time periods. In fact, Malamuth and Ceniti (1986) examined whether repeated exposure to sexually violent or nonviolent soft-core materials during a 4-week period contributed to male laboratory aggression against women 1 week later. They failed to find any effect. College students, by and large, tend to have previous sexual experiences, and perhaps persisting modeling effects only occur with sexually inexperienced adolescents or preadolescents.

No research has explicitly related the availability of sexually violent materials per se to changes in the rates of sex crimes such as rape. Court (1984) reported that the availability of sexually explicit materials was associated with increased rape reports in areas such as Australia and the state of Hawaii. He attempted to argue, based on other studies conducted in the laboratory, that the cause of this relationship is likely due to the impact of violent sexual materials on aggression. The data were thus consistent with modeling and other effects of media violence. Nonetheless, a variety of other possible interpretations, such as changes in crime reporting rates, remain. Perhaps future research could relate changes in restriction of sexual materials to rates of crimes that involve both murder and rape on the assumption that such data would be more valid.

In any case, any causal effect of availability on increased rape rates may not occur in all cultures. Japan, in which sexual films often include bondage and rape themes (without visually displaying human genitals), nonetheless has a microscopic rape rate in comparison with the United States (Abramson & Hayashi, 1984). Of course, cultural differences in reporting rates may confound any such comparison.

Researchers have also related violent sexual materials to various measures of behavioral predispositions. In one experiment, Check and Guloien (1989) reported that repeated exposure to violent materials depicting rape contributed to increased self-reported likelihood of raping, measured 1 week after exposure stopped, among Canadian males drawn from college student and general populations. The effect was particularly strong for males scoring relatively high in psychoticism, especially among students. Such a measure taps one component of an attitude as commonly conceptualized (see chap. 7). Their results thus were consistent with a social learning theory prediction of greater effects among those who are still learning about sex (Check & Guloien, 1989). Of course, whether self-reported predispositions will predict actual behavior is problematic. Marking a questionnaire may or may not indicate much about whether someone will rape, an act that would occur in a very different situation.

The Effects of Nonviolent Sexual Materials
on Aggression

Experimental Evidence. Researchers have examined whether nonviolent sexual materials contribute to or defuse forms of nonsexual aggression. Available evidence suggests that either effect can occur, under the right circumstances, if people are angry or (possibly) chronically aggressive. Meta-analytic work suggests that increased aggressiveness may be the more typical outcome (Paik & Comstock, 1994).

E. Donnerstein, Donnerstein, and Evans (1975) found that highly erotic stimuli (pictures with full nudity and implied sexual activity) tend to increase laboratory aggression if male subjects are angered subsequent to exposure, whereas mildly erotic materials (e.g., *Playboy* type pictures) tend to reduce aggression among those previously angered. The authors suggested that two separate theoretical processes explain these results. Sexual materials can shift one's attention away from anger, but they also contribute to enhanced arousal. A key variable in determining which process in dominant may be the level of arousal produced. L.A. White (1979) conducted research demonstrating that a person's emotional reaction to sexual materials also influences whether they enhance or diminish aggressive predispositions. He exposed angered male subjects to either affectively positive stimuli (e.g., depicting sexual intercourse) or affectively negative (e.g., explicit cunnilingus). The positive stimuli defused laboratory aggression. Consistent with mood theory, the negative stimuli enhanced it, although only slightly. These two studies concerned aggression directed by males against males. When nonviolent sexual materials increase aggression against women in experimental studies, the effect generally seems weaker than against men perhaps because of social inhibitions against such behavior (Check & Malamuth, 1986). Whether these effects occur outside the laboratory and persist longer than a few minutes remains unclear.

Finally, Check and Guloien (1989) reported that repeated exposure to nonviolent, dehumanizing video sexual materials (which depicted verbal abuse and domination of a woman depicted as hysterically responsive to male demands) increased males' self-reported likelihood of raping as measured 1 week after exposure stopped. The effect occurred primarily (and perhaps only) for male college students who were high in psychoticism, rather than for males drawn from the general adult population. These researchers also found no effect for explicit sexual video that contained no dehumanizing or violent content. This suggests that inconsistencies in earlier studies may have resulted from research that failed to distinguish carefully between the effects of nonviolent sexual materials that depict degradation and those that do not.

Adult Magazine Circulation and Rape: Correlational Evidence.   Most research into the effects of media contents uses the level of analysis of the individual person. In a different approach, L. Baron and Straus (1984) hypothesized that U.S. states in which sex magazines (e.g., *Chic, Hustler,* and *Playboy*) are popular tend to have higher rates of reported rapes. Feminist theory about rape yielded the hypothesis. Using a multiple regression analysis, they found that increased per capita sex magazine circulation covaried with higher rape rates, even with controls for numerous other variables, such as rates of other violent crimes and certain demographic characteristics of states.

Nonetheless, interpreting these results requires a good deal of caution. To the extent that cultural differences among different states affect the likelihood that rape will be reported, relying on crime reports for this sort of analysis is more dangerous than with trend studies (e.g., Court, 1984) that examine the same geographic area during different time periods. In addition, the correlational nature of the design leaves open numerous alternative explanations to any conclusion that circulation of the magazines increases sexual battery. For instance, states may differ in the presence of *compulsive masculinity*, which could increase both sex magazine readership and rape and result in a spurious association between the two (Baron & Straus, 1984). In fact, a more recent study found rape rates associated with circulation of outdoor magazines (e.g., *Field and Stream*), but not with the presence of adult theaters and book stores in states (Scott, 1985; cited in E. Donnerstein et al., 1987). This adds credence to the compulsive masculinity interpretation.

Cultivation of Sexually Callous Attitudes

One prominent study examined the effects of exposure to sexually explicit materials on perceptions of rape and sexuality, rather than on aggressive behavior. This study was reminiscent of media cultivation research (see chap. 9), in which researchers look at the long-term impact of media contents on audience perceptions of the world. Unlike conventional cultivation research, however, it used an experimental design. At the University of Massachusetts, 80 male and 80 female students participated in an experiment lasting some 9 weeks (Zillmann & Bryant, 1982). The stimuli consisted of sexually explicit stag films depicting heterosexual activities such as anal and vaginal intercourse, as well as cunnilingus and fellatio. None of the films contained deliberate infliction of pain. Each stag film lasted about 8 minutes. Researchers randomly assigned the students to one of four treatment groups. One group, a massive exposure condition, saw six films per weekly session for 6 weeks. Students in an intermediate exposure condition saw three erotic and three nonerotic films in each session. Those in a no-exposure condition saw six nonerotic films per session. A fourth group received no treatment.

About 3 weeks after the experimental treatments ended, the students returned. They read a newspaper account concerning a man convicted of rape and were asked to recommend a prison sentence. Perhaps not surprisingly, women recommended tougher sentences than did men, but the patterns were similar. Overall, those who saw no treatment film recommended an average sentence of about 9 years, and those who saw only nonerotic films recommended a sentence of about 10 years. In the intermediate condition, students recommended about 7.5 years, and massively exposed students suggested average sentences of about 5.3 years. The authors interpreted these results, and the fact that relatively large numbers of students massively exposed recommended minimal sentences of less than 1 year, as reflecting a trivialization of rape in the minds of the students exposed to nonviolent filmed sex resulting from an apparent loss of compassion for rape victims (Zillmann & Bryant, 1982).

Newspaper headlines and scholarly controversy, some of it quite amusing, followed. Cultivation researcher Larry Gross (1983) suggested that students who viewed the sexual films figured out the point of the research and repaid the researchers for an enjoyable experience by giving the researchers what they wanted (i.e., the results reflected a scientifically meaningless demand characteristic; see chap. 2). In response, the authors suggested that Gross merely "got carried away in defense of something of value to him" (Zillmann & Bryant, 1983, p. 114). Canadian philosophy professor Ferrel Christensen (1986) argued that young people typically are raised with a great amount of anxiety about sex and that becoming acquainted with a source of anxiety tends to reduce it. Hence, the lesser rape sentences recommended by those exposed to sexual films may have reflected less anxiety about sex, he argued, rather than a loss of compassion for the suffering of victims. Zillmann and Bryant (1986a) responded by citing more direct evidence collected subsequent to the 1982 study that sexual materials contribute to a loss of compassion. The earlier discussed incident in Madison, Wisconsin, suggests another possible, but probably at best partial, interpretation. Perhaps the sexual films somehow lowered the extent to which students assumed the rapist was responsible for his behavior. The students doubtlessly experienced sexual arousal. Because of the common tendency for people to assume that media contents affect others more than themselves, the *third-person effect* (Perloff, 1989), arousal perhaps caused some students to conclude that the forces beyond the rapist's control produced his behavior.

One can only speculate (with much trepidation) as to the behavioral consequences of this finding. One possibility is that, with the widespread presence or sexual materials in society, convicted rapists could receive more lenient treatment by judges and juries. However, if the public expects rapists to receive shorter sentences, juries paradoxically might convict offenders more readily.

This effect may occur only with stag films and not with standard X-rated movies, which at least have some semblance of a plot (however stupid) to them. Linz, Donnerstein, and Penrod (1988) found no evidence that prolonged exposure to either nonviolent, X-rated adult films or R-rated sexually nonexplicit films affected sentences recommended to a convicted rapist. They suggested that the film images of women engaged in nonsexual activities (e.g., driving a car or holding a job) may have counteracted the effect of the sex scenes, and the apparent implications about wanton female promiscuity perhaps cultivated in the minds of viewers.

The 1982 Zillmann and Bryant study also contained other evidence of interest, suggesting both first- and second-order cultivation-type effects (see chap. 9). Students were asked to estimate percentages of persons in society who engage in various behaviors, such as group sex, bestiality, and anal intercourse. Massively exposed subjects believed these activities to be more common than did other students (Zillmann & Bryant, 1982). In some instances, however, the films may have resulted in more accurate impressions about the amount of sex in society, which many people evidently underestimate (Zillmann & Bryant, 1982). In addition, the study found that exposure to sexual materials increased sexual callousness toward women and resulted in less agreement with the goals of the women's liberation movement among subjects (Zillmann & Bryant, 1982).

In another experiment, these researchers found evidence that repeated exposure to nonviolent sexual materials causes people (including college students and others drawn from the general population) to attach less significance to the institution of marriage and to experience less desire to have children (Zillmann & Bryant, 1988a). It also makes them feel less satisfied with their current sexual partners (Zillmann & Bryant, 1988b). Conceivably, such sexual dissatisfaction may occur both because men and women perceive their partners as inadequate and because they find themselves deficient in comparison with what they see on the screen, hence experiencing reluctance to take chances (Zillmann & Bryant, 1988b).

Of course, whether one views certain of these second-order type effects as negative depends both one's values and the extent to which one assumes that they have behavioral consequences. For example, something that makes people less satisfied with their spouse and less attached to marriage as an institution could contribute to the breakdown of the nuclear family, leading to a variety of social problems. Yet some people feel that the world is already overpopulated. In this light, something that results in less desire among humans to produce children may seem welcome. In any case, these possible consequences assume (perhaps with great danger) that human feelings or attitudes will tend to correspond with actual behavior.

Children, Adolescents, and Sexual Media Contents

The presence of the Internet, which provides access to a vast variety of sexual contents, raises many questions about the possible future impact of mediated sex on both children and adolescents. Ethical issues have prevented study of this, and existing regulation in the past has kept explicit materials away from young people to an extent. The Internet "ensures ready access to all conceivable forms of sexual material, and any effective curtailment of such liberal access is unlikely" (Zillmann, 2000, p. 43). One can easily find pictures of almost any conceivable form of sexual activity, written descriptions of sexually oriented businesses such as prostitution, commercial sites allowing observers to watch ad hoc sexual activity, and so on. The impact of sexually explicit materials on children and adolescents may be much greater than their effect on college students and other adults. In the future, researchers will have many opportunities to observe the consequences of natural exposure. In 40 years or so, perhaps a Centerwall-type study will link the presence of the Internet with who knows what.

At present, research offers little guidance concerning what to expect. Only a few studies link the sexual fare of media contents such as soap operas to changes in adolescents' sexual attitudes or behaviors. For instance, available evidence correlates exposure to televised sexual contents and soap operas with earlier sexual activity and teenage pregnancy, respectively (see the review in Strasburger & Donnerstein, 1999). Of course, such evidence is by no means inconsequential given the links between teenage pregnancy and factors such as poverty.

Consequences of Research Concerning Sexual Materials

Policymakers who wish to rely on research concerning the impact of sexually explicit materials face greater problems than do those relying on research concerning media violence. For one thing, the previously discussed shortcomings of research due to ethics and (sometimes) measurement validity make policy judgments especially difficult. That the evidence available is at least arguably more contradictory (and perhaps less coherent, theoretically) than that regarding mediated violence also does not help things. Thus, those attempting to answer the most important, practical questions (e.g., do these materials contribute to increased rates of sexual battery) may risk attempting an impossible inferential leap across a cognitive Grand Canyon. Yet recent evidence (Kim & Hunter, 1993a, 1993b) linking attitudes and behavioral predispositions much more strongly to volitional behavior than was believed previously may have shortened the leap considerably. In fact, if one (unlike the present author) accepts the idea that experimentation constitutes the method par excellence of science, one might argue that the evidence linking sexual materials to antisocial behavior is stronger than the evidence concerning media violence. In any case, the possibility that sexual contents contribute to sexual crimes such as sexual battery seems rather high or at least very plausible. That they contribute, in certain contexts, to negative attitudes toward women seems even more plausible.

In this light, one possibility is to assume the worst (i.e., that the conclusions of the Meese Commission are substantially justified or even understated, but that society may never know it with complete or even reasonable scientific certainty). If so, a number of immediate remedies are possible. That commission recommended vigorous enforcement of existing laws against obscenity, rather than new legislation. Arguments in favor of regulation (e.g., Sears, 1989) usually assume that harmful effects exist and stress that constitutional protections against free speech do not give people carte blanche rights to express themselves, however they wish, whenever they wish. Courts have upheld restrictions against obscenity and a number of other harmful forms of speech. These include conspiring to commit a murder, false and misleading advertising, and shouting that a fire is present in a crowded theater. Some advocates of regulation express amazement that video depictions of sexual intercourse could be considered speech in the first place. In contrast, opponents of regulation (e.g., Linsley, 1989) usually argue that any attempt to stamp out offensive expression is likely to be dangerous if only because it will open the door to restriction of additional materials. For example, if sexual materials are restricted because they degrade or lower the status of women, what will prevent others from claiming that nonsexual materials (e.g., the Bible) also lower the status of women and should be banned? They also sometimes question why sexual or violent media contents should be singled out for restriction when other activities that may contribute more clearly to violence or sexual battery, such as alcohol consumption, remain legal. Some civil libertarians have advocated the use of prostitution laws to pursue makers of X-rated films. Of course, performers are paid to commit sex acts. For better or for worse, this would not restrict adult access to sexual materials once they are made.

That obscenity laws make restriction uniquely possible with sexual materials, and that the Meese Commission found little reason for additional legislation, indicate that the courts and lawmakers in the United States have sided largely with the advocates of restriction. Nonetheless, there is little reason to expect that these materials will become substantially less available in the foreseeable future. For one thing, a large increase in enforcement of existing laws probably will not occur and might not substantially reduce the presence of sexual materials in society today anyway. Law enforcement agencies and prosecutors usually avoid allocating a lot of resources to minor crimes, especially if the behavior occurs discreetly, such as fornication, prostitution, and sodomy. Many see these as involving mere sexual peccadilloes. Not surprisingly, enforcement of obscenity law often has had a similar priority and probably will continue to do so perhaps unless research more clearly links sexual materials to serious crime. Even when enforcement occurs, as with the federal government's recent attempts to use racketeering statutes to prosecute distributors of sexual materials, the results often are not clearly successful.

Given certain of these problems with legal controls, some concerned persons have recommended use of a variety of extralegal measures to deal with mediated sex, ranging from education (E. Donnerstein et al., 1987) to legalized prostitution (Abramson & Hayashi, 1984) to picketing businesses that carry such materials. Certainly education about the possible effects of mediated sex, conducted in a manner that respects the academic freedom of students, could be included in the curriculum of high schools. It could occur alongside that dealing with other aspects of sexuality and with media violence and alcohol or drug abuse. Such an approach probably would create little controversy. What is less clear is whether it would do much good. In large part because few school systems have included this content in their curricula, there is little evidence about its effectiveness, but that available suggests optimism is in order (Fisher & Barak, 1989; Linz, Fuson, & Donnerstein, 1990). Put to this use, research may not change the world, but it does not have to leave it the same either.

11

Conclusion

This chapter focuses on the potential future of the field in light of contemporary social concerns. Prior to this, it discusses the possibility that in focusing on specific media contents, such as TV violence, researchers have missed the most significant effects.

TV AND ONE'S SENSE OF PLACE

Meyrowitz (1985, 1986) argued that TV caused much of the social change in the United States since the 1950s, such as the massive movement of women into the labor force. Building on the ideas of scholars such as Marshall McLuhan, Meyrowitz's contextualist theory in some way resembles the mainstreaming idea from cultivation theory (see chap. 9). He maintained that TV has reduced the traditional separations of people into different experiential worlds. Such separation

> fostered different world views, allowed for sharp distinctions between people's "onstage" and "backstage" behaviors, and permitted people to play complementary — rather than reciprocal roles. Such distinctions in situations were supported by the diffusion of literacy and printed materials, which tended to divide people into very different informational worlds based on different levels of reading skill and on training and interest in different "literatures." These distinctions were also supported by the isolation of different people in different places, which led to different social identities based on the specific and limited experiences available in given locations. By bringing many different types of people to the same "place," electronic me-

261

dia have fostered a blurring of many formerly distinct social roles. (Meyro-witz, 1985, pp. 5–6)

Thus, TV has fogged distinctions between masculinity and femininity, as well as adults and children. Meyrowitz's theory is not simple techno-logical determinism, however. Human beings exercise their freedom within the bounds set by physical and mediated environmental con-straints, he argued. Thus, the theory potentially "offers a means of gaining further control over our destiny by allowing us to be more conscious of the ways in which the media we create can, in turn, function to re-create us" (Meyrowitz, 1986, p. 250). To empiricists, it may sound like uncon-firmed speculation. Yet after some 15 years, it remains "rich with provoca-tive ideas waiting to be sifted and winnowed by enterprising researchers into testable hypotheses" (Rosnow, 1985, p. 206).

THE NEED TO ADDRESS THE PUBLIC'S RESEARCH AGENDA

If we are to manage the fruits of the unprecedented explosion of knowledge in virtually every scientific field in our generation, we have to stimulate and create, in my view, a much deeper and more profound, more involved and sustained dialogue between science and the public about the meaning of sci-ence, the meaning of new discoveries and the implications of those discover-ies for the society in which they take place, and for the civilization that allo-cates resources for such discoveries. (Al Gore, Jr., cited in Cialdini, 1988, p. 781)

Effectively addressing the needs and research agendas of the public repre-sents one key to the future of mass communication research. Of course, throughout history, the field has examined widespread social concerns about the media, although often in a rather unsystematic, haphazard way. Therefore, an important question to the field's social usefulness concerns its ability to address public concerns more effectively. Obviously, what is needed is a means to promote transactions between science and society in ways that will not circumvent the autonomy of inquiry necessary for sci-entific progress. In her 1993 address to the annual conference of the Inter-national Communication Association, its president put it well: "Commu-nication scholarship (as all scholarship) needs to be addressing the public issues. How we maneuver through the public agenda, select problems, and frame research about them in terms of our theoretical understanding is up to each individual scholar" (Wartella, 1994, p. 59).

In this light, Zillmann (1992) offered a number of suggestions that could improve scientific responses to social concerns about the media. After reviewing barriers to the influence of psychological research on public policy concerning sexually explicit materials, Zillmann discussed three steps to make research more meaningful. First, a committee could assess citizen concerns and develop a comprehensive list of perceived problems. Interested researchers would then receive funding to conduct the investigations needed to address these problems.

> It should be noted that such an agenda in no way limits the freedom of investigators to conduct whatever studies they deem important, even studies that are extraneous to the agenda. Research extraneous to the agenda would, in fact, complement agenda research in a most positive fashion, potentially serving as a corrective for incomplete agendas. (Zillmann, 1992, p. 176)

Second, a committee consisting of social scientists could assess the technical merits of and integrate all pertinent research regardless of its policy implications using the language of laypersons. Third, another committee, consisting of those experienced in dealing with political constituencies, could recommend appropriate policy. Conceivably, those conclusions and recommendations could be presented before either elite policymakers, the masses, or even both groups.

The role for social scientists, as Dewey said, is to perfect the processes of inquiry and disseminate their conclusions, not execute policy. The fact that the presence of TV violence may contribute to increased rates of violent crime does not mean automatically that society should adopt censorship. Rather, in a world in which inquiry replaces dogmatism, in which humans no longer impose fixed ideals on unexamined situations, responses to research evidence often take on a tragic but healthy quality (Nisbet, 1983). According to Hook (1974; cited in Nisbet, 1983),

> every genuine experience of moral doubt and perplexity in which we ask "What should I do?" takes place in a situation where good conflicts with good . . . No matter how we resolve the opposition some good will be sacrificed, some interest whose immediate craving for satisfaction may be every whit as intense and authentic as its fellow will be modified, frustrated, or even suppressed. (p. 306)

In short, even if fully enlightened by research evidence, the public debate about TV violence (to use one salient example) necessarily must represent a battle between two perhaps mutually exclusive goods (as well as, if viewed somewhat differently, the lesser of two evils). One side would avoid the threats to legitimate expression brought about by governmental intervention to reduce the availability of mediated violence (at least to children) at the risk of tolerating more violent crime in society. The other would sacrifice a degree of freedom in society in favor of the possibility of

greater security for its citizens. Because research evidence can never satisfy a Platonic quest for certainty, it can amount to no more than one voice,
although presumably not an insignificant one, among many in public debate. In any case, whatever policies come out of debate will rely on, or perhaps choose to ignore, only necessarily tentative forms of scientific dialogue. In one sense, the role of research is as much to try to change the
world as to understand it. In another sense, researchers perhaps should
feel a degree of satisfaction if they help clarify socially significant issues
for the broader human community.

CONCLUDING THOUGHTS

Shortly after the first Reagan administration took office and as the social
sciences faced potentially drastic cutbacks in government support for
their work, the editors of *Public Opinion* magazine interviewed a group of
distinguished social scientists. The resulting symposium, entitled "Is Social Science a God That Failed?" (1981), reflected a widespread feeling that
the social sciences have not lived up to their potential. Instead of facilitating the scientific transformation of modern society and the solution of
pressing social issues, they often appeared to accomplish little beyond of-
fering extremely qualified answers to important issues. Of course, such
highly qualified answers ("In some circumstances, exposure to some
types of mediated violence may have harmful effects on some individuals") can hamper effective application of research findings.

  Clearly, overblown hopes existed in various periods of the 20th century for the social sciences. These hopes appeared during the early 20th
century, when the social sciences largely began the task of applying the
scientific method to human behavior. They were also evident during the
1960s, when the rapid improvement in computer technology made it possible to perform complex data-analytic operations in seconds that previously required months of hand calculations from dozens of people. Complex methods seemed to hold the key to explaining, predicting, and
(where appropriate) controlling human behavior. As of the early 1980s, this
clearly had not happened. Instead, many findings appeared to apply only
to very narrow, even idiosyncratic contexts, caricaturing pragmatist ideas
about the variable and provisional nature of knowledge (cf. Gergen, 1973).

  By the late 1990s, some developments suggested a somewhat more optimistic view about the potential value of mass communication research.
For instance, Centerwall's (1989) epidemiological study of TV and homicide suggested at least the possibility of some substantively important
findings. Kim and Hunter's (1993a, 1993b) meta-analytic studies strongly
linking attitudes with behavior appeared to enhance the significance of re-

search into the impact of sexual media contents. Of course, due to ethical constraints such research often has relied on attitudes and behavioral intentions as the outcomes of experimental interest, rather than forms of conduct such as sexual assault. In addition, evidence implicating TV and other forms of media with health problems seemed likely to continue growing. For example, Andersen, Crespo, Bartlett, Cheskin, and Pratt (1998) correlated TV exposure with less physical activity and increased obesity among children. Such a finding seemed of particular import because medical authorities noted a substantial increase during the 1990s in Type 2 diabetes among various age groups. In fact, some doctors suggested that TV and the Internet play a major role in this by promoting a sedentary lifestyle (Kluger, 2000). The evidentiary basis of such claims, however, largely awaits future assessment. Research also continued to demonstrate almost undeniable positive influences of TV as well (see chap. 6). These influences seemed largely tied to the relatively small amounts of intentionally prosocial programming, however.

Beyond this, the high level of researcher consensus concerning TV violence (see chap. 10) contributed to public policy initiatives designed to address the issue. Public concerns about media violence showed signs of having an impact as well. Yet these concerns may be linked as much to anecdotal evidence as to formal research (Nisbett & Ross, 1980; Taylor & Thompson, 1972). For one thing, when journalists cover available research, their tendencies to seek comments from both sides may create an impression that fails to convey the existing overwhelming scholarly consensus. In addition, reported anecdotes often are quite striking. For example,

> the influence of professional wrestling has been linked by news outlets, including Court TV, to the deaths of children aged 6, 3, and 18 months. The 6-year-old was thrown repeatedly into the iron stairway railing; the 3-year-old died after his brother performed a "running clothesline" move across his throat; the 18-month-old was body-slammed on a couch until his cousin got bored and returned to watching TV before finally noticing blood foaming from the unconscious baby's nose. (Malkin, 2000)

Such examples may or may not be true. The first evidently refers to claims made by a criminal defense attorney. In any case, anecdotal evidence cannot substitute for scientific work, in part, because it is impossible to isolate causes in individual instances. Here, watching wrestling might affect the form, but not the substance, of fatal aggressiveness among children. In addition, formal research offers insights into possible solutions to such problems, such as what mitigation strategies to include in media literacy classes and what form of v-chip may be most useful (see Cantor, 2000).

Trained first as a journalist and then as a communication scientist, I have attempted to reach students with research about mass communication that is of potential social benefit. I hope it helps inform not only future media practitioners, but a much wider variety of college students and, thereby indirectly, society. Certain mass communication programs today are taking more seriously than in their past the social obligation to educate students about the media and their impact, instead of merely training large numbers of people in the minutiae of their first job. Conceivably, technological changes in the media and educational reform could cause more programs to find a place in the liberal arts mission of the academy and attempt to contribute to the education of all students, rather than just of future practitioners (see Blanchard & Christ, 1993). A common theme through the various chapters is a call for education in the public schools about critical media consumption. Perhaps this can help reduce harmful consequences of media and enhance the beneficial so that future writers can present a brighter picture. In short, education about media effects has the potential to change, and sometimes limit, such effects.

This volume has attempted to interpret the current state of mass communication theory and research. It has also discussed the pragmatic and/or pragmatist roots of substantial portions of the field. Yet to paraphrase William James, the ultimate meaning and importance of the field lies more in its fruits than in its roots, pragmatic or otherwise. To date, the corporate sector often has reaped the fruits of media studies — for instance, with improved advertising techniques. In a free (and perhaps in any) society, social benefit perhaps will result more from the enlightened actions of ordinary citizens, following the dissemination of research by education, than from the acts of censors or governmental regulators. Despite society's more serious treatment of the TV violence issue, such fruits sometimes die on the vine or remain mostly out of sight — perhaps part of a distant horizon. Therefore, this book represents a small attempt to stimulate the transactive processes of education as well as those of change.

Appendix
The Philosophical Context

Many important theorists and researchers in mass communication probably do their work without ever seriously considering its metaphysical and
epistemological underpinnings. Metaphysics is the branch of philosophy
that seeks to explain the nature of reality and the structure of the world.
Epistemology, closely related to metaphysics, deals with the nature and
limits of knowledge. This appendix discusses implicit philosophical foundations of research. In the light of a pragmatist orientation, the very term
metaphysics, implying that human thought can somehow transcend the
natural world of which it is a part, becomes something of a misnomer.
Thus, this section treats such ideas not with reference to any ultimate reality, but in terms of their consequences for research.

About 60 years ago, philosopher Stephen C. Pepper (1942) examined a
number of then influential philosophical worldviews and concluded that
only a few were relatively adequate. Those views were based on distinc-
tive root metaphors, such as defining the world as a machine. They included the formism of Plato and Aristotle; the mechanism of Descartes,
Hume and Locke; the organicism of Hegel and Royce; and the contextualism of Peirce, James, and Dewey. Pepper attempted to pull out the essence of each philosophical position, rather than the details associated
with any particular writer. Individuals tended to slip into eclecticism, as
when Dewey's work reflected aspects of both contextualism and organicism. Pepper believed that such combination only created unnecessary confusion.

According to Reck (1982), Pepper's ideas likely contributed to Kuhn's
notion of the paradigm (see chap. 1). Pepper (1982) stated that

there is practically no difference between the function of the paradigm as a guiding conceptual pattern in scientific procedure and that of the root metaphor as a guiding conceptual pattern in world hypotheses except the restricted scope of the former. (p. 204)

Fundamentally, these worldviews differ from one another along two dimensions. First, formism and mechanism are analytic: The essence of an event or object is found in its parts, not in its whole. To properly understand something, one should examine its pieces. Contextualism and organicism are synthetic: The essence is found in the synthesized whole, not its parts. The whole is something qualitatively different from the sum of its parts, and to analyze an event or object (i.e., break it down into its parts) is to distort it. Second, formism and contextualism are dispersive: The world is not necessarily orderly, nor is everything inherently related to everything else. These views do not assume that a cause exists for everything; things may occur by pure chance. Note that these positions do not assume the existence of spontaneity; they merely allow it as a possibility. Mechanism and organicism are integrative: They assume that order is categorical—that everything has its cause.

Each worldview contains a somewhat different conception of what truth is. The three major conceptions of truth found in Pepper's world hypotheses—correspondence, coherence, and instrumentalism—are all likely are to come into play in research. In particular, each may have a role in the validation of scientific ideas. As Kaplan (1964) said, "a theory is not validated merely because it is accepted; rather, it is accepted—by scientists, at any rate—because it is believed to be validated" (p. 312).

Formism

To a formist, the basic metaphor for the world is the similarity of forms (e.g., as when a charcoal drawing resembles a person's face). An idea is true if it corresponds in form with the external world. Even a verbal or mathematical description of a theoretical scientific law is true if it allows one to visualize the form of whatever it describes. Given the dispersive nature of formism, scientific laws (e.g., those relating to gravitation and inertia) are seen as possibly unrelated to one another, rather than inherently linked as part of the cosmic structure of the universe. Although few, if any, mass communication researchers really qualify as formists, influence from this worldview occurs in the research literature. For instance, it is common to see references to a theoretical idea corresponding to the facts. In addition, such research concepts as the *stereotype* and *schemata* (see chaps. 6 and 9) are sometimes used in formistic ways. Finally, traditional notions of universal scientific laws often take formistic forms.

Because of its considerable influence (if questioned, most people probably would define truth in these terms), the *correspondence idea* merits further consideration. It can be defined as "the theory of truth that a statement is rendered true by the existence of a fact with corresponding elements and a similar structure" (Flexner, 1987, p. 455). Many traditional correspondence notions of truth are both *objective* and *absolute* ones (Popper, 1983). That is to say, they both assume that truth is a property independent of human knowledge about an object or event (e.g., something may be true even if no one is aware of or believes in it) and can be, in principle, complete and final. Despite its intuitive appeal, philosophers have failed to explain adequately the puzzling notion of how human thought can correspond with the world.

Formists are philosophical *realists* in the specialized sense that they believe universal entitles such as forms, laws, or essences (e.g., of an object such as a blue jay) are real rather than mind-imposed. Thus, their position contrasts with *nominalism*—the dominant tendency among modern philosophers (see Lewis & Smith, 1980). Nominalists deny the existence of mind-independent universals. The work of Charles Darwin, with its emphasis on process and change rather than permanence, contributed to the nominalists' predominance today. One should not confuse this issue with the question of the existence of a physical world. In this sense, both formistic realists and many nominalists accept the existence of a world beyond human perception.

Mechanism

In communication and related fields, one commonly hears humanists vaguely criticize quantitative, social-scientific researchers for being mechanists. Often this probably means that the scientific study of human behavior dehumanizes people. For scientists, however, mechanism is a very influential philosophical position. Mechanism assumes that the world (or, less commonly, some part of it) metaphorically is some sort of a machine (e.g., the clock of Newtonian mechanics or the computer of cognitive psychology). The job of the scientist becomes one of describing the parts of the cosmic machine, their relation to each other, and the interrelated laws that regulate its operation. A significant implication of mechanism is that, in principle, one can attain complete and final knowledge through analysis (Hayes et al., 1988). That is to say, some basic element exists (perhaps a subatomic particle) that will allow the scientist to describe the world completely. If so, the successful scientific study of communication, or any other phenomenon, might eventually force all researchers to become physicists.

Mechanists believe in a philosophical separation of mind and matter (e.g., mind and body). Because of their acceptance of this mind–matter dualism, mechanists distinguish primary qualities—those aspects of the physical world (such as the mass, weight, or electronic charge of an object) that one cannot observe directly from secondary qualities (e.g., color and sound) that are characteristics of objects only as people perceive them. Most mechanists are concerned primarily with matter—with the physical world. In fact, a few mechanists, such as the behaviorist psychologist J.B. Watson, have denied the existence of the human mind, arguing that researchers should only concern themselves with primary qualities (e.g., human behavior). Yet others (e.g., George Berkeley) denied the existence of the physical world and argued that inquiry should be limited to the mind or secondary qualities.

To most mechanists, perception occurs purely within the mind, but it is somehow related to physiological processes in a human being that the outside environment sets off. Thus, one cannot experience the physical world directly. Instead, to understand the cosmic machine, one must infer the relations both between mental experience and one's physiology and between this physiology and the world outside. To a mechanist, *truth* is a name for physiological reactions that are adjusted causally with the outside environment. For example, one perceives an object and orally identifies it as an automobile. The stimulus has set off physical reactions, which are correlated somehow with perception. Because of the impossibility of perceiving the physical world directly, mechanists often stress the need for many observers to validate an observation independently (Hayes et al., 1988). Mechanists typically embrace nominalism, which prevents traditional formistic notions of truth as correspondence from fitting in with their philosophy (see Pepper, 1942). Their ideas mesh with forms of empiricism—a prototypically nominalist philosophy. Empiricists tend to limit the real world to that which can be perceived. Mechanism shows up in mass communication research in various ways—most obviously when a researcher studies media effects on the assumption that the cause and effect are independent, separable entities.

Organicism

Unlike mechanism, organicism assumes that one reaches absolute knowledge by working up, rather than down, to it. Pepper (1942) described the metaphor for organicism as a more or less concealed organic process, but he also expressed some dissatisfaction with the metaphor. Intellectually, an organicist's search for knowledge in some ways is akin to walking up a mountain, from the top of which one can see the whole of the universe, on a graded path that winds around all sides of the elevation. On the way up, one can see fragments of the surrounding countryside, but these often provide a contradictory or entirely false impression. For instance, one may see smaller peaks surrounding the mountain and assume that they continue for some distance, only to notice on reaching a higher elevation that a level plain starts a short distance away. When one reaches the top, the synthesized organic whole, which Hegel called the *absolute*, comes into view.

The organicist theory of truth is one of coherence, which occurs when all observational inconsistencies and contradictions vanish, and the whole is seen as having been implicit in the previously misleading parts. Clearly, coherence comes into play in research—for instance, when modern psychologists reject ideas from parapsychology because they contradict other knowledge. Nonetheless, too much emphasis on it "ruthlessly suppresses as rebellion any movement of thought which might make for a scientific revolution" (Kaplan, 1964, p. 315).

Until absolute knowledge is reached, a dualism persists between *appearances* and *reality*. Organicism views scientific knowledge as proceeding from the integration of fragments, as when Newtonian astronomy integrated the previous work of Aristotle, Copernicus, Kepler, and so on and took the field closer to its piece of the absolute. Organicism, typically a form of nominalism, has had influence on mass media researchers. For example, those using cognitive developmental theories to study the media influences on children (see chap. 7) may be implicit organicists.

Contextualism

This is Pepper's name for pragmatism. Pragmatism, often described as the only uniquely U.S. contribution to philosophy, was especially prominent during the early 20th century. Hook (1974) provided perhaps the most general definition. According to Hook, *pragmatism* is "the theory and practice of enlarging human freedom in a precarious and tragic world by the arts of intelligent social control" (p. 25).

Pepper evidently substituted the term *contextualism* for pragmatism in part because he wished to avoid the popular association during the 1940s of pragmatism with sheer practicality. Many scholars have also seen contextualism as closely linked to organicism, as indicated by occasional statements that "pragmatism is simply idealism with the absolute left out" (Pepper, 1942, p. 280). However, Pepper preferred, to separate them for good reason. For example, many pragmatists describe epistemology and methodology as identical. According to Kurtz (1992),

> [the] problem of epistemology—to try to penetrate the veil of perception and plumb the nature of reality—is considered to be illusory. On the contrary, the central issue is to delineate the methodology by which human intelligence and experience can cope with the world. (p. 69)

According to contextualism, the essence of the universe is found in the synthesized historical, yet categorically changing, event. Any event—inventing a scientific theory, driving a car, laughing at a joke—contains this essence. As Pepper (1942) wrote: "The quality of blowing your nose is just as cosmic and ultimate as Newton's writing down his gravitational formula. The fact that his formula is much more useful to many more people doesn't make it any more real" (p. 251).

Events are considered historical not in the common usage of the word (i.e., in the past), but because they change continuously and point both to past antecedents and future outcomes. Change is viewed as categorical; thus, knowledge always must remain provisional and relative (Georgoudi & Rosnow, 1985b). Therefore, researchers must avoid "the supposition that whatever is found true under certain conditions may forthwith be asserted universally or without limits and conditions. Because a thirsty man gets satisfaction in drinking water, bliss consists in being drowned" (Dewey, 1922/1957, p. 175). For example, researchers should exercise caution in using static, hypothetico-deductive models (see chap. 2) to explain dynamic phenomena (Georgoudi & Rosnow, 1985b). However, contextualists do not ignore, "the possibility that some forms of change are much slower than others so as to give the impression of timeless structures or qualities in the events examined" (Georgoudi & Rosnow, 1985b, p. 11). In short, scientific ideas are only tentative guides to action that may or may not apply in future situations.

To a contextualist, disorder is also a categorical feature of the universe — so much so that it does not even preclude order. Therefore, change is not an appearance that dualistically masks the reality of permanent structures in nature, whether these consist of underlying mechanics or overarching organicist integrations (Pepper, 1942). Rather, it represents the essence of the world.

A discussion of other categories of contextualism, linked to its ineradicable features of change and disorder or novelty, can help provide the reader with a feel for the worldview. Most basic are the quality and texture of the changing event. *Quality* refers to the total meaning of the event, and *texture* consists of the details that define a quality. These details become fused to varying degrees in the eyes of observers. Pepper (1942) illustrated fusion with a musical chord; if a musician changes one of the tones, an entirely different quality results (e.g., a major vs. minor chord). In turn, the texture includes strands, a context, and references. A strand contributes directly and the context indirectly to the quality of a texture, although formally the two are inseparable (Pepper, 1942). The references are temporal strands linking the event with its earlier initiations and its anticipated consummations. That is to say, both prior events and an observer's expectations about where an event is leading help determine its fused meaning.

According to contextualism, a person watching TV drama experiences synthesized yet constantly changing events, the quality of which is defined at a given point in time by the nature of the medium, the specific content seen, the emotional state of the reader or viewer, the room temperature, the presence of others, and so forth. To the individual viewer, the specifics of content seen at any moment would be the strands, and earlier scenes would make up part of the context. The fused meaning of a scene reflects temporal senses of direction both back toward earlier scenes and forward toward the viewer's expectations about subsequent scenes and the outcome of the episode. Of course, if the strands or context are altered, the meaning of the event likely will change. For example, a viewer who turns the set on in the middle of a dramatic episode will have to interpret what he or she sees without the temporal references to earlier scenes.

Labeling something a *texture*, rather than a strand or context, is arbitrary (Pepper, 1942). For example, the viewer could focus momentarily on the facial features of a character. The viewer would perceive the face as a texture with its own quality (fused appearance), strands (mouth, nose, and eyes), and context (whatever is in the background), instead of as a contributing strand in the texture of the ongoing scene. With further relaxation of fusion, the viewer could perceive the mouth and nose as textures in their own right. As a result of the view that nothing can be studied in isolation from its context, contextualists recognize the utility of analysis, but argue that knowledge never can be absolute, complete, or final. Unlike in mechanism, there is no ultimate bottom to the world. The most basic unit of an object or event is its textural quality, which results from a fusion of strands and the context. "In the extended analysis of any event we presently find ourselves in the context of that event, and so on from event to event as long as we wish to go, which would be forever or until we got tired" (Pepper, 1942, p. 249). Because of its arbitrary nature, analysis must be at least indirectly practical in the broad sense of helping to attain some goal. It matters not whether the goal is to understand the world or change it; pragmatism imposes no restrictions on one's goals. Of analysis for its own sake, however, the contextualist asks: "What is the good of it, except as the mere fun of paddling about in the ocean of things?" (Pepper, 1942, p. 250).

In contextualism, the distinction between mind and matter also vanishes. Knowledge comes from the transaction (see chap. 4) of the knower and the known as someone acts on objects in the world. Perception is not some spiritual phenomenon correlated in a puzzling way with the physical world. Rather, the quality of any observed event or object results from a texture of strands partly derived from the event and partly from the observer and the means of observation (Pepper, 1934). As the tools of observation change, the perceived qualities of events are likely to as well. By definition, an observer can never know what qualities an event or object has outside of perception. Thus, a contextualist judges the truth of a scientific idea by its usefulness for solving practical problems or attaining the goals of science (see chap. 2), rather than by whether it somehow copies or mirrors a phenomenon of interest. Science does not provide the human race with a "God's-eye" view of the world, as contemporary pragmatists like to point out. "But what outside reality may be, in and for itself, abstracted from all human behavioral needs and all human behavioral capacities, we do not, cannot, and need not know" (Tolman, 1932, p. 431).

No pragmatist would equate the fused quality of a potentially useful idea with the qualities of events to which it refers. For example, early contextualists such as Tolman (1932) viewed scientific ideas as maps that guide people in dealing with the world. However, a person reading a road map experiences a quite different texture and quality than does someone who actually drives a given route. Nonetheless, if the map works, "idea and thing become one" (p. 429)

Contextualism is not without its detractors, however, especially regarding its notion of truth. For example, mechanistic-oriented scientists are likely to see contextualists as "merely technicians, more interested in changing events than understanding them" (Hayes et al., 1988, p. 106). Given the contextualist categories, however, any event can be factored in any number of ways, and whatever advances some purpose provides the only basis of choice. The supposed association of contextualist truth with naked expediency, which James' loose use of language unfortunately encouraged, has long made the pragmatists the target of much humor and caricature. Perhaps because of such criticisms, some modern contextualist writers (e.g., Jenkins, 1974; McGuire, 1983) have tended to deemphasize or modify its theory of truth, *instrumentalism*, a term borrowed from Dewey.

Based on the influence of Darwin and his theory of evolution, pragmatists saw thinking and knowledge as mental capacities that human beings evolved to help them adapt to their environment. As discussed by James (1907/1975), "ideas (which themselves are but parts of our experience) become true just in so far as they help us to get into satisfactory relations with other parts of our experience" (p. 34). An idea is truer than another only if it is more helpful. Nor is knowledge changeless or stagnant, according to instrumentalists. Ideas are not true or false inherently. Rather, they become true as part of events in the world, as they prove useful, as their consequences become known. There are no eternal truths in pragmatism. Rather, new evidence can modify or change any belief. Contextualism rejects extreme forms of both philosophical idealism and materialism (Georgoudi & Rosnow, 1985b). The world is not constructed solely from human ideas or intentions, nor are human ideas merely a product of an external reality. If ideas are merely mirror images that the outside world imposes on an individual, how can one account for their ability to change the world (Hook, 1987)?

Common sense probably suggests, to most people, the correspondence theory of truth of formism. Some pragmatists, notably Peirce and James, actually retained the idea of correspondence as part of their notions about truth. Contextualists, however, define correspondence in their own way. Ideas and the objects and events they describe are not static entities, nor can an idea correspond with external reality without being linked to it through action, as when a key corresponds to a lock when one opens a door (Hook, 1987). As Pepper (1942) described the argument, formism "goes wrong in thinking that events can correspond without an active operational juncture of one with the other" (p. 277). That is to say, there is no inherent similarity between reading a road map and the act of driving from one place to another or between the map and the portion of the planet that one observes when traveling. The "dynamic correspondence" (J.E. Smith, 1978, p. 77) of contextualism only occurs when one successfully uses the map to navigate a given route or identify one's location. According to Almeder (1986):

> The scientific method is valid . . . because it produces beliefs that are useful in that they allow us to adapt successfully, and that particular quality is impossible to explain unless we suppose that the same beliefs are saying in some epistemologically privileged way how the world is. (p. 81)

Contextualists find a grain of accuracy in the coherence conception of knowledge as well. The coherence theory of organicism tends to confuse the nature and the results of pragmatist truth (Pepper, 1942). By nature, truth is the successful working of an idea, which then results in a sense of coherence.

Despite Pepper's warning about eclecticism, contextualism is rather unique in that it allows one to borrow ideas from the other views (e.g., the mechanistic conception of the human mind as a computer that underlies much of modern cognitive psychology). Such borrowing remains acceptable as long as one ultimately assesses the truth or adequacy of a borrowed idea against the contextualistic standard (Hayes et al., 1988).

As articulated by Pepper, pragmatic contextualism tends toward nominalism. The classical pragmatists, however, disagreed about this issue. Peirce fervently embraced realism, James was a clear nominalist, and Dewey and Mead displayed elements of each (Lewis & Smith, 1980). Viewed pragmatically, the debate has serious consequences for science and human life. Nominalists typically stress individualism, chance, Darwinism, capitalism, and free will; realists often embrace collectivism, law, Christianity, communalism, altruism, and determinism (Lewis & Smith, 1980). Pragmatic instrumentalism has nominalist overtones, but the communitarian or social component in the thought of Dewey, Mead, and Peirce fits in with realism. Lewis and Smith (1980) alleged that combining nominalism and realism is akin to trying to mix oil and water. Matthews (1982) disagreed, "Pragmatism was in great part a rebellion against the tyranny of absolute categories, an insistence that the demands of theory taken with absolute rigidity could distort and imprison, that by human results should theories be judged" (p. 476). In short, thou shall not crucify fertile, consequential scholarship upon a cross of philosophical consistency.

Mead's ideas, for example, about the human mind (see chap. 1) neatly illustrate a place for both nominalist and realist elements. He assumed that the human mind emerges from a matrix that is both biologically Darwinian (i.e., nominalist) and social (i.e., realist). In some ways, the theory may illustrate realist philosopher Morris Cohen's (1931/1953) *principle of polarity*—the idea that opposite categories such as individuality and universality (or, presumably, nominalism and realism) "must always be kept together though never identified" (p. xi). A neo-Hegelian idea, it assumes that opposites rely on each other for their meaningfulness. Thus, "positive gains in philosophy can be made not by simply trying to prove that one side or the other is the truth, but by trying to get at the difficulty and determining in what respect and to what extent each side is justified" (p. xi).

Especially in its Deweyan form, contextualism undermines many other traditional philosophical dualisms. Throughout his life, Dewey argued that these result from erecting "the results of analysis into real entities" (cited in Rorty, 1982, p. 80). In addition to the mind–matter (and theory–practice) separation, the dualisms between art and science, facts and values, thinking and doing, and means and ends also vanish.

Dewey (1927/1946) believed both art and science represented potentially interlinked means of coping with the environment. For example, only a small number of people within academia often read and understand the results of social-scientific investigation. Artistic presentation can create public appeal for such material, by breaking "through the crust of conventionalized and routine consciousness" (Dewey, 1927/1946, p. 183). To Dewey (1934/1958), the arts of history, poetry, and science

> all have finally the same *material*; that which is constituted by the interaction of the live creature with his surroundings. . . . Science uses the medium that is adapted to the purpose of control and prediction, of increase of power; it is an art. (pp. 319–320)

Similarly, many scientists pursuing pure research traditionally have seen their work as value free probably because they believe that the mathematical vocabulary that has worked so well in the natural sciences since Galileo, and that seems free of moral significance, mirrors reality (Rorty,

1982). Instead of somehow capturing nature's own language, Rorty suggested that Galileo just lucked out and found an especially useful vocabulary for his purposes. Pure science (see chap. 1) is allegedly only concerned with what is, rather than with normative matters or practical use. At present, many scholars would argue that science is never really free of values for a variety of reasons (see the discussion in Kaplan, 1964). For example, university researchers today who use human subjects in their work must obtain approval from their peer-review committees. These concerns with research ethics typically address both the possible harm done to human subjects by research (e.g., by exposing the young to televised violence) and the possible social harm creating by not doing research (e.g., into the causes of violence). Thus, they emphasize the inevitable context of values within which inquiry occurs (Georgoudi & Rosnow, 1985b).

Beyond the fact that advocacy of value freedom in science reflects an obvious value, what a scientist (or anyone else) concludes depends on human valuation. For instance, scientists can never be absolutely certain that their conclusions are sound; they have to live with a certain risk of error. As previously discussed, they normally behave conservatively in forming conclusions. The greater danger perhaps is not so much that values influence what questions scientists address, but that they may intrude inappropriately into the interpretation that researchers place on research findings. The political views of social scientists, for instance, might cause them to set impossibly high (or low) criteria before concluding that certain media contents have harmful or beneficial social effects. Yet values obtain a kind of objective status to the degree that they are informed by (without being strictly deduced from) facts.

Similarly, thinking and doing are not separate forms of behavior, but interlinked means of environmental adjustment. Speaking of the early pragmatists, Wilcox (1992) said: "Maybe the mind or mental phenomena are something that comes out of a relationship between people and their environments, as opposed to being something that is inside people" (p. 39). Hence, theory and practice cannot be viewed in isolation from each other.

In this light, there are no absolute ends in life (other than death), and what serves as an end for one purpose becomes a means to another. Scientific knowledge is no exception. Often it simply may serve as a means to more knowledge, as when scientists value experiments because their results suggest a need for many other studies. However, knowledge often can have a practical effect on the world, changing it in ways that require additional inquiry.

References

Abel, R. (1966-1967). Pragmatism and the outlook of modern science. *Philosophy and Phenomenological Research, 27*, 45–54.

Abramson, P. R., & Hayashi, H. (1984). Pornography in Japan: Cross-cultural and theoretical considerations. In N. M. Malamuth & E. Donnerstein (Eds.), *Pornography and sexual aggression* (pp. 173–183). Orlando, FL: Academic Press.

Ajzen, I., & Fishbein, M. (1980). *Understanding attitudes and predicting social behavior*. Englewood Cliffs, NJ: Prentice-Hall.

Akhavan-Majid, R., & Wolf, G. (1991). American mass media and the myth of libertarianism: Toward an "elite power group" theory. *Critical Studies in Mass Communication, 8*, 139–151.

Allen, M., D'Alessio, D., & Brezgel, K. (1995). A meta-analysis summarizing the effects of pornography: II. Aggression after exposure. *Human Communication Research, 22*, 258–283.

Allen, M., & Reynolds, R. (1993). The elaboration likelihood model and the sleeper effect: An assessment of attitude change over time. *Communication Theory, 3*, 73–82.

Allen, M., & Stiff, J. (1989). Testing three models for the sleeper effect. *Western Journal of Speech Communication, 53*, 411–426.

Almeder, R. (1986). A definition of pragmatism. *History of Philosophy Quarterly, 31*, 79–88.

Altschull, J. H. (1984). *Agents of power: The role of news media in human affairs*. New York: Longman.

American politics: Self-centered [Review of the book *Bowling alone: The collapse and revival of American community*]. (2000, July 8). *The Economist, 356*, 86–87.

Andersen, R. H., Crespo, C. J., Bartlett, S. J., Cheskin, L. J., & Pratt, M. (1998). Relationship of physical activity and television watching with body weight and level of fatness among children. *Journal of the American Medical Association, 279*, 938–942.

Anderson, D. R., Bryant, J., Wilder, A., Santomero, A., Williams, M., & Crawley, A. M. (2000). Researching Blue's Clues: Viewing behavior and impact. *Media Psychology, 2*, 179–194.

Anderson, J. R. (1980). *Cognitive psychology and its implications*. San Francisco: Freeman.

Apel, K. (1977). The a priori of communication and the foundation of the humanities. In F. R. Dallmayr & T. A. McCarthy (Eds.), *Understanding and social inquiry* (pp. 292–315). Notre Dame, IN: University of Notre Dame Press.

Armstrong, G. B., Boiarsky, G. A., & Mares, M. (1991). Background television and reading performance. *Communication Monographs, 58*, 235–253.

Asch, S. E. (1952). *Social psychology*. New York: Houghton Mifflin.

Asher, H. B. (1976). *Causal modeling*. Sage University Paper series on Quantitative Applications in the Social Sciences, 07-003. Beverly Hills: Sage Publications.

Attorney General's Commission on Pornography: Final Report. (1986, July). Washington, DC: U.S. Department of Justice.

Babrow, A. S., & Swanson, D. L. (1988). Disentangling antecedents of audience exposure levels: Extending expectancy-value analyses of gratifications sought from television news. *Communication Monographs, 55*, 1–21.

Ball-Rokeach, S. J. (1998). A theory of media power and a theory of media use: Different stories, questions, and ways of thinking. *Mass Communication & Society, 1*, 5–40.

Ball-Rokeach, S. J., & DeFleur, M. L. (1976). A dependency model of mass-media effects. *Communication Research, 3*, 3–21.

Ball-Rokeach, S. J., Rokeach, M., & Grube, J. W. (1984). *The Great American Values Test: Influencing behavior and belief through television*. New York: The Free Press.

Bandura, A. (1969). *Principles of behavioral modification*. New York: Holt, Rinehart & Winston.

Bandura, A. (1973). *Aggression: A social learning analysis*. Englewood Cliffs, NJ: Prentice-Hall.

Barber, B. R. (2000, August). The crack in the picture window [Review of the book *Bowling alone: The collapse and revival of American community*]. *The Nation, 271*, pp. 29–32, 34.

Baron, J. N., & Reiss, P. C. (1985). Same time, next year: Aggregate analyses of the mass media and violent behavior. *American Sociological Review, 50*, 347–363.

Baron, L., & Straus, M. A. (1984). Sexual stratification, pornography, and rape in the United States. In N. M. Malamuth & E. Donnerstein (Eds.), *Pornography and sexual aggression* (pp. 185–209). Orlando, FL: Academic Press.

Bartlett, F. C. (1932). *Remembering: A study in experimental and social psychology*. Cambridge: Cambridge University Press.

Bass, A. Z. (1969). Refining the "gatekeeper" concept: A UN radio case study. *Journalism Quarterly, 46*, 69–72.

Bauer, R. A. (1963). The initiative of the audience. *Journal of Advertising Research, 3*, 2–7.

Bauer, R. A. (1964). The obstinate audience: The influence process from the point of view of social communication. *American Psychologist, 19*, 319–328.

Beaman, A. L. (1991). An empirical comparison of meta-analytic and traditional reviews. *Personality and Social Psychology Bulletin, 17*, 252–257.

Beaman, A. L., Barnes, B. K., Klentz, B., & McQuirk, B. (1978). Increasing helping rates through information dissemination: Teaching pays. *Personality and Social Psychology Bulletin, 4*, 406–411.

Becker, L. B., & Whitney, D. C. (1980). Effects of media dependencies: Audience assessment of government. *Communication Research, 7*, 95–120.

Behr, R. L., & Iyengar, S. (1985). Television news, real-world cues, and changes in the public agenda. *Public Opinion Quarterly, 49*, 38–57.

Bell, D. (1947). Adjusting men to machines: Social scientists explore the world of the factory. *Commentary, 3*, 79–88.

Belson, W. A. (1978). *Television violence and the adolescent boy*. Westmead, England: Saxon House.

Beltran, L. R. (1976). Alien premises, objects, and methods in Latin-American communication research. *Communication Research, 3*, 107–134.

Beniger, J. R. (1987). Toward an old new paradigm: The half-century flirtation with mass society. *Public Opinion Quarterly, 51*, S46–S66.

Berelson, B. (1949). What "missing" the newspaper means. In P. F. Lazarsfeld & F. N. Stanton (Eds.), *Communications research 1948–49* (pp. 111–129). New York: Harper.

Berelson, B. (1952). *Content analysis in communication research*. Glencoe, IL: The Free Press.

Berelson, B. (1959). The state of communication research. *Public Opinion Quarterly, 23*, 1–6.

Berger, P., & Luckmann, T. (1966). *The social construction of reality.* Garden City, NY: Doubleday.

Berkowitz, D. (1992). Who sets the media agenda? The ability of policy makers to determine news decisions. In J. D. Kennamer (Ed.), *Public opinion, the press, and public policy* (pp. 81–102). Westport, CT: Praeger.

Berkowitz, L. (1971, December). Sex and violence: We can't have it both ways. *Psychology Today,* pp. 14, 18, 20, 22–23.

Berkowitz, L., & Donnerstein, E. (1982). External validity is more than skin deep: Some answers to criticisms of laboratory experiments. *American Psychologist, 37,* 245–257.

Berry, W. E., Braman, S., Christians, C., Guback, T. G., Helle, S. J., Liebovich, L. W., Nerone, J. C., & Rotzoll, K. B. (1995). *Last rights: Revisiting four theories of the press.* Urbana, IL: University of Illinois Press.

Biddle, W. W. (1932). *Propaganda and education.* New York: Teachers College, Columbia University.

Biocca, F. (2000). New media technology and youth: Trends in the evolution of new media. *Journal of Adolescent Health, 27S,* 22–29.

Black, J., & Whitney, F. C. (1988). *Introduction to mass communication* (2nd ed.). Dubuque, IA: Brown.

Blanchard, R. O., & Christ, W. G. (1993). *Media education and the liberal arts: A blueprint for the new professionalism.* Hillsdale, NJ: Lawrence Erlbaum Associates.

Blumer, H. (1946). Elementary collective groupings. In A. M. Lee (Ed.), *New outline of the principles of sociology* (pp. 178–198). New York: Barnes & Noble.

Blumer, H. (1948). Public opinion and public opinion polling. *American Sociological Review, 13,* 542–549.

Blumer, H., & Hauser, P. M. (1933). *Movies, delinquency, and crime.* New York: Macmillan.

Blumler, J. G., & Katz, E. (1974). Forward. In J. G. Blumler & E. Katz (Eds.), *The uses of mass communications: Current perspectives on gratifications research* (pp. 13–16). Beverly Hills, CA: Sage.

Bogart, L. (Ed.). (1987). The future study of public opinion: A symposium. *Public Opinion Quarterly, 51,* S173–S191.

Bogart, L. (1991, August). The pollster and the Nazis. *Commentary,* pp. 47–49.

Bornstein, R. F. (1989a). Exposure and affect: Overview and meta-analysis of research, 1968–1987. *Psychological Bulletin, 106,* 265–289.

Bornstein, R. F. (1989b). Subliminal techniques and propaganda tools: Review and critique. *The Journal of Mind and Behavior, 10,* 231–262.

Boster, F. J., & Mongeau, P. (1984). Fear-arousing persuasive messages. In R. N. Bostrom (Ed.), *Communication yearbook 8* (pp. 330–375). Beverly Hills, CA: Sage.

Boush, D. M., Friestad, M., & Rose, G. M. (1994). Adolescent skepticism toward TV advertising and knowledge of advertising tactics. *Journal of Consumer Research, 21,* 165–175.

Bransford, J. D., Barclay, J. R., & Franks, J. J. (1972). Sentence memory: A constructive versus interpretive approach. *Cognitive Psychology, 2,* 331–350.

Bransford, J. D., & Franks, J. J. (1971). The abstraction of linguistic ideas. *Cognitive Psychology, 2,* 331–350.

Brewer, W. F., & Nakamura, G. V. (1984). The nature and functions of schemas. In R. S. Wyer & T. K. Srull (Eds.), *Handbook of social cognition* (Vol. 1, pp. 119–160). Hillsdale, NJ: Lawrence Erlbaum Associates.

Bryce, J. (1981). The nature of public opinion. In M. Janowitz & P. Hirsch (Eds.), *Reader in public opinion and mass communication* (pp. 3–9). New York: The Free Press.

Brown, H. I. (1977). *Perception, theory and commitment: The new philosophy of science.* Chicago: University of Chicago Press.

Brown, J. A. (1991). *Television "critical-viewing skills" education: Major media literacy projects in the United States and selected countries.* Hillsdale, NJ: Lawrence Erlbaum Associates.

Brown, R. (1958). *Words and things*. New York: The Free Press.

Bryant, J., & Brown, D. (1989). Uses of pornography. In D. Zillmann & J. Bryant (Eds.), *Pornography: Research advances and policy considerations* (pp. 25–55). Hillsdale, NJ: Lawrence Erlbaum Associates.

Bryant, J., & Zillmann, D. (1984). Using television to alleviate boredom and stress: Selective exposure as a function of induced excitational states. *Journal of Broadcasting, 28,* 1–20.

Campbell, J. (1995). Community without fusion: Dewey, Mead, Tufts. In R. Hollinger & D. Depew (Eds.), *Pragmatism from progressivism to postmodernism* (pp. 56–71). Westport, CT: Praeger.

Cancian, F. M. (1968). Varieties of functional analysis. In D. L. Sills (Ed.), *International encyclopedia of the social sciences* (Vol. 6, pp. 29–43). New York: Macmillan.

Cantor, J. (1994). Fright reactions to mass media. In J. Bryant & D. Zillmann (Eds.), *Media effects: Advances in theory and research* (pp. 213–245). Hillsdale, NJ: Lawrence Erlbaum Associates.

Cantor, J. (2000). Media violence. *Journal of Adolescent Health, 27S,* 30–34.

Cantor, J., Harrison, K., & Krcmar, M. (1998). Ratings and advisories: Implications for the new ratings system for television. In J. T. Hamilton (Ed.), *Television violence and public policy* (pp. 179–211). Ann Arbor, MI: The University of Michigan Press.

Cantril, H. (1952). *The invasion from Mars: A study in the psychology of panic.* Princeton, NJ: Princeton University Press.

Carey, J. W. (1989). *Communication as culture: Essays on media and society.* Boston: Unwin Hyman.

Carey, J. W., & Kreiling, A. L. (1974). Popular culture and uses and gratifications: Notes toward an accommodation. In J. G. Blumler & E. Katz (Eds.), *The uses of mass communications: Current perspectives on gratifications research* (pp. 225–248). Beverly Hills, CA: Sage.

Carter, R. F. (1989). On paradigmatic productivity. In B. Dervin, L. Grossberg, B. J. O'Keefe, & E. Wartella (Eds.), *Rethinking communication: Volume 1. Paradigm issues* (pp. 144–147). Newbury Park, CA: Sage.

Carter, R. F. (1990). Our future research agenda: Confronting challenges . . . or our dying gasp? *Journalism Quarterly, 67,* 282–285.

Carter, R. F., Stamm, K. R., & Heintz-Knowles, K. (1992). Agenda-setting and consequentiality. *Journalism Quarterly, 69,* 868–877.

Carveth, R., & Alexander, A. (1985). Soap opera viewing motivations and the cultivation process. *Journal of Broadcasting & Electronic Media, 29,* 259–273.

Centerwall, B. S. (1989). Exposure to television as a cause of violence. In G. Comstock (Ed.), *Public communication and behavior* (Vol. 2, pp. 1–58). Orlando, FL: Academic Press.

Centerwall, B. S. (1992). Television and violence: The scale of the problem and where to go from here. *Journal of the American Medical Association, 267,* 3059–3063.

Centerwall, B. S. (1996). Penetrating the mind: Television as a cause of violence. In R. R. Ivatury & C. G. Cayton (Eds.), *Handbook of penetrating trauma* (pp. 70–78). Baltimore, MD: Williams & Wilkins.

Chaffee, S. H. (1988). Differentiating the hypodermic model from empirical research: A comment on Bineham's commentaries. *Communication Monographs, 55,* 247–249.

Chaffee, S. H. (1991). *Communication concepts 1: Explication.* Newbury Park, CA: Sage.

Chaffee, S. H., & Rogers, E. M. (1997). Wilbur Schramm: The founder. In W. Schramm, *The beginnings of communication study in America: A personal memoir* (pp. 125–153). Thousand Oaks, CA: Sage.

Chaffee, S. H., & Roser, C. (1986). Involvement and the consistency of knowledge, attitudes, and behavior. *Communication Research, 13,* 373–399.

Chaffee, S. H., & Schleuder, J. (1986). Measurement and effects of attention to media news. *Human Communication Research, 13,* 76–107.

Chaffee, S. H., & Wilson, D. G. (1977). Media rich, media poor: Two studies of diversity in agenda-holding. *Journalism Quarterly, 54,* 466–476.

Chaiken S., & Eagly, A. H. (1976). Communication modality as a determinant of message persuasiveness and message comprehensibility. *Journal of Personality and Social Psychology, 34,* 605–614.

Chaiken, S., & Eagly, A. H. (1983). Communication modality as a determinant of persuasion: The role of communicator salience. *Journal of Personality and Social Psychology, 45,* 241–256.

Check, J. V. P., & Guloien, T. H. (1989). Reported proclivity for coercive sex following repeated exposure to sexually violent pornography, nonviolent dehumanizing pornography, and erotica. In D. Zillmann & J. Bryant (Eds.), *Pornography: Research advances and policy considerations* (pp. 159–184). Hillsdale, NJ: Lawrence Erlbaum Associates.

Check, J. V. P., & Malamuth, N. M. (1986). Pornography and sexual aggression: A social learning theory analysis. In M. L. McLaughlin (Ed.), *Communication yearbook 9* (pp. 181–213). Beverly Hills, CA: Sage.

Chen, S., & Chaiken, S. (1999). The heuristic-systematic model in its broader context. In S. Chaiken & Y. Trope (Eds.), *Dual-process theories in social psychology* (pp. 73–96). New York: Guilford.

Christensen, F. (1986). Sexual callousness re-examined: A critique. *Journal of Communication, 36*(1), 174–183.

Cialdini, R. B. (1988). Communicating responsibly with the public: Researcher as edifier. *Communication Research, 15,* 781–792.

Cohen, B. C. (1963). *The press and foreign policy.* Princeton, NJ: Princeton University Press.

Cohen, J., & Cohen, P. (1983). *Applied multiple regression/correlation analysis for the behavioral sciences* (2nd ed.). Hillsdale, NJ: Lawrence Erlbaum Associates.

Cohen, M. (1931/1953). *Reason and nature: An essay on the meaning of scientific method.* Glencoe, IL: The Free Press.

Coleman, J. S. (1988). Social capital in the creation of human capital. *American Journal of Sociology, 94,* S95–S120.

Combs, S., & Slovic, P. (1979). Newspaper coverage of causes of death. *Journalism Quarterly, 56,* 837–843, 849.

Commission on Freedom of the Press. (1947). *A free and responsible press.* Chicago: The University of Chicago Press.

Commission on Obscenity and Pornography. (1970). *The report of the Commission on Obscenity and Pornography.* Washington, DC: U.S. Government Printing Office.

Compaine, B. M. (2000a). Distinguishing between concentration and competition. In B. M. Compaine & D. Gomery (Eds.), *Who owns the media?: Competition and concentration in the mass media industry* (3rd ed., pp. 507–535). Mahwah, NJ: Lawrence Erlbaum Associates.

Compaine, B. M. (2000b). The newspaper industry. In B. M. Compaine & D. Gomery (Eds.), *Who owns the media?: Competition and concentration in the mass media industry* (3rd ed., pp. 1–59). Mahwah, NJ: Lawrence Erlbaum Associates.

Converse, P. E. (1987). Changing conceptions of public opinion in the political process. *Public Opinion Quarterly, 51,* S12–S24.

Conway, J. C., & Rubin, A. M. (1991). Psychological predictors of television viewing motivation. *Communication Research, 18,* 443–463.

Cook, R. F., & Fosen, R. H. (1971). Pornography and the sex offender: Patterns of exposure and immediate arousal effects of pornographic stimuli. In *Technical Reports of the Commission on Obscenity and Pornography* (Vol. 7, pp. 149–162). Washington, DC: U.S. Government Printing Office.

Cook, T. D., & Campbell, D. T. (1979). *Quasi-experimentation: Design and analysis issues for field settings.* Chicago: Rand McNally College Publishing Co.

Cook, T. D., & Conner, R. F. (1976). Sesame Street Around the World: The educational impact. *Journal of Communication, 26*(2), 155–164.

Cook, T. D., Kendzierski, D. A., & Thomas, S. V. (1983). The implicit assumptions of television research: An analysis of the 1982 NIMH report on *"Television and behavior."* *Public Opinion Quarterly, 47,* 143–202.

Corteen, R. S., & Williams, T. M. (1986). Television and reading skills. In T. M. Williams (Ed.), *The impact of television: A natural experiment in three communities* (pp. 39–86). Orlando, FL: Academic Press.

Cotton, J. L. (1986). Cognitive dissonance in selective exposure. In D. Zillmann & J. Bryant (Eds.), *Selective exposure to communication* (pp. 11–33). Hillsdale, NJ: Lawrence Erlbaum Associates.

Court, J. H. (1984). Sex and violence: A ripple effect. In N. M. Malamuth & E. Donnerstein (Eds.), *Pornography and sexual aggression* (pp. 143–172). Orlando, FL: Academic Press.

Craig, R. T. (1989). Communication as a practical discipline. In B. Dervin, L. Grossberg, B. J. O'Keefe, & E. Wartella (Eds.), *Rethinking communication: Volume 1. Paradigm issues* (pp. 97–122). Newbury Park, CA: Sage.

Craig, R. T. (1993). Why are there so *many* communication theories? *Journal of Communication, 43*(3), 26–33.

Crespi, I. (1989). *Public opinion, polls, and democracy.* Boulder, CO: Westview.

Cressey, P. G. (1932/1968). *The taxi-dance hall: A sociological study in commercialized recreation and city life.* New York: Greenwood.

Cronbach, L. J. (1975). Beyond the two disciplines of scientific psychology. *American Psychologist, 30,* 116–127.

Cronen, V. E. (1995). Coordinated management of meaning: The consequentiality of communication and the recapturing of experience. In S. J. Sigman (Ed.), *The consequentiality of communication* (pp. 17–65). Hillsdale, NJ: Lawrence Erlbaum Associates.

Croteau, D., & Hoynes, W. (2000). *Media/society: Industries, images, and audiences* (2nd ed.). Thousand Oaks, CA: Pine Forge Press.

Danielson, W. A. (2000). Review of *Origins of mass commmunications research during the American Cold War: Educational effects and contemporary implications. Journalism Quarterly, 77,* 433–434.

Davis, D. K., & Robinson, J. P. (1989). Newsflow and democratic society in an age of electronic media. In G. Comstock (Ed.), *Political communication and behavior* (Vol. 2, pp. 59–102). Orlando, FL: Academic Press.

Deen, T. (1999, March 4). *U.N. health arm seeks global treaty against smoking.* Inter Press Service. Available: Lexis-Nexis, allnews files.

DeFleur, M. L., & Ball-Rokeach, S. J. (1989). *Theories of mass communication* (5th ed.). New York: Longman.

Delia, J. G. (1987). Communication research: A history. In C. R. Berger & S. H. Chaffee (Eds.), *Handbook of communication science* (pp. 20–98). Beverly Hills, CA: Sage.

Dershowitz, A. (1992). *Contrary to popular opinion.* New York: Pharos Books.

Dervin, B., Grossberg, L., O'Keefe, B. J., & Wartella, E. (Eds.). (1989). *Rethinking communication: Volume 1. Paradigm issues.* Newbury Park, CA: Sage.

Deutsch, K. W. (1952). On communication models in the social sciences. *Public Opinion Quarterly, 16,* 356–380.

Deutschmann, P. J., & Danielson, W. A. (1960). Diffusion of knowledge of the major news story. *Journalism Quarterly, 37,* 345–355.

Dewey, J. (1896). The reflex arc concept in psychology. *The Psychological Review, 3,* 357–370.

Dewey, J. (1916). *Democracy and education.* New York: Macmillan.

Dewey, J. (1922/1957). *Human nature and conduct.* New York: The Modern Library.

Dewey, J. (1925/1973). The development of American pragmatism. In J. J. McDermott (Ed.), *The philosophy of John Dewey: Vol. 1. The structure of experience* (pp. 41–58). New York: Putnam Sons.

Dewey, J. (1927/1946). *The public and its problems.* Denver, CO: Alan Swallow.

Dewey, J. (1929). *The quest for certainty: A study of the relation of knowledge and action.* New York: Minton, Balch.

Dewey, J. (1930/1981). Individuality in our day. In J. A. Boydston (Ed.), *The later works, 1925–1953/John Dewey* (Vol. 5, pp. 111–123). Carbondale, IL: Southern Illinois University Press.

Dewey, J. (1934/1958). *Art as experience.* New York: Capricorn Books.

Dewey, J. (1947). Liberating the social scientist: A plea to unshackle the study of man. *Commentary, 4,* 378–385.

Dewey, J., & Bentley, A. F. (1949). *Knowing and the known.* Boston: Beacon.

Diener, E., & DeFour, D. (1978). Does television violence enhance program popularity? *Journal of Personality and Social Psychology, 36,* 333–341.

Diesing, P. (1991). *How does social science work?: Reflections on practice.* Pittsburgh, PA: University of Pittsburgh Press.

Donnerstein, E. (1980). Aggressive erotica and violence against women. *Journal of Personality and Social Psychology, 39,* 269–277.

Donnerstein, E., Berkowitz, L., & Linz, E. (1986). *Role of aggressive and sexual images in violent pornography.* Unpublished manuscript, University of Wisconsin, MA.

Donnerstein, E., Donnerstein, M., & Evans, R. (1975). Erotic stimuli and aggression: Facilitation or inhibition? *Journal of Personality and Social Psychology, 32,* 237–244.

Donnerstein, E., Linz, D., & Penrod, S. (1987). *The question of pornography: Research findings and policy implications.* New York: The Free Press.

Donohew, L., Palmgreen, P., & Rayburn, J. D. (1987). Social and psychological origins of media use: A lifestyle analysis. *Journal of Broadcasting & Electronic Media, 31,* 255–278.

Donohue, G. A., Tichenor, P. J., & Olien, C. N. (1975). Mass media and the knowledge gap: A hypothesis reconsidered. *Communication Research, 2,* 3–23.

Donohue, G. A., Olien, C. N., & Tichenor, P. J. (1987). Media access and knowledge gaps. *Critical Studies in Mass Communication, 4,* 87–92.

Drabman, R. S., & Thomas, M. H. (1974). Does media violence increase children's toleration of real-life aggression? *Developmental Psychology, 10,* 418–421.

Eagly, A. H., & Chaiken, S. (1993). *The psychology of attitudes.* Fort Worth, TX: Harcourt Brace Jovanovich.

Elliott, S. (1999, August 2). Reversing the message, ad agencies switch sides. *The New York Times,* pp. C1, C13.

Entman, R. M. (1989). *Democracy without citizens: Media and the decay of American politics.* New York: Oxford University Press.

Eron, L. D., & Huesmann, L. R. (1984). The control of aggressive behavior by changes in attitudes, values, and the conditions of learning. In R. J. Blanchard & D. C. Blanchard (Eds.), *Advances in the study of aggression* (pp. 139–171). Orlando: Academic Press.

Ettema, J. S., & Kline, G. F. (1977). Deficits, differences, and ceilings: Contingent conditions for understanding the knowledge gap. *Communication Research, 4,* 179–202.

Fazio, R. H. (1990). Model processes by which attitudes guide behavior: The MODE model as an integrative framework. In L. Berkowitz (Ed.), *Advances in experimental social psychology* (Vol. 23, pp. 75–109). New York: Academic Press.

Fazio, R. H., Powell, M. C., & Herr, P. M. (1983). Toward a process model of the attitude–behavior relation: Accessing one's attitudes upon mere observation of the attitude object. *Journal of Personality and Social Psychology, 44,* 723–735.

Fazio, R. H., Powell, M. C., & Williams, C. J. (1989). The role of attitude accessibility in the attitude-to-behavior process. *Journal of Consumer Research, 16,* 280–287.

Fazio, R. H., & Roskos-Ewoldsen, D. R. (1994). Acting as we feel: When and how attitudes affect behavior. In S. Shavitt & T. C. Brock (Eds.), *Psychology of persuasion* (pp. 71–93). Needham Heights, MA: Allyn & Bacon.

Ferguson, D. A., & Perse, E. M. (2000). The World Wide Web as a functional alternative to television. *Journal of Broadcasting & Electronic Media, 44*, 155–174.

Feshbach, S. (1955). The drive-reducing function of fantasy behavior. *Journal of Abnormal and Social Psychology, 50*, 3–11.

Festinger, L. (1957). *A theory of cognitive dissonance.* Stanford, CA: Stanford University Press.

Final report: National Commission on Excellence in Education. (1983). *Education Digest, 49*, 36–40.

Finn, S., & Gorr, M. B. (1988). Social isolation and social support as correlates of television viewing motivations. *Communication Research, 15*, 135–158.

Finn, S., & Roberts, D. F. (1984). Source, destination, and entropy: Reassessing the role of information theory in communication research. *Communication Research, 11*, 453–476.

Fisch, S. M., Truglio, R. T., & Cole, C. F. (1999). The impact of *Sesame Street* on preschool children: A review and synthesis of 30 years' research. *Media Psychology, 1*, 165–190.

Fishbein, M., & Ajzen, I. (1975). *Belief, attitude, intention, and behavior.* Reading, MA: Addison-Wesley.

Fisher, W. A., & Barak, A. (1989). Sex education as a corrective: Immunizing against possible effects of pornography. In D. Zillmann & J. Bryant (Eds.), *Pornography: Research advances and policy considerations* (pp. 289–320). Hillsdale, NJ: Lawrence Erlbaum Associates.

Flexner, S. B. (Ed.). (1987). *The Random House dictionary of the English language.* New York: Random House.

Floyd, D. L., Prentice-Dunn, S., & Rogers, R. W. (2000). A meta-analysis of research on protection motivation theory. *Journal of Applied Social Psychology, 30*, 427–429.

Frazier, P. J., & Gaziano, C. (1979). Robert Ezra Park's theory of news, public opinion, and social control. *Journalism Monographs* (64).

Freedman, J. L. (1992). Television violence and aggression: What psychologists should tell the public. In P. Suedfeld & P. E. Tetlock (Eds.), *Psychology and social policy* (pp. 179–189). New York: Hemisphere.

Friestad, M., & Wright, P. (1994). The persuasion knowledge model: How people cope with persuasion attempts. *Journal of Consumer Research, 21*, 1–31.

Friis, R. H., & Sellers, T. A. (1996). *Epidemiology for public health practice.* Gaithersburg, MD: Aspen Publishing.

Gaddy, G. D. (1986). Television's impact on high school achievement. *Public Opinion Quarterly, 50*, 340–359.

Galtung, J. (1974). A rejoiner. *Journal of Peace Research, 11*, 157–160.

Galtung, J., & Ruge, M. H. (1965). The structure of foreign news. *Journal of Peace Research, 2*, 64–91.

Garramone, G. M. (1984). Audience motivation effects: More evidence. *Communication Research, 11*, 79–96.

Gary, B. (1996). Communication research, the Rockefeller Foundation, and mobilization for the war on words, 1938–1944. *Journal of Communication, 46*(3), 124–147.

Gaziano, C. (1983). The knowledge gap: An analytical review of media effects. *Communication Research, 10*, 447–486.

Gebotys, R. J., & Claxton-Oldfield, S. P. (1989). Errors in the quantification of uncertainty: A product of heuristics or minimal probability knowledge base. *Applied Cognitive Psychology, 3*, 237–250.

Genova, B. K. L., & Greenberg, B. S. (1979). Interest in news and the knowledge gap. *Public Opinion Quarterly, 43*, 79–91.

Georgoudi, M., & Rosnow, R. L. (1985a). The emergence of contextualism. *Journal of Communication, 35*(1), 76–88.

Georgoudi, M., & Rosnow, R. L. (1985b). Notes toward a contextualist understanding of social psychology. *Personality and Social Psychology Bulletin, 11*, 5–22.

Gerbner, G. (1956). Toward a general model of communication. *Audio-Visual Communication Review, 4,* 171–199.

Gerbner, G. (Ed.). (1983). Ferment in the field (Special Issue). *Journal of Communication, 33*(3).

Gerbner, G. (1986). The symbolic context of action and communication. In R. L. Rosnow & M. Georgoudi (Eds.), *Contextualism and understanding in behavioral science* (pp. 251–268). New York: Praeger.

Gerbner, G., Gross, L., Morgan, M., & Signorielli, N. (1980). The "mainstreaming" of America: Violence profile no. 11. *Journal of Communication, 30*(3), 10–29.

Gerbner, G., Gross, L., Morgan, M., & Signorielli, N. (1981). A curious journey into the scary world of Paul Hirsch. *Communication Research, 8,* 39–72.

Gerbner, G., Gross, L., Morgan, M., & Signorielli, N. (1982). Charting the mainstream: Television's contributions to political orientations. *Journal of Communication, 32*(2), 100–127.

Gerbner, G., Gross, L., Morgan, M., & Signorielli, N. (1994). Growing up with television: The cultivation perspective. In J. Bryant & D. Zillmann (Eds.), *Media effects: Advances in theory and research* (pp. 17–41). Hillsdale, NJ: Lawrence Erlbaum Associates.

Gerbner, G., Gross, L., Signorielli, N., & Morgan, M. (1980). Aging with television: Images on television drama and conceptions of social reality. *Journal of Communication, 30*(1), 37–47.

Gerbner, G., Gross, L., Signorielli, N., Morgan, M., & Jackson-Beeck, M. (1979). Demonstration of power: Violence profile no. 10. *Journal of Communication, 29*(3), 177–196.

Gergen, K. J. (1973). Social psychology as history. *Journal of Personality and Social Psychology, 26,* 309–320.

Gibson, J. J. (1979). *The ecological approach to visual perception.* Boston: Houghton Mifflin.

Gillespie, D. (1992). *The mind's we: Contextualism in cognitive psychology.* Carbondale, IL: Southern Illinois University Press.

Gitlin, T. (1981). Media sociology: The dominant paradigm. In G. C. Wilhoit & H. de Bock (Eds.), *Mass communication review yearbook* (Vol. 2, pp. 73–121). Beverly Hills, CA: Sage.

Glander, T. (2000). *Origins of mass communications research during the American cold war: Educational effects and contemporary implications.* Mahwah, NJ: Lawrence Erlbaum Associates.

Glazer, N. (1946). Government by manipulation: The social scientist reports for service. *Commentary, 2,* 81–86.

Glynn, C. J., Hayes, A. F., & Shanahan, J. (1997). Perceived support for one's opinions and willingness to speak out: A meta-analysis of survey studies on the "spiral of silence." *Public Opinion Quarterly, 61,* 452–463.

Goldman, L. K., & Glantz, S. A. (1998). Evaluation of antismoking advertising campaigns. *Journal of the American Medical Association, 279,* 772–777.

Gomery, D. (2000). Interpreting media ownership. In B. M. Compaine & D. Gomery (Eds.), *Who owns the media?: Competition & concentration in the mass media industry* (3rd ed., pp. 507–535). Mahwah, NJ: Lawrence Erlbaum Associates.

Gonzenbach, W. J. (1992). The conformity hypothesis: Empirical considerations for the spiral of silence's first link. *Journalism Quarterly, 69,* 633–645.

Goranson, R. E. (1970). Media violence and aggressive behavior. In L. Berkowitz (Ed.), *Advances in experimental social psychology* (Vol. 5, pp. 2–33). New York: Academic Press.

Gortmaker, S. L., Salter, C. A., Walker, D. K., & Dietz, W. H., Jr. (1990). The impact of television viewing on mental aptitude and achievement: A longitudinal study. *Public Opinion Quarterly, 54,* 594–604.

Graber, D. A. (1988). *Processing the news: How people tame the information tide* (2nd ed.). New York: Longman.

Grant, A. E., Guthrie, E. K., & Ball-Rokeach, S. J. (1991). Television shopping: A media system dependency perspective. *Communication Research, 6,* 773–798.

Greenberg, B. S. (1974). Gratifications of television viewing and their correlates for British children. In J. G. Blumler & E. Katz (Eds.), *The uses of mass communications: Current perspectives on gratifications research* (pp. 71–92). Beverly Hills, CA: Sage.

Groebel, J. (1983). Federal Republic of Germany: Aggression and aggression research. In A. P. Goldstein & M. H. Segall (Eds.), *Aggression in global perspective* (pp. 75–103). New York: Pergamon.

Gross, L. (1983). Pornography and social science research: Serious questions. . . . *Journal of Communication, 33*(4), 107–111.

Grossman, D. (1998, August 10). Trained to kill. *Christianity Today*, pp. 1–8.

Grossman, D., & DeGaetano, G. (1998). *Stop teaching our kids to kill*. New York: Crown Publishers.

Growing support found for ban on sex, violence in movies, magazines. (1986, August). *Gallup Report No. 251*, pp. 2–10.

Gunter, B., Furnham, A., & Griffiths, S. (2000). Children's memory for news: A comparison of three presentation media. *Media Psychology, 2*, 93–118.

Hamilton, J. T. (1998). Media violence and public policy. In J. T. Hamilton (Ed.), *Television violence and public policy* (pp. 1–12). Ann Arbor, MI: The University of Michigan Press.

Hamilton, M. A., Hunter, J. E., & Boster, F. J. (1993). The elaboration likelihood model as a theory of attitude formation: A mathematical analysis. *Communication Theory, 3*, 51–65.

Harris, R. J. (1977). Comprehension of pragmatic implications in advertising. *Journal of Applied Psychology, 63*, 603–608.

Harris, R. J. (1989). *A cognitive psychology of mass communication*. Hillsdale, NJ: Lawrence Erlbaum Associates.

Harrison, K., & Cantor, J. (1999). Tales from the screen: Enduring fright reactions to scary media. *Media Psychology, 1*, 97–116.

Hastorf, A. H., & Cantril, H. (1954). They saw a game: A case study. *Journal of Abnormal and Social Psychology, 49*, 129–134.

Hawkins, R. P., & Pingree, S. (1990). Divergent psychological processes in constructing social reality from mass media content. In N. Signorielli & M. Morgan (Eds.), *Cultivation analysis: New directions in media effects research* (pp. 35–50). Newbury Park, CA: Sage.

Hawkins, R. P., Pingree, S., & Adler, I. (1987). Searching for cognitive processes in the cultivation effect: Adult and adolescent samples in the United States and Australia. *Human Communication Research, 13*, 553–557.

Hayes, S. C., Hayes, L. J., & Reese, H. W. (1988). Finding the philosophical core: A review of Stephen C. Pepper's *World hypotheses: A study in evidence. Journal of the Experimental Analysis of Behavior, 50*, 97–111.

Heath, R. L., & Bryant, J. (1992). *Human communication theory and research: Concepts, contexts, and challenges*. Hillsdale, NJ: Lawrence Erlbaum Associates.

Heider, F. (1946). Attitudes and cognitive organization. *Journal of Psychology, 21*, 107–112.

Heider, F. (1958). *The psychology of interpersonal relations*. New York: Wiley.

Herzog, H. (1940). Professor Quiz: A gratification study. In P. Lazarsfeld (Ed.), *Radio and the printed page* (pp. 64–93). New York: Duell, Sloan & Pearce.

Herzog, H. (1944). What do we really know about daytime serial listeners? In P. F. Lazarsfeld & F. N. Stanton (Eds.), *Radio research 1942–1943* (pp. 3–33). New York: Duell, Sloan & Pearce.

Hesse, M. (1980). *Revolutions and reconstructions in the philosophy of science*. Bloomington: Indiana University Press.

Hickman, L. A. (1995). Pragmatism, technology, and scientism. Are the methods of the scientific-technical disciplines relevant to social problems? In R. Hollinger & D. Depew (Eds.), *Pragmatism from progressivism to postmodernism* (pp. 72–87). Westport, CT: Praeger.

Himmelweit, H. T., Oppenheim, A. N., & Vance, P. (1958). *Television and the child: An empirical study of the effect of television on the young*. London: Oxford University Press.

Hirsch, P. M. (1980). The "scary world" of the nonviewer and other anomalies: A reanalysis of Gerbner et al.'s findings on cultivation analysis, part 1. *Communication Research, 7*, 403–456.

Hirsch, P. M. (1981). On not learning from one's own mistakes: A reanalysis of Gerbner et al.'s findings on cultivation analysis, part 2. *Communication Research, 8*, 3–37.

Hirsch, P. M. (Ed.). (1992). Globalization of mass media ownership (Special Issue). *Communication Research, 19*(6).

Hoffman, R. R., & Nead, J. M. (1983). General contextualism, ecological science and cognitive research. *The Journal of Mind and Behavior, 4*, 507–560.

Hook, S. (1938/1995). *John Dewey: An intellectual portrait.* Amherst, NY: Prometheus Books.

Hook, S. (1974). *Pragmatism and the tragic sense of life.* New York: Basic Books.

Hook, S. (1987). *Out of step.* New York: Harper & Row.

Hornik, R. (1981). Out-of-school television and schooling: Hypotheses and methods. *Review of Educational Research, 51*, 193–214.

Hornik, R. (1989). The knowledge-behavior gap in public information campaigns: A development communication view. In C. T. Salmon (Ed.), *Information campaigns: Balancing social values and social change* (pp. 113–138). Newbury Park, CA: Sage.

Horton, D., & Wohl, R. R. (1956). Mass communication and para-social interaction: Observations on intimacy at a distance. *Psychiatry, 19*, 215–229.

Hovland, C. I., Janis, I. L., & Kelley, H. H. (1953). *Communication and persuasion: Psychological studies of opinion change.* New Haven, CT: Yale University Press.

Hovland, C. I., Lumsdaine, A. A., & Sheffield, F. D. (1949). *Studies in social psychology in World War II: Vol. 3. Experiments on mass communication.* Princeton, NJ: Princeton University Press.

Hovland, C. I., & Weiss, W. (1951–1952). The influence of source credibility on communication effectiveness. *Public Opinion Quarterly, 15*, 635–650.

Howard, J. L., Liptzin, M. B., & Reifler, C. B. (1973). Is pornography a problem? *Journal of Social Issues, 29*, 133–145.

Hu, T.-W., Sung, H.-Y., & Keeler, T. E. (1995). Reducing cigarette consumption in California: Tobacco taxes versus an anti-smoking media campaign. *American Journal of Public Health, 89*, 1218–1222.

Huesmann, L. R. (1986). Cross-national communalities in the learning of aggression from media violence. In L. R. Huesmann & L. D. Eron (Eds.), *Television and the aggressive child: A cross-national comparison* (pp. 239–257). Hillsdale, NJ: Lawrence Erlbaum Associates.

Huesmann, L. R., & Eron, L. D. (1986a). The development of aggression in American children as a consequence of television violence viewing. In L. R. Huesmann & L. D. Eron (Eds.), *Television and the aggressive child: A cross-national comparison* (pp. 45–80). Hillsdale, NJ: Lawrence Erlbaum Associates.

Huesmann, L. R., & Eron, L. D. (1986b). The development of aggression in children of different cultures: Psychological processes and exposure to violence. In L. R. Huesmann & L. D. Eron (Eds.), *Television and the aggressive child: A cross-national comparison* (pp. 1–27). Hillsdale, NJ: Lawrence Erlbaum Associates.

Huesmann, L. R., & Eron, L. D. (Eds.). (1986c). *Television and the aggressive child: A cross-national comparison.* Hillsdale, NJ: Lawrence Erlbaum Associates.

Huesmann, L. R., Eron, L. D., Berkowitz, L., & Chaffee, S. (1992). The effects of television violence on aggression: A reply to a skeptic. In P. Suedfeld & P. E. Tetlock (Eds.), *Psychology and social policy* (pp. 191–200). New York: Hemisphere.

Huesmann, L. R., Eron, L. D., Klein, R., Brice, P., & Fischer, P. (1983). Mitigating the imitation of aggressive behaviors by changing children's attitudes about media violence. *Journal of Personality and Social Psychology, 44*, 899–910.

Hunt, S. D. (1991). *Modern marketing theory: Critical issues in the philosophy of marketing science.* Cincinnati, OH: South-Western.

Hunter, J. E., Schmidt, F. L., & Jackson, G. B. (1982). *Meta-analysis: Cumulating research findings across studies.* Beverly Hills, CA: Sage.

Huston, A. C. (1987). Television and aggression around the world [Review of *Television and the aggressive child: A cross-national comparison*]. *Contemporary Psychology, 32,* 942–943.

Is social science a God that failed? (1981, October/November). *Public Opinion,* pp. 11–15.

Iyengar, S., & Kinder, D. R. (1987). *News that matters: Agenda-setting and priming in a television age.* Chicago: University of Chicago Press.

Iyengar, S., Peters, M. D., & Kinder, D. R. (1982). Experimental demonstrations of the "not-so-minimal" consequences of television news programs. *American Political Science Review, 76,* 848–858.

Jackman, R. W., & Miller, R. A. (1996). A renaissance of political culture? *American Journal of Political Science, 40,* 632–659.

Jacobson, T. L. (1993). A pragmatist account of participatory communication research for national development. *Communication Theory, 3,* 214–230.

James, W. (1890/1907). *The principles of psychology* (Vols. I & II). New York: Macmillan.

James, W. (1898/1960). *The will to believe and other essays in popular philosophy.* New York: Dover.

James, W. (1907/1975). *Pragmatism.* Cambridge, MA: Harvard University Press.

Jenkins, J. J. (1974). Remember that old theory of memory? Well, forget it. *American Psychologist, 29,* 785–795.

Jo, E., & Berkowitz, L. (1994). A priming effect analysis of media influences: An update. In J. Bryant & D. Zillmann (Eds.), *Media effects: Advances in theory and research* (pp. 43–60). Hillsdale, NJ: Lawrence Erlbaum Associates.

Johansson, G. (1973). Visual perception of biological motion and a model for its analysis. *Perception and Psychophysics, 14,* 201–211.

Johnson, B. T., & Eagly, A. H. (1989). Effects of involvement on persuasion: A meta-analysis. *Psychological Bulletin, 106,* 290–314.

Johnston, W. A., & Dark, V. J. (1986). Selective attention. In M. R. Rosenzweig & L. W. Porter (Eds.), *Annual review of psychology* (Vol. 37, pp. 43–75). Palo Alto, CA: Annual Reviews.

Joy, L. A., Kimball, M. M., & Zabrack, M. L. (1986). Television and children's aggressive behavior. In T. M. Williams (Ed.), *The impact of television: A natural experiment in three communities* (pp. 303–360). Orlando, FL: Academic Press.

Kaplan, A. (1961). *The new world of philosophy.* New York: Random House.

Kaplan, A. (1964). *The conduct of inquiry.* San Francisco, CA: Chandler.

Kariel, H. G., & Rosenvall, L. A. (1984). Factors influencing international news flow. *Journalism Quarterly, 61,* 509–516, 666.

Katz, D. (1960). The functional approach to the study of attitudes. *Public Opinion Quarterly, 24,* 163–204.

Katz, E. (1959). Mass communication research and the study of popular culture: An editorial note on a possible future for this journal. *Studies in Public Communication, 2,* 1–6.

Katz, E. (1979). The uses of Becker, Blumler, and Swansom. *Communication Research, 6,* 74–83.

Katz, E., Blumler, J. G., & Gurevitch, M. (1974). Utilization of mass communication by the individual. In J. G. Blumler & E. Katz (Eds.), *The uses of mass communications: Current perspectives on gratifications research* (pp. 19–32). Beverly Hills, CA: Sage.

Katz, E., & Lazarsfeld, P. F. (1955). *Personal influence.* Glencoe, IL: The Free Press.

Katz, J. E., & Aspden, P. (1997). A nation of strangers? *Communications of the ACM, 40*(12), 81–86.

Katzev, R., & Brownstein, R. (1989). The influence of enlightenment on compliance. *The Journal of Social Psychology, 129,* 335–347.

Kelman, H. (1958). Compliance, identification and internalization: Three processes of attitude change. *Journal of Conflict Resolution, 2,* 51–60.

Kenny, D. A. (1984). The NBC study and television violence. *Journal of Communication, 34*(1), 176–182.

Kepplinger, H. M. (1997). Political correctness and academic principles: A reply to Simpson. *Journal of Communication, 47*, 102–117.

Key, V. O., Jr. (1967). *Public opinion and American democracy.* New York: Alfred A. Knopf.

Key, W. B. (1972). *Subliminal seduction: Ad media's manipulation of a not-so-innocent America.* New York: Signet.

Kiesler, C. A., Collins, B. E., & Miller, N. (1969). *Attitude change: A critical analysis of theoretical approaches.* New York: Wiley.

Kilpatrick, F. P. (1988). Hadley Cantril (1906–1969): The transactional point of view. In A. H. Cantril (Ed.), *Psychology, humanism, and scientific inquiry: The selected essays of Hadley Cantril* (pp. 229–234). New Brunswick, NJ: Transaction.

Kim, J., & Rubin, A. M. (1997). The variable influence of audience activity on media effects. *Communication Research, 24*, 107–135.

Kim, M., & Hunter, J. E. (1993a). Attitude–behavior relations: A meta-analysis of attitudinal relevance and topic. *Journal of Communication, 43*(1), 101–142.

Kim, M., & Hunter, J. E. (1993b). Relationships among attitudes, behavioral intentions, and behavior: A meta-analysis of past research, part 2. *Communication Research, 20*, 331–364.

Kincaid, D. L., & Schramm, W. (1975). *Fundamental human communication* (Module text). Honolulu, HI: East-West Communication Institute.

Klapper, J. T. (1960). *The effects of mass communication.* New York: The Free Press.

Kluger, J. (2000, September 4). The diabetes explosion. *Time, 156,* p. 58.

Kodaira, S. I. (1998). A review of research on media violence in Japan. In U. Carlsson & C. von Feilitzen (Eds.), *Children and media violence* (pp. 81–105). Gotenberg, Sweden: The UNESCO International Clearinghouse on Children and Violence on the Screen.

Kosicki, G. M. (1993). Problems and opportunities in agenda-setting research. *Journal of Communication, 43*(2), 100–127.

Kraut, R., Lundmark, V., Patterson, M., Kiesler, S., Mukopadhyay, T., & Scherlis, W. (1998). Internet paradox, A social technology that reduces social involvement and psychological well-being? *The American Psychologist, 53*, 1017–1031.

Krippendorff, K. (1989). The ethics of constructing communication. In B. Dervin, L. Grossberg, B. J. O'Keefe, & E. Wartella (Eds.), *Rethinking communication: Volume 1. Paradigm issues* (pp. 66–96). Newbury Park, CA: Sage.

Krosnick, J. A., & Kinder, D. R. (1990). Altering the foundations of support for the President through priming. *American Political Science Review, 84*, 497–512.

Kruglanski, A. W., & Thompson, E. P. (1999). Persuasion by a single route: A view from the unimodel. *Psychological Inquiry, 10*, 83–109.

Kuhn, T. S., (1970). *The structure of scientific revolutions* (2nd ed.). Chicago: The University of Chicago Press.

Kunkel, D. (1991). Crafting media policy: The genesis and implications of the Children's Television Act of 1990. *American Behavioral Scientist, 35*, 181–202.

Kunkel, D. (1992). Children's television advertising in the multichannel environment. *Journal of Communication, 42*(3), 134–152.

Kunkel, D., & Roberts, D. F. (1991). Young minds and marketplace values: Issues in children's television advertising. *Journal of Social Issues, 47*(1), 57–72.

Kurtz, P. (1990). *Philosophical essays in pragmatic naturalism.* Buffalo, NY: Prometheus Books.

Kurtz, P. (1992). *The new skepticism: Inquiry and reliable knowledge.* Buffalo, NY: Prometheus Books.

Kutchinsky, B. (1973). The effect of easy availability of pornography on the incidence of sex crimes: The Danish experience. *Journal of Social Issues, 29*, 163–181.

Ladd, E. C. (1999). *The Ladd Report.* New York: The Free Press.

Lakatos, I. (1970). Falsification and the methodology of scientific research programmes. In I. Lakatos & A. Musgrave (Eds.), *Criticism and the growth of knowledge* (pp. 91–195). New York: Cambridge University Press.

Larvor, B. (1999). *Lakatos: An introduction.* Routledge: New York.

LaPiere, R. T. (1934). Attitudes versus action. *Social Forces, 13,* 230–237.

Lasswell, H. D. (1927). *Propaganda technique in the world war.* New York: Alfred A. Knopf.

Lasswell, H. D. (1948). The structure and function of communication in society. In L. Bryson (Ed.), *The communication of ideas* (pp. 37–51). New York: Harper & Brothers.

Lasswell, H. D. (1951). The policy orientation. In D. Lerner & H. D. Lasswell (Eds.), *The policy sciences* (pp. 3–15). Stanford, CA: Stanford University Press.

Lazarsfeld, P. F., Berelson, B., & Gaudet, H. (1968). *The people's choice* (3rd ed.). New York: Columbia University Press.

Lee, A. M., & Lee, E. B. (Eds.). (1939). *The fine art of propaganda: A study of Father Coughlin's speeches.* New York: Harcourt, Brace.

Lerner, D. (1958). *The passing of traditional society: Modernizing the Middle East.* New York: The Free Press.

Lesser, G. S. (1974). *Children and television: Lessons from Sesame Street.* New York: Random House.

Levy, M. R., & Windahl, S. (1984). Audience activity and gratifications: A conceptual clarification and exploration. *Communication Research, 11,* 51–78.

Levy, M. R., & Windahl, S. (1985). The concept of audience activity. In K. E. Rosengren, L. A. Wenner, & P. Palmgreen (Eds.), *Media gratifications research: Current perspectives* (pp. 109–122). Beverly Hills, CA: Sage.

Lewis, K. (1947). Frontiers in group dynamics: II. Channels of group life; social planning and action research. *Human Relations, 1,* 143–153.

Lewin, K. (1948). *Resolving social conflicts.* New York: Harper & Row.

Lewis, J. D., & Smith, R. L. (1980). *American sociology and pragmatism: Mead, Chicago sociology, and symbolic interaction.* Chicago: University of Chicago Press.

Linsley, W. A. (1989). The case against censorship of pornography. In D. Zillmann & J. Bryant (Eds.), *Pornography: Research advances and policy considerations* (pp. 343–359). Hillsdale, NJ: Lawrence Erlbaum Associates.

Linz, D., Fuson, I. A., & Donnerstein, E. (1990). Mitigating the negative effects of sexually violent mass communications through preexposure briefings. *Communication Research, 17,* 641–674.

Linz, D. G., Donnerstein, E., & Penrod, S. (1988). Effects of long-term exposure to violent and sexually degrading depictions of women. *Journal of Personality and Social Psychology, 55,* 758–768.

Lippmann, W. (1922). *Public opinion.* New York: Macmillan.

Lippmann, W. (1925). *The phantom public.* New York: Harcourt, Brace.

Lockhardt, R. S., & Craik, F. I. M. (1990). Levels of processing: A retrospective commentary on a framework for memory research. *Canadian Journal of Psychology, 44,* 87–112.

Lord, C. G., Ross, L., & Lepper, M. R. (1979). Biased assimilation and attitude polarization: The effects of prior theories on subsequently considered evidence. *Journal of Personality and Social Psychology, 37,* 2098–2109.

Lowery, S. A., & DeFleur, M. L. (1983). *Milestones in mass communication research.* New York: Longman.

Lowery, S. A., & DeFleur, M. L. (1988). *Milestones in mass communication research* (2nd ed.). New York: Longman.

Lundin, R. W. (1987). Functionalism. In R. J. Corsini (Ed.), *Concise encyclopedia of psychology* (pp. 446–447). New York: Wiley.

Lynd, R. S. (1939). *Knowledge for what?: The place of social science in American culture.* Princeton, NJ: Princeton University Press.

Maccoby, E. E. (1954). Why do children watch television? *Public Opinion Quarterly, 18,* 239–244.

Mahaney, E. (1969, June 30). Partners for profit: Children, toys and TV. *Broadcasting,* p. 18.

Malamuth, N. M., & Ceniti, J. (1986). Repeated exposure to violent and nonviolent pornography: Likelihood of raping ratings and laboratory aggression against women. *Aggressive Behavior, 12*, 129–137.

Malkin, M. (2000, December, 23). Wrestling group body slams group exercising free speech. *The Florida Times-Union*, p. B7.

Manis, M., & Landman, J. (1992). Functionalism and social psychology. In D. A. Owens & M. Wagner (Eds.), *Progress in modern psychology: The legacy of American functionalism* (pp. 230–240). Westport, CT: Praeger.

Mares, M. (1996). The role of source confusions in television's cultivation of social reality judgments. *Human Communication Research, 23*, 278–297.

Marshall, W. L. (1989). Pornography and sex offenders. In D. Zillmann & J. Bryant (Eds.), *Pornography: Research advances and policy considerations* (pp. 185–214). Hillsdale, NJ: Lawrence Erlbaum Associates.

Maryanski, A., & Turner, J. H. (1991). Functionalism. In E. F. Borgatta & M. L. Borgatta (Eds.), *Encyclopedia of sociology* (Vol. 2, pp. 730–736). New York: Macmillan.

Matthews, F. (1982). Review of *American Sociology and pragmatism: Mead, Chicago sociology, and symbolic interaction*. *Journal of American History, 69*, 475–476.

McChesney, R. W. (1993). *Telecommunications, mass media, and democracy: The battle for the control of U.S. broadcasting, 1928–1935*. New York: Oxford University Press.

McChesney, R. W. (1997). *Corporate media and the threat to democracy*. New York: Seven Stories Press.

McCombs, M. E., & Reynolds, A. (Eds.). (1999). *The poll with a human face: The National Issues Convention experiment in political communication*. Mahwah, NJ: Lawrence Erlbaum Associates.

McCombs, M. E., & Shaw, D. L. (1972). The agenda-setting function of mass media. *Public Opinion Quarterly, 36*, 176–187.

McCracken, K. W. J. (1987). Australia and Australians: View from New York Times. *Journalism Quarterly, 64*, 183–187.

McGuire, W. J. (1962). Persistence of the resistance to persuasion induced by various types of prior belief defenses. *Journal of Abnormal and Social Psychology, 64*, 241–248.

McGuire, W. J. (1968). Personality and susceptibility to social influence. In E. F. Borgotta & W. W. Lambert (Eds.), *Handbook of personality theory and research* (pp. 1130–1187). Chicago: Rand McNally.

McGuire, W. J. (1973a). Persuasion, resistance, and attitude change. In I. Pool, W. Schramm, F. Frey, N. Maccoby, & E. B. Parker (Eds.), *Handbook of communication* (pp. 216–252). Chicago: Rand McNally.

McGuire, W. J. (1973b). The yin and yang of progress in social psychology: Seven koan. *Journal of Personality and Social Psychology, 26*, 446–456.

McGuire, W. J. (1974). Psychological motives and communication gratification. In J. G. Blumler & E. Katz (Eds.), *The uses of mass communications: Current perspectives on gratifications research* (pp. 167–196). Beverly Hills, CA: Sage.

McGuire, W. J. (1983). A contextualist theory of knowledge: Its implications for innovation and reform in psychological research. In L. Berkowitz (Ed.), *Advances in experimental social psychology* (Vol. 16, pp. 1–47). Orlando, FL: Academic Press.

McGuire, W. J. (1985). Attitudes and attitude change. In G. Lindzey & A. Aronson (Eds.), *Handbook of social psychology* (Vol. 2, 3rd ed., pp. 233–246). New York: Random House.

McGuire, W. J. (1986a). The myth of massive media impact: Savagings and salvagings. In G. Comstock (Ed.), *Public communication and behavior* (Vol. 1, pp. 173–257). Orlando, FL: Academic Press.

McGuire, W. J. (1986b). A perspectivist looks at contextualism and the future of behavioral science. In R. L. Rosnow & M. Georgoudi (Eds.), *Contextualism and understanding in behavioral science* (pp. 271–301). New York: Praeger.

McGuire, W. J. (1986c). The vicissitudes of attitudes and similar representational constructs in twentieth century psychology. *European Journal of Social Psychology, 16,* 89–130.

McGuire, W. J. (1989). The structure of individual attitudes and attitude systems. In A. R. Pratkanis, S. J. Breckler, & A. G. Greenwald (Eds.), *Attitude structure and function* (pp. 37–69). Hillsdale, NJ: Lawrence Erlbaum Associates.

McGuire, W. J. (1997). Creative hypothesis generating in psychology: Some useful heuristics. *Annual Review of Psychology, 48,* 1–30.

McGuire, W. J., & Papageorgis, D. (1961). The relative efficacy of various types of prior belief-defense in producing immunity against persuasion. *Journal of Abnormal and Social Psychology, 62,* 327–337.

McLeod, J. M., & Becker, L. B. (1974). Testing the validity of gratifications measures through political effects analysis. In J. G. Blumler & E. Katz (Eds.), *The uses of mass communications: Current perspectives on gratifications research* (pp. 137–164). Beverly Hills, CA: Sage.

McLeod, J. M., & Becker, L. B. (1981). The uses and gratifications approach. In D. D. Nimmo & K. R. Sanders (Eds.), *Handbook of political communication* (pp. 67–99). Beverly Hills, CA: Sage.

McLeod, J. M., & McDonald, D. G. (1985). Beyond simple exposure: Media orientations and their impact on political processes. *Communication Research, 12,* 3–33.

McLeod, J. M., & Reeves, B. (1980). On the nature of mass media effects. In S. B. Withey & R. P. Abeles (Eds.), *Television and social behavior: Beyond violence and children* (pp. 17–54). Hillsdale, NJ: Lawrence Erlbaum Associates.

McNelly, J. T. (1959). Intermediary communicators in the international flow of news. *Journalism Quarterly, 36,* 23–26.

Mead, G. H. (1934). *Mind, self and society from the standpoint of a social behaviorist.* Chicago: The University of Chicago Press.

Meadowcroft, J. M., & Reeves, B. (1989). Influence of story schema development on children's attention to television. *Communication Research, 16,* 352–374.

Meadowcroft, J. M., & Zillmann, D. (1987). Women's comedy preferences during the menstrual cycle. *Communication Research, 14,* 204–218.

Medved, M. (1999, April 29). Nonstop kids' TV: It's time to face the real media culprit. *USA Today,* p. 15A.

Mendelsohn, H. (1973). Some reasons why information campaigns can succeed. *Public Opinion Quarterly, 37,* 50–61.

Mendelsohn, H. (1974). Some policy implications of the uses and gratifications paradigm. In J. G. Blumler & E. Katz (Eds.), *The uses of mass communications: Current perspectives on gratifications research* (pp. 303–318). Beverly Hills, CA: Sage.

Merritt, D. (1998). *Public journalism and public life: Why telling the news is not enough* (2nd ed.). Hillsdale, NJ: Lawrence Erlbaum Associates.

Meyer, A. J., Nash, J. D., McAlister, A. L., Maccoby, N., & Farquhar, J. W. (1980). Skills training in a cardiovascular health education campaign. *Journal of Consulting and Clinical Psychology, 48,* 129–142.

Meyer, P. (1991). *The new precision journalism.* Bloomington and Indianapolis: Indiana University Press.

Meyrowitz, J. (1985). *No sense of place: The impact of electronic media on social behavior.* New York: Oxford University Press.

Meyrowitz, J. (1986). Media as social contexts. In R. L. Rosnow & M. Georgoudi (Eds.), *Contextualism and understanding in behavioral science* (pp. 229–250). New York: Praeger.

Miedema, S., & Biesta, G. J. J. (1994). Constructivism and pragmatism: How to solve the problematic relation between methodology and epistemology in the debate about replication. In R. van der Veer, M. van IJzendoorn, & J. Valsiner (Eds.), *Reconstructing the mind: Replicability in research on human development* (pp. 71–92). Norwood, NJ: Ablex.

Milavsky, J. R., Kessler, R. C., Stipp, H., & Rubens, W. S. (1982). *Television and aggression: A panel study*. New York: Academic Press.

Miller, G. R. (1987). Persuasion. In C. R. Berger & S. H. Chaffee (Eds.), *Handbook of communication science* (pp. 446–483). Newbury Park, CA: Sage.

Miller, J. M., & Krosnick, J. A. (2000). News media impact on the ingredients of presidential evaluations: Politically knowledgeable citizens are guided by a trusted source. *American Journal of Political Science, 44*, 295–309.

Miller, M. M., & Hurd, R. (1982). Conformity to standards in newspaper reporting of public opinion polls. *Public Opinion Quarterly, 46*, 243–249.

Miller, N., & Campbell, D. T. (1959). Recency and primacy in persuasion as a function of timing of speeches and measurement. *Journal of Abnormal and Social Psychology, 59*, 1–9.

Mills, C. W. (1959). *The sociological imagination*. New York: Oxford University Press.

Moca, D. J. (1993, August 2). Station managers: Television is too violent. *Electronic Media*, pp. 1–2.

Mongeau, P. A., & Stiff, J. B. (1993). Specifying causal relationships in the elaboration likelihood model. *Communication Theory, 3*, 65–72.

Moore, D. W. (1987). Political campaigns and the knowledge-gap hypothesis. *Public Opinion Quarterly, 51*, 186–200.

Morgan, M. (1986). Television and the erosion of regional diversity. *Journal of Broadcasting & Electronic Media, 30*, 123–139.

Morgan, M., & Gross, L. (1980). Television viewing, IQ, and academic achievement. *Journal of Broadcasting, 24*, 117–133.

Morgan, M., Leggett, S., & Shanahan, J. (1999). Television and family values: Was Dan Quayle right? *Mass Communication & Society, 2*, 47–63.

Morgan, M., & Shanahan, J. (1997). Two decades of cultivation research: An appraisal and meta-analysis. In B. R. Burleson (Ed.), *Communication yearbook 20* (pp. 1–45). Thousand Oaks, CA: Sage.

Morgan, M., & Signorelli, N. (1990). Cultivation analysis: Conceptualization and methodology. In N. Signorielli & M. Morgan (Eds.), *Cultivation analysis: New directions in media effects research* (pp. 13–34). Newbury Park, CA: Sage.

Morris, C. W. (1932). *Six theories of mind*. Chicago: The University of Chicago Press.

Morris, C. W. (1934). Introduction: George H. Mead as social psychologist and social philosopher. In G. H. Mead (Ed.), *Mind, self and society from the standpoint of a social behaviorist* (pp. ix–xxxv). Chicago: The University of Chicago Press.

Mounce, H. O. (1997). *The two pragmatisms: From Peirce to Rorty*. London: Routledge.

Moy, P., Scheufele, D. A., & Holbert, R. L. (1999). Television use and social capital: Testing Putnam's time displacement hypothesis. *Mass Communication & Society, 2*(1/2), 27–45.

Murphy, J. P. (1990). *Pragmatism: From Peirce to Davidson*. Boulder, CO: Westview.

National Television Violence Study (Vols. 1–3) (1997–1998). Thousand Oaks, CA: Sage.

Neisser, U. (1976). *Cognition and reality: Principles and implications of cognitive psychology*. San Francisco: Freeman.

Nelson, H. L., & Teeter, D. L., Jr. (1973). *Law of mass communications* (2nd ed.). Mineola, NY: The Foundation Press.

Neuharth, A. (1989). *Confessions of an S.O.B.* New York: Doubleday.

Newcomb, T. M. (1953). An approach to the study of communicative acts. *Psychological Review, 60*, 393–404.

Nisbet, L. (1983). Hook's "Pragmatism and the tragic sense of life." In P. Kurtz (Ed.), *Sidney Hook: Philosopher of democracy and humanism* (pp. 305–309). Buffalo, NY: Prometheus Books.

Nisbett, R. E., & Ross, L. (1980). *Human inference: Strategies and shortcomings of social judgment*. Englewood Cliffs, NJ: Prentice-Hall.

Noelle-Neumann, E. (1974). Turbulences in the climate of opinion: Methodological applications of the spiral of silence theory. *Public Opinion Quarterly, 41,* 143–158.

Noelle-Neumann, E. (1977). The spiral of silence: A theory of public opinion. *Journal of Communication, 24*(2), 43–51.

Noelle-Neumann, E. (1979). Public opinion and the classical tradition: A re-evaluation. *Public Opinion Quarterly, 43,* 143–156.

Noelle-Neumann, E. (1983). The effect of media on media effects research. *Journal of Communication, 33*(3), 157–165.

Noelle-Neumann, E. (1992, January). The pollster and the Nazis (letter to the editor). *Commentary,* pp. 9–11, 14–15.

Nomani, A.Q., & Carroll, P. B. (1993, August 27). Critics of Perot's new book on Nafta charge co-authors twist or omit some crucial facts. *The Wall Street Journal,* p. A8.

Norris, P. (1996). Does television erode social capital? A reply to Putnam. *PS: Political Science & Politics, 29,* 474–480.

O'Brien, R. M. (1985). *Crime and victimization data.* Beverly Hills, CA: Sage.

O'Brien, R. M. (1996). Police productivity and crime rates. *Criminology, 34,* 183–207.

Office of Technology Assessment. (1990). *Critical connections: Communication for the future.* Washington, DC: U.S. Government Printing Office.

Owens, D. A., & Wagner, M. (Eds.). (1992). *Progress in modern psychology: The legacy of American functionalism.* Westport, CT: Praeger.

Packard, V. (1957). *The hidden persuaders.* New York: Pocket Books.

Page, B. I., & Shapiro, R. Y. (1983). Effects of public opinion on policy. *American Political Science Review, 77,* 175–190.

Paik, H. (1995). Prosocial television programs and altruistic behavior: A meta-analysis. *Mass Communication Review, 22,* 147–165.

Paik, H., & Comstock, G. (1994). The effects of television violence on antisocial behavior: A meta-analysis. *Communication Research, 21,* 516–546.

Paisley, W. (1984). Communication in the communication sciences. In B. Dervin & M. J. Voight (Eds.), *Progress in communication sciences* (Vol. 5, pp. 1–43). Norwood, NJ: Ablex.

Paivio, A. (1971). *Imagery and verbal processes.* New York: Holt, Rinehart & Winston.

Palmgreen, P., & Rayburn, J. D. (1979). Uses and gratifications and exposure to public television: A discrepancy approach. *Communication Research, 6,* 155–180.

Palmgreen, P., & Rayburn, J. D. (1982). Gratifications sought and media exposure: An expectancy value model. *Communication Research, 9,* 561–580.

Palmgreen, P., & Rayburn, J. D. (1985). An expectancy-value approach to media gratifications. In K. E. Rosengren, L. A. Wenner, & P. Palmgreen (Eds.), *Media gratifications research: Current perspectives* (pp. 61–72). Beverly Hills, CA: Sage.

Palmgreen, P., Wenner, L. A., & Rayburn, J. D. (1980). Relations between gratifications sought and obtained: A study of television news. *Communication Research, 7,* 161–192.

Palmgreen, P., Wenner, L. A., & Rosengren, K. E. (1985). Uses and gratifications research: The past ten years. In K. E. Rosengren, L. A. Wenner, & P. Palmgreen (Eds.), *Media gratifications research: Current perspectives* (pp. 11–37). Beverly Hills, CA: Sage.

Papacharissi, Z., & Rubin, A. M. (2000). Predictors of internet use. *Journal of Broadcasting & Electronic Media, 44,* 175–196.

Papageorgis, D., & McGuire, W. J. (1961). The generality of immunity to persuasion produced by pre-exposure to weakened counterarguments. *Journal of Abnormal and Social Psychology, 62,* 475–481.

Park, R. E. (1940). News as a form of knowledge: A chapter in the sociology of knowledge. *American Journal of Sociology, 45,* 669–686.

Park, R. E., & Burgess, E. W. (1921/1924). *Introduction to the science of sociology.* Chicago: The University of Chicago Press.

Peirce, C. S. (1878/1957). How to make our ideas clear. In V. Tomas (Ed.), *Charles S. Peirce: Essays in the philosophy of science* (pp. 31–56). New York: The Liberal Arts Press.

Peled, T., & Katz, E. (1974). Media functions in wartime: The Israel home front in October 1973. In J. G. Blumler & E. Katz (Eds.), *The uses of mass communications: Current perspectives on gratifications research* (pp. 49–69). Beverly Hills, CA: Sage.

Pepper, S. C. (1934). The conceptual framework of Tolman's purposive behaviorism. *Psychological Review, 41*, 108–133.

Pepper, S. C. (1942). *World hypotheses.* Berkeley, CA: University of California Press.

Pepper, S. C. (1982). Metaphor in philosophy. *The Journal of Mind and Behavior, 3*, 197–206.

Perloff, R. M. (1989). Ego-involvement and the third person effect of television news coverage. *Communication Research, 16*, 236–262.

Perloff, R. M. (1993). *The dynamics of persuasion.* Hillsdale, NJ: Lawrence Erlbaum Associates.

Perry, D. K. (1992). Assessing the import of media-related effects: Some contextualist considerations. *World Communication, 21*, 69–82.

Perry, D. K. (1998, October). *Civic journalism, nominalism, and realism.* Paper presented to the Second Annual Conference for the Center for Mass Communications Research, University of South Carolina, Columbia.

Perry, D. K., Howard, T., & Zillmann, D. (1992). Predicting retention of the contents of film drama based upon a fictional or historical context. *Communication Research Reports, 9*, 195–203.

Perse, E. M. (1986). Soap opera viewing patterns of college students and cultivation. *Journal of Broadcasting & Electronic Media, 30*, 175–193.

Perse, E. M. (1990). Cultivation and involvement with local television news. In N. Signorielli & M. Morgan (Eds.), *Cultivation analysis: New directions in media effects research* (pp. 51–69). Newbury Park, CA: Sage.

Perse, E. M., & Rubin, A. M. (1990). Chronic loneliness and television use. *Journal of Broadcasting & Electronic Media, 34*, 37–53.

Peters, J. D. (1986). Institutional sources of intellectual poverty in communication research. *Communication Research, 13*, 527–559.

Peters, J. D. (1989a). Democracy and American communication theory: Dewey, Lippmann, Lazarsfeld. *Communication, 11*, 199–220.

Peters, J. D. (1989b). Satan and savior: Mass communication in progressive thought. *Critical Studies in Mass Communication, 6*, 247–263.

Petty, R. E., & Cacioppo, J. T. (1979). Issue involvement can increase or decrease persuasion by enhancing message-relevant cognitive responses. *Journal of Personality and Social Psychology, 37*, 1915–1926.

Petty, R. E., & Cacioppo, J. T. (1986). The elaboration likelihood model of persuasion. In L. Berkowitz (Ed.), *Advances in experimental social psychology* (Vol. 19, pp. 123–205). New York: Academic Press.

Petty, R. E., & Priester, J. R. (1994). Mass media attitude change: Implications of the elaboration likelihood model of persuasion. In J. Bryant & D. Zillmann (Eds.), *Media effects: Advances in theory and research* (pp. 91–122). Hillsdale, NJ: Lawrence Erlbaum Associates.

Petty, R. E., & Wegener, D. T. (1999). The elaboration likelihood model: Current status and controversies. In S. Chaiken & Y. Trope (Eds.), *Dual-process theories in social psychology* (pp. 41–72). New York: Guilford.

Petty, R. E., Wegener, D. T., Fabrigar, L. R., Priester, J. R., & Cacioppo, J. T. (1993). Conceptual and methodological issues in the elaboration likelihood model of persuasion: A reply to the Michigan State critics. *Communication Theory, 3*, 336–362.

Petty, R. E., Wheeler, S. C., & Bizer, G. Y. (1999). Is there one persuasion process or more? Lumping versus splitting in attitude change theories. *Psychological Inquiry, 10*, 156–163.

Pfau, M. (1992). The potential of inoculation in promoting resistance to the effectiveness of comparative advertising messages. *Communication Quarterly, 40*, 26–44.

Phillips, D. P., & Bollen, K. A. (1985). Same time, last year: Selective data dredging for negative findings. *American Sociological Review, 50,* 364–371.

Picard, R. G. (1985). *The press and the decline of democracy: The democratic socialist response in public policy.* Westport, CT: Greenwood.

Pierce, J. P., Choi, W. S., Gilpin, E. A., Farkas, A. J., & Berry, C. C. (1998). Tobacco industry promotion of cigarettes and adolescent smoking. *Journal of the American Medical Association, 279,* 511–515.

Pierce, J. P., & Gilpin, E. A. (1995). A historical analysis of tobacco marketing and the uptake of smoking by youth in the United States: 1890–1977. *Health Psychology, 14,* 500–508.

Pollay, R. W., Siddarth, S., Siegel, M., Haddix, A., Merritt, R. K., Giavino, G. A., & Eriksen, M. D. (1996). The last straw? Cigarette advertising and realized market shares among youths and adults, 1979–1993. *Journal of Marketing, 60*(2), 1–16.

Popper, K. R. (1965). *Conjectures and refutations: The growth of scientific knowledge.* Oxford: Oxford University Press.

Popper, K. R. (1983). Truth and approximation to truth. In D. Miller (Ed.), *A pocket Popper* (pp. 181–198). Oxford: Fontana.

Potter, W. J. (1987). Does television hinder academic achievement among adolescents? *Human Communication Research, 14,* 27–46.

Potter, W. J. (1988). Perceived reality in television effects research. *Journal of Broadcasting and Electronic Media, 32,* 23–41.

Potter, W. J. (1991). Examining cultivation from a psychological perspective. *Communication Research, 18,* 77–102.

Potter, W. J. (1993). Cultivation theory and research: A conceptual critique. *Human Communication Research, 19,* 564–601.

Potter, W. J., Cooper, R., & Dupagne, M. (1993). The three paradigms of mass media research in mainstream communication journals. *Communication Theory, 3,* 317–335.

Pratkanis, A. R., Leippe, M. R., Greenwald, A. G., & Baumgardner, M. H. (1988). In search of reliable persuasion effects: III. The sleeper effect is dead. Long live the sleeper effect. *Journal of Personality and Social Psychology, 54,* 203–218.

Price, M. E. (Ed.). (1998). *The v-chip debate: Content filtering from television to the internet.* Mahwah, NJ: Lawrence Erlbaum Associates.

Price, V. (1988). On the public aspects of opinion: Linking levels of analysis in public opinion research. *Communication Research, 15,* 659–679.

Price, V. (1989). Social identification and public opinion: Effects of communicating group conflicts. *Public Opinion Quarterly, 53,* 197–224.

Price, V. (1992). *Communication concepts 4: Public opinion.* Newbury Park, CA: Sage.

Price, V., & Allen, S. (1990). Opinion spirals, silent and otherwise: Applying small-group research to public opinion phenomena. *Communication Research, 17,* 369–392.

Price, V., & Roberts, D. F. (1987). Public opinion processes. In C. R. Berger & S. H. Chaffee (Eds.), *Handbook of communication science* (pp. 781–816). Newbury Park, CA: Sage.

Pritchard, D. (1986). Homicide and bargained justice: The agenda-setting effect of crime news on prosecutors. *Public Opinion Quarterly, 49,* 19–37.

Pritchard, D., Dilts, J. P., & Berkowitz, D. (1987). Prosecutors' use of external agendas in prosecuting pornography cases. *Journalism Quarterly, 64,* 392–398.

Putnam, R. D. (1993). *Making democracy work: Civic traditions in modern Italy.* Princeton, NJ: Princeton University Press.

Putnam, R. D. (1995). Tuning in, tuning out: The strange disappearance of social capital in America. *PS: Political Science & Politics, 28,* 664–683.

Putnam, R. D. (2000). *Bowling alone: The collapse and revival of American community.* New York: Simon & Schuster.

Quine, W. V. (1951/1980). Two dogmas of empiricism. In W. V. Quine (Ed.), *From a logical point of view* (2nd ed., pp. 20–46). Cambridge, MA: Harvard University Press.

Rayburn, J. D., & Palmgreen, P. (1984). Merging uses and gratifications and expectancy-value theory. *Communication Research, 11*, 537–562.

Reck, A. J. (1982). Pepper and recent metaphilosophy. *The Journal of Mind and Behavior, 3*, 207–216.

Reeves, B., & Anderson, D. R. (1991). Media studies and psychology. *Communication Research, 18*, 597–600.

Reynolds, P. D. (1971). *A primer in theory construction.* Indianapolis, IN: Bobbs-Merrill.

Rhodes, N., & Wood, W. (1992). Self-esteem and intelligence affect influenceability: The mediating role of message reception. *Psychological Bulletin, 111*, 156–171.

Ritchie, D., Price, V., & Roberts, D. F. (1987). Television, reading, and reading achievement. *Communication Research, 14*, 292–315.

Roberts, D. F. (1983). Children and commercials: Issues, evidence, interventions. *Prevention in Human Services, 2*, 19–35.

Roberts, D. F. (2000). Media and youth: Access, exposure, and privatization. *Journal of Adolescent Health, 27S*, 8–14.

Roberts, D. F., & Bachen, C. M. (1981). Mass communication effects. *Annual Review of Psychology, 32*, 307–356.

Roberts, D. F., & Maccoby, N. (1985). Effects of mass communication. In G. Lindzey & E. Aronson (Eds.), *Handbook of social psychology* (3rd ed., pp. 539–598). New York: Random House.

Roberts, J. V. (1985). The attitude–memory relationship after 40 years: A meta-analysis of the literature. *Basic and Applied Social Psychology, 6*, 221–241.

Robinson, J. P., & Levy, M. R. (1986). *The main source: Learning from television news.* Beverly Hills, CA: Sage.

Rogers, E. M. (1976). Communication and development: The passing of the dominant paradigm. *Communication Research, 3*, 213–240.

Rogers, E. M. (1983). *Diffusion of innovations* (3rd ed.). New York: The Free Press.

Rogers, E. M. (1986). *Communication technology: The new media in society.* New York: The Free Press.

Rogers, E. M. (1989). Inquiry in development communication. In M. K. Asante & W. B. Gudykunst (Eds.), *Handbook of international and intercultural communication* (pp. 67–86). Newbury Park, CA: Sage.

Rogers, E. M. (1992). On early mass communication study. *Journal of Broadcasting & Electronic Media, 36*, 467–471.

Rogers, E. M. (1994). *A history of communication study: A biographical approach.* New York: The Free Press.

Rogers, E. M. (1995). *Diffusion of innovations* (4th ed.). New York: The Free Press.

Rogers, E. M., & Dearing, J. W. (1988). Agenda-setting research: Where has it been, where is it going? In J. A. Anderson (Ed.), *Communication yearbook 11* (pp. 555–594). Newbury Park, CA: Sage.

Rogers, E. M., Dearing, J. W., & Bregman, D. (1993). The anatomy of agenda-setting research. *Journal of Communication, 43*(2), 68–84.

Rogers, E. M., & Kincaid, D. L. (1981). *Communication networks: Toward a new paradigm for research.* New York: The Free Press.

Rogers, E. M., & Storey, J. D. (1987). Communication campaigns. In C. R. Berger & S. H. Chaffee (Eds.), *Handbook of communication science* (pp. 817–846). Newbury Park, CA: Sage.

Rogers, M., & Smith, K. H. (1993). Public perceptions of subliminal advertising: Why practitioners shouldn't ignore this issue. *Journal of Advertising Research, 33*(2), 11–18.

Rogers, R. W. (1975). A protection motivation theory of fear appeals and attitude change. *The Journal of Psychology, 91*, 93–114.

Rogosa, C. (1980). A critique of cross-lagged correlations. *Psychological Bulletin, 88*, 245–258.

Rorty, R. (1979). *Philosophy and the mirror of nature.* Princeton, NJ: Princeton University Press.

Rorty, R. (1982). *Consequences of pragmatism.* Minneapolis: University of Minnesota Press.

Rorty, R. (1983). Method and morality. In N. Haan, R. N. Bellah, P. Rabinow, & W. M. Sullivan (Eds.), *Social science as moral inquiry* (pp. 155–176). New York: Columbia University Press.

Rosengren, K. E. (1974). International news: Methods, data, and theory. *Journal of Peace Research, 11,* 145–156.

Rosengren, K. E., Wenner, L. A., & Palmgreen, P. (Eds.). (1985). *Media gratifications research: Current perspectives.* Beverly Hills, CA: Sage.

Rosengren, K. E., & Windahl, S. (1989). *Media matter: TV use in childhood and adolescence.* Norwood, NJ: Ablex.

Rosenstiel, T. B. (1993, March 25). Views on TV violence reflect generation gap. *Los Angeles Times,* p. 2.

Rosenthal, R. (1986). Media violence, antisocial behavior, and the social consequences of small effects. *Journal of Social Issues, 42,* 141–154.

Roskos-Ewoldsen, D. (1997). Implicit theories of persuasion. *Human Communication Research, 24,* 31–63.

Rosnow, R. L. (1985). A tour de force [Review of *No sense of place: The impact of electronic media on social behavior*]. *Journal of Communication, 35*(3), 204–206.

Rowland, W. D. (1983). *The politics of TV violence: Policy uses of communication research.* Beverly Hills, CA: Sage.

Rubin, A. M. (1993). Audience activity and media use. *Communication Monographs, 60,* 98–105.

Rubin, A. M. (1994). Media uses and effects: A uses-and-gratifications perspective. In J. Bryant & D. Zillmann (Eds.), *Media effects: Advances in theory and research* (pp. 417–436). Hillsdale, NJ: Lawrence Erlbaum Associates.

Rubin, A. M., & Perse, E. M. (1987a). Audience activity and soap opera involvement: A uses and effects investigation. *Human Communication Research, 14,* 246–268.

Rubin, A. M., & Perse, E. M. (1987b). Audience activity and television news gratifications. *Communication Research, 14,* 58–84.

Rubin, A. M., Perse, E. M., & Powell, R. A. (1985). Loneliness, parasocial interaction, and local television news viewing. *Human Communication Research, 12,* 155–180.

Rubin, A. M., Perse, E. M., & Taylor, D. S. (1988). A methodological examination of cultivation. *Communication Research, 15,* 107–134.

Rubin, A. M., & Rubin, R. B. (1982). Contextual age and television use. *Human Communication Research, 8,* 228–244.

Ruggiero, T. E. (2000). Uses and gratifications theory in the 21st century. *Mass Communication & Society, 3,* 3–37.

Rummel, R. J. (1972). *The dimensions of nations.* Beverly Hills, CA: Sage.

Saffer, H. (1991). Alcohol advertising bans and alcohol abuse: An international perspective. *Journal of Health Economics, 10,* 65–79.

Sallach, D. L. (1974). Class domination and ideological hegemony. *The Sociological Quarterly, 15,* 38–50.

Salmon, C. T. (1986). Perspectives on involvement in consumer and communication research. In B. Dervin & M. J. Voight (Eds.), *Progress in communication sciences* (Vol. 7, pp. 243–268). Norwood, NJ: Ablex.

Salmon, C. T., & Glasser, T. L. (1995). The politics of polling and the limits of consent. In T. L. Glasser & C. T. Salmon (Eds.), *Public opinion and the communication of consent* (pp. 437–458). New York: Guilford.

Salmon, C. T., & Mou, C. (1992). The spiral of silence: Linking individual and society through communication. In J. D. Kennamer (Ed.), *Public opinion, the press, and public policy* (pp. 145–161). Westport, CT: Praeger.

Salmon, C. T., & Neuwirth, K. (1990). Perceptions of opinion "climate" and willingness to discuss the issue of abortion. *Journalism Quarterly, 67*, 567–577.

Schiller, H. I. (1976). *Communication and cultural domination*. White Plains, NY: International Arts and Sciences Press.

Schramm, W. (1964). *Mass media and national development*. Stanford, CA: Stanford University Press.

Schramm, W. (1997). *The beginnings of communication study in America: A personal memoir* (S. H. Chaffee & E. M. Rogers, Eds.). Thousand Oaks, CA: Sage.

Schramm, W., Lyle, J., & Parker, E. (1961). *Television in the lives of our children*. Stanford, CA: Stanford University Press.

Sears, A. E. (1989). The legal case for restricting pornography. In D. Zillmann & J. Bryant (Eds.), *Pornography: Research advances and policy considerations* (pp. 343–359). Hillsdale, NJ: Lawrence Erlbaum Associates.

Self, C. C. (1974). *A transactional model of communication*. Paper presented to the annual convention of the International Communication Associations, New Orleans, LA.

Shah, D. V. (1998). Civic engagement, interpersonal trust, and television use: An individual-level assessment of social capital. *Political Psychology, 19*, 469–496.

Shannon, C., & Weaver, W. (1949). *The mathematical theory of communication*. Urbana: University of Illinois Press.

Shapiro, J. S. (1999). Loneliness: Paradox or artifact? *The American Psychologist, 54*, 782–783.

Shapiro, M. (1991). Memory and decision processes in the construction of social reality. *Communication Research, 18*, 3–24.

Shavitt, S. (1990). The role of attitude objects in attitude functions. *Journal of Experimental Social Psychology, 26*, 124–148.

Sherif, M., & Sherif, C. (1967). Attitude as the individual's own categories: The social judgment-involvement approach to attitude and attitude change. In C. W. Sherif & M. Sherif (Eds.), *Attitude, ego-involvement and change* (pp. 105–139). New York: Wiley.

Shoemaker, P. J. (1989). Introduction. In P. J. Shoemaker (Ed.), *Communication campaigns about drugs: Government, media, and the public* (pp. 1–5). Hillsdale, NJ: Lawrence Erlbaum Associates.

Shoemaker, P. J. (1991). *Communication concepts 3: Gatekeeping*. Newbury Park, CA: Sage.

Shoemaker, P. J., & Reese, S. D. (1991). *Mediating the message: Theories of influences of mass media content*. New York: Longman.

Shoemaker, P. J., & Reese, S. D. (1996). *Mediating the message: Theories of influences of mass media content* (2nd ed.). New York: Longman.

Shrum, L. J. (1996). Psychological processes underlying cultivation effects: Further tests of construct accessibility. *Human Communication Research, 22*, 482–509.

Shrum, L. J., & O'Guinn, T. C. (1993). Processes and effects in the construction of social reality: Construct accessibility as an explanatory variable. *Communication Research, 20*, 436–471.

Shusterman, R. (1997). *Practicing philosophy: Pragmatism and the philosophical life*. New York: Routledge.

Siebert, F. S., Peterson, T., & Schramm, W. (1956). *Four theories of the press*. Urbana, IL: University of Illinois Press.

Signorielli, N. (Ed.). (1985). *Role portrayal and stereotyping on television: An annotated bibliography of studies relating to women, minorities, aging, sexual behavior, health and handicaps*. Westport, CT: Greenwood.

Signorielli, N., McLeod, D., & Healy, E. (1994). Gender stereotypes in MTV commercials: The beat goes on. *Journal of Broadcasting & Electronic Media, 38*, 91–101.

Simonson, P. (2001). Varieties of pragmatism and communication: Visions and revisions from Peirce to Peters. In D. K. Perry (Ed.), *American pragmatism and communication research* (pp. 1–26). Mahwah, NJ: Lawrence Erlbaum Associates.

Simpson, C. (1994). *Science of coercion: Communication research and psychological warfare 1945–1960*. New York: Oxford University Press.

Simpson, C. (1996). Elisabeth Noelle-Neumann's "spiral of silence" and the historical context of communication theory. *Journal of Communication, 46*(3), 149–171.

Singer, E. (1987). Editors's introduction. *Public Opinion Quarterly, 51*, S1–S3.

Smith, J. E. (1978). *Purpose and thought: The meaning of pragmatism*. New Haven, CT: Yale University Press.

Smith, L. D. (1986). *Behaviorism and logical positivism*. Stanford, CA: Stanford University Press.

Star, S., & Hughes, H. M. (1950). Report of an educational campaign: The Cincinnati plan for the United Nations. *American Journal of Sociology, 55*, 389–397.

Steinem, G. (1980). Erotica and pornography: A clear and present difference. In L. Lederer (Ed.), *Take back the night: Women on pornography* (pp. 35–39). New York: William Morrow.

Sterling, C. H. (2000). Foreword: Considering who owns the media. In B. M. Compaine & D. Gomery (Eds.), *Who owns the media?: Competition and concentration in the mass media industry* (3rd ed., pp. xv–xviii). Mahwah, NJ: Lawrence Erlbaum Associates.

Stevenson, R. L. (1988). *Communication, development, and the third world: The global politics of information*. New York: Longman.

Strasburger, V. C., & Donnerstein, E. (1999). Children, adolescents, and the media: Issues and solutions. *Pediatrics, 103*, 129–139.

Sundar, S. S. (2000). Multimedia effects on processing and perception of online news: A study of picture, audio, and video downloads. *Journalism Quarterly, 77*, 480–499.

Surgeon General's Scientific Advisory Committee on Television and Social Behavior. (1972). *Television and growing up: The impact of televised violence*. Washington, DC: U.S. Government Printing Office.

Swanson, D. L. (1992). Understanding audiences: Continuing contributions of gratifications research. *Poetics, 21*, 305–328.

Tan, A. S. (1977). Why TV is missed: A functional analysis. *Journal of Broadcasting, 21*, 371–380.

Tankard, J. W., Jr. (1990a). Donohue, Olien, and Tichenor and the structural approach. In W. D. Sloan (Ed.), *Makers of the media mind* (pp. 258–267). Hillsdale, NJ: Lawrence Erlbaum Associates.

Tankard, J. W., Jr. (1990b). Maxwell McCombs, Donald Shaw, and agenda-setting. In W. D. Sloan (Ed.), *Makers of the media mind* (pp. 278–286). Hillsdale, NJ: Lawrence Erlbaum Associates.

Tankard, J. W., Jr. (1990c). Wilbur Schramm, definer of a field. In W. D. Sloan (Ed.), *Makers of the media mind* (pp. 239–248). Hillsdale, NJ: Lawrence Erlbaum Associates.

Tarrow, S. (1996). Making social science work across space and time: A critical reflection on Robert Putnam's *Making democracy work*. *American Political Science Review, 90*, 389–397.

Taylor, S. E., & Thompson, S. C. (1982). Stalking the elusive "vividness" effect. *Psychological Review, 89*, 155–181.

Tewksbury, D., & Althaus, S. (2000). Differences in knowledge acquisition among readers of the paper and online versions of a national newspaper. *Journalism Quarterly, 77*, 457–479.

Thompson, M. E., Chaffee, S. H., & Oshagan, H. H. (1990). Regulating pornography: A public dilemma. *Journal of Communication, 40*(3), 73–83.

Thorson, E. (1989). Processing television commercials. In B. Dervin, L. Grossberg, B. J. O'Keefe, & E. Wartella (Eds.), *Rethinking communication: Volume 2. Paradigm exemplars* (pp. 397–410). Newbury Park, CA: Sage.

Tichenor, P. J., Donohue, G. A., & Olien, C. N. (1970). Mass media flow and differential growth in knowledge. *Public Opinion Quarterly, 34*, 159–170.

Toch, H., & MacLean, M. S., Jr. (1962). Perception, communication and educational research: A transactional view. *Audio Visual Communication Review, 10*(5), 55–77.

Tolman, E. C. (1932). *Purposive behavior in animals and men*. New York: Century.

Troldahl, V. C. (1966-1967). A field test of a modified two-step flow of communication model. *Public Opinion Quarterly, 30*, 609–623.

Tuchman, G. (1978). *Making news: A study in the construction of reality.* New York: The Free Press.

Turow, J. (1984). Pressure groups and television entertainment: A framework for analysis. In W. D. Rowland, Jr., & B. Watkins (Eds.), *Interpreting television: Current research perspectives* (pp. 142–162). Beverly Hills, CA: Sage.

Tversky, A., & Kahneman, D. (1971). Belief in the law of small numbers. *Psychological Bulletin, 76*, 105–110.

Tversky, A., & Kahneman, D. (1973). Availability: A heuristic for judging frequency and probability. *Cognitive Psychology, 5*, 207–232.

Tversky, A., & Kahneman, D. (1974). Judgment under uncertainty: Heuristics and biases. *Science, 185*, 1124–1131.

U.S. Bureau of the Census. (1975). *Historical statistics of the United States, colonial times to 1970, bicentennial edition, part 1.* Washington, DC: U.S. Department of Commerce.

U.S. Bureau of the Census. (1992). *Statistical abstract of the United States 1992.* Washington, DC: U.S. Department of Commerce.

U.S. Federal Bureau of Investigation (annual volumes). *Uniform crime reports for the United States.* Washington, DC: U.S. Government Printing Office.

Uslander, E. M. (1998). Social capital, television, and the "mean-world": Trust, optimism, and civic participation. *Political Psychology, 19*, 441–467.

Vallone, R. P., Ross, L., & Lepper, M. R. (1985). The hostile media phenomenon: Biased perception and perceptions of media bias in coverage of the Beirut Massacre. *Journal of Personality and Social Psychology, 49*, 577–585.

Viswanath, K., & Finnegan, J. R. (1996). The knowledge gap hypothesis: Twenty-five years later. In B. R. Burleson (Ed.), *Communication yearbook 19* (pp. 186–227). Thousand Oaks, CA: Sage.

Wackman, D. B., & Wartella, E. (1977). A review of cognitive development theory and research and the implication for research on children's responses to television. *Communication Research, 4*, 203–224.

Wagner, M., & Owens, D. A. (1992). Introduction: Modern psychology and early functionalism. In D. A. Owens & M. Wagner (Eds.), *Progress in modern psychology: The legacy of American functionalism* (pp. 3–16). Westport, CT: Praeger.

Walker, J. L., Jr. (1977). Setting the agenda in the U.S. Senate: A theory of problem selection. *British Journal of Political Science, 7*, 423–445.

Wartella, E. (1994). Challenge to the profession. *Communication Education, 43*, 54–62.

Wartella, E., & Reeves, B. (1985). Historical trends in research on children and the media. *Journal of Communication, 35*(2), 118–133.

Weaver, D. (1991). Issue salience and public opinion: Are there consequences of agenda-setting? *International Journal of Public Opinion Research, 3*, 53–68.

Wells, A. (1972). *Picture-tube imperialism?: The impact of U.S. television on Latin America.* Maryknoll, NY: Orbis.

Wenner, L. A. (1985). Transaction and media gratifications research. In K. E. Rosengren, L. A. Wenner, & P. Palmgreen (Eds.), *Media gratifications research: Current perspectives* (pp. 73–94). Beverly Hills, CA: Sage.

Wenner, L. A. (1986). Model specification and theoretical development in gratifications sought and obtained research: A comparison of discrepancy and transactional approaches. *Communication Monographs, 53*, 160–179.

Westbrook, R. B. (1991). *John Dewey and American democracy.* Ithaca, NY: Cornell University Press.

Westley, B. H., & MacLean, M. S., Jr. (1957). A conceptual model for communications research. *Journalism Quarterly, 34*, 31–38.

Whitby, G. L., & Whitby, L. K. (1990). James Carey and the cultural approach. In W. D. Sloan (Ed.), *Makers of the media mind* (pp. 167–175). Hillsdale, NJ: Lawrence Erlbaum Associates.

White, D. M. (1950). The "gate keeper": A case study in the selection of news. *Journalism Quarterly, 27*, 383–390.

White, L. A. (1979). Erotica and aggression: The influence of sexual arousal, positive affect, and negative affect on aggressive behavior. *Journal of Personality and Social Psychology, 37*, 591–601.

Whitney, D. C. (2000). Review of *The case for television violence. Journalism Quarterly, 77*, 195.

Wicker, A. W. (1969). Attitudes versus actions: The relationship of verbal and overt behavioral responses to attitude objects. *Journal of Social Issues, 25*, 41–78.

Wilcox, S. B. (1992). Functionalism then and now. In D. A. Owens & M. Wagner (Eds.), *Progress in modern psychology: The legacy of American functionalism* (pp. 31–51). Westport, CT: Praeger.

Wilson, B. J., Kunkel, D., Linz, D., Potter, W. J., Donnerstein, E., Smith, S. L., Blumenthal, E., Berry, M., & Federman, J. (1998). The nature and context of violence on American television. In U. Carlsson & C. von Feilitzen (Eds.), *Children and media violence* (pp. 63–79). Gotenberg, Sweden: The UNESCO International Clearinghouse on Children and Violence on the Screen.

Wilson, B. J., & Weiss, A. J. (1992). Developmental differences in children's reactions to a toy advertisement linked to a toy-based cartoon. *Journal of Broadcasting & Electronic Media, 36*, 371–394.

Windahl, S., & Signitzer, B. H. (1992). *Using communication theory: An introduction to planned communication.* Newbury Park, CA: Sage.

Witte, K. (1992). Putting the fear back into fear appeals: The extended parallel process model. *Communication Monographs, 59*, 329–349.

Witte, K. (1994). Fear control and danger control: A test of the extended parallel process model (EPPM). *Communication Monographs, 61*, 113–134.

Wood, W., Wong, F. Y., & Chachere, J. S. (1991). Effects of media violence on viewers' aggression in unconstrained social interaction. *Psychological Bulletin, 109*, 371–383.

World Health Organization (annual volumes). *World health statistics annual.* Geneva, Switzerland: Author.

Wright, C. R. (1960). Functional analysis and mass communication. *Public Opinion Quarterly, 24*, 605–620.

Zajonc, R. B. (1968). Attitudinal effect of mere exposure. *Journal of Personality and Social Psychology* (Suppl. 9, Part 2), 1–27.

Zillmann, D. (1971). Excitation transfer in communication-mediated aggressive behavior. *Journal of Experimental Social Psychology, 7*, 419–434.

Zillmann, D. (1985). The experimental exploration of gratifications from media entertainment. In K. E. Rosengren, L. A. Wenner, & P. Palmgreen (Eds.), *Media gratifications research: Current perspectives* (pp. 225–239). Beverly Hills, CA: Sage.

Zillmann, D. (1992). Pornography research, social advocacy, and public policy. In P. Suedfeld & P. E. Tetlock (Eds.), *Psychology and social policy* (pp. 165–178). New York: Hemisphere.

Zillmann D. (2000). Influence of unrestrained access to erotica on adolescents' and young adults' dispositions toward sexuality. *Journal of Adolescent Health, 27S*, 41–44.

Zillmann, D., & Bryant, J. (1982). Pornography, sexual callousness, and the trivialization of rape. *Journal of Communication, 32*(4), 10–21.

Zillmann, D., & Bryant, J. (1983). Pornography and social science research: Higher moralities. *Journal of Communication, 33*(4), 111–114.

Zillmann, D., & Bryant, J. (1986a). Sexual callousness re-examined: A response. *Journal of Communication, 36*(1), 184–188.

Zillmann, D., & Bryant, J. (1986b). Shifting preferences in pornography consumption. *Communication Research, 13,* 560–578.

Zillmann, D., & Bryant, J. (1988a). Effects of prolonged consumption of pornography on family values. *Journal of Family Issues, 9,* 518–544.

Zillmann, D., & Bryant, J. (1988b). Pornography's impact on sexual satisfaction. *Journal of Applied Social Psychology, 18,* 438–453.

Zillmann, D., & Bryant, J. (1994). Entertainment as media effect. In J. Bryant & D. Zillmann (Eds.), *Media effects: Advances in theory and research* (pp. 437–461). Hillsdale, NJ: Lawrence Erlbaum Associates.

Zimmerman, B. F. (1983). Social learning theory: A contextualist account of cognitive functioning. In C. J. Brainerd (Ed.), *Recent advances in cognitive-developmental theory* (pp. 1–50). New York: Springer-Verlag.

Zimring, F. E., & Hawkins, G. (1997). *Crime is not the problem: Lethal violence in America.* New York: Oxford University Press.

Author Index

Subject Index